The war next door

A study of second-track intervention during the war in ex-Yugoslavia

By

Judith Large

HAWTHORN PRESS

Cover photo: Children's Peace Wall, Pakrac 1994, courtesy of Vesna Terselic.

Published by Hawthorn Press,
Hawthorn House, 1 Lansdown Lane, Lansdown, Stroud,
Gloucestershire, GL5 1BJ
Tel (01453 757040) Fax (01453) 751138

The ideas expressed within this book are not necessarily those of the publisher.

Designed and typeset by Lynda Smith
Cover artwork and typography by Bill Hicks
Printed by Quorum, Cheltenham
British Library Cataloguing in Publication Data
A catalogue record for this book is available from the British Library.

ISBN 1 869 890 97-3

This book is dedicated to Prof. Martin Wight and his past profound influence, to Martin Large and the present, and to Lana, age 1, in Zagreb, and the future of her region (all of former Yugoslavia) and its diverse peoples.

Table of contents

Glossary of acronyms

AI	Anmesty International
ARK	Anti-War Campaign, Zagreb
BPP	Balkan Peace Project
BPT	Balkan Peace Team
BSV	Bund für soziale Verteidigung
CAA	Centre for Anti-War Action, Belgrade
CCCRTE	Co-ordinating Committee for Conflict Resolution Training in Europe
COS	Centrum voor Internationele Samenwerking
CSCE	Conference on Security and Co-operation in Europe
DHA	United Nations Department of Humanitarian Affairs
DSHV	Democratic Alliance of Croats in Vojvodina
EC	European Community
EU	European Union
GONGO	Government affiliated NGOs
HCA	Helsinki Citizens Assembly
HDZ	Croatian Democratic Union
HRT	Hrtvatska Radio-Televizija
ICRC	International Committee of the Red Cross
ICTY	International Criminal Tribunal for the Former Yugoslavia
ICVA	International Council for Voluntary Agencies
IGOs	International Intergovernmental Organisations
INGO	International Non-Governmental Organisation
IR	International Relations
IWPR	Institute of War and Peace Reporting
JNA	Yugoslav People's Army (Jugoslovenska narodna armija)
LCY	League of Communists in Yugoslavia
MEDACT	Medical Action for Global Security
NATO	North Atlantic Treaty Organization
NGO	Non-Governmental Organization
NSMs	New Social Movements
NVC	Non-violent Communication
ODI	Overseas Development Institute
OSCE	Organisation for Security and Co-operation in Europe
PBI	Peace Brigades International
PSRP	Pakrac Social Reconstruction Project
PTSD	Post Traumatic Stress Disorder
QUANGO	Quasi-NGO
QUNO, Geneva	Quaker United Nations Office
QPS	Quaker Peace and Service
RSK	Republic of Serbian Krajina
SAO	Serbian Autonomous Region
SDF	Serbian Democratic Forum
SDS	Serbian Democratic Party
SIPRI	Stockholm International Peace Research Institute
SPS	Socialist Party of Serbia
UN	United Nations
UNDP	United Nations Development Programme
UNFICYP	UN Peacekeeping Force, Cyprus
UNHCR	United Nations High Commissioner for Refugees
UNICEF	United Nations Children Fund
UNIFIL	UN Peacekeeping Force, Lebanon
UNOV	UN Office Vienna
UNPAs	United Nations Protected Areas
UNPROFOR	United Nations Protection Force in former Yugoslavia
UNTAES	United Nations Temporary Administration
USAID	United States Agency for International Development
VMDK	The Democratic Community of Vojvodina Hungarians
WATFY	Women's Aid to Former Yugoslavia
WEU	Western European Union
WFP	World Food Programme
WHO	World Health Organization
WRI	War Resistors International

Acknowledgements

There are many thank-yous and acknowledgements to be extended on the completion of this report.

The study has been made possible through the generosity of the Joseph Rowntree Charitable Trust, through archive support from the Institute of War and Peace Reporting, and by the Fire Service College of Moreton-in-Marsh. The Fire Service College and the University of Coventry have jointly pioneered an interdisciplinary approach to international disaster management and their BSc. International Disaster Engineering and Management Course reflects this approach. Both colleagues and students have been helpful in seeing the project through. Having a 'base' as a fellow at The University of Kent, Canterbury. has been a great help, for which my appreciation is extended to Prof. A. J. R. Groom and Dr. Keith Webb.

Many thanks are due to Fritz Behrendt for the use of his vivid political cartoons as published originally in Tus za slobodu (Ink for Freedom), (1992) MCG Zagreb, to Penguin UK for kind permission to quote from Misha Glenny's The Fall of Yugoslavia (1992) pp 124-126, and to Alexander Weisner and the Pancevo Peace Group for use of photographs and their own visual work. The cover photo and Pakrac photos were provided by Vesna Terselic of ARK. The extract from 'The Game' by Edvard Kocbek is taken from the full poem's translation in Daniel Weissbort (ed.) The Poetry of Survival 1991, Penguin Books, London, p.48.

Karlo Miklausic and Nina Pecnic were instrumental in raising and talking through initial questions and dilemmas, and enormously supportive in friendship and sheer patience. I'm indebted to Branislava Kostic for her COS study, and to Rik Hendriks for his assistance. Colleagues who contributed unreservedly in conducting interviews, digging out factual information and helping with practical organisation include Ute Caspers, Nicholas and Rosemary Street, and Judith Wainwright. Prof. Hugh Miall of Lancaster University, Alan Pleydell of Quaker Peace and Service, and debates within both the UK Network for Conflict, Development and Peace (CODEP) and the Co-ordinating Committee for Conflict Resolution Training (CCCRTE) have helped with ideas and insights. Grateful acknowledgement also to the Erasmus Foundation and ARK (Anti-War Campaign) of Zagreb, the Local Democracy Embassy and the Centre for Peace in Osijek, UNTAES of former Sector East, Bert and Tanja van der Linde, peace groups and activists in Baranja, Novi Sad, Subotica, Pancevo and Group 484 of Belgrade. Thanks also to Trish Dickinson and Nada Ignjatovic-Savic.

Lynda Smith, Martin, Abigail and all the team at Hawthorn Press have been positive, enthusiastic and competent in their continual 'back-up' and in seeing to the editing and production of this document. Bill Hicks, graphic designer, is to be thanked for his ideas as much as for his technical expertise. (For any errors or mistakes in this document the credit must be solely mine.)

Finally, within and behind these pages stand individuals in ex-Yugoslavia and its new states who continually offered hospitality, honest accounts, and friendship as they quite literally made their own history. All I have done is to try to interpret this and I hope the resulting interpretation will stand up in their eyes.

Introduction

Sarajevo 14 January 1992

Today I, Mirad Balic from Foca, (age 13)
start a diary
because a new life begins.
I am staying a couple of days
with my uncle Djuka and my
aunt Fazila
here in Sarajevo.
We celebrated the orthodox
new year
with Serbian friends of uncle Djuka.
Until yesterday I still felt
a schoolboy
And I was.
*But since the speech of Nenad Pejic**
on Sarajevo television
I feel quite different.
As if I'm awake for the first time.
I never understood anything
about politics,
Just like my friends.
But suddenly, last night
I understood it's about ourselves.
All about ordinary people.

(*Nenad Pejic broadcast his concern that the words and actions of political parties were leading to a crisis point of civil war, and asked the Sarajevo public to switch off their house lights if they agreed that what was needed was peace and co-operation. '...the whole city became dark within five minutes.')

Extracts from 'Mirad A Boy from Bosnia' a play by Ad De Bont, translated by Marian Buijs (unpublished).

This study was conceived at a time when it was apparent that traditional means of diplomatic and/or military interventions were failing in response to the war in what we once knew as Yugoslavia, in part it seemed because of a legitimacy problem in the leadership which was being honoured by conventional western political mechanisms, and in part because of a fumbling in foreign policy on the part of governments distracted by the Gulf war and unprepared for post-cold war conflicts in closer proximity.

At the same time it was obvious that *internal* voices and constituencies were working against, and opposed to war. Non-official response from external groups and agencies to these initiatives proliferated, both solicited and imposed. The question then which seemed to loom to the 'outside' practitioner was one of good practice—what was appropriate response? What was 'good practice' as opposed to interference? Even five years ago the gap between 'first track' official diplomacy and summit politics and 'second track' or multi-level approaches to community building (and violence reduction) was enormous.

Since then there have been three major changes. Firstly there is now a sound emergent body of literature on good practice and guidelines for intervenors, at least with regard to humanitarian interventions.[1] The prevention of war, once the domain of foreign policy and statecraft, is now a concern of relief and development agencies as well. The new 'contract culture' of governments and aid budgets means the privatisation of peace building. Chapter One considers the implications of this for the fields of international relations and development of social policy.

Secondly, the gap between first and second track diplomacy has narrowed, almost to the point of convergence. The post-Dayton rebuilding of Bosnia is underlined by emphasis on community and NGO development, human rights work, social reconstruction and the language of 'civil society'. If there has been any learning from the violent disintegration of Yugoslavia it is perhaps that elections alone do not equal democracy. The U.S. government funds independent media initiatives in the former republics. ECHO funds a myriad of new civic groups and enterprises on a grant basis. The OSCE has field officers working on specific democratisation and human rights initiatives which stress grass roots and municipality involvement, and UN agencies use the language of 'empowerment'. Chapter II presents a framework for levels of intervention and the approaches to violent conflict which these represent.

Thirdly, however, there is a new, often acrimonious debate on the nature of second track interventions, particularly those with a 'conflict resolution' label or claim. At the heart of this debate is what Mark Duffield calls 'the old sociological chestnut of whether you can modify social structures by working on the attitudes and behaviour of the individual',[2] i.e., is it possible to 'socially engineer' peace? We may be on the verge of a new orthodoxy in which 'psycho-social' and conflict resolution approaches are seen to be somehow both ineffective and negative, based on false premises rooted in some false western liberal consciousness. Chapters III and IV look at specific contexts and the responses of local populations to their experience of disintegration and the onset of war, and considers what 'capacity building' in such situations might look like. Chapter V looks in detail at a scheme of entry points used by second-track intervenors. Chapters VI and VII examine 'Contested concepts' and the question of social change. As far as possible this is done from the point of view of citizens 'in the field', as key participants for their specific standpoints as opposed to only social science definitions. Contested concepts under scrutiny here are 'conflict resolution' (theory and practice) and 'civil society'.

In light of the developments identified above the emphasis for the WAR-NEXT-DOOR study has somewhat changed. It seeks to address the question of impact and efficacy of second track interventions and in particular the struggle of citizens themselves to 'peace-build' from 'below'. The central question is whether there are ways in which outsiders can intervene *early enough and in any meaningful way to assist and strengthen local capacity for violence reduction*: if so, how do we measure or evaluate the impact of the same? This approach sees the destructiveness and violence of war as the problem—not conflict itself. Conflicts, even those over 'ethnicity', territory or 'self-determination' can be settled peaceably—witness the dissolution of Czechoslovakia, or the emergence (shaky and fragile at times) of Macedonia. Moreover, while the international community did not have the mechanisms to respond to dissident voices in old Yugoslavia who spoke in the name of 'civil society' and 'multiculturalism' in 1990/91, the same language is now incorporated into INGO post-war reconstruction planning and implementation. The interim was too bloody, too costly, not to try to learn alternative approaches.

Rationale

There is justification for a critical debate on 'second track' interventions.[3] For example, the work of Derek Summerfield has highlighted how western research *agendas* and psychological *doctrines* generated trauma counselling and psycho-social interventions as much as any genuine needs-based context approach in the ex-Yugoslavia republics, with varying degrees of relevance and efficacy. His critique is constructive in that it aims for clear basic principles which improve practice. A similar critical analysis is needed for conflict resolution work which, based on a pure 'communications' model of misperception (the subjectivist school) could not address military or strategic power questions in any measurable degree. On the other hand, the direct action or strategic school does address this dimension.

This study does not see psychological trauma work and conflict resolution as the same thing, but it is true that there is a **spectrum of conflict resolution activities** which has at one end a 'psycho-social' pole. It will address this spectrum in order to de-construct and examine components of a much used and loaded term.

It seems to me that if we conclude on impressionistic rather than detailed evidence and enquiry that conflict resolution does not work we are on a slippery slope to a position which says that force and violence do work and are therefore acceptable. For instance, in her scathing critique of UNICEF peace culture programmes in Serbian schools Vanessa Pupavac (1997) states 'Moreover for all the peace education initiatives in former Yugoslavia, the use of force is seen as having been the actual way of dealing with conflict...'[4] Pupavac implies an acceptance of the inevitability of violence, and seems to place no moral differentiation on who uses it, how, and where. More frightening, in my opinion, is a collection of essays on 'Emerging Norms of Justified Intervention' published by the Committee on International Security Studies, (American Academy of Arts and Sciences) (Trachtenberg, 1995) who ought to know better. Consider the following:

> 'If the problem in what used to be Yugoslavia is that the different ethnic groups there can no longer live together peacefully, and if for reasons having to do with precedent, proximity, and spillover effects in general, the Western world decides that the continuation of such violence is intolerable, then there is no compelling reason that intervention should be limited to preventing starvation or controlling atrocities—that is, to action aimed only at the most extreme violations of international norms. There is no reason why the outside powers should rule out as illegitimate the very idea of trying to get at the root of the problem—for example, by arranging for an orderly, equitable, and humane exchange of populations' (Trachtenberg, p. 31).

(Perhaps we should have arranged an orderly form of apartheid in South Africa?) Such a statement is offensive to the thousands of former Yugoslavians who resisted propaganda, sheltered friends, lived out mixed marriages and fought for the ideals of multi-culturalism throughout this war. It 'buys into' the carefully constructed demonization carried out prior to and during this war, as evidenced now in the painfully and artificially cantonized nature of post-Dayton Bosnia.

Breaking the Impasse

The quotation above takes a limited view of the 'root of the problem', as it implies de facto or inherent ethnic hatred. As such, this narrowness exemplifies the critical impasse of Duffield's 'chestnut' (the question of individual attitudes vs. socio-political change. **Psychology** deals with personal hatreds. If hatreds become collective, this is a **political** problem, and never the twain shall meet.

The chestnut is actually a useful allegory if we are to break the impasse in theory and in practice. On the face of it, a chestnut is an enclosed object with a hard shell. It is both the product and the seed of a large tree, and as such part of a living system. Biologically speaking it contains the potential for the reproduction of another tree, or by implication, many trees eventually, depending on internal and external conditions. It does not have the capacity for behaviour to alter or change those conditions. Human beings have not only biological capacities but also behavioural and attitudinal ones. If the collective mobilisation of these were not possible, civilisations would not exist, revolutions would not happen, slavery would not have been abolished. Unless one argues for the spontaneous outbreak of war, it must be that the mobilisation of humans comes into play for this as well.[5] Presumably there are wars which people—the majority of people, believe in, and wars which the majority feel are waged against them.[6] The country which was once Yugoslavia is full of new majority and minority peoples. In the final analysis their war was hardly spontaneous. The problem of the impasse is not conflict—it is destructive unwarranted violence, and the conditions which deem this possible. It must be possible to identify precipitating factors, to prevent, whole-scale collective violence. Coser's theories on structural conduceiveness may offer the kind of linkage between the micro and macro levels of understanding necessary for awareness and preventative action. (See Chapter III and conclusions.) It is this kind of linkage which can inform practice and move the debate forward.

For indigenous anti-war groups in Croatia and Serbia the debate has been real, practical, and lived out in terms of a tension between 'therapeutic' and 'direct action' approaches to conflict resolution.

Moreover it has been lived out in terms of opposition to militarised states and often intimidating elites. The experience has been valuable and at times painful learning. For critics from outside, such as Pupavac or Voutira and Brown (1995) it was pointless to think that because an individual worked on his or her attitudes, war policies would alter. For activists inside, it mattered too much not to try. For the critics, it was pointless because of realistic 'power and structure' considerations. For activists inside, power took on new meanings. They see clearly how power manifested in old Yugoslav structures, but structure is something we are part of and can potentially shape; it is not constant deterministic form. The key to breaking the impasse is strategy, reflective analysis, and daring to learn even when this is from mistakes as much as successes.[7]

Notes for Introduction

1. Lewer and Ramsbottom (1993) put forward ten framework principles for humanitarian intervention in 'international-social conflict.' These have been followed by Mary Anderson's 'do no harm' ethic and 'local capacities for peace' work in Cambridge, USA. (See Menkhaus, 1995). Minnear and Weiss introduced their 'providence principles' in *Mercy under Fire*, 1995. These ideas and guidelines, as well as the 'state of the debate' are reviewed in Chapter VIII.

   See also RRN Network Paper 7, 1994, 'Code of Conduct for the International Red Cross and Red Crescent Movement and NGOs in Disaster Relief', September. ODI London.

   Commonwealth Foundation, 1995, 'Non-Governmental Organisations: Guidelines for Good Policy and Practice'. London.

   People in Aid, 1997. 'Code of Best Practice on Management and Support of Aid Personnel'. London: People in Aid, ODI London.

2. Mark Duffield, personal conversation at the University of Birmingham, 6 April 1997.

3. Derek Summerfield, 'The Impact of War and Atrocity on Civilian Populations: Basic Principles for NGO Interventions and a Critique of Psychosocial Trauma Projects', Relief and Rehabilitation Network Paper 14, April 1996 ODI London.

4. Pupavac, (1997). 'Moreover for all the peace education initiatives in former Yugoslavia, the use of force is seen as having been the actual way of dealing with conflict. Whilst people may have been involved in internationally funded non-violent conflict resolution programmes, they were aware of the demands of the West for UN or US military intervention and they witnessed it being successful or even morally justified. It was Serbian armed forces which took Srebenica and elsewhere, it was the Croatian and Bosnian armies that took Krajina and Western Bosnia, and it was the power of the US army, not non-violent conflict resolution initiatives that resulted in the Dayton Agreement. The staff in the Most (Bridge) project in Western Slavonia which had been attempting to try to encourage dialogue and peaceful ethnic conflict resolution between Croats and Serbs in the divided town of Pakrac were devastated by the destruction of their work in the Croatian offensive Operation Lightning in May 1995 in which their office on the Serbian side in Pakrac was destroyed and people they knew killed.'

5. 'Even violence is not an eruption of latent tensions and frustrations that takes place in an organizational vacuum, but an outcome of a continuous process of mobilization and conflictual interaction' (W. Gamson, B. Fireman and S. Rytina, 1982).

6. For an overview of the 'objective' and 'subjective' elements deeming group positions and perceptions in society, see Henri Tajfel, 'The Social Psychology of Minorities', a Minority Rights Group International Report, London, reprinted in 1992.

7. One of the conclusions of Paul Stubbs in his summary research report 'Social Reconstruction and Social Development in Croatia and Slovenia : the role of the NGO sector' June 1996 for ODA identified a need for 'a shift from a technical approach to NGO development, evaluation, and peacebuilding, to a concern with social processes, cultural imperialism, and violence' (p28).

Chapter I

The war next door

..Oh damned lies of Heaven and Homeland/
When wise man is silent/and newspapers are barking

Miroslav Krleza (1893—1981), Croatian writer

'It is better to talk one million years than to make war one day...'

student in Belgrade, 1994

The warlords will hardly seek peace, by definition they can only hope to benefit by war—and actually and unfortunately they indeed do. Therefore it becomes more and more urgent to involve other and more constructive forces in negotiations, to give international support to anti-nationalistic civic forces, to assist independent media and groups, to stress the role of those who in civil society appear to be more capable than governments in achieving peace, dialogue and inter-ethnic coexistence. Mediation cannot neglect elementary justice and preservation from future conflict sources.

Extract from the Verona Forum Statement Geneva, 6 January 1993.

Western leaders used to miss no opportunity to set up photo-opportunities with Soviet dissidents. Who pays attention to those willing to be 'nationalist traitors' now? Projects such as an independent experts' committee and other citizens' groups are supported solely by western non-governmental organisations, not western governments. The official explanation is that peace can only come by speaking to the people who are doing the killing. But can no official place be found for those who really have a stake in peace?

Anthony Borden, Petar Lukovic and Dan Plesch 'The Gentle Path' in *New Statesman*
15 January 1993

'...I can't stop looking at images,
a procession of ghosts, spirits on pilgrimage,
the winking of truths, the revelation of fates.
Someone has changed and defined us,
as though shuffling a pack of cards.'

from 'The Game' by Edvard Kochek, Slovene poet.

I. The war next door

1.1 The onset of war: international response

When war rapidly followed the 1991 Slovenian and Croatian declarations of independence, it was pursued with a ferocity not seen in Europe since the end of the Second World War. Modern communications and media images left the viewing public gaping in shock or incredulity at major crisis and brought words like 'ethnic cleansing' into the popular vocabulary. Initially it seemed that terminology of response centred around two key words, 'mediation' and 'intervention'. Both received media coverage and academic attention as 'first track' areas of activity; that is, affairs conducted by governmental officials on the basis of major international policy decisions and implemented by such **formal** institutions as the United Nations. In a sense the conflict in Yugoslavia had taken the international community by surprise. The dominant theme of strategic studies had for some time been nuclear war; NATO had not yet formulated its new post-Cold War security stance in Europe. Here was a country literally *next door* to the 'European Community'; a state once known for affluent, articulate promotion of 'non-alignment'; that now seemed to be imploding with political violence. 'You Westerners were too caught up in the Gulf War to notice what was happening to us' was a charge levelled at me by a delegate from Zagreb at an international conference in early 1992.

1.2 Mediation

The EC initiated early **mediation** attempts but European efforts were often hampered by either lack of co-ordination or outright disagreement among the mediators. The first agreed plan for a comprehensive solution was the *Common Declaration on the Peaceful Resolution of the Yugoslav Crisis*, known as the **Brioni Declaration,** signed in July 1991 by the Federal Presidency, Slovenia, and the European Community. This confirmed the cease-fire in Slovenia and paved the way for the Yugoslav Army to withdraw from that republic. It deferred implementation of Slovenia's and Croatia's declarations of independence for a period of three months and committed all sides to refrain from unilateral acts, especially of violence. Guidelines were set for an international observer mission to Slovenia by the Conference on Security and Co-operation in Europe (CSCE); and provided for on-going negotiations on the future of Yugoslavia.

In the words of the International Commission on the Balkans (Tindemans, 1996, p. 43) '...the EC mediators suffered from a basic misunderstanding of what was happening'[1]: Serbia's leadership was less concerned about keeping Slovenia in a united Yugoslavia than with gaining control over Serb-populated areas of Croatia and Bosnia-Herzegovina. Opposed by (then) Federal Prime Minister Ante Markovic, the Brioni Declaration left the JNA free to regroup in Croatia and Bosnia, 'where Serbia was preparing local Serb communities to wage war' (Ibid.). This was not 'mediation' then in the sense of two hostile sides being assisted in resolving an issue; rather it was the first of many diplomatic 'peace plans' which (while well-intended) fell short of fully addressing the military and political interests at work in the situation. Subsequently the Badinter Commission acknowledged a process of dissolution and set in place criteria for recognition (on succession) for Serbia to reject and Croatia to gain statehood by. The Carrington Plan came and went.[2] European, American, and UN response was embodied in series of plans.

1.3 Intervention

Intervention was heralded with the Vance plans for a peacekeeping operation in Yugoslavia. With a mandate of 'prevention of new conflict by interposition', UN 'blue helmets' were deployed in areas of Croatia designated as United Nations Protected Areas (UNPAs). In practice, these were in the Serb-controlled parts of the republic, except in Western Slavonia, where control was divided. The population in these areas were to be protected 'from fear of armed attack'—hence the mission's name: United Nations Protection Force, or UNPROFOR. Its 14,000 strong force was supposed to disband and disarm the militias, supervise the withdrawal of the JNA, and help 500,000 displaced persons return to the protected areas. 600 UN policemen were given the task of safeguarding human rights, with a theoretical mandate to register complaints and investigate offences. The problems with this conventional peacekeeping force soon became apparent: though intended as an interim authority, pending a political solution, it had no effective means of fulfilling its mandate. Though initially preventing the renewal of fighting between Serbs and Croats in the Krajina, UNPROFOR's presence actually maintained the *status quo,* freezing the military solution to the advantage of the Serb militias, which proceeded to set up a government. 'Moreover, the slow deployment of the UN peace keepers permitted the Serb militias to complete their "ethnic cleansing": once in place, although United Nations were pleased to report the end of the "clean-up", in fact all non-Serbs had by then been killed or driven out, and the new police force was simply the old militia in new uniforms' (Jean, 1993). Disarmament and demobilisation were soon forgotten, and not one of the 500,000 refugees was able to return home. The safety of the UN contingents soon became more important than protecting civilians, and the deployment of UNPROFOR troops seemed a self-sustaining end in itself.

'Intervention' then, has generally been taken to mean the deployment of UN peacekeeping troops, and the implementation of sanctions on Serbia beginning with Resolution 713 of 25 September 1991 by the UN Security Council. The word also encompasses massive efforts by agencies such as UNHCR and ICRC, subsequent occasional use or threat of air strikes over Bosnia and the training of Croatian army officers by US military contacts in leadership and team efficiency.[3]

1.4 Other actors

In fact, both mediation and intervention have had direct relevance to localised grass-roots groups in ex-Yugoslavia who have struggled to keep multi-ethnic and civic ideas alive, and to act for the protection of human rights. As the theatre of war spread and centralised in Bosnia during late 1992, there began an uneasy new 'status quo' for communities in Croatia and 'rump' Yugoslavia* who had to adapt to new demarcation lines of occupied territory and statehood while dealing both with their own post-war trauma and the continual awareness of ongoing or ever threatening hostilities 'next door' and the possible spillover of these. Secondly, abroad in a country like Britain the immediacy of the Balkan situation and the close geographic proximity of ex-Yugoslavia motivated civilians to care and relate in a fashion perhaps unprecedented since the Spanish Civil War. In this sense, the war was also, indeed, next door.

The War-Next-Door prompted non-official humanitarianism, relief, and 'diplomatic' initiatives on a large scale. New charity initiatives sprang up as self-drive lorries crossed borders to take blankets and medicines. Dentists and doctors organised links to offer their services, and women's groups offered everything from postal delivery of shoe-boxes full of baby goods to the personal arrival of Women's Aid to Former Yugoslavia solidarity. It must be said that 'peace' and 'conflict resolution' initiatives and offerings have also flooded in. In the UK the Co-ordinating Committee for Conflict Resolution Training in Europe was established in response to personal requests from Zagreb and Belgrade, and linked internationally with an ever-growing network. The National Peace Council regularly updated its listings of anti-war networks.

* Hereafter referred to as simply Serbia, but with emphasis in this study on Serbia and Vojvodina.

Full directories became available: *Hilfe fur Ex-Jugoslawien* is a twenty-five page listing of German groups working for peace in ex-Yugoslavia, first published in August 1995, *Oorlog in Voormalig Joegoslavie* is a hundred page listing of Dutch and Balkan peace groups, first produced in September 1995 by Pax Christi/Netherlands, and from across the Atlantic, *Working for Peace in the Balkans: A Guide to US Organizations* is a 1996 directory available both in print and on the internet.

There is a need for analysis of the role of local anti-war groups in their society, the capacity of these groups to make an impact on their society and an assessment of how far outside interventions were a response to specific needs of these groups.

Mixed motives or intentions may inform given interventions into a conflict configuration. Outcomes and/or risks are not always fully comprehended. Individuals and groups local to the post- or pre-war zone must work with multiple levels of stress, change, needs, and responses to these. Their goals will range from survival to making an impact on the wider situation. It is precisely these individuals and groups who form the social fabric at once at risk from and also possible determinants as to whether violence returns. For the trainer or practitioner from outside then, the following questions must be addressed: Do we know fully what we are doing? What is the range of possible results directly or indirectly from our actions? Can we do it better? Are there situations in which we might either change what we do or do nothing at all? What can we learn from three or four years intense experience in former Yugoslavia?

Dr. Andrew Williams, who has worked in a 'second-track' diplomatic capacity in several conflicts (if not in ex-Yugoslavia) captures the nature of these questions:

> 'I take our role to have therefore been threefold: (i) *analytical*, (ii) *facilitatory*, and (iii) *advisory*...
>
> *Use and abuse of our role by others?* Were we used to legitimise actors that might not otherwise have been so legitimised? *Access to relevant information?* It is often very difficult indeed to have access to what other "tracks" are doing. This is understandable, given the normal practise of diplomacy, but it does run the risk of making others assume we know what we do not know, with potentially disastrous consequences. Conversely, it may be argued that this enhances our ability to help the parties to talk to each other with us being part of the wallpaper. *Can we provide the necessary expertise?* It seems to me quite clear that the answer to this has often to be 'no, but I know a man who can'. We have to

be very direct in explaining this... *What difference did we make?* and *What criteria for knowing?* Statements by the parties, public or private? Results "on the ground"?'[4]

1.5 Project objectives

The War-Next-Door project attempts to address two issues current to our understanding of conflict:

1. The theoretical and applied gaps in the study and practice of international relations, in that emphasis on first track diplomacy and models of policy do not fully take into account the internal dynamics of the modern state, nor 'civil society', nor moral as opposed to political or military legitimacy. We know how to 'map' activity of such entities as the UN, NATO, OSCE, EU or the WEU in their response to crisis in the former Yugoslavia. Less clear is the range of responses that have ensued from civic groups and social movements in Croatia, Serbia, Vojvodina and Bosnia. Far from being only 'victims' of power struggles and militarism, many of the population have worked on their own strategies to try to influence a complex situation.

2. The question of long-term structural impact efficacy, and intended/unintended consequences of second track intervention, from grass-roots relief and resource initiatives to training for mediation, non-violent action, trauma counselling, peace education or human rights advocacy. Some hard questions need asking here. Did ideas from outside assist a group in becoming more effective? Was 'help' ever actual interference? Did it lead to the creation of new elites? How do we measure effectiveness? Is it possible to speak of a relationship between personal change and social change in wartime? Are there viable entry points from which to change culture and structures of militarism?

1.6 Background and analytical framework

At the 1992 Bratislava meeting of the Helsinki Citizens Assembly (HCA) various working groups and discussions with representatives from ex-Yugoslavia highlighted the acute need for conflict handling/mediation skills for individuals engaged in situations of war, rapid social change leading to violence, or civic initiatives for reconstruction. The Bratislava workshops were one platform for networking by groups from east and west which led to a plethora of activities and exchanges. A range of alliances and meetings ensued, often conducted under the umbrella vocabulary of 'conflict resolution'.

In both Croatia and Serbia over the next five years the language and processes of 'workshops' moved to 'projects' and finally 'NGO' constructs, as individuals sought to articulate and embody values in opposition to war. Meanwhile the 'international community' in the form of statesmen and inter-government institutions used traditional 'first track' diplomacy to treat these two populations very differently. To Croatia went the carrot, and to Serbia the stick. One favoured westward-leaning state received Blue Helmets to police new borders, US. military training, and weaponry which slipped in under the noses of the UN and Peter Galbraith. To the perceived eastward-leaning 'pariah' state, sanctions were proclaimed.

Writing in *Mercy under Fire* Minear and Weiss document the politicisation of humanitarian aid due to the punishment policy of sanctions. Refugees in Serbia and Montenegro received far less attention than other victims of the break-up of the former Yugoslavia. The world was making the Federal Republic of Yugoslavia suffer for a war for which other parties—the Croatians in Croatia and Bosnia, the Bosnian Muslims, and the Bosnian Serbs—also bore responsibility:

> 'Moreover, by levying economic sanctions against Serbia and Montenegro in May 1992 and tightening them in April 1993, the international community sought to force the Milosevic government to change its policies of "ethnic cleansing". Although the arms embargo of September 1991 had benefited the Serbs, who controlled the bulk of the military assets of the armed forces of the former Yugoslavia, the economic sanctions were seen as singling them out for punishment.
>
> The impact on humanitarian activities of the perceived anti-Serb animus was demonstrably negative. The strategy introduced what the UN chief of humanitarian operations in Serbia and Montenegro, UNHCR's Judith Kumin, termed "a fundamental contradiction: trying to implement a humanitarian program in a sanctions environment". The UN was, in effect, trying to deny assistance and to provide it at one and the same time' (Minear and Weiss, 1995).

In hindsight, there have been many fundamental contradictions in official responses to the war in former Yugoslavia. Western intervention aimed at mediation and crisis management. Instead, as Susan Woodward demonstrates in *Balkan Tragedy*, it provided the irreversible turning point in crisis escalation toward nationalist extremism and war. Failing to engage with the mounting debacle of 1989-90, actions were taken in 1991 which redefined origins and aspects of complex conflict as ethnic and nationalist revolution. To quote Woodward, the result was self-fulfilling:

> 'External intervention continued to reinforce the pressures of the preceding decade that made *states*—political control over territory, its economic assets, and coercive power - the most valuable goal. Nationalist party leaders who had gained legitimacy with the first democratic elections in 1990 but whose programs and performance had not yet been tested by a second election were promoted by EC, CSCE, and UN negotiators to the status of statesmen, leaders of nations struggling for independence. While intervention gave even more authority to the leaders of the republics than in the decentralised federation, it weakened the supports for opponents of their nationalism who considered the creation of democratic procedures, market relations, and guarantees of individual rights within states to be more important. By abandoning the Yugoslav federal government, which depended on international support for its economic and political reforms; prejudging the army as nationalist and its actions to restore order in the republics as illegitimate intervention; and ignoring the many citizens' groups working to foster countrywide co-operation, the West deprived Yugoslav citizens of the last of the protections for their individual rights and the last alternatives to nationalist or treasonous loyalties within their republics of residence' (Woodward, 1995).

Woodward argues that by accepting the principle of national self-determination for the independence of states - without regard to the Yugoslav conditions of multi-nationality or shared rights to national sovereignty, or a willingness to enforce their unilateral decision on borders - Western powers made war over territory inevitable. The struggle to create new states out of the Yugoslav federation was a struggle to get international recognition. The fight for international opinion was as important as the fight on the ground.

This study will seek to make visible some of the citizens' groups mentioned above, using particular case studies from Zagreb, Osijek, Pakrac, Laslavo, Baranja, Subotica, Pancevo and Belgrade. Before setting out the practical methodology used in this endeavour, two particular points must be made.

Firstly, we need new models of understanding which move away from the over-emphasis on 'state' so critically captured in Woodward's observation. It is not enough to frame policy according to how central government in Zagreb relates to the same in Belgrade. Populations relate to each other as well, and sometimes oppose their governments.

Diagram 1 attempts to show the internal tensions manifest when social movements are in opposition to the government of a given state's 'official' policy. There are relationships between social movement (what de Waal refers to as 'primary movements'[5] and governments, between social movements and social movements, and between governments and governments.

Secondly, this study will suggest that Croatian and Serbian populations alike between 1992—1996 became caught up in the overlapping, sometimes competing agendas of two western imports: 'development', and 'conflict resolution' advocacy.

1.7 Development

'No-one told us about development' stated a social worker and grass roots organiser in Zagreb in November 1995. She was looking back at the evolution of local women's work with refugees and the displaced from 1991 onwards. 'What is this word development?' asked a psychologist from Osijek, student on a course in Birmingham, England 1992. By 1996 development ideology and structures were firmly in place in Croatia and making great headway in parts of Bosnia.[6]

The flow of aid and ideas from the west into former Yugoslavia took place in a wider world context for agencies caught increasingly in harsh realities represented by the 'relief to development' debate. Since the end of the cold war there has been a marked proliferation of so-called 'complex emergencies'. The term 'complex emergency' emerged in Africa in the late 1980s to describe situations where natural disaster, drought and/or famine, massive population dislocation and political violence or war were intermingled, sometimes seemingly inextricably, as in Ethiopia, Angola, or Sudan. In the aftermath of the Gulf War (and particularly when the UN's Department of Humanitarian Affairs was established in 1991) it entered the mainstream intervention vocabulary. Duffield (1994) suggests that apart from flagging the term 'multicausal', the definition is largely operational—that is, it tells us more about organisational response than the concrete situation that 'complex emergencies' represent. Response is viewed as equally multi-faceted; UN agencies, donor governments, associated NGOs, as well as diplomacy and sometimes (Somalia, Bosnia) military action.

If it is suggested that 'definition is largely operational', it remains that *complexity* has also been the experience of local populations as well, as was evident in the surveys for this study. Although

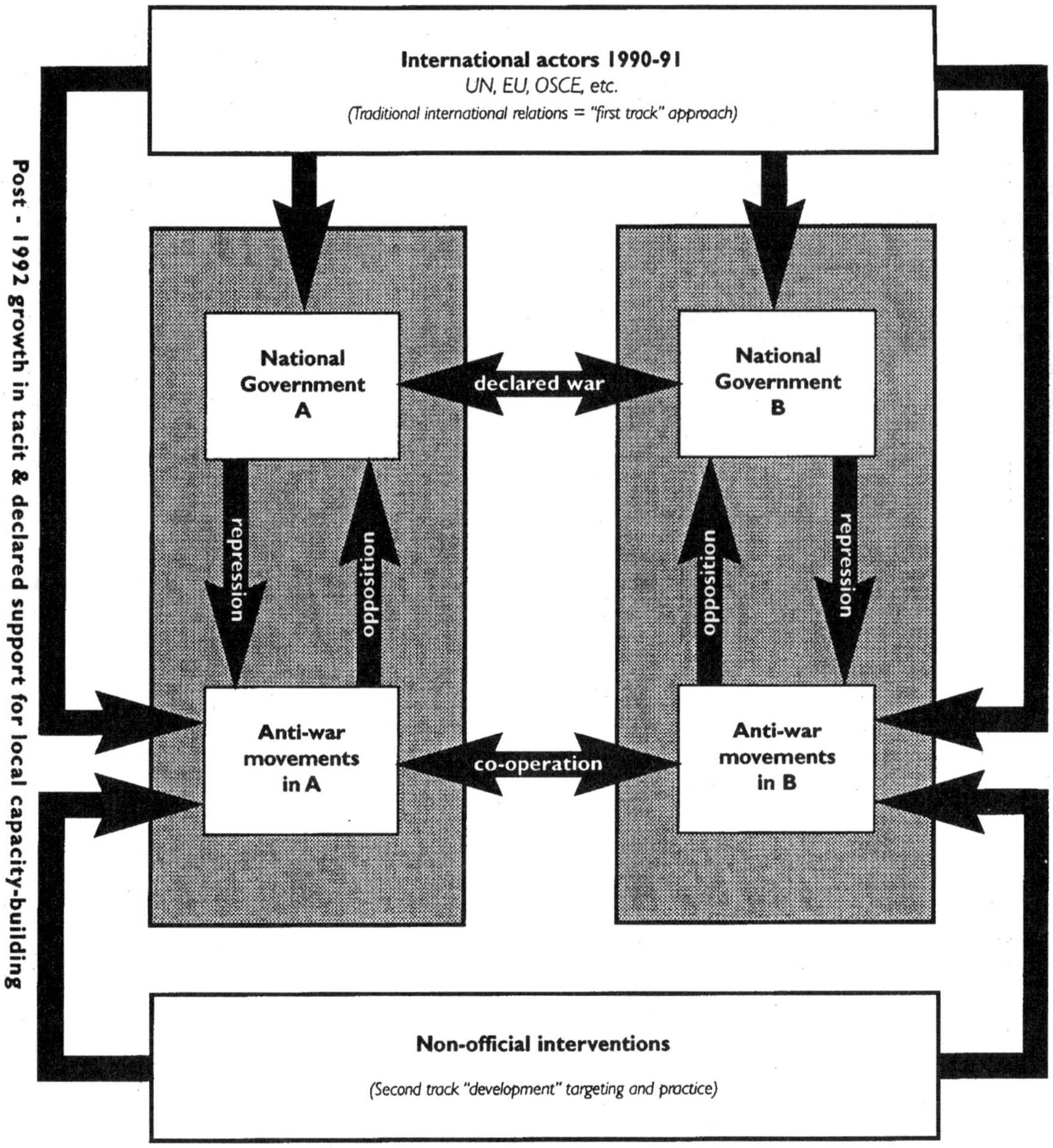

Diagram 1
Primary Movements, Governments and External Actors

Yugoslavia had extreme regional variations ('the ox cart and the jet airliner') it was by and large a successful socio-economic experiment, with levels of prosperity peaking in the late 1970s. In the words of one economist from Sombor, 'What my country has done in socio-economic terms is equivalent to climbing the highest of diving boards and then jumping off—into an empty concrete pool.' Modernity breeds its own complexity; people who stayed in Osijek in 1991/92 often lived in flats on ninth, tenth, or eleventh floors with no electricity for the lift, stranding the elderly, rendering the carrying of water and fuel (as in Sarajevo) doubly difficult. There was concern in Novi Sad about the inability (due to sanctions) to treat the city's water supply, and the unavailability of specialist medication for people with multiple sclerosis, epilepsy, or diabetes.

Technological complexity is one thing. The breakdown of governance, the emergence of intimidating predatory warlords, the politics of coercion and the moral dilemmas posed by witnessing atrocity or compromising from fear are probably far worse. Biserka Tompak was a child in Osijek during the Second World War, and remembers being shot at by German soldiers when she and her brother collected firewood. 'In those days,' she says, 'we had our own confusion, but you knew who was who, and what ideals people were fighting for. In those days too, we knew real, biting hunger. Not so in this war. This is a different nightmare. We can eat, but we do not know what is going on around us' (1992). Mara, displaced from Tenja and living in Osijek now, echoed the same sentiments in a separate conversation a year later.

A key aspect of this study's analytical framework will be to unravel and seek to clarify specific contexts and specific experiences.

As per complex emergencies in general, the culminative effect has been increased donor support for relief assistance, and concern for the 'relief-development continuum'. This is a major shift in the structure of international aid and in western governments donor policy.[7] In its simplest form, the idea is that 'relief should be made developmental' (Ibid.). People should not just be helped in the crisis event, but enabled to address their needs in a sustainable fashion afterwards. Consider the following extract from a paper analysing different approaches to housing the refugees and displaced in Croatia:

> 'In war it is important that relief programmes do not just bring the "...food, medical care, shelter and personnel..." that will save and preserve lives. If we are to provide relief programmes that promote sustainable development in war, then our actions must promote peace; without it, development is both unsustainable and unfeasible. It is not enough simply to give aid or bring relief; in a war situation there is also a need to assist in rebuilding shattered lives and communities, and to take practical steps towards bridging the social and economic divides that war causes. The programmes of aid agencies "... need to be planned in a manner that encourages peace and reduces the level of conflict..."
>
> Peace can be built at all levels and in many ways. While it may not be possible for donors or agencies to stop the war outright, it is within the power of all to act in a manner that does nothing to increase ethnic rifts or levels of tension within communities. Peace is a necessary background for development; if we wish our relief projects to be developmental, then we must address how to build peace as well as physical and social capacity' (Ellis and Barakat, 1995).

The incorporation into development usage of this view of peace 'building' from below is problematic, if well-intended. The emphasis on reconstruction, physical and social, and working to heal severed communities draws charges of both naive 'functionalism' and a predisposition towards illusions of political harmony. Duffield cites 'the growing interest in conflict resolution' as an example of a trend towards 'the unthinking advocation of "development" in increasingly debatable conditions' (Duffield, 1995).

1.8 Conflict resolution

Voutira and W. Brown claim that 'the different models of NGO activities all operate within the same functionalist model of society that views interventions as restoring order and balance disrupted by conflict. The metaphors used to describe the causes of conflict often include "health" and "disease"' (Voutira and Brown, 1995). In order to reach this conclusion Voutira and Brown spent two months studying mission statements and narratives of relevant US and European-based NGOs. They take 'conflict resolution' per se and claim this as a literal objective, then tear apart the term as one with conflicting definitions and meanings. They as well as Duffield (1997) gear their observations through an NGO 'lens'; that is, an issue of concern for the donor. With its stated objectives (1. and 2. above) *The War next door* attempts to open questions both broader analytically and at the same time more personal in terms of recipients'/participants' voices.

This study will approach conflict resolution as an emergent body of applied social and behavioural science as well as a process-based movement for change. The very term needs 'unpacking'. It will explore whether conflict resolution initiatives have become inextricably bound up with humanitarian ones, and examine what this has meant in practice for host communities. While some agency initiatives on 'evaluation' will be considered, the primary emphasis will be on the impact of interventions. Different time scales will be considered; immediate/short, medium, or long-term change, and always in the context of the local community. As such, it will borrow from development studies theory the idea of 'capacity building'. Capacity building may be described as enhancing the systems in place which allow for individuals and groups to realise their goals and potential for socio-political change in a coherent sustainable fashion. Anderson and Woodrow (1989) suggest that 'capacity' can be seen as physical, material, social, organisational. motivational, or attitudinal. International agencies and NGOs with a relief/development 'brief' now 'factor in' conflict as an anticipated problem for organisational positioning (Small, 1996).

The convergence of conflict studies and development policy marks a watershed test for conflict resolution 'theory to practice' in second-track interventions. Development practice and policy are undergoing a major transformation in framing responses to violent conflict and adopting measures for 'peace building'. At the same time initiatives under a 'conflict resolution' banner are increasingly identified as 'humanitarian' in nature. Note the following statement from David Atwood of QUNO, Geneva:

> 'In the aftermath of the Cold War, we are in an important evolutionary period in the practice and understanding of different forms of humanitarian intervention. "Non-official non-coercive" intervention, like the role of non-governmental actors generally, receives less attention in official and academic circles than do the other forms. Witness the relative inattention to this area in Boutros Boutros-Ghali's *Agenda for Peace*. Despite this, there is a tremendous flowering of this form of activity in response to the types of conflict now prevalent in the world. Among the types of "non-official non-coercive" conflict intervention activities... are such things as active mediation; counselling; creating mediation/reconciliation contexts; economic and humanitarian aid; fact-finding; empowering and supporting internal non-official groups; human rights monitoring; problem-solving and process-promoting workshops; training and education in non-violence and conflict resolution; independent media.
>
> It is important to come to a better understanding of the possibilities and limits of forms of "non-official non-coercive" intervention as part of the repertoire of responses available to the "international community" in the face of potential or actual violent conflict situations. It is also important to learn more about the relationship between this form of activity and "official" forms of conflict intervention' (Atwood, 1994).

1.9 Methodology

In international relations as a discipline the problem of conflict studies has long been fraught with the 'level of analysis' problem. For example, Barry Buzan's (1991) *People, States and Fear* starts from the assumption that there are basic levels of security, 'individual', 'national' and 'international', and notes that concepts of 'national' security have tended to organise the other two levels (p.1). Buzan further notes the historic 'militarization' of the concept to which this framework generally gave rise, and the growing criticism of this notion of security 'bound to the level of individual states and military issues', which he points out is 'inherently inadequate' (p.5).

Security from the point of view held in development studies, on the other hand, may refer to food supplies, social acceptance, economic opportunity, access to health care and clean water, shelter and community. Populations are vulnerable not only to armed attack. They are vulnerable to deprivation, fear, persecution, hatred or exhausted resources. Development is perceived as 'a process of increasing people's capacity to reduce their vulnerability,' and such vulnerable areas may include that of susceptibility to violence, itself. All these areas may be at stake during war.

Even when we talk about 'state' security we refer ultimately to an institution constructed by human beings, and involving individuals and groups in many ways. In the words of Martin Shaw, writing in 'There is no such thing as society: beyond individualism and statism in international security studies':

> 'We cannot, from a methodological point of view, simply assume the fiction of political theory according to which states represent their citizens in a general sense. We have to examine the particular connections which individual members of society (we cannot simply consider them as citizens)—both those involved in running the state and those 'outside' it—really have with the state' (Shaw, 1993).

The standpoint of this study is that qualitative research based on testing theories about inter-relationships between variable levels and groupings can result in valuable input into our *gradual* understanding of conflict as a form of human behaviour. My concern is those primary social movements mentioned above; mobilised citizens who opposed war and tried to change their own situation. Their efforts echoed resistance in 1940 Nazi Germany (Stoltzfus, 1996). Like their German predecessors, they were accused of 'treason to soldiers at the front'; their choices of tactics are also comparable—avoidance of state orders, pamphlets, demonstrations, helping the persecuted, possible sabotage, speaking to external actors.[8] My subjective understanding is that these modern groups looked to 'conflict resolution' (whatever that is) as a means for *furthering struggle in a non-violent way, so as not to replicate the very violence they sought to oppose.* I am somewhat baffled at the charge of an 'emphasis on harmony' levelled at conflict resolution in the current debate.

Using case-studies in conflict research provides an opportunity of relating theoretical propositions, which in themselves derive from observation of empirical events and (at times) intuition, to a situation of reality. The process of relating theory to empirical events provides the opportunity of continual adjustment and readjustment of ideas in the deepening of our understanding of social phenomena. I have attempted not only to observe social phenomena (as an outsider looking in), but more importantly to listen to those experiencing it. The role of narrative has been vital in what may also be termed an interpretative study. Some 200 interviews and conversations have been conducted over a four year period. I should say here that I started taking field notes long before the research idea was formulated, and I should declare an interest as participant/observer. In many cases people have been visited and revisited (on invitation) perhaps five times in the period, so there is some sense of continuity, 'history' and development. My role has been one of neo-academic 'solidarity' (speaking in public forums, facilitating group meetings at times, representing donor or support organisations such as Quaker Peace and Service), friend, and sometimes advisor or contact-person. It is local voices which have both informed and helped to shape the substance of argument in these pages. It is hoped that this has been a participative strategy which has involved those on the receiving end of intervention activity.

Evaluation process, when approached from what might be called a traditional perspective, is understood as a retrospective review of what has happened in order to consolidate present or shift future directions of effort by measuring success and failure. This has usually meant the elaboration of standards or suitable indicators of achievement by outsiders. As such, evaluation is much considered currently by 'conflict resolution' initiatives and 'trainers' as they seek—in the UK and the USA at any rate—to both learn, codify and aim for good practice. (See Chapter VIII)

When approached from an interpretative perspective, however, evaluation acquires a very different and more central function; one which questions the very nature of the premises on which the intervention is based. 'Impact analysis' seeks to broaden scope yet further, to seek some understanding of intended and unintended consequences. In a changing world, it is hoped that impact analysis will become a tool for 'rooting' current inter-relationships, and clarifying what might be called the knock-on effects of becoming involved. It may be used for reflection on policy. There are of course, dilemmas and limitations. How can we impose a set of values associated with particular understandings of concepts such as accountability, effectiveness, and outcome onto circumstances and conditions which are informed by sometimes differing sets of values? Western conceptions of the environment, for example, may reasonably be questioned by others who see themselves facing a very different set of problems. Who is the arbiter of what 'good government' should be? Different value systems reflect different priorities and if partnerships are to be developed which can accommodate those different sets of values, then methodologies need to be evolved that make those values explicit and inscribe them in understandings agreed by all. (See Marsden, *Measuring the Process* 1994).

As much as possible then this study will stress the experience of primary actors in local and historical context. It will take the following form:

1. A review, based on international relations theory, of levels of intervention which aim to alter the power relations of war.
2. An examination of popular responses to war in ex-Yugoslavia; actions, group formations, and organising principles such as 'civil society', 'peace culture', and 'new communications'.
3. Focus on two specific contexts, East Slavonia and Vojvodina, for an understanding of structural conduciveness to war; and capacity building for peace.
4. An attempt at a framework of 'the intervenors', extracting from this a spectrum of activities purporting to be 'conflict resolution'.
5. Consideration of the theory and practice evident in this spectrum, including dilemmas of training.
6. An exploration of 'impact', intended and unintended, with particular emphasis on the transition from social movements to NGO formations, and on value changes in society.
7. Conclusions.

In his ground-breaking 1990 *Personal Identity, National Identity and International Relations* William Bloom tackled the 'unit of analysis' question by examining identity theory:

> '...one of the results of the introduction of a more scientific approach to the study of International Relations was that the mass of a state's people—the *nation* indeed—became disengaged from any analysis of inter-state behaviour, as the discipline became self-aware of the fact that it did not have the theoretical tools to handle the issue. The movements, communications and transactions of the national population were, in fact, excluded from the mainstream power political analysis. A certain irony can be perceived here, for in an 'era of the masses'—or, at least, professed popular democracy (and is there any state

which, in its public statements, eschews this?)—an analysis of inter-state behaviour that does not include the mass national population as a major variable is obviously lacking holistic perspective' (Bloom, 1990, p.3).

It is hoped that the spirit of his enquiry will be reflected in this far more modest attempt to find a theoretically coherent way of understanding the current proliferation of second track interventions and patterns—if there are any—of impact.[9]

Notes for Chapter I

1. In 1914 the Carnegie Endowment for International Peace published the 'Report of the International Commission to enquire into the Causes and Conduct of the Balkan Wars of 1912 and 1913'. The chair of the investigating International Commission was Baron d'Estournelle de Constant, a French diplomat who had been present at peace conferences in 1899 and 1907. According to Leo Tindemans, d'Estournelle de Constant noted that the 'powers of Europe' had spent billions contributing to arsenals in the region instead of assisting with what today would be called 'development' needs, i.e., roads, waterways, laboratories, hospitals, and public works. He recognised that a more suitable title for his report might have been 'Divided Europe and her Demoralising Action in the Balkans'. This criticism, though, 'might have been unjust...In reality there is no solution, no way out either for small states or for great countries except by union and conciliation' (preface to 1996 report). The modern study was conducted by the Carnegie Endowment and Aspen Institute together with other European and American foundations.

2. In early October 1991, Carrington reached verbal agreement with Presidents Tudjman and Milosevic, and the Federal Minister of Defence, General Kadijevic, that negotiations should seek to reorganise Yugoslavia as 'a loose association or alliance of sovereign or independent republics,' with guarantees for human and minority rights, and no unilateral border changes. This was formalised as an *Outline of the Arrangements for a General Settlement*, known as the **Carrington Plan**. In addition to framing 'new relations between the republics,' the plan envisioned a 'special status' for areas where minority 'national or ethnic groups' formed a majority of the population. Milosevic soon rejected Article 1 of the Outline, which proposed, *inter alia*, 'sovereign and independent Republics with an international personality for those that wish it'; and, in the framework of a general settlement, 'recognition of the independence, within the existing borders, unless otherwise agreed, of those Republics wishing it' (Report, Ibid., p.44).

3. See, for example, Charlotte Eager's 'Croatian Army success made in America' in *The Observer*, 7 May 1995, p. 17.

4. Extract from a piece by Williams in the University of Kent International Relations Alumni Newsletter Vol. 1, Issue 2 Dec. 1995.

5. Writing in the *Times Literary Supplement*, 21 February 1997, Alex De Waal describes 'primary' movements as 'mobilised citizens in non-violent pursuit of specific political principles that would change these citizens' own lives.' See 'Becoming shameless', p.3.

6. By 1996/97 the social and public policy issues almost seemed to dominate research concerns over ex-Yugoslavia. (What happened to political violence and war?). One researcher in social policy acknowledged the need for broader scope of enquiry, at least mentioning 'social visions at supranational, state, regional, and community levels...acute questions about how to address causes rather than symptoms...' See Paul Stubbs, 'The Role of NGOs in social reconstruction in post-Yugoslav countries' in the *Relief and Rehabilitation Network Newsletter* No. 8, May 1997, ODI London. Sorensen (1997) makes the point that in Eastern Europe the term 'transition' often is substituted for 'development'.

   According to the International Council for Voluntary Agencies (ICVA) some 320 aid organisations (international and local) were operating in Bosnia by 1996. Sorensen (1997) estimated that 44 of these were engaged in social reconstruction. The research of Dave Bekkering (Goni Vakuf NGO unit) suggested that many local groups by then felt it was time for their realm to 'develop more by itself' rather than being moulded by outside agencies. See the 'assistance to local NGOs' section of Dave Bekkering's NGO survey (UNOV—GV@ZAMIR-ZG.ZTN.APC.ORG).

7. For a comprehensive view of this theoretical and policy shift, see the IDS Bulletin Vol. 25 No. 4 Oct. 1994, which takes 'Linking Relief and Development' as its overall theme (Institute of Development Studies, University of Sussex).

   > 'The concept of a relief to development continuum is increasingly controversial and has been attacked by critics concerned that humanitarian response has superseded political response to political violence. Intended as an inclusive approach to affected populations with an eye to long term recovery, it has nonetheless drawn accusations of 'organisational accommodation with the external crisis' (Duffield, 1996).

8. See Geschichte und Geschehen 10, Ausgabe N Gymnasium, Klett Schulbuch Verlag, Stuttgart 1988.

9. According to Imre Lakatos,'... a series of theories is theoretically progressive ... if each new theory has some excess empirical content over its predecessor, that is, if it predicts some novel, hitherto unexpected fact' (Lakatos, 1970).

   Habermas's discourse theory implies a consensual theory of truth, the discourse aims at universally valid truths as an ideal. Eisner (1991) has argued for qualitative research as art, based on connoisseurship and criticism, accepting the personal, literary, and even poetic as valid sources of knowledge. The aim here is consensus. See 'The Social Construction of Validity' by Steinar Kvale, *Qualitative Inquiry* Vol. 1, No. 1 1995

Chapter II

Contextualizing intervention

'In trying to distinguish intervention from other actions that have consequences across frontiers, one can only set outer limits: intervention is any action, beginning with deliberate or remediable interaction among nations, that significantly affects the public internal realm of another sovereign state and which stops short of aggressive crossing of international frontiers. Intervention is action along a continuum of possible choices. The range of alternative courses once men have decided to intervene (or indeed, not to intervene) is far greater than is usually thought of when men debate intervention. Our political and moral responsibility in the realm of intervention is therefore far greater than we usually assume.'

Manifred Halpern 'Morality and Politics of Intervention',
International Aspects of Civil Strife, ed. J. Rosenau, 1964

'Third party intervention is not without its risks, and I would caution disputants against automatically turning to outside intervenors for assistance. For one thing, such intervenors may prove to be incompetent; they may render an already bad situation even worse through ineffectual intervention. Second, they may have their own axes to grind, in the form of vested interests that, although remaining undisclosed, nevertheless guide the third party's particular point of view. Finally, third party intervention risks taking the initiative toward settlement out of the disputants' hands and placing it with someone else. Ultimately, if an agreement is to be reached that has a chance of enduring, it is important that the disputants create an agreement that makes sense to them, that is "owned" by them, to which they feel responsible because they have devised it.'

Jeffrey Z. Rubin, 'The Timing of Ripeness,' *Timing the De-escalation of International Conflicts*
ed. Kriesberg and Thorson, 1991.

'You outsiders just do not understand how we feel.'

Woman in Osijek to German mediator, November 1995.

II. Contextualizing intervention

Debates within the international relations discipline have long linked the concept of intervention to that of sovereignty (Weber, 1992, Evans and Newnham, 1990, Little, 1987). Cynthia Weber (1990. p. 200) argued for a 'recognition that the meanings of sovereignty and intervention are inscribed, contested, erased and re-inscribed through historical practices.' She called for theorists to think about sovereign statehood in terms of authority relations which are worked out in practice, seeing the sovereignty/intervention boundary as an important locale where authority relations are contested.[1] James Rosenau in his early calls for a scientific study of intervention (1968, 1969) shifted the debate from diplomatic and legalistic norms (concerned with the sending of armed forces into another state) and defined intervention as a deviation in the relations between an intervener and a target state which is aimed at altering the authority structure in the target state (1968).

Within this interpretation from almost thirty years ago lies the key to the importance of 'development' in the intervention debate today. Non-military aid and development policy was used by both 'super powers' in the cold war era to obtain allies, and to significantly alter authority structures in target states. Since then measures which promote literacy, reduce inequality, empower minority groups, ensure economic livelihood, or ideologically inform (significantly altering authority structures) have been aimed quite specifically at 'feudal' states. In what Duffield calls the 'modernist paradigm' of developmentalism (Duffield 1994)[2], today there is active linkage of development and conflict reduction. Consider the following quotation from an address by Baroness Chalker to the Institute for International Affairs, Stockholm, October 1996: 'Support from development assistance budgets can help diffuse violent conflicts through strengthening civic groups and allowing "voices of reason" to speak out.'[3]

Development agencies now conduct their own debates on intervention, with important contributions such as John Harris, ed. *The Politics of Humanitarian Intervention* (1995) and the Médecins Sans Frontières Report on World Crisis Intervention *Life, Death and Aid* (1993).[4]

Jonathan Goodhand and Peter Chamberlain offer their own shrewd assessment of this new state of affairs in comments from 'the field', in this case, Afghanistan:

> 'In the era of democratisation and good governance, NGOs have become the donors' "favoured child", with access to growing resources and influence...They are viewed both as "market actors" which are more efficient and cost-effective than governments, and as the agents of democratisation, an integral part of a thriving civil society...Underpinning this consensus is the presumption that political democracy and socio-economic development are mutually enforcing. The State, market, and civil society—which, following Korten (1990), we shall refer to as *prince*, *merchant* and *citizen* —are related in a series of virtuous circles. A basic tenet of 'NGO lore' is that NGOs promote and strengthen civil society, thus subject the prince and merchant to greater public accountability.
>
> There is, however, an element of triumphalism in the discourse about New World Order, and the belief that NGOs are "part of the warp and weft of democracy." Such words ring hollow in a world characterised by instability, fragmentation, and deepening poverty' (Goodhand and Chamberlain, 1996. p. 196).

At its most basic, and in essence *intervention means to interfere with or become involved in the affairs of another.*[5] In capturing the images of 'prince, merchant, and citizen' Goodhand and Chamberlain offer levels of dominant international theory and thus practice vis a vis violent conflict.

2.1 On people and paradigms: international relations theory and approaches to intervention

A cursory overview would reveal that those studies of war and peace which derive from the discipline of international relations have at least three broad approaches to causes of conflict, often categorised as realism, structuralism and modern idealism (or the world society school of thought). These and a range of complementary theories have been outlined by Light and Groom (1985). Each approach also encompasses ideas for the processes, analysis, management and outcome of a given conflict:

1. The Prince

Realism claims Machiavelli as a spokesman but is most often associated in modern times with Hans Morgenthau for his widely-used text *Politics among Nations*. Morgenthau argued that the drive to dominate is universal among individuals and, through them, on the part of social groups. If individuals have a drive to dominate then those that are dominated will always strive, whenever it is possible, to escape their fate. This view of a hostile world and malign intent reflects a long tradition in political thought which includes not only Hobbes, but Machiavelli as well as Thucydides. In a 1989 lecture at the University of Kent A. J. R. Groom suggested that it also reflects a 'Calvinistic view of the political process in IR and it is one that is largely shared by diplomats and journalists. After all, diplomats are congenitally cautious and by making prudent prognostications they can claim, if good fortune prevails, that it was because of their warning and hard work that the worst did not prevail! Journalists, proverbially cynical, are well aware that bad news is the news that sells best!'[6]

Often state-centric, advocating 'the balance of power' and rational use of war as part of state-craft, this view accepts rigid hierarchy and absolute victory or defeat as political and natural norms. Realism calls for diplomatic intervention, military preparedness and 'conflict management'. The stunning book by Laura Silber and Alan Little *The Death of Yugoslavia* could be called a realist interpretation of the war in that it focuses on the manoeuvrings of plotting politicians and the foils of opportunism. As such, this work gives lie to early western explanations of the conflict as 'ethnic'.

The images given for realism are often either the chess board of calculating players or the billiard game.

2. The Merchant

Structuralism as a school of thought has a different starting point. It rejects notions of actor control over residual socio-political form. People are rather positioned in and shaped by 'structures' in society.[7] Some are dominated in such a way (due to history and economic exploitation) as to never realise their full potential.

Collective, often imbalanced, relationships are central to structuralism. Marx is often cited as one of the first major thinkers in this vein, although the Chinese could well claim Mencius. The debate on imperialism earlier this century framed by such thinkers as Luxemberg, Hilferding, Lenin and Hobson influenced this approach, as did the more recent work by R. Prebisch on 'dependencia' in Latin America.

Galtung, Curle, and Webb have written on conflict and structures, each contributing to the debate on 'structural violence'[8], as well.

With the expansion of the Deutsch Mark as legitimate currency throughout the former republics, and the carrot of investment held out at Dayton there can be no question about the validity of approaches which involve economic functions. Regional economic disparities were themselves a factor in the disintegration leading to secession and war. But structure can also involve organisational principles...how the forms and organisation of society shape action, internally, and on different levels. So social-psychology offers interpretation of the dynamics of affiliation, with a greater emphasis on the fears and misperceptions arising between communities, what is taken (or given) from the past and present which shapes current and future relationships. It addresses questions of group identity, motivation, aggression and violence (Volkan) The approach of the Community Relations Council in Northern Ireland and 'psycho-cultural' dimension addressed by cultural traditions, symbols and perceptions work pioneered by Marie Fitzduff is one example of this particular theory in practice[9] (Fitzduff, 1993).

Structuralism then as a broad approach will include both revolution and resolution as responses or possible outcomes; since conflict is built into structures, the only way of broaching it is to change the structures. Once there is an awareness of structural conflict, and demands for change from those that are victims of it, then open conflict may ensue as the beneficiaries of structural privileges come to the defence of their favoured position. But not always. The finer points of perception and relationships may be worked on in a myriad of meeting points. Determining factors will include power; whether it is symmetrical or asymmetrical, resources, and awareness.

The layer cake is an image sometimes given for this approach: strata of needs, capabilities, and resources.

3. The Citizen

Modern idealism.

The work of John Burton is often credited with bringing a 'world society' approach to the fore. Light and Groom refer to it in their introduction:

> 'This approach has no generally accepted definition, although there is a measure of agreement that both the level of analysis and the unit of analysis are a function of the research problem. But it is not merely the question of an interdisciplinary approach. Rather the focus is upon the adisciplinary treatment of phenomena such as conflict, decision-making, development, integration or identity seen in the context of world society (and social science) as a whole. Systems of transactions, their structures no less than their processes, are the focus of attention, as is the degree to which such structures and processes are legitimized. This points to decision-making

as an important concern. But beyond the decision-making process and structures, the needs theorists have pointed to the individual, with his unchanging needs and implacable search for their fulfilment, as the irreducible unit of analysis, thus ensuring that the old debate between 'nature' and 'nurture' lives on in the world society approach. The question is ultimately an empirical one and a utilitarian one: does it help us to know and accomplish better what we want as individuals in society?' (Light and Groom, 1985).

Michael Banks argued in *Conflict in World Society* that 'pluralism'[10] reflected a changing world as The Cold War ebbed, multi-lateralism came to the fore and purist realism could not deal with new realities.

This argument draws on integration theory or functionalism, articulated by I. Claude (1971) and earlier Mitrany (1943) whose work stood in polar opposition to Morgenthau's. Here we find an emphasis on co-operation and the desirability of peace:

> 'Functionalism begins its analysis with the deceptively simple proposition that the provision of common needs can unite peoples across STATE boundaries. This has produced a concentration by functionalist writers on what has been called the wealth-welfare dimension in WORLD POLITICS and to the avoidance of HIGH POLITICS. The functionalist logic, that there are wide and significant areas for the provision of common services and for the meeting of common needs, served to inspire the UN to establish a host of Specialized Agencies—such as the WORLD HEALTH ORGANIZATION (WHO). By avoiding the most politically contentious issue areas and concentrating instead upon wealth-welfare provisions, functionalists tried to focus upon areas of unity rather than disunity between people and states. Functionalists assumed that a natural HARMONY OF INTERESTS existed in these matters' (Evans and Newnham, 1990).

Communications Theory (Deutsch 1991) and social psychology influence this multi-level view in its approach to conflict. Modern Idealism accepted aspects of both the state centric framework and differentiations which could be called structural. Chris Mitchell's *The Structure of International Conflict* is a classic analytic formulation of the universality of mechanisms, behaviours, cycles, and outcomes at different levels. As economics lends itself to structuralism, social science has influenced the 'world society' school of thought. It is often given the image of a 'cobweb', or a system of interacting points and actors, it is an image used for the world society approach.

2.2 View from 'real life'

On the 'receiving end' of intimidation, militarism, and a conflict he sees as both realist and structural in origins, Aleksander Weisner wrote from Serbia in a way which echoes this multiplicity of concerns:

> *'The problem of conflict resolution is directly connected to the nature of the conflict, i.e. the cause of the conflict and the relations in it, which depends on a person's position in the society and his formation and expression on the way from individual to social. This formation expresses itself through needs (through levels), feelings, experience, habits, knowledge, social status, accepted system of values... Religion., politics, economy, nation ... all of this are means of manipulation and through that manipulation the primary conflict is being re-established. This explains why many conflicts through history are identical, but also, this is the answer to the question why those persons who know the skill of conflict resolution sometimes cause the conflict, do not use those skills, or find them ineffective.*
>
> *That is why I believe that, for a thorough approach to conflict resolution, a complexity of various fields, that we must not ignore, is required: social-psychotherapy, various pedagogical methods, animation.. Thus, the change in the approach to the problem of training design would be mostly in the methods that are not separated from the psycho-dynamics of the group, and in the wider meaning-contents of the conflict ...'* [11]

At worst the contending dominant views (realism, structuralism, idealism) become guarded positions in their own right, and cease giving actual perspective or understanding for real events. At best they are differing lenses with which to examine complex phenomena.

2.3 From theory to action

Dennis Sandole 'Paradigms, theories and metaphors in conflict and conflict resolution: coherence or confusion?' (Sandole and van der Merwe, 1993) refers to the work of Thomas Kuhn (1970) who pointed to societal determination of internalised thought frameworks or 'paradigms': 'Different paradigms, different mappings of the "same thing", mean different "realities"—different descriptions and explanations of the 'same thing', plus a different sense of problems appropriate to that 'thing' and of methods relevant to solving them—whether for members of different communities at one point in time or for members of the same community undergoing radical change over time.' Sandole is concerned with theories of conflict and conflict resolution, 'world-views' or ideological positions on how we understand conflict and whether we 'conflict analysts, conflict resolution theorists and practitioners, peace researchers and "concerned others" have anything to say about, or to offer the parties in protracted violent conflict situations.' The potential for the explanation of violent conflict, judging by his chapter and a wealth of literature on the subject, far exceeds our potential for response to it.

Yet 'paradigms' affect modes of action as much as they frame analysis. International institutional capacity to respond to the post-cold war phenomena of disintegration conflicts has been poor. Sandole suggests that *Realpolitik* dominated the perceptions and behaviour of 'Serbs and Croats' during their wars in Croatia and Bosnia-Herzegovina (and of Armenians and Azerbaijanis in Nagorno-Karabakh) and that it continues to dominate behaviour elsewhere. There emerge two problem areas here. Firstly, it may be time to turn the question around to asking what parties in protracted violent conflict have to say to the analyst and practitioner about their experience. Secondly, let us be clear about who the parties are—who are the 'Serbs' and the 'Croats' in this case, and would it not be more useful to distinguish between types of leadership, types of community, and the wide range or spectrum of activity undertaken during times of war? This must include not only decisions for military action but also coping strategies, opposition or resistance, adaptation to new status quo conditions and recovery. It may also entail the transformation of attitudes and choices, and the active creation of alternatives to violence.

2.4 Levels of operationality

Galtung takes a lively approach to what is traditionally called 'first track' diplomacy:

> 'Major actors are, of course, states in general and governments in particular. They tend to define the tool on which they presumably have monopoly, military force, as relevant, and see military problems and enemies everywhere. In addition they tend to be arrogant, patriarchic, secretive, exclusive and jealous of non-governmental forces, and of course to pursue their own interests, thereby often deforming conflicts rather than transforming them in any useful way. Their academic training is usually in international law, mainstream economics and area studies, including the history and the culture of the region. Useful, but also dangerous. International law tends to legitimize as negotiation partners those who exercise **de facto** territorial control, meaning that war lords can shoot themselves into the conference room. Moreover, the perspective is strongly punishment oriented, with measures like economic sanctions and war crimes tribunals. Economics tends to be blind to the countless side-effects of market behaviour. Area studies tend to isolate regions from contexts, e.g., Ottoman Turks, Germany and Habsburg Austrians/Hungarians from Yugoslavia' (Galtung, 1994).

He continues to outline 'levels' in society from which interventions may ensue in situations of violent conflict or the threat of violence. Corporations and business people may play a role, Galtung argues, but 'capital actors ...' are money-oriented in their approach rather than force oriented.

> 'Capital, the corporations, are underestimated as peace actors. And yet they could participate with plans for rebuilding the country, donate computers, modems etc. for peace work.
>
> Another forgotten actor that is playing a positive role in Yugoslavia is the municipality, a territorial unit with some ability to mobilize positive resources, yet without that negative resource, the military. Municipalities abroad can adopt municipalities in Yugoslavia as is done through the Belgian/Swiss organization **Cause commune/Gemeinde gemeinsam**, and in principle help refugees, protect conscientious objectors, contribute food and clothes and medicaments, send doctors and nurses etc. One day they could send local police and mediators.
>
> And then there are all the NGOs ...And there are the many peace organizations and institutes that have come into being recently. All of this activity is seriously under-reported by the media that by and large have played a horrible role, fanning the flames of the conflict rather than stimulating the positive forces. We have too many war journalists, too few peace journalists who know how to report peace activities away from the prominent conference table in Geneva where state logic is being enacted. The media focus on blood and elites, not on peace at the grassroots level.
>
> Literally thousands of conferences take place every day in war torn Yugoslavia. But unconnected, unheard of, unseen. Even in our information age we do not manage to bring them together, so that we could launch a standing "peace lord conference" in the room next door to the "war lord conference" in Palais

des Nations in Geneva. The dialogue between those two rooms holds much of the key; and that dialogue is absent from the process' (Galtaus, 1994).

These latter observations describe what may be called 'track two', multi-track,[12] or unofficial diplomacy and intervention. Multi-track diplomacy is a multi-disciplinary approach to involvement. It assumes that 'ethnic' and regional conflict situations involve a large and intricate web of parties and influences which require a systems[13] approach. It also operates on the premise that change can come from 'below' and is not simply imposed from 'above' as in first-track operations, i.e., outright military victory, judicial 'settlement', political take-over or occupation forces. J. P. Lederach has put in visual triangular form this hierarchy of complementary levels (see **Diagram 2**). He states, 'It seems increasingly clear that peacemaking activity works in at least three levels. The highest level involves very few people, the well known leaders and personalities, the processes are usually highly public, and tend to focus on cease-fires and political solutions. The middle-range level has more people, who may be well known within a given sector, ethnic group, or by religious affiliation, but they have more room to manoeuvre, given that they are not directly in the lime light. The most populous is the grassroots level where people often experience the devastation of the conflict and are concerned primarily with daily survival. A comprehensive approach must recognize that sustainable peace builds across the levels of society and does not rely exclusively on peace trickling down'. Lederach further argues, 'It is crucial that peacemaking efforts emerge from and be connected to the context and setting within which the conflicts/problems are raging.' Therefore, he argues, it is important to 'Encourage and provide space for peacemaking approaches that emerge from the setting. More specifically this suggests we must respect and support indigenous ways of approaching peacemaking, as opposed to relying on transferring or prescribing our ways.' Also, it is crucial to 'Encourage and provide space for indigenous peacemakers. We are not primarily about the task of introducing ourselves as mediators or peacemakers, we are about the task of supporting and encouraging people from the setting as they have the vision and undertake this task' (Lederach 1993).

Non-state actors and international outcomes is an area deserving increased study and attention. They operate against an historical background of entrenched social forms and precedent. Writing in 1979, Philip Reynolds characterised emergent challenges to state-centric control. From when the modern state system came into existence in Western Europe in the sixteenth and seventeenth centuries until the end of the second world war, it could be argued that the use or threat of force was a common component of international relationships, that the control of the means of violence was effectively monopolised by states, and that governments accordingly regarded the maintenance of armed forces sufficient for defence against attack or for optimum exploitation of opportunities for advancing purposes (frequently in the form of territorial gains) as being of paramount importance. Since the second world war control of the means of violence is no longer monopolised by states. At the same time non-military transactions have increased in range and quantity, so the dominant influence on international outcomes exercised by states as a result of their monopolistic military position is now no longer so decisive.

> 'Within the realm of security...the central question is the extent to which non-state actors now play a role...In the first place control of information of strategic significance may not be wholly in the hands of governments. Many multi-national corporations are involved both with research and development and with the production of critical components of weapons systems (computers for instance), and it is very difficult for governments of parent countries to be aware in sufficient detail of the operations of corporation subsidiaries in other countries to be able to ensure that information of strategic importance does not pass out of the country...
>
> A much more obvious incursion of non-state actors in the security field is to be seen in the activity of guerrilla groups and terrorists, some of which at least may be viewed as international non-governmental organizations. Whatever the reason for their rise (such as the decline of governments' competence, the reduced level of satisfaction with or acceptance of value systems, the development of new loyalties across as well as within state frontiers, the availability or ease of manufacture of means of destruction, the swift global passage of information promoting emulative behaviour) the influence of such groups on international outcomes is evident'(Reynolds, 1979).

Exactly a decade after Reynold's article appeared the potential of new social movements (NSMs) and independent media came to the fore, achieving what cold war confrontational politics never did: the collapse of Eastern European communist regimes.

State centred 'realism' with its emphasis on coercion and high politics of 'national interest' has prompted both sharp theoretical criticism and practical soul-searching. Realist notions cannot handle systemic change because interactive levels of adaptation are too subtle for win/lose equations. Vasquez argued in the *Power of Power Politics* (1983), that power politics does not explain. It may describe competitive or fighting stances but it does not interpret or explain. It needs to be explained.

2.5 Track one

The supposed basis for international governmental responses to conflict situations is the UN Charter. Article 1 of the Charter defines the first purpose of the UN to be 'to maintain international peace and security, and to that end: to take effective collective measures for the prevention and removal of threats to the peace, and for the suppression of acts of aggression or other breaches of the peace.' To this end, the Charter gives the Security Council 'primary responsibility for the maintenance of international peace and security' and the power to 'determine the existence of any threat to the peace, breach of the peace, or act of aggression' and to 'make recommendations, or decide what measures shall be taken' (Roberts, 1993). Decisions made by the Security Council in this area are binding. Thus, the Charter gives the Security Council the central role in responding to conflicts and grants it effectively unlimited powers to take action in this area. It is within this context, that the Security Council has, since the end of the Cold War, taken action in response to a growing number of conflicts and authorised a range of enforcement actions in response to the conflicts in Iraq, Bosnia and Somalia.

Central to the ongoing debate on military or other intervention is the tension between the Security Council's mandate and the nature of most current conflicts. Although broad, the powers given to the Security Council under the Charter were clearly intended to relate to conflicts between states rather than within them, as indicated by the Charter's reference to '**international** peace and security' (emphasis added). Yet, almost all contemporary conflicts are occurring not between states, but within them. The Security Council has dealt with this by defining intra-state conflicts, most specifically in the cases of Iraq, Bosnia, Somalia and Rwanda, as 'threats to international peace and security' and therefore falling within its remit. It is this ambiguous use of the term 'threat to international peace and security' which has led to the current situation of ad hoc and inconsistent responses to crisis. The ambiguity of the term allows the Security Council to take action in response to some situations and not in response to others and leads to glaring inconsistencies.

Some learning has taken place with regard to preventative work. The deployment of the UN peacekeeping force to Macedonia was a significant step to promote confidence and deter conflict in Macedonia—notably, being the first time the UN Security Council had authorised the deployment of a peacekeeping force in a preventative mode before violence had broken out (Cottey, 1996).

One clear lesson of the Yugoslav conflict is that the negotiation of cease-fires and the deployment of peacekeeping forces once violence has broken out is only likely to be successful if and when the participants to the conflict have accepted the need for a cease-fire. Similarly, mediation can only be successful when the circumstances are already ripe for some form of cease-fire or settlement. Furthermore, the Yugoslav conflict has highlighted the fact that the negotiation of cease-fires and the deployment of peacekeeping forces often only serves to freeze the situation on the ground in favour of gains achieved through aggression, without resolving underlying political issues.

First track measures for military action have limitations simply because they are 'top-down' and restricted in how much change they can effect. This is increasingly evident. Sadaam Hussein, and other seemingly corrupt but less demonised governments, are still in power in spite of a stunning Western, high-tech, military 'victory' in the Gulf.

Inter-positional peacekeeping forces installed with conviction now have 'track records' of their own, which raise questions about the viability of 'conflict management'.

It is obvious that unresolved causes of conflicts may eventually result in the renewal of new violence which can shatter the work of even the best manager. Consider Cyprus where the UN peace-keeping force (UNFICYP) contained the inter-communal conflict between 1964-74 but did not achieve a political settlement. Underlying tensions developed into open warfare in July 1974 when a Greek sponsored coup that installed a puppet government led by Nicos Sampson provoked a Turkish invasion. In Lebanon, UN force (UNIFIL) were in a similar situation in 1982 when Israeli Defence Force tanks advanced through its positions on their way to lay siege to Beirut.

In an early and optimistic article (1993), James Gow argued that the EC's and UN's 'successes all came as a result of coercion.' He refers to coercion as 'one of the instruments of diplomacy.' Woodward takes a strikingly different view. She suggests that while refusing to enforce its own rulings or to impose forces between armed parties, the EC (and then the UN and the United States) nonetheless interposed itself politically. All the while that it insisted on the norms of sovereignty and prohibited interference in the internal affairs of a sovereign state without consent, the EC in fact stepped into the shoes of that sovereign state. Because it ignored the compromises that Yugoslavia represented in guaranteeing nations the right to self-determination in a nationally mixed area, ignored the security guarantee that Yugoslavia had provided for territories of mixed population, and did little to reassure those relegated to minority status that they would be protected, it could not alter the downward spiral of suspicion and insecurity that led to war. It then assumed the role of mediator to obtain cease-fire agreements. That meant talking to leaders who were fighting because they could not agree, while insisting that no agreement achieved by the use of force would be recognised. It could negotiate cease-fires, but it could not persuade parties to disarm without providing a constructive alternative to those whose national rights were denied by the international insistence on the republican borders. To avoid recognising rights until there was an overall political settlement for the whole country, for example, the Vance plan for a cease-fire in Croatia placed 14,000 UN peacekeeping troops at "flash points" in four UN protected areas. Sent to monitor the withdrawal of the JNA, the disarming of Serb militia, and the restoration of control over police and government to local majorities in the UNPAs, the UN operation was viewed by both the Croatian government and the Serb authorities in *Krajina* as legitimating their territorial claims as per rights to self-determination.

> 'Moreover, despite the resort to violence, there was no military solution to these conflicts without the extermination or expulsion of large numbers of people. Military control over territory would still have to return to the constitutional issues of national, ethnic, minority and citizens' rights' (Woodward, 1995).

If there are problems associated with the first track approach when applied without attempts to resolve underlying factors in the conflict, there are also problems that will arise if the resolution approach is attempted without effective response to violence. For the continuing violence will feed several destructive processes that if unchecked will destroy the work of the resolvers. These destructive processes ... include polarisation, incitement, stereotyping, scapegoating, militarisation and entrenched positions for revenge. They are likely to continue to feed the conflict, and to feed off it, until direct violence is brought under some control, often the pre-condition for successful conflict resolution. Otherwise the 'logic of violence' will be too strong for resolution attempts to be successful.

> 'The key point to be made here is that managers/peace-keepers can do no more than reduce physical violence. But this direct violence will often be the symptom of deeper conflicts that have their roots in the pursuit of justice, equality, dignity and freedom. There is a very real danger, therefore, that effective management will create not a situation of peace but of pacification. That is, a situation where an unjust, unfree society is perpetuated though the suppression of violent opposition. This can only be avoided if the management approach is accompanied by attempts to resolve these deeper, underlying causes of the violence' (Ryan 1992).

As an international community we have lost confidence as to what intervention is appropriate when. After a generation of strategic and popular thought devoted to the possibility of a nuclear holocaust, we find ourselves facing moral dilemmas of human behaviour on a much more ancient basis —how men and women treat other men and women.

The majority of politicians and public are hesitant about sending 'our boys' anywhere to defend others. The dead soldiers of the Gulf War, or the Battle of Goose Green, or in Vietnam do not bring the same honour and glory to their grieving families as was once claimed, in a time-honoured fashion for the fallen warrior. Our uncertainty regarding moral obligation and practical involvement was evident in Bosnia. Journalist Martin Bell took a strong position on the ambivalence:

> 'We came up with limited, symbolic measures, which may have prolonged the conflict. One was using UN troops to escort aid to the victims of war rather than to prevent the aggression. This was to pass food in through the window while the murderer stood at the door. Another was the plan for UN designated safe areas without the troops and the mandate which would have made them safe' (Bell, 1996).

Bell sees war as diplomacy's failure. After an extended tour of duty in Bosnia he can no longer accept the 'national interest' as a sole basis for foreign policy.

2.6 Track two

At the 1994 Conference on Security and Co-operation in Europe (CSCE, now the OSCE) Review meeting in Budapest, the agenda included new approaches to security. The resulting document included sections on conflict management and the following statement: 'The participating States and CSCE institutions will provide opportunities for increased involvement of NGOs in CSCE activities as foreseen in Chapter IV of the Helsinki Document 1992.' (Budapest Document 1994, Decisions, Chapter viii, para. 17). The OSCE initiative is aimed particularly at non-governmental actors involved in a wide range of non-violent conflict resolution activities or unofficial 'track two' work for communication, dialogue, mediation or reconciliation. (Gutlove and Thompson, Helsinki Monitor, Vol. 6 1995 No. 3). Although the Budapest document has a whiff of old-fashioned diplomatic hierarchy, i.e., 'They will search for ways in which the CSCE can best make use of the work and information provided by the NGOs', it is nonetheless revealing about new realities and trends in war and peace. On the one hand, diplomats and governmental organisations no longer command immediate respect or access; it may be that international intergovernmental organisations (IGOS) have neither the funds, expertise or legitimacy to deal effectively with post cold-war security questions. On the other hand war itself is increasingly not about formal declarations, state armies and rules of engagement. It is about new re-forming configurations in the social fabric itself.

Track two diplomacy has been defined as 'unofficial, informal interaction between members of adversarial groups or nations which aims to develop strategies, influence public opinion, and organize human and material resources in ways that resolve their conflict' (Montville, 1991 p.162). It is in no way a substitute for official, formal 'track one' government-to-government or leader-to-leader channels, but offers complementarity in its emphasis on relationships and change from 'below'.

Berman and Johnson refer to the range of private international relations as 'unofficial diplomacy', a category which includes different kinds of participants, channels and approaches: 'It should be made clear that our concern is not with domestic groups that work to influence only their own government, but with individuals and groups who have contact with private citizens or government officials from other countries as well as with their own government' (*Unofficial Diplomats,*, Columbia University Press 1977, p.5).

Berman and Johnson still see international relations as state centric although they look to John Burton's term 'global society' as a useful/inclusive phrase. Their 1977 study emphasises the 'intermediary' function of unofficial diplomacy, that is the third party communicative function which unofficial channels may have which then assist the formal and the official. They stress that private individuals or organisations can offer neither threats nor offer promises: 'In terms of the resources that government officials control—money, armies, economies—they are feeble. Nevertheless, sometimes alone, other times in concert with official efforts, private initiatives may contribute to the alleviation of problems in communication that may result whenever different nations speak or conduct their relations. By providing auxiliary channels...serving as intermediaries between governments, by performing various third party functions including negotiating and mediating in conflict situations, and by contributing to a climate in which policy-makers can usefully work, private citizens may augment and facilitate official diplomacy.'

The potential and validity of grassroots activism has been addressed by Curle and Boulding who have written mainly about 'global transformation' but whose ideas can be applied equally well to situations of inter-communal conflict. Curle (1990), for example, has identified three 'tools for transformation': peacemaking, development (defined as 'purposeful growth and change'), and education. Whilst Boulding has pointed out the need to create 'learning sites' to ensure contact and dialogue between different groups (1990, p. xxii), Alger (1991, p.245) has noted a broadening of the definition of peace in recent years which reveals 'that a diversity of sectors of any society and a diversity of sectors of relationships between societies, contribute to peacelessness...This does not mean that governmental and non-governmental institutions and leaders no longer have important roles in peace building. But it does mean that they cannot attain a strong and lasting peace alone without widespread knowledge, participation and support from people of the world'. Finally, in a recent study Walker (1998) has examined the 'transformative assault on our inherited notions of authority, legitimacy. and power' undertaken by 'critical social movements'. He also points out areas where such movements can concentrate their analysis: economic development, gender, environment, militarisation, human rights and culture. Such items are as relevant for the agenda of 'disintegration' conflict as they are for global politics. Indeed, they may have a more urgent relevance in such situations. All of these studies emphasise the importance of social movements. Using a classification developed by Giddens (1990), they can therefore be said to exhibit responses to modern problems known as 'radical engagement'. This can be compared with other responses which Giddens has labelled 'pragmatic acceptance' (where the emphasis is on day-to-day problems and tasks and which often involves a numbness arising out of deep underlying anxieties); 'sustained optimism' (based on an Enlightenment faith in reason and science); and 'cynical

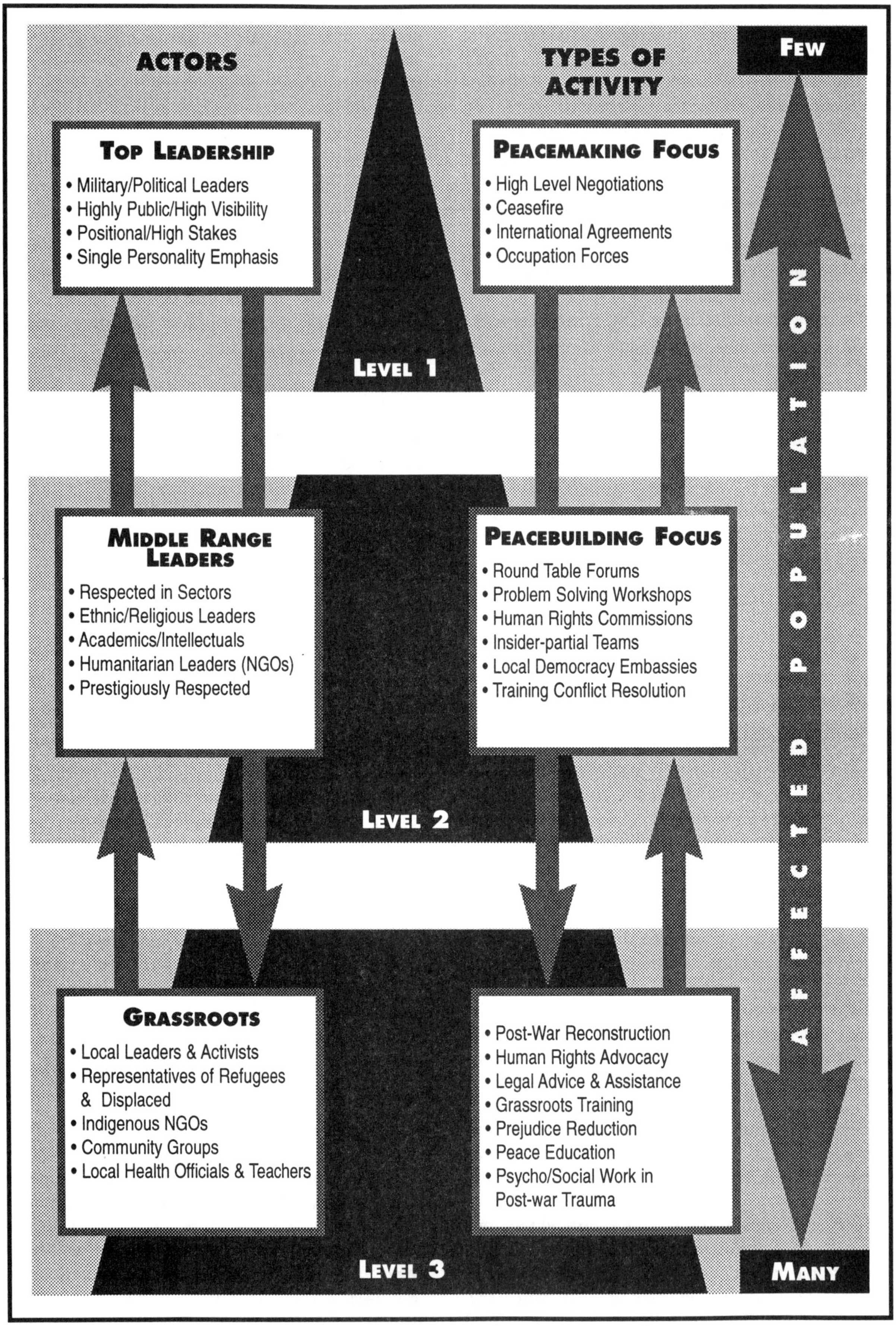

Diagram 2

Three Types of Actors in the Affected Population and Peacemaking Foci

Based on: Lederach, JP: Pacificism in Contemporary Conflict, July 1993

pessimism' (based on the neutralising of emotion and the potential for black humour). Unlike any of these alternative approaches radical engagement emphasises the need to transcend major problems through mobilization.

'Even in periods of political upheaval, economic crises, rising social intolerance—and in the case of Yugoslavia, open warfare—society goes on. Regardless of a general fall in living standards and the inadequacy of *ad hoc* measures of social compensation, people somehow patch their lives together with resources husbanded from diverse and parallel economies. Some work in the formal sector, some work in the semi-legal second economy, some work on family garden plots, some exchange skills and abilities with neighbours and friends, and large amounts of the uncosted work of women and female children and some reliance on minimal state benefits make life viable.' (Deacon, 1993, p.229). Radical engagement is not disproportionate to levels of violence in the environment at a given time. Dr. Katarina Kruhonja described the 'black box' she felt engulfed by during the worst of the bombing of Osijek in winter 1991/1992. It was some months before she and colleagues would contemplate their own approach to peace work. Peace building at the grassroots level will not have immediate dramatic effects on conflict situations. It works to a different time frame and agenda. When effective it may lead to the establishment of new networks and new institutions. According to Walker (1998), critical social movements can explore new political spaces, extend horizons and establish connections. They may develop a new language of dialogue to replace the language of conflict and sectarianism. In doing so they may help to 'deconstruct' and reconceptualise the inherited history of myth and symbol that fuels confrontation. External assistance or enabling of such work may be seen as track two work, and a type of third party involvement given the wider configuration of conflict. Lane and Cormick (1978) suggest that third party roles include those of 'advocate', 'mediator', 'researcher', and 'enforcer'. The latter term may refer to someone overseeing funding or indeed the reorganisation of local police.

2.7 Conclusion

The image of 'prince, merchant and citizen' reflects schools of thought about actors and processes in international conflict, i.e. realism, structuralism and modern idealism. These views in turn are represented by intervention approaches and levels, as pictured in the adaptation of Lederach's tiered triangle.

In spite of how they are named, theorised, or pictured however, these levels are not a static form of socio-political stratification, but dynamic and cross-referential. For example, at the start of the war, when opposition to Serbia's president Slobodan Milosevic managed to bring out tens of thousands of protesters in Belgrade, David Owen and the other international negotiators sometimes met the grassroots social action group 'Women in Black.'[14] Grassroots volunteers in Western Slavonia were instrumental in monitoring and gathering human rights violations data during military action in 1995, which could then be documented by appropriate INGOs and governments and influenced decisions taken not to admit Croatia to the Council of Europe.[15]

Taken together in response to complex emergencies and political disintegration, these contemporary responses are seen by Kelman and Warwick as 'social intervention':

> 'Social intervention is any act, planned or unplanned, that alters the characteristics of another individual or the pattern of relationships between individuals. The range of acts covered in this definition is intentionally broad. It includes such macro phenomena as national planning, military intervention in the affairs of other nations, population policy and technical assistance. It also applies to psychotherapy, sensitivity training, neighbourhood action programs, experiments done with human beings and other micro changes' (Kelman and Warwick, 1978).

The efficacy of social intervention will lie in specific understandings of context and conditions. Above all, 'second track' initiatives will only be effective if they link directly to localised internal responses to war.

Notes for Chapter II

1. Robert Jackson did precisely this for the concept of sovereignty in his 1990 study Quasi-States: Sovereignty, International Relations and the Third World, Cambridge University Press:

   'The old colonial regime withheld independence from under-developed countries until they were considered "fit" for self-government. The new post-colonial regime extends independence as a matter of right in the expectation or at least hope of subsequently assisting them to develop their capacities of self-government and thereby enable them to deliver civil and socio-economic goods to their populations. International aid is justified on the affirmative action grounds that independence is necessary but not sufficient to enable ex-colonial states to become their own masters. *Consequently, the positive norms and activities of contemporary international organization can be understood as an attempt (to date not very successful) to compensate for the shortage of positive sovereignty of quasi-states.*

What is most significant in all of this is not variations in empirical statehood which have always existed but changes of international norms and expectations concerning underdevelopment. What was once considered a *prima facie* ground for denying membership in international society is now regarded as a claim to additional international support and assistance: sovereignty plus. The following chapter outlines the contrasting *modus operandi* of these very different sovereignty regimes' (p. 31. Italics my own).

2. See also M. Buchanan-Smith and Simon Maxwell "Linking Relief and Development" IDS Bulletin Vol. 25 No. 4 October 1994.

3. 'Can Development Programmes Reduce Conflict?' Baroness Chalker's address to the Institute for International Affairs, Stockholm, 1 October 1996, available from The Overseas Development Administration, London.

4. See also 'interven/e v.i. Come in as something extraneous; occur in the meantime; come between so as to prevent or modify result etc.intervention n. [L. inter (*venire vent*–come)]' from *The Concise Oxford Dictionary*, 1976, O.U.P.

5. As per popular usage and *Chambers 20th Century Dictionary*, 1983.

6. Personal lecture notes, University of Kent, winter 1989.

   A young Serbian film maker submitted a television documentary synopsis/proposal on 'Peace Groups in the Yugoslav Republics' to the BBC in London, late 1991. It was rejected on the grounds that the content was 'not sexy' (Personal conversation with Vanda Krajinovic).

7. Structures being autonomous, independent phenomena separate from actors but influencing actors: wholes bigger than their parts.

8. Johan Galtung's notion of structural violence refers to the institutionalised nature of social injustice which preserves a gap between an individual's aspirations and reality. The aim of peace should therefore not simply be the absence of overt physical violence ('negative peace') but also the transformation of society to overcome injustice ('positive peace').which involves the dissolution of structural violence.

   See:

   Adam Curle, *Making Peace*, Tavistock Publications, London, 1971

   Johan Galtung, *A Structural Theory of Imperialism*, Journal of Peace Research 1 (8), 1971

   Keith Webb, 'Structural Violence and the Definition of Conflict', *Encyclopaedia of Social Services*

9. See *Community Conflict Skills*, 1988 by Marie Fitzduff, Express Litho, Belfast. A handbook for group work, this approach was undertaken by the Community Relations Council of N.I. from its inception in 1990.

10. **Pluralism** This term is used in two senses. First, as a perspective on the structure of the system, pluralism may be taken as a portmanteau term covering all those who reject the assumptions of STATE-CENTRISM in preference for some kind of MIXED ACTOR MODEL. Secondly, pluralism is derived from political sociology where it is used to identify political systems where power is shared amongst a plurality of competing parties and interest groups. Pluralism is thus a theory both of inter-state, intra-state and domestic politics.

    Pluralism in the first sense argues that the assumptions of the traditional state-centred view of international relations were derived from a period when the level of interconnectedness between states was significantly lower than at present. Pluralists believe that certain economic goals—or 'wealth/welfare issues'—can only be realised by states becoming more collaborative with other state and non-state actors. The state is seen as more integrated into the global system by pluralists than by REALISTS. Because the system is one of mixed actors, the defining characteristic of the actor becomes AUTONOMY rather than SOVEREIGNTY.

11. Personal correspondence from Pancevo, June 1996

12. Lewer and Ramsbottom (1993) cite multi-track ideas from U.S. former Ambassador McDonald, which stipulate five possible 'tracks' of diplomatic activity:

    Track 1 Official government-government interaction.

    Track 2 Un-official, non-governmental, analytical, policy-oriented, problem-solving efforts by skilled, educated, experienced and informed private citizens interacting with other private citizens.

    Track 3 Businessman-businessman, private sector, free enterprise, multi-national corporations. (McDonald claims that the contribution is much undervalued).

    Track 4 Citizen-citizen exchange programmes of all kinds such as scientific, cultural, film, student, etc.

    Track 5 Media-media based efforts designed to expose and educate large segments of the population in conflict to the philosophy, ideas, culture and needs of the other nation, society or ethnic group with which they are in conflict.

13. For further reading on the 'systems' approach, see Capra (1997) and Czempiel (1989).

14. See Jonathan Steele's 'Silent Sentinels for Peace', in *The Guardian* 16 Aug. 1995

15. See 'Crisis and Co-ordination: May-August 1995' (p. 23) in Paul Stubbs, 1996, *Social Reconstruction and Social Development in Croatia and Slovenia: the role of the NGO sector*.

Chapter III

Responses to war

»Rana vježba«
»Early exercise« 1971

III. Responses to war

In retrospect, responses to war in Croatia and Serbia developed along contrasting organisational lines. There proved to be fundamental differences in style, what one ARK activist referred to in early 1996 as 'new communicative way versus old dissident traditions.' What she meant was that the Zagreb centre spurned conventional politics, preferring to work in 'horizontal' networking 'new social movement' mode (Mastnak, 1990), whereas the Belgrade centre head Vesna Pusic consolidated a major political foothold in Zajedno (the main opposition coalition) and CAA organised itself rather more 'hierarchically.' In Croatia groups grew, proliferated, multiplied. In Serbia one had the impression of many splits, divisions, and firmer positioning style. Three factors must be considered here: personalities, geography, and ethos.

That leading personalities in each movement were exceptional is in no doubt, as evidenced by the nominations of Vesna Terselic (ARK, Zagreb) and Vesna Pesic (CAA, Belgrade), along with Selim Beslagic, Mayor of Tuzla, for the 1997 Nobel Peace Prize. Group composition in either centre drew on different constituencies. The atmosphere at ARK in November 1995 was not prone to electioneering ('Why vote?') while CAA headquarters were essentially fielding their own candidate in 1996 Serbian elections. *The recognised need for change was shared but the styles were different.*

Geographical location must have had its own influence on style. Belgrade had been/is a federal capital, a centralised urban setting of decisions and control. Amid the Milosevic purges and heavy-handed police tactics employed periodically there was scant scope for 'alternative' cultural radicalism to thrive. Zagreb, on the other hand, was a stone's throw from Slovenia, home of the late 70's punk subculture, and by the mid-80's a site for alternative networks Mastnak (Ibid.) characterised as 'pacifist, environmentalist, feminist, gay, and spiritual "new age".' In other words it imbibed more of what he deemed 'civil society... initially conceived as an alternative, rather than as an opposition' (Ibid. pp. 305-306).

Finally, post 1992 ethos in Croatia became that of New Nation, New Member of the UN, and a new collective revival and celebration of folk tradition, as in the greeting 'Bok' and language claims. There was a view westward, for new investment, for consumer goods, for a future again in tourism. There was a carefully cultivated feeling that a war had been won, in spite of goings-on in Bosnia, or unfinished SAO business. In Serbia international sanctions resounded as punishment of a pariah state, business activity, news, commodities and travel possibilities dried up. Greece and Bulgaria remained fairly friendly neighbours, but the internal sense was one of loss, confusion, and a curious combination of guilt and victimhood.

Whatever general differences emerged, there were also evident dichotomies groups 'on both sides' were to share. They struggled with a tension between 'therapeutic' and 'direct action' approaches to activity. There was a change in emphasis which induced growth from anti-war solidarity to 'NGO development'; from informal group work and organising to proposal-writing, donor-funded, registered organisations; from radical minority to new computerised, 'westernised' professionals. These developments notwithstanding, it is important to recall the urgency, shock, disbelief and desperate need for response as a once unified nation-state, a leader of the 'non-aligned' world, quite literally fell apart.

3.1 Protest

Early 1991 saw thousands of protesters in street marches in Belgrade, with shouts of 'Slobo-Sadaam'. Workers went on strike in Belgrade, Nice and Pancevo, for want of pay as much as political sentiment. Later that spring one third of all Serbian workers were on strike[1]. By the second half of the year, when fighting had broken out in Croatia, some 40,000 JNA soldiers deserted *while in uniform* (Vasi, 1995). 'Almost nobody was prosecuted. The political opposition, obsessed by its own nationalism, didn't notice those expressions of the popular will' (Ibid.). In Sept. 1991 army reservists and some civilians led an anti-war 'uprising' in Velika Plana, central Serbia, according to a report on the independent Belgrade radio station B-92. The group's leader, an unnamed member of the Serbian Democratic Party, said the reservists refused to fight while the borders of Serbia remained undefined by the republic's parliament.[2]

The previous July had seen the launch of the charter of the Anti-War Campaign written in Zagreb, and signed by both individuals and organisations. By the end of 1991, 76 groups and organisations from ex-Yugoslav republics signed the Charter and about 500 individuals. Movement for Peace and Non-violence from Ljubljana (Slovenia), the Sarajevo Peace Centre of Civil Forum (Bosnia and Herzegovina), the Belgrade Centre of Antiwar Actions (Serbia), the Titograd Peace and Civil Committee (Montenegro) were among the signers of the Charter. In this way the Charter became the basis of an unofficial gathering of peace activists against war in Croatia and other regions of already ex-Yugoslavia. A 'Basic Information' document published by the Antiwar Campaign Council, Croatia in February 1992 stated the following:

Responses to War - Pancevo 1991

Responses to War - Pancevo 1991

'With the escalation of war in Yugoslavia, peace initiatives in all republics started to take place in July last year. They emerged spontaneously, were organized in various ways and started numerous actions...All these groups and organizations are facing the same problems: political pressure by the authorities and war-mongering political parties and movements (especially pronounced in Serbia), the media blockade, the lack of knowledge and experience and the lack of money and other material facilities. Apart from that, war operations aggravate communication exchange considerably (traffic blockade, the blockade of telephone and mail exchange). The Campaign is also faced with various problems due to different political attitudes which we try to overcome by our common principles of non-violence, democracy, co-operation and the right of dissimilarity.'[3]

Box 1 shows only a partial list of projects contained in this early document. Its first paragraphs would be as relevant five years later as it was then:

PROJECTS OF ANTIWAR CAMPAIGN COUNCIL

Training for non-violence, conflict resolution and mediation

In the forthcoming months conflict resolution and peace mediation will be one of the most important activities of AWCC. Return of over 500,000 refugees will be accompanied with much violence. The hatred between Serbs and Croats is deeper than ever. One could easily imagine what is going to happen when refugees will return to their destroyed villages, seeing only the ruins of their houses, hearing stories about murdered relatives and friends, seeing the landscape of burned trees and fields. An extreme need for revenge is already burning in their hearts. Some of them will choose the violent and some the non-violent solution.

Antiwar Campaign would like to point out the ways of non-violent solution. We will be organizing a number of workshops in the damaged towns and villages. People from Osijek, Rijeka, Karlovac, Slavonska Pozega and Zadar have already expressed their interest. Over ten workshops were held so far owing primarily to the help of Bund für Soziale Verteidigung from Germany. There will be several more workshops in the forthcoming months. We also hope to organize the first seminar for trainers, which will thus enable us to prepare workshops on our own. We would be interested to find an experienced trainer who could stay in Croatia for six months, as a mentor and supervisor working with our trainers.

Publication of newsletter (ARKzin)

The newsletter is published bimonthly. It provides information on peace and antiwar groups in all republics of ex-Yugoslavia and includes reports, interviews, essays, poems and cartoons, etc. It is also distributed to workers from Yugoslavia in West Europe and is entirely translated into German owing to the help of our friends involved in the peace initiative there. The summary will be translated into English and distributed abroad by fax and computer network.

'War in the media' research

The aim of the research is a comparative analysis of war propaganda in media as to point out manipulation mechanism and spreading of negative emotions and prejudices. Teams of enquirers have been formed in Ljubljana, Zagreb and Belgrade. Two meetings of researchers have been held so far, trying to define patterns of investigation.

Peace entrance

The so-called Peace Entrance (in the centre of Zagreb) has been the stage of happenings and concerts of spiritual music since last autumn. There was a break during the winter months when concerts were held at St Martin's Church in Zagreb, but are again planned for the outdoor stage. The project also includes stone-dressing of a nearby wall with peace messages and the erection of the Pillar of Peace (such as many towns in the world already have).

Human rights protection

Protection of human rights from illegal and illegitimate violence from the state and its bodies becomes more important with the cease of war operations. All forms of violence are interconnected and are getting more pronounced. The Council has therefore initiated an action aimed at protecting the Serbs in Croatia from revanchism and such laws and regulations which violate rights of civilians in Croatia and from other tendencies which try to establish authoritative rather than democratic relations.

War crime research

The research includes gathering data on war crimes, their analysis and instituting legal proceedings in front of proper authorities or international court. News articles are analysed and reported accidents gathered according to standardized pattern. We cooperate with the Belgrade Centre for Antiwar Actions in this project. The initiative is starting to gather European non-government peace and human rights organizations at a meeting suggested for March this year in Geneva which would plead to the UN for establishing a special commission for war crime research in ex-Yugoslavia.

Peace policy and demilitarisation

Working out of peace policy within non-violent framework and general mobilisation. Attempts to influence the official politics of the Croatian government as well as of the international participants in the crisis solution. Finding of common ground together with other peace initiatives in ex-Yugoslav republics. Several appeals to Croatian government and public have been published so far.

(From ODBAR ANTIRATNE KAMPANJE/HRVATSKA 'Basic Information' Document Feb. 1992, Zagreb.)

Other focus areas included support for the right of conscientious objection and alternatives to military service, organising volunteers to help with post-war reconstruction, enabling women's empowerment and protest organisation, translation of literature on non-violence, 're-socialisation' of former soldiers (with assistance from Vietnam Veterans Against the War, USA) and practical training in 'mediation and negotiation.' The Belgrade Centre operated along similar lines:

> 'The Center for Antiwar Action is a citizen's association established in Belgrade in July 1991. It answers the need of many citizens to resist the war and prevent its escalation. A number of non-party and non-governmental organizations opposing war and advocating peaceful resolution of the crisis are among its founding members. The enthusiastic participation of numerous volunteers, has kept the Center running and made its activities possible. The Center became known to the public through its slogans: *negotiations instead of war and violence and the right to desert from the civil war*' (Center for Antiwar Action leaflet, Kralja Petra, 46 Beograd, September 1993).

3.2 The importance of networking and the problem of patriotism

The early initiators of antiwar action were activists representing what Mastnak characterised as new social movements or simply the 'Alternative' (Mastnak, 1990): students, ecology groups, feminist groups, 'youth culture' and artistic circles, as well as journalists and 'enquiring' professionals (social workers, psychologists, economists, scientists), many of whom had links and connections in Western Europe. The concern with conscription, and the flood of young men over borders to Hungary, Austria, Germany, Italy and Scandinavia to avoid service meant contact with War Resisters International and 'training' by Christine Schweitzer and Kurt Südmeisen in Zagreb as early as September 1991.

At the same time as activists in Zagreb and Belgrade embraced a framework of 'rights' and 'alternatives', i.e., conscientious objection and non-violent conflict resolution, spontaneous protests took new forms. The mothers of young conscripts organised as Bedem Ljubavi or Shield of Love, claiming that many young soldiers had been illegally retained to fight even though their national service period was over. They argued that their sons were being held hostage by the JNA. Organised by

Shield of Love, mothers from Croatia, Bosnia-Herzegovina, Macedonia and Kosovo initiated a series of demonstrations from Belgrade to Brussels. Despite intervention from Serbian authorities, a group protested outside Belgrade's parliament building, demanding peace and the release of their sons.

Shield of Love continued on to Brussels and assembled before the European Parliament, holding candles and waving EC flags to which they added a dove of peace. Representatives handed the European Commission member for human rights a seven-point appeal, demanding peace, the release of conscripts, the return to barracks of the federal army, and an amnesty for deserters.

The question of rights and universal values which subsumed national loyalty was to become a key element for sustained anti-war work. Without a wider mandate including non-violence or peaceful settlement, Shield of Love mothers eventually fell back on national identity:

> 'Some Serbian mothers want their sons back from the federal army too, but those demanding peace are in a minority and their pleas are ignored by the tightly controlled Serbian media. Others support the army's actions in defending, as they see it, endangered Serbs in bloodthirsty Croatia.
>
> Nor is Shield of Love the stereotypical women's peace organisation. They want peace, but not at any price; they view Croatian military action as justifiable self-defence against Serbian aggression. Antonija Bilic, who went to Brussels, describes the reactions of a mother whose son was fighting in the federal army. She was overjoyed when he deserted, but only because he had then joined the Croatian National Guard. "My heart is singing and I am happy," she said' (Holmes, 1991).

'Peace' after all is a normative word representing a state of affairs which can be fought for and won, as much as imposed or negotiated. In some circles it was no contradiction to be 'pro-peace' and 'pro-war' in Croatia and Serbia. The problem with a stated 'anti-war' stance was the implied disloyalty to whichever state was conducting it. So it was, that Women in Black, silent protesters who appeared in the streets of Belgrade and Pancevo in October 1991 were 'occasionally attacked' (Steele, J., 1996) by paramilitary groups, had their placards smashed, and were shouted at and abused by passers-by.[4] This type of response ebbed and waned: weekly Wednesday vigils continued unabated for the next five years.

Women in Pancevo held candlelight vigils from Nov. 1991 to August 1994 *every day* in the town's main square, and after that at weekends. 'Originally,' says Jasenka M., 'we mourned for all the war's victims and attracted hundreds of ordinary people—some who were more concerned, admittedly, with Serb deaths.' They were ignored by national media, and tolerated by local authorities. Jasenka now says ruefully of the Serbian (Milosovec's) government, 'They may be criminals and thieves but they are not stupid.' Such isolated cases of 'repressive tolerance'[5] heightened the need for contacts outside. It was vital to affirm stances by communicating with external agents. The claim to externally verified validity was crucial for group formation in Pancevo, Subotica, Sombor, Novi Sad, and (over the new border) in Osijek, Rijeka, Karlovatz, Split, as well as in Belgrade and Zagreb centres.

If it is possible to identify patterns in anti-war group formation and issue areas (see below) it is far more difficult to ascertain the degree of non-compliance, or 'everyday resistance' to war.

3.3 Everyday resistance

The work of James Scott (1985) points to the possibility of localised forms of resistance which is embedded in everyday struggles for survival.[6] He defines these as actions which deploy 'weapons of the weak', including 'foot dragging, dissimulation, false compliance, pilfering, feigned ignorance, slander, arson, sabotage, and so forth' (Ibid. p.29).

'The nature of such resistance means it does not require strategic co-ordination. It avoids direct confrontation with authority, and it encapsulates some notion of "individual self-help" (Ibid.). It is gradual, piecemeal, and to a large extent 'invisible.'

Examples would include the family in Osijek who hid their (Croat) daughter's (Serb) fiancé for eight months lest he become a local target; the Belgrade restaurateur who considered herself 'not political' but was appalled by the 'Nazi style' (her words) commandeering of Bosnian Serb refugee men (by military police) at gun point for forced return to the front-line, and subsequently found hiding places for a dozen such men until they could melt into the countryside, find forged papers or be smuggled out of the country. 'It was only when police stormed my very own café,' said G., 'and caused total crazy panic at gun point, that I realised I had to act.'

'Going slow' on bureaucratic demands was another tactic: teachers and administrators who lost, misplaced and lost again the government forms on which they were to declare ethnicity statistics; teachers who attempted to bypass new 'guidelines'

Voice from Sarajevo:
February 1992

'Publication for Human Rights and Peace'

EDITORIAL

The time of civic initiatives has gained its full affirmation in the choice between war and peace, between hopelessness and hope. The paralysing fear that was blinding our mind's eye is beginning to disperse owing to the great world initiative to bring peace back to Yugoslavia. This is just the beginning of hope. Yet, the citizens of Bosnia-Herzegovina have a major event before them: to decide at the Referendum about the future status of their Republic. But the international recognition of human and civil rights and freedoms, which stood behind the peacemaking mediations of the EC and the world implies acknowledgement of Bosnia-Herzegovina as a civil state.

Another acknowledgement for Bosnia-Herzegovina and Sarajevo in particular as a natural peace zone is the proposal of Mr. Boutros Ghali, the UN Secretary General from Egypt, to locate the UN peace forces' mainstaff in our city. The commander-in-chief will be a general from India. It is another proof that the centuries-old wisdom of tolerance learned by living together in a multi-confessional, multi-national, and civilizational mix has provided a basis for emanation of an undestroyable peace-loving culture recognized at home and the world over.

This issue of our publication for human rights and peace dedicates a considerable space to the opinions of renowned intellectuals from the country and abroad on the crisis resolution. But what seems to be common to most of them is the Spynx-like answer: wait for Godot.

Visually, this issue is dominated by the installations full of top hats for solemn occasions , coconuts for last survival resources in the spiritual and economic desert, and lions roaring from the top. No need to ask why.

But the resolute yet non-demanding steps of Mahatma Ghandi and his nieces on the back cover of the paper represent the only meaningful answer to all those who wonder why so many institutes for the research of peace, tolerance, future... Why so many movements for peace, non-violence, justice ... It is the only weapon to stop the riders of Apocalypse. ■

Ibrahim Spahić

on the teaching of much re-written histories of both Croatia and Serbia. 'When it came to teaching "the Vatican as Comintern", admits V. from Nice, 'I digressed and avoided as much as possible. But I was in a minority, and much cold-shouldered by patriotic colleagues.'

Z., a young Serb who let down the tyres of buses and mini-buses used for the forced expulsion of Croats, Slovaks and Hungarians from his area of Ilok, was caught and given a beating so severe that he is now partially deaf. 'People were being shot in the cornfields,' he remembers. 'I was tired of the tyranny of non-reaction, and sickened by the stench of silence.' According to UN figures some 1,200 non-Serb villagers were forcibly expelled from the Ilok-Erdut area in April/May 1992 alone (Traynor, 1992).

3.4 Group formation and issue areas

Anti-war groups formed where individuals could opt for a collective identity and a degree of visibility. In Ilok, for example, such organisation would have been impractical verging on suicidal given 'the armed thugs who have a license to terrorise' (Ibid.) and the relative rural isolation which is a feature of the area.[7]

Townspeople, on the other hand, had a relatively more cosmopolitan base in which to begin, although urban paramilitary activity was not to be underestimated. As urban areas, Zagreb and Belgrade offered the communications and networks on which to build links with European bodies such as The Helsinki Citizens Association, ecumenical church agencies, environmental and civic groups (particularly in Netherlands, Switzerland, Germany, Italy) or with international activists and advisors, i.e. the work of Gene Sharp (1985) on non-violent action and Hodgkinson and Stewart's (1991) *Handbook of Disaster Management* were both evident in early meetings in Zagreb and Belgrade.

Intellectuals and activists from these two cities tried to stay in contact with each other and shared voice with those from a third capital: Sarajevo. The February 1992 edition of the 'Publication for Human Rights and Peace' (produced by the Citizens' Forum of Sarajevo)[8] is a poignant reminder of the rigour with which claims to multi-culturalism, diversity and human rights were then articulated. Page 34 reproduces the frontpiece editorial from this issue. In it, Ibrahim Spahic voiced his tenuous optimism that the institutions of track one would still save Bosnia-Herzegovina. Spahic was president of the Centre for Peace, Sarajevo.

The articulation of claims to non-violence, conscientious objection, multi-culturalism and human rights were vital issue areas. So, as the war developed, were the questions of self-help and religio-spiritual renewal.

Self-help and social-engagement

The propensity for self-help was informal and spontaneous in the early days of the war, particularly in Croatia where both the new national independence and status as 'victim' state ascribed 'meaning' to being bombed or displaced. Initially people sought refuge with relations or friends, (as was the case in Serbia for those fleeing the new 'Croatian' side of hostilities).

The population of Osijek emerged from a night's mortar fire or bombing to sweep up, place board over blasted-out windows, shift rubble and retain some sense of normalcy, if casualties were low enough to render this possible. Sixty per cent of the city's 21,000 flats were damaged during the siege Osijek experienced. Psychologists and teachers worked as volunteers in setting up and running 'S.O.S. Telephone,' a 'help line' patterned after continental services designed for people needing support because of domestic violence or depressive/suicidal tendencies. S.O.S. Telephone functioned from a tiny office in an underground arcade which had previously held shops and services for subway users. It advertised its help line number in the local paper, (which took pride in maintaining production and delivery during the war!), on posters glued to fences and street lamps and on local radio. The idea was that anyone who felt alone, isolated, in need of help, or seeking information could ring. Remarkably, given the vulnerability of telephone systems in modern war, some 2,000 calls were logged during a six month period from October 1991 to March 1992.[9]

Callers ranged from a six year old whose mother had 'gone out for a loaf of bread,' to an eighty-one year old in need of assistance due to mobility problems. 'In the beginning calls were very short,' explained Bozica Stumfol, volunteer at that time. 'After the "cease-fire" of 3 January, people rang for long tellings of their own tension, for relief of it, and we got 1/2 hour to 2 hour calls.'

In 1991 and 1992 Subotica (Vojvodina) was confronted with its first wave of refugees. About three thousand registered refugees entered the city which, unlike devastated Osijek, could offer some prospects for employment and integration. At least two hundred found full time work, more found casual labour or part-time jobs (Hendriks and van der Berg, 1995). There were at least as many 'informal' as registered incomes, however. Churches (Adventists, Catholics, Hari Krishna, to name a few) organised meal centres, offering soup and bread to the indigent.

By the end of 1992 there were over 700,000 registered refugees and displaced in Croatia.[10] In early summer 1992 anti-war activists and other concerned colleagues began 'enabling activities' on a personal scale in the collective centres near them in Zagreb; taking in a box of toys to enable play, ingredients for a meal, materials to make things with etc. The origins of 'Suncokret' (Sunflower) were thus informal and needs-based. As an early Croatian NGO, Suncokret's stated aims included 'social engagement':

> 'If we define politics in terms of power, then Suncokret is a political initiative and movement, in the sense that it is committed to grassroots work, to peace and to the principles of non-violence. Suncokret works *with*, or alongside, people rather than *for* them and values the importance of cultural diversity and of challenging oppression. Suncokret seeks to provide opportunities for people to empower themselves, to exercise their right to choose and make decisions, to take more control over their lives...'(Pecnik and Stubbs, 1995).

The Suncokret initiative developed into a programme using international volunteers, and was recognised by UNHCR as a conduit for 'international aid.' It became a channel for donors and had rapid institutional growth.

A radical 'social engagement' philosophy was also espoused by Belgrade radio station B-92 which operated without a license from the end of 1989. When the first barricades went up in Sarajevo at the beginning of the war in Bosnia, B-92 barricaded off a street in Belgrade to show what it would feel like in Sarajevo. 'We blocked a one-way street because we didn't want to disturb anyone,' says Sasa Vucinic. 'When anyone wanted to pass, we said: "Just pass." We wanted to show people how stupid it is. Every individual should think about society.'[11]

The station organised peace concerts attracting up to 50,000 in Belgrade, demonstrations against the wars in Croatia and Bosnia, and even 400 babies at Milosevic's residence after he imposed a 44% tax on children's goods. (B-92 urged mothers to 'give' the government babies which the government was making it impossible to support. Any baby who cried or made a noise was judged to have voted against Milosevic and handed back to its mother. The tax was reduced to 14%). Because of its limited frequency range B-92 could broadcast to only a million people in Belgrade in a geographical bloc which voted consistently 'oppositional' in elections. To a disgruntled Pancevo peace activist, 'B-92 reaches the converted. They may as well be on the moon, for all we on the periphery are concerned.'[12] Like Suncokret however, it attracted international interest. The International Media Fund (Washington D.C.) sponsored management and engineering study of Radio B-92 in August 1991 which resulted in subsequent provision and installation of transmitting and sound-mixing equipment.[13]

Elections were held in both Croatia and Serbia in 1992; in each case the outcome was a consolidated mandate for the regime in power. The USA-based International Republican Institute monitored each election and voiced serious concern in their reports. In Croatia these concerns included the manipulation of citizenship laws and identity cards for voters, questionable participation of displaced persons in the voting, composition of voter registries, the misuse of the media, lack of civic education, and some instances of intimidation. The Serbian minority was completely excluded from voting in the elections.[14]

In Serbia the IRI mission found that the post-Dec. 1992 election period had brought 'dramatic changes in various opinion-framing institutions. For instance, purges have been conducted in the University of Belgrade, including the dismissal of the student leaders, the National Theater, in the official radio and television service and in the Belgrade medical school. In addition, vital equipment sent from the West for the opposition electronic media "disappeared" in transit.'[15]

In what had been previously an opposition stronghold, the political dynamics in the province of Vojvodina changed dramatically with the December election results. The Serbian Socialist Party and its political allies in the Radical Party won a majority of seats in the Vojvodina Assembly. The new mayor of Novi Sad, the capital of Vojvodina, was a member of the Radical Party, in circumstances of 'potential large scale vote fraud.' [16]

With dominant power structures and figureheads in place, the triumph of new formal nationhood setting in in Croatia, and a 'siege' sense under internationally imposed sanctions in Serbia, fewer and fewer people took to the streets in any number to register opinion about the fate of Bosnia. Sonja Biserko would reflect two years later that at demonstrations in Belgrade in 1992, tens of thousands of people came out into the streets to criticise Milosevic because of the sanctions: 'But few in the crowd dared—or perhaps even thought—to carry signs criticising the war in Bosnia. Milosevic easily exploited this political naiveté—shifting blame to the outside world and branding all domestic opponents as traitors. A great many people from Serbia who opposed the war—estimated at 200,000—did so simply because they themselves did not want to fight, and expressed this opposition merely by leaving the country' (Biserko, 1994).

Religio-spiritual renewal

The role of religion and the war is a subject deserving of economic study in itself. It is highlighted with regard to second track intervention

Organizations formed in response to the war: Vojvodina

Organizations pleading for peace, supporting conscientious objectors, striving for tolerance, inter-ethnic co-operation and respect for human rights and freedom

None of these organizations consider themselves as political, but they act as ones, or better to say groups for pressure aiming at political conflicts resolution. However, they cannot be identified with either political organizations or groups for pressure. Compared to political organizations these NGOs do not wish to come to power, and compared to other pressure groups, they are not orientated only to pressurize authorities. They concentrate on several basic activities:

- *promotion of their attitudes*
- *gathering like-minded individuals*
- *education (directed against untrue information launched by authorities)*
- *providing legal, material and psychological support*
- *establishing contacts with international organizations supporting peace movements and international promotion of their attitudes.*

The following organizations belong to this group:

- *peace movements: Centre for Antiwar Actions Belgrade—branch in Ada, Crepaja for Peace, Spiritual Republic 'Zitzer' in Tresnevac, Group for Peace Actions 'M' in Pancevo, Initiative group 'Society for Peace and Tolerance' in Backa Palanka, Movement for Peace in Voivodina with initiative groups in Temerin and Becej, Movement for Peace in Pancevo, Peace group in Sombor and Action for Peace in Subotica.*
- *women's organizations: Women's center 'Isidora' in Pancevo and The Women in Black in Pancevo. This group has 11 peace groups and 2 women's organizations. Listed women's organizations carry out some activities which are not connected with war and its consequences (medical and psychological help).*

Some of these organizations appeared as a reaction to compulsory mobilization which endangered their local community, but when the danger passed, these groups ceased to exist (Spiritual Republic 'Zitzer'). When the state disassociated itself from the war in Bosnia and Herzegovina, these organizations started losing their actuality. Only large organizations, such as Movement for Peace in Vojvodina, remained in action, and they were pleading not only for peace, but for human rights and liberties protection, inter-ethnic tolerance and co-operation, and providing legal and psychological help. One of the most interesting organizations was the Center for Antiwar actions in Ada. It was a small organization, but one of the most successful in times when demonstrations for peace were organized (in Senta and Ada these demonstrations reached a climax when the local authorities were dismissed from their position and the whole action was brought to an end when the organizers were arrested), Although in a small town, practically without any equipment, this organization has remained active even today (1993).

Although the war in former Yugoslavia still continues, it seems that peace movements are looking for new forms of activities. They have directed their activities to work with refugees (Movement for Peace in Vojvodina), and humanitarian aid, which confirms the position that the war, although far enough, can disturb people and make them do something. In the meantime, the regime has turned into a 'peace-making one,' and thus influenced the process of their gradual disappearing.

Branislava Kostic 1994

here because it had a direct bearing on particular interpretations of the term 'conflict resolution' and because for many people one response to war was an inward search for spiritual renewal. It must be said that one response to war was also to join the given state religion so as to be marked an 'insider,' a member of the primary 'ethnic' majority. So it was that families of 'questionable' allegiance/ background (newcomers, people with mixed marriages, or 'minority' members), in both Zagreb and Belgrade flocked to have their children blessed and baptised for political as well as divine acceptance.

On 26 November 1992, representatives of the Serbian Orthodox, Croatian Catholic, and Muslim hierarchies signed an "Appeal for Peace in Bosnia and Hercegovina,' in which they called for an end to the war, the distribution of humanitarian assistance without respect to faith or persuasion, the closing of all prison camps and the release of all prisoners, an end to ethnic cleansing, the return of all refugees and displaced persons, and an end to any use of religious symbols to foster hatred or war.[17] This statement marked the first time leaders of the three primary religious traditions in the former Yugoslavia spoke with one voice to oppose the war (Shenk, 1993). In spite of this the leaders of both the Catholic and Orthodox churches experienced the strains and obligations of patriotic necessity in their official status as adjunct to the state. For some of the population affiliation with the official church was akin to nationalist allegiance [18]; for others it was a source of solace and hope[19]. For some the question of traditional state religion offered more uncertainties than answers. Gerald Shenk noted the propaganda and 'disinformation' surrounding faith on his several visits to the region:

> 'For example, in February 1993, it was commonly believed in Zagreb that the Mufti of Belgrade had fled for reasons of safety. However, during a visit to Belgrade the first week of March, he was there. Likewise, I had been told in Serbia, during a March 1993 visit, that an Orthodox church in Osijek (Croatia) had been damaged by Croats. Both in August 1992 and in May 1993, when I visited Osijek, I was driven by the church premises in Donji Grad and told that Protestant and Catholic churches had contributed toward repair of the building, damaged by Serb shells.
>
> In addition to these specific examples, conspiracy theories about the roots of the conflict abounded. Serbs spoke of both a Catholic plot masterminded by the Vatican, and Muslim fundamentalist domination of Bosnian politics. Muslims spoke of a Christian plot to rid Europe of Islam. Croats spoke of a Serbian communist attempt to exert control over them, aided by the United Nations' (Ibid. p.56).

Religious allegiance was often an important conduit for the relief of suffering. The Muslim humanitarian organisation Merchamet ran a warehouse in Zagreb and co-operated with Suncokret as well as the leading Jewish aid agency, La Benevolencia. CARITAS assisted with rehabilitation of physically disabled veterans in Osijek, European ecumenical organisations sent medicine and food into Novi Sad during peak influxes of refugees. Greek Orthodox church donations found their way to commodity-starved Belgrade.

As early as 1989/90 Franciscan Mako Matausic of Zagreb had 'noticed the virus of war by observing growing ethnic hatred' and appealed to Pax Christi International for help.[20] Response came later in the visits of Rev. H. Fröhlich and representatives of the International Fellowship of Reconciliation, who gave seminars on faith and non-violence. The virus, however, had taken hold.

Meanwhile many had sought alternative religion. There had been growing popularity (since the mid-80s) for eastern religions, which was only accentuated by war. The works of Belgrade literary figure Vesna Krmpotic were sought after in Croatia, for their poetic invocations of the Indian master Si Baba, and her own near legendary conversion to his path after the death of one of her children. Krmpotic spoke in Osijek in the summer of 1993 to capacity audiences after negotiating safe passage 'across the line.' In Zagreb the literature of Buddhism, scientology and American-style Evangelical Christianity shared space in book shop windows. In Belgrade Hare Krishna followers distributed whole food donations to the second wave of incoming refugees. Osijek became the chosen centre for the 'Course in Miracles,' for Pentecostal and 'born again' initiatives. In the words of Jasenka H., 'It is a great possibility to be born again, if you are killed in Osijek.'

3.5 Accessing the network

The German Bund für Soziale Verteidigung (Federation for Social Defence) had contacts with Slovenian students through their campaign 'Bundes-Republik Deutschland ohne Armee' (Germany without an army). When the war broke out in Slovenia,[21] German representatives asked their Slovenian counterparts how they could be of help. They received invitations to Ljubljana and were also put in touch with Zagreb dissidents who made it known in July 1991, that they wished to have non-violence training.[22] In response to this request, seminars were given on non-violent action, conflict resolution and mediation in Zagreb 28 Sept.—7 Oct. 1991 (see Chapter VI). Subsequently the BSV trainers travelled to Belgrade (via Budapest) 'to make contact with the peace movement there' (Schweitzer, 1992). They were received by a member of the IPPNW (International Physicians for the Prevention of Nuclear War) who introduced them to people at the Centre of Antiwar Action. As all road and telecommunications between Zagreb and Belgrade were cut off completely, the pair were 'treated like emissaries and post couriers' (Ibid.), in itself a useful function. Erich Bachman of BSV later became almost legendary for his introduction of E-mail skills and equipment to the region to break this communication barrier.

CAA Belgrade subsequently framed a project called 'Community Building through Non-violent Conflict Resolution Workshops in Local Settings,' with Vesna Pesic, president, also requesting BSU trainers and support.

The beginning of war with Slovenia had coincided with a major meeting in Finland which resulted in active networking and project formation. The International Society for Political Psychology (ISPP) was holding a scientific symposium featuring presentations and discussions by 'conflict resolution practitioners' (Gutlove, 1992) who made contacts in Croatia, Serbia and Bosnia through a member resident in Slovenia:

> 'Members of these organizations expressed interest in learning more about non-violent conflict resolution techniques and their application to the current crisis. Among these groups was the Physicians Against War (PAW), a newly formed organization of Serbian and Croat physicians. PAW planned many projects, ranging from a meeting with federal officials of the former Parliament (a surprising number of whose elected members were physicians) to community-level conflict resolution interventions where the physicians patient populations spanned ethnic and cultural boundaries. Members of PAW thought exposure to conflict resolution theory and technique would be an important aid to them in both endeavours. Other interested organizations included the Ljubljana Peace Institute, the newly formed Croatian Anti-War Campaign, the Forum for Ethnic Relations, the Helsinki Citizens Assembly, and the European Civic Center for Conflict Resolution in Subotica' (Ibid.).

The 'Balkan Peace Project', as it became known, offered conflict resolution as an interactive approach, emphasising the social and psychological dimensions of conflict, with focus upon meeting basic human needs (i.e. identity, recognition, security, and equity). Plans for the workshops were finalised during a meeting in Schlaining, Austria during November 1991 that was sponsored by the Austrian Institute for Peace Research and Peace Education (APRI). The meeting was the second in a series initiated by APRI and the Ljubljana Peace Institute that considered non-violent conflict resolution in Yugoslavia. Representatives from the PAW and the Anti-War Campaign in Croatia, the Ljubljana Peace Institute in Slovenia, and the European Civic Center for Conflict Resolution in Subotica agreed to host each of the three workshops. Representatives from the Helsinki Citizens Assembly and the Center for Anti-War Action in Belgrade were also present.

Another international networking site was the 1992 Bratislava meeting of the Helsinki Citizens Assembly (HCA). At a session on demilitarisation and peace politics, participants heard from Vesna Terselic (ARK) about the activism and urgency in former Yugoslavia as the arrival of the 'Blue Helmets' was anticipated. The UN presence, she stressed, would be of a peace keeping nature, not a peace building one. Meanwhile, much of the population suffered from physical displacement, trauma, grieving, tendencies towards revenge or personal violence, and basic needs such as shelter and mine clearance. She identified needs in co-ordinating information, 'peace culture education' and training skills for those trying to build strong centres for non-violent change in each of the former republics. Delegates from Belgrade were also present, including Sonja Licht, then of HCA and later of Soros, as well as Vedran Vucic from Subotica. Prof. Adam Curle proposed that a network be established for training in mediation and related skills; many NGOs present at the conference had experience to offer, such as War Registers International (WRI), Peace Brigades International (PBI), Quaker Peace and Service (QPS), Pax Christi, etc.

An invitation was extended for Curle and two colleagues to visit Osijek that spring as part of an ARK sponsored meeting with crisis groups there and civic leaders. Also, as a result of Curle's proposal, the UK based 'Co-ordinating Committee for Conflict Resolution Training in Europe' (CCCRTE) was formed. The original intention was that this committee should work for 18 months, following which, if necessary, it should be superseded by a less British dominated and more fully European body. Grant funding was obtained from foundations and trusts to form a budget amid firm basis for the committee. Christine Merkel, of Pax Christi Netherlands and co-convenor of the HCA's Peace Politics Commission, wrote to the funding group in March 1992 highlighting the need

Current listing of anti-war centres in former-Yugoslavia

Bosnia-Herzegovina:

International Peace Centre, Dobrovoljacka 3, Sarajevo (Ibrahim Spahic +38 71 646455; fax +38 71 663730 or 663626; email zlatljiljan@gn.apc.org)
Centre for Anti-War Activities, U1 Hasana Kikica br 8, 71000 Sarajevo (+38 71 650660).

Croatia:

Centre for Peace, Nonviolence and Human Rights, Tkalclceva 38, 41000 Zagreb (+38 41 422495; fax 271143; email mir_zg.@zamir-zgcomlink.dc)
Antiwar Campaign Croatia (ARK), Tkalciceva 38, 41000 Zagreb (+38 41 422495; fax 271143; email mir_zg@zamir-zg.comlink.de)
Dalmatian Committee of Solidarity, Kruziceva 2, pp 583, 58000 Split (+38 58 362 060; fax 517 036)
Movement for Peace Rijeka, Korzo 2, 51000 Rijeka (+38 51 213 280; fax 713 291)
Centre for Peace, Nonviolence and Human Rights, J Cesmickog 10, 54000 Osijek (+38 54 559948; fax 45934; email czm_osijek@zamir-zg.comlink.de)
SunCokret Centre, Marusevacka 8, 41000 Zagreb (+38 41 318576; fax 339715; email suncokret_zg@zamir-zgcomlink.de)

Kosova

Democratic League of Kosova, Prishtine (+38 38 24234; fax 27660)
Kosova Helsinki Committee, Taslixhe 1 36a, 38000 Prishtine (+38 38 34 786)

Macedonia

Committee for Peace, ul Nakoden Front 31/3, 91000 Skopje (+38 91 210 627; fax 236856)
Green Action Skopje, c/o Jovan Nansijevski (+38 91 213 966; fax 201 75)
HCA Macedonia, Manapo 41/1, 91000 Skopje (Slobodanka +38 91 257 356; fax 256979)
Forum for Human Rights of Macedonia, c/o Meto Jovanovski, St. P. Zografski 51, 91000 Skopje (+38 91 219 067)
Women for Peace, Skopje (+38 91 210627; fax 236856)

Montenegro

Citizens Commitee for Peace, Hercegovacka 15, 81000 Podgorica (+38 81 41914)

Serbia

Centre for Anti-War Action, Kralja Petra 46, 11000 Belgrade (+38 11 635 813;email caa_beograd@zamir-bg.comlink.de)
GAMA (Citizens Action for Peace), Prof Miladin Zivotic, Dom Omladine, Makedonska 22, 11000 Belgrade
Women in Black, c/o Stasa Zajovic, Dragoslava Popovica 9/10, 11 Belgrade (+38 11 624 701)

Slovenia

Peace Institute, Mestni trg 13, 61000 Ljubljana (+38 61 224 666; email mirovniki@uniljacmail.yu)
Association of Preventative and Voluntary Work, Linhartova 13, 61000 Ljubljana (refugee support)

Vojvodina

Anti War Centre of Ada, Vera Vebel, Sencanski Put 27, 24430 Ada
Anti-War Centre of Novi Sad, c/o Nenad Mirovic, Narodnog Fronta 43, 21000 Novi Sad (+38 21 363 302; fax 57797)
European Civic Centre for Conflict Resolution, trg Cara Jovana Nenada 15, 24000 Subotica (+38 24 24600; fax 37116)
Peace Movement of Pancevo, c/o Sasa Marinkovic, Br Jovanovica 62a, 26001 Pancevo, Vojvodina (+38 13 3882; fax 41735; email ppm_pancevo@zamir-bg.comlink.de)
Peace Movement Vojvodina, c/o Slavenka Ljubic, Maksima Gorkog 10/III, 21000 Novi Sad (+38 21 619 019)
Women in Black, Biljana Regeodic, Vojvodanska 53, 26000 Pancevo (+38 13 512 641)

> *Statement from the Sarajevo Peace Centre*
> *We, Serbs, Yugoslavs of Serbian ethnic origin, Bosnians of Serbian ethnic origin, as well as other citizens of Serbian ethnic origin who live in Sarajevo and Bosnia and Herzegovina declare that:*
>
> *The Serbian Democratic Party (SDS) does not represent the interests of the majority of the Serbian people; equally, we are convinced that the interests of Croats and Muslims are not represented by national parties. We do not agree with the statement that it is ethnic conflict that Bosnia and Herzegovina is faced with. The disastrous conditions we experience today resulted from the insatiable nationalistic policies of the governing parties. We do not accept the solution of our faiths and our future by arms and killings. Our interest is in indivisible common life with Muslims, Croats, and other nations.*

Please continue to keep writing to these groups and publicising their work within your networks.

NPC February newsletter 1993

for clarity with the term 'conflict resolution' if it was to be used, the danger of high expectations and the need for proactive rather than reactive initiatives.[23]

The above network examples include early German, American, and British-based initiatives which responded to the crisis in 'Yugoslavia.' All three used the language of 'conflict resolution' and all three had value-based approaches centred on training workshops. Importantly, they also all attempted to address the subject of evaluation. Questions of style, content and impact will be further addressed in this study, particularly in chapters VI and VIII.

If international activists could share the ideal of 'peace' with their hosts and colleagues in Croatia and Serbia, they could not fully understand—indeed *had not experienced*—the fullness of historical, political and social dimensions which they were entering. They brought ideals and methods into a context which was new to them. Sweitzer (1992) put it well in one of her early recommendations: 'Trainers who are new to this area should plan some extra days to get familiar with the situation.'

Notes for Chapter III

1. This is the estimate of Martin Woollacott, 'Sorry, it's more bad news in Yugoslavia,' *The Guardian* 11.1.97. Higher figures have been quoted to me by workers in industrial towns of Serbia and Vojvodina.

2. See 'YugoFax' No.3, 21 Sept. 1991

3. From ARK 'Basic Information' Document, Feb. 1992, Zagreb, with thanks to Vesna Terselic.

4. See also 'Women in Black against war' in *Peace News* educational offprints 1/1993, p.22.

5. A term introduced by Herbert Marcuse to imply the manner in which authority structures deny the validity of protest by allowing rather than reacting to it, thus absorbing it into a repressive system.

6. I am indebted to Eleanor O'Gorman for discussions on everyday resistance and an introduction to Scott's work. Note: James Scott based his work on peasant struggle. The idea of non-compliance seems applicable to all 'classes' of former Yugoslavia in this study given the consistent non-payment of salaries, spiralling inflation trends and unavailability at times of basic commodities. Non-compliance is also perceived as 'strategy' by Henrietta Moore in *Feminism and Anthropology*, 1988 Cambridge, Polity Press p. 180.

7. An embryonic group did exist, making use of meeting points in Hungary to keep up contact with relatives and friends from the other side. A formal proposal for an 'Association for Peace and Human Rights' of Baranja was put to local authorities for registration in 1994 and an application for a working grant for the same went to the International Rescue Committee in late 1995.

8 'Why?' Publication for Human Rights and Peace, February 1992, No. 2, Citizens' Forum, Sarajevo.

9. Interview with Bozica Stumfol, S.O.S. Telephone volunteer, in Osijek May 1992.

10. This figure is from Pecnik and Stubbs (1995) who also explain the distinction between two categories of forced migrants: displaced persons (from Serbian held areas of Croatia), or refugees (Mainly those who have fled from Bosnia and Herzegovina). It is the status of the border you have crossed which determines your personal status if you have been made homeless and forced to move on by war.

11. Quoted by Julie Flint, *The Guardian* 16 Feb. 1993, reprinted in Spring edition of *Republika*, Belgrade 1993. Vucinic continued: 'Another message is: "Believe no one - not even us." Thus, on one occasion, the station organised an elaborate deception to show the extent of its support in Belgrade. It announced that its regular team had been replaced by a new crew and the station's name changed to SPS Radio, the initials of Milosevic's Socialist Party. "We completely changed our programming," says Vucinic. "We said only good things about the SPS and very bad things about the opposition. We said the whole editorial board was on vacation and the new board wanted to change editorial policy. We received 600 phone calls. People shouted and threatened. We taped it all and broadcast it the next day to protest the fact that we still do not have a frequency licence.'

12. Interview with Mirko Mandrino, Pancevo, May 1996.

13. Final Report of the International Media Forum 1992 (Washington D.C.) p.18.

14. IRI Croatian Report on 'The Elections' 2 August 1992, pp.3-12.

15. IRI Post-Election and Program Assessment Mission to Republics of Serbia and Montenegro 2 - 10 February, 1993. p.2.

16. Ibid., p.4. Note other concerns from this report: 'The political situation in Vojvodina is clearly deteriorating, because of indications of:

    1. potential large scale vote fraud in the province, as the region was previously an area of great opposition support; or

    2. the political impact of the large number of Serbian refugees from Bosnia-Herzegovina and Croatia relocated in the province, which may result in short and long term political controversies; and/or

    3. strong signs that Serbian authorities may systematically usurp the little remaining autonomy from the province.'

17. 'Appeal for Peace in Bosnia and Hercegovina,' Appeal of Conscience Foundation, Wolfsberg (ZH/Switzerland), 26 November 1992.

18. Personal conversations in Zagreb, Karlovatz, Belgrade, Nice and Pancevo 1992—1995.

19. Dr. Katarina Kruhonja of The Osijek Centre took a particular interest in working with the churches through visitations, roundtables and dialogues and received funding to devote a full year to such work

focus. The 1996 centre leaflet includes a quote from Bishop mons di. Ciril Kos.

20. From the interview of Herbert Fröhlich, Catholic priest in Heidelberg by Ute Caspers, 20 February 1996.

21. For an indication of groups operating in Slovenia see the National Peace Council Listing p.*

22. Interview with Christine Schweitzer by Ute Caspers, Köln, 17 Feb. 1996. Note, Marko Hren of Ljubljana was a member of the Council of War Resisters International.

23. Letter from Christine Merkel to Adam Curle, David Atwood (IFOR), Andrew Clark (QPS), Howard Clark (URI) and Simon Fisher (Responding to Conflict), March 1992.

Chapter IV

Contexts and conducivity: the case for capacity building

»Halo, dozvolite da se obratimo...«
»Hello, excuse us...« 1992

IV. Contexts and conducivity

4.1 The powder keg experience of war

B. is a veteran of the Second World War and sits smoking his pipe on a doorstep in Osijek on fair mornings. He lives with his daughter now, having left behind his own home, vegetable garden, fruit trees, neighbours and friends in Baranja when he joined the exodus from there in winter 1991. He muses over the nature of this most recent war, which he calls a 'powder keg' experience: 'It is,' he sighs, 'as though little kegs of gun powder were all gathered to the same place—our East Slavonia—and then fuses put in place. One by one the fuses were lit. In the end we got an explosion we could not deal with.' His daughter approves of the analogy, and adds to it while serving strong coffee. 'I suppose some of the gun powder itself was just the standard of living going down, blaming others and the wrong people seeming to take control after so many (post-communist) changes. But we knew fuses had been lit when we heard about Borovo Selo, and most of all when the murder came of the Police Chief Kir.'

B.'s 'powder keg' picture is apt in its identification of 'precipitating factors' in the building-up (or slide in) to war.[1] His daughter offered a candid opinion ('standard of living...wrong people...so many changes...') suggesting events and components which may have rendered her society 'prone' to war. The events leading to Kir's death were a tragic personal unfolding for the population in the region, and for ex-Yugoslavia as a whole. *They also represent, in their stages of provocation, incident, spread of fear, and hardening positions, classic social patterns conducive to war.*[2] The story goes roughly like this: Joseph Reihl-Kir was murdered by HDZ extremists on 1st July 1991. His death followed several tense months during which he had attempted moderation and mediation in volatile local situations. The murder shocked the majority of citizens in Osijek; spontaneous gatherings protested it and mourned it. Candles were lit and placed on kerbsides and in the city parks in his memory.

Kir was of mixed German and Slovene descent, which is not uncommon for the area, and considered himself Croatian. In the middle of April a group of highly placed HDZ members visited him with a particular request. Grojko Susak[3] asked Kir to lead him along country paths and through fields to the outskirts of Borovo Selo, a Serb-populated village near the town of Vukovar on the Danube. Kir knew this excursion would inflame the local Serbs but under intimidation, he agreed.

From outside the village, Susak and his companions fired three shoulder-launched Ambrust missiles into the village. 'They're crazy,' Kir later confided, in disgust and disbelief, to a colleague (Silber and Little, 1995. p.154). One rocket hit a house, another landed in a potato field, failed to explode and was later exhibited on Belgrade television as evidence of Croat aggression. The Federal Interior Minister, took the unexploded shell to a meeting of the Federal Presidency to wave it in the face of the Croat representative Stipe Mesic and demand an explanation. Mesic could offer no defence for what was 'undisputedly, an unprovoked act of aggression, by extremists in Mesic's own party, designed to provoke ethnic conflict' (Ibid.). The three rockets caused no casualties in Borovo Selo, but gave Serb villages every excuse they needed to strengthen their defences. Kir continued to try to restore confidence and relations between Serbs and Croats...

On the first of May, (traditionally a workers' holiday) the villagers of Borovo Selo put out flags, Yugoslav flags, carrying the Communist five-pointed star. Four Osijek (Croat) policemen drove into the village in the dead of night, past the unmanned barricade, determined to remove the Yugoslav flag and replace it with the Croatian one carrying the symbol the Serbs hated—the red-and-white checkerboard shield, the *sahovnica*.[4] They were met by a hail of gunfire. Two were wounded, two escaped, and the wounded men were taken prisoner.

Hard-line HDZ officials had gained the upper hand in both the police and the civil administration. Precisely who gave the order for what came next, on the morning of 2 May, is not known.

The policemen who had escaped returned to Osijek and described what had happened to their colleagues. In the morning, a bus-load of Croatian policemen gathered at Vinkovci and set off for Borovo Selo, determined to rescue the wounded men. Serb militiamen were waiting in force. The visit in the night had put the entire village on alert. Between 10 a.m. and 11 a.m., when the Croatian police bus entered the village, waiting Serb militiamen opened fire. There were twelve Croats killed and more than twenty wounded.

> 'Borovo Selo caused a sea-change in Croatian public opinion. The Serb "enemy within" was now demonized beyond all reason. The Croatian media launched a campaign that pandered to the worst excesses of Croatian "Serbophobia". Croatian Radio and television began, routinely, to refer to the Serbs of Slavonia as "chetniks" or, frequently,

"terrorists". Zagreb television carried photographs of the bodies of the twelve men, claiming autopsy evidence that they had been tortured to death, and subsequently mutilated. The newspapers did not stint in their use of the vocabulary of horror. They said the policemen had died at the "bestial hands" of chetniks' (Ibid. p.155).

Angry exchanges were now made by nationalist leaders. Seselj boasted on Belgrade television that his 'chetniks' had taken part in the Borovo Selo events. Ministers in Zagreb conferred and the idea of an immediate declaration of sovereignty gained new momentum. Misha Glenny says of Borovo Selo, 'there is no doubt that the incident raised the violence of the conflict to a new level, resulting in a complete breakdown of trust between Serbs and Croats in the Vukovar—Vinkovci region, thus clearing the ground for one of the bloodiest and most inhumane struggles of the entire conflict' (Glenny, 1992. p.75). Vukovar became the symbolic centre of a radius of violence, disintegration and confusion which took in East Slavonia, Vojvodina, Croatia and Serbia, and was ultimately to prove a portent of the wholesale destruction of Bosnia itself.

4.2 Understanding contexts

The basis and rationale of 'track one' diplomacy lie surely in the belief in legitimate centralized leadership and the control that leadership holds over populations. It assumes the mandate or power to govern. This chapter will attempt to shed light on regional complexity and problems with the 'unitary actor' view of war, which assumes master plans and unified chains of command. For while Tudjman and Milosevic are now recognised for their personal *realpolitik* in the break-up of Yugoslavia, evidence indicates that neither were in full control all of the time. The ideologies they unleashed, on the other hand, may have been.[5]

A 'thumbnail sketch' will be given of two particular regions, E. Slavonia and Vojvodina. While international interventions such as UN occupation or the imposition of sanctions impacted on local populations in these areas, at the same time their respective capitals and 'national' policy often seemed very far away. With the political partition in E. Slavonia, for example, there was immediate experience of violence and disintegration plus unmet expectations of assistance (Osijek looking to Zagreb) and/or affiliation (Baranja looking to Belgrade). Moreover, it was local warlords and the divide and rule politics of intimidation that defined experience, irrespective of international negotiations and talks with Tudjman and Milosevic far away.[6]

Two defining features render this area an essential case study for 'second track' intervention and capacity building: 1) the type of **disintegration** leading to war, (as above), and 2) the **lack of legitimate governance.**

As well as offering brief regional profiles this chapter will seek to:

1. indicate how local populations experienced and identified their own critical problems.
2. introduce the idea of 'structural conduceiveness' and corresponding capacity-building needs, and
3. describe early initiatives to respond to these needs which emerged in 1991-1992.

4.3 Regional Profiles

Eastern Slavonia

Eastern Slavonia saw some of the fiercest fighting of the 1991 Serb-Croat war. Writing in *Balkan Tragedy*, S. Woodward observes that the 'first stage' of fighting (seen in both the wars in Croatia and Bosnia-Herzegovina, when the world was least attentive or prepared to react) was 'not a calculated strategy between contending armies or between Yugoslav army and republican militias. The situation was, instead, chaotic. Competing militias and gangs marauded, only loosely linked to centers of command and control or fully freewheeling, and paramilitary extremists escalated small confrontations to force political leaders to greater militancy. The declining number of regular troops and difficulty finding conscripts willing to fight led to supplementation with militant extremist volunteers and criminals released from jails, who were more often motivated by the invitation to loot and plunder than nationalist fervour. The worst excesses of reported massacres, rape and mutilations emerged because of such conditions' (Woodward, 1995. p. 266).

Conflict and confusion *within* national and military organisations over political goals and strategies, the absence of adequate equipment for communication among local units, and both local intimidation and loyalties interfered throughout the period with efforts to impose central control or impose negotiated agreements:

> 'It remains unclear whether there would have been a three-month siege (Aug.24-November 17, 1991) and destruction of Vukovar, the worst battle of the Croatian war, had renegade forces from the Croatian National Guard (called the Wolves of Vukovar) and neo-fascist Ustasha bands such as the Zebras, who were loyal to local politicians (particularly the right wing radical in the HDZ, Tomislav Mercep), not

EASTERN SLAVONIA AREA

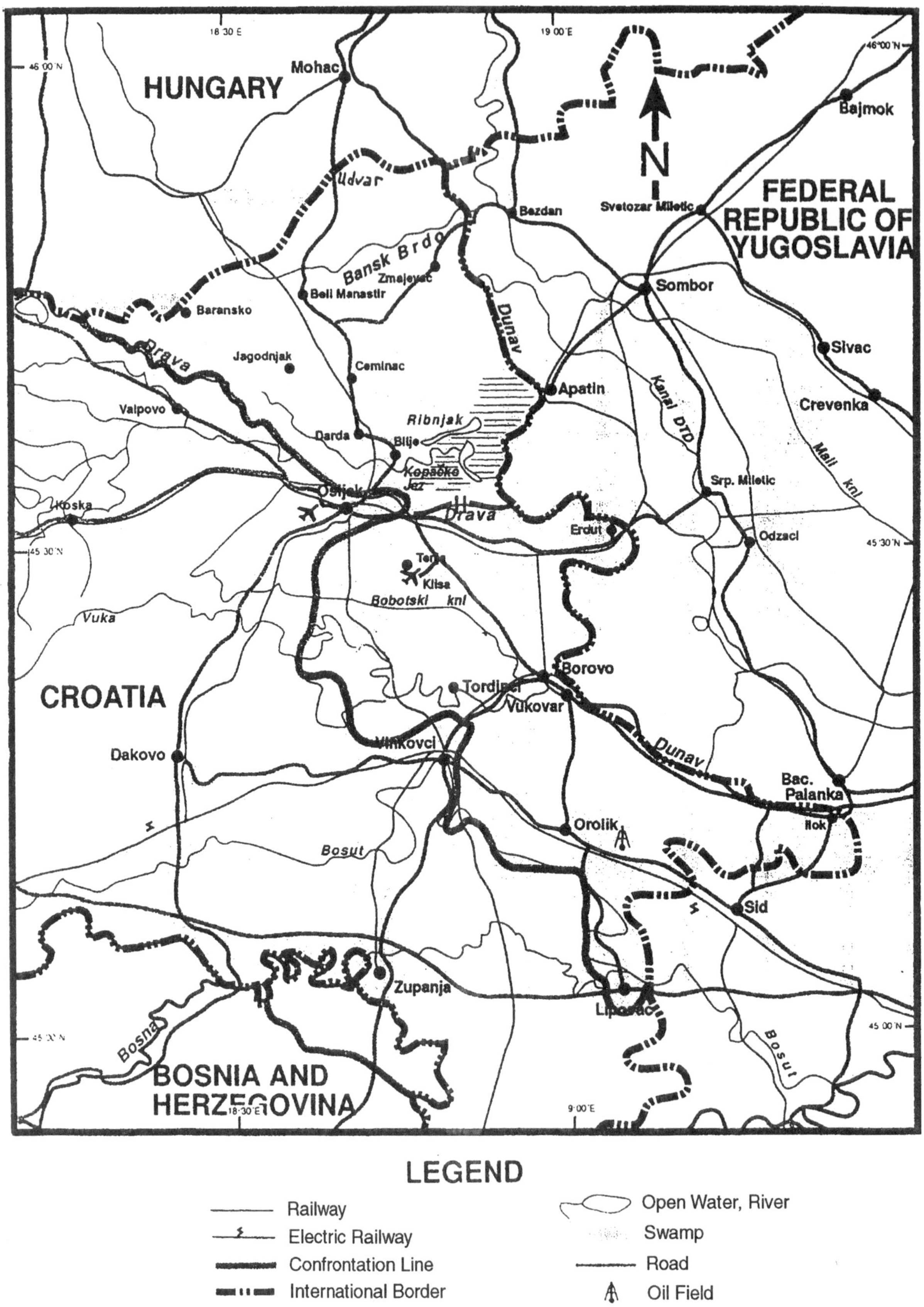

Map of the area showing highlighted East Slavonia Region

> chosen to ignore Zagreb authority and put up a stiff resistance in order to draw the government into a more aggressive strategy. They succeeded in escalating the war because they were matched on the Serb side by right wing radicals from Serbia, such as Seselj, who had attempted to make eastern Slavonia a Chetnik base through radicalising campaigns during the spring...' (Ibid.)

Despite the cease-fire which Cyrus Vance, UN envoy, had negotiated in Croatia, Croatian forces retaliated for Vukovar with a counter-offensive on Papuk at the end of November.

The JNA had pulled out of its Osijek barracks in mid-September to new positions in the south and east from which it bombarded the city with artillery and mortar fire for the next three months. There was massive population dislocation due to fear, people fleeing in their thousands to Austria, Hungary, Germany or further afield. As local power generators and buses took direct hits, electricity supplies and transport dissolved. Curfew was imposed, an 'SOS telefon' functioned from underground when telephones worked, sand-bags and protective boards were erected to what seemed like semi-permanent positions.

Strategically Osijek was a key site and seemed certain to be destined for a fate like that of Vukovar. At one point Arkan even entered the city and boasted that he would have it. For a combination of reasons, the city did not fall. Mayor Kramaric took the view that his 'town was defended by words and by internationalising the problem of Osijek' (a reference to his appeals to 6,000 other mayors world-wide for international assistance to stop the war).[7]

Meanwhile Croatia had built an army and routed the JNA on many fronts, and Milosevic had agreed to the deployment of international peace-keeping troops in such a way that partitioned Serb and Croat entities. Osijek became part of UN protected zone E, formally separated from the Baranja—its rich agricultural hinterland on the other side of the river Sava, part of the now designated 'Sector East'.

An internationally brokered cease-fire in late 1991 was followed by the implementation of the Vance Plan. This plan introduced United Nations Protection Forces (UNPROFOR) into the territory, assisted the withdrawal of the JNA, and designated the region as one of four 'protected areas' (known as UNPAs).

Expectations of the role of UNPROFOR differed on the two sides. The Croatians expected the forces to help with the return of Croatian persons displaced out of the area and a return of the territories to the control of Zagreb. Conversely, the Serbs in the UNPAs were counting on the UN forces to maintain their protected status, and even hoped to have their self-proclaimed new state, Republic of Serbian Krajina (RSK), recognised. After the Vance Plan was signed, Croatia was recognised by most members of the international community inside borders that included the RSK, and was accepted into the UN as a full member.

For the next four years the situation remained at an impasse, apart from numerous clashes and a number of smaller offensives from the Croatian side (e.g., Maslenica in the end of January 1993). While the front lines changed little, politically the situation was increasingly tense, as this status quo was unacceptable for Croatia. Despite a little progress in negotiations which began to ease life for both sides (highway opening, oil pipeline connections, electrical grid repairs) there was no significant movement on the overall conflict: that of determining who would govern the territory...

Osijek

Croatia's third largest city and provincial capital of eastern Slavonia, Osijek, had a 1991 pre-war population of just over 160,000 with an estimated 66 per cent Croatian, 20 per cent Serbian, and the balance a mixture of Hungarian, German and others. In spite of the efforts in early '91 of local police chief Josip Reich-Kir to mediate and build confidence between local Serb and Croat communities, hard-line HDZ activists gained control and Kir was himself murdered (see above). There was an escalation of local incidents and confrontation, notably in Borovo Selo and Erdut.

It has been estimated that the subsequent war-induced mass exodus (see above) reduced the population by one half. The sound of singing was heard from cellars and shelters at nightfall in attempts to drown out the sounds of war. People emerged each morning to sweep up broken glass and plaster from pavements.

During the peak of its bombardment Osijek became a city without children. Schools were closed and used as a barracks for the new Croatian army soldiers. By March '92 approximately 22,000 incoming displaced and refugees were housed in improvised centres or 'squats', and the remaining Serb population was reckoned at 6—7 per cent.[8]

A loyalty oath (to the new Croatia) was compulsory in many workplaces, including the university. The hospital administrator reported some 700 casualties, approximately 400 of whom were civilian.[9]

By 1992/3 it was possible to identify multiple parties and constituents in Osijek and conflicts on distinct, often intersecting levels. Examples would be:

1. Personal—in crises of loyalty and allegiance, in unemployment or housing situations, and in families and friendships according to now pronounced 'ethnic' difference. For example, the Croatian wife following (or not) her Serbian husband into exodus in Baranja, or conversely the Croatian family in Osijek hiding their daughter's Serb fiancé from neighbours and authorities.
2. Group—tensions between citizens who had stayed during the war and citizens who had fled and were now returning.
3. Community—the displaced and an influx of refugees from Bosnia versus professionals attempting to help them and local authorities, as the lack of resources and poor communications complicated tense uncertainty about the future.
4. Political—emergent organisations of the displaced on both sides of the Sava, local elected officials versus Glavas, peace activists versus militant patriots and nationalist leaders.
5. National/international—dictates (or not) from Zagreb and the new Croatian army, international UNPROFOR forces occupying the region.

Vojvodina

According to the 1974 Constitution, because of its diversified ethnic makeup, the Vojvodina was made into an Autonomous Province within the Serbian republic, similar to Kosovo. To satisfy the various national traditions the province had five official languages: Serbo-Croat, Hungarian, Slovak, Romanian and Rusyn. Minorities were granted a number of cultural and educational rights. For example, the Hungarians had about 200 elementary schools, a daily newspaper, *Magyar Szo*,

'Ethnic cleansing' comes to crunch in limbo land

Baranja

Victoria Clark

BARANJA is a sad limbo land. Everyone is marking time in this United Nations protectorate — once Croatia but for the past year Serb-controlled and now 70 per cent 'ethnically cleansed' of Croats and Hungarians.

Even Serbs, uprooted from their homes in Croatia by the war last year and resettled in the conquered territories, are not living the dream of Greater Serbia these days.

In the village of Petlovac, a Serb schoolteacher from Osijek, 15 miles away across Croat lines, stands outside a strange school, waving goodbye to strange schoolchildren, counting the days of her exile: 'It is a year to the day since I left Osijek,' she says. 'Who wouldn't go back to their own home, if they could?' Another teacher warned her not to speak to us.

Last month an elderly Croat couple, the Andrics, from the village of Branjin Vrh, were murdered. The husband was gutted with a knife; his wife had been clubbed over the head.

For the past three weeks the incidence of terrorism has been high and rising. It is always directed against non-Serbs. There were three murders last week alone, more than 50 since the UN's Belgian battalion arrived in April.

The village of Luc is deathly quiet. The door of the Roman Catholic church has been vandalised, and last week three grenades were thrown into houses.

UN patrols have been stepped up but the 17-man UN police force — comprising Bangladeshis, Jordanians, Swedes, French and Colombians — is fully stretched. They monitor the activities of the local police but cannot do any 'direct policing' because that would exceed their UN mandate. Without enough men or cars, all they can do is watch and report what they see to higher UN authorities, and help those under threat leave if they want to. But they have little idea how many Serb police there are, what part they play in forcing people from their homes to make way for Serbs, or how many Bosnian Serbs are still arriving in Baranja. The local Serb authorities will not tell them.

In the village of Petrovo Selo, a Bosnian Serb refugee and former railwayman claimed he was now 'a policeman' — although the Cyrus Vance plan lays down that the ethnic composition of the police should match that of the region before the war, when Serbs comprised only a quarter of the population.

Selo is confident the Croats and ethnic Hungarians will never come back and that is why he chose to settle in this fertile, prosperous region near Hungary.

Only the Vance peace plan does not mark time around here. But the step-by-step demilitarisation of areas under UN control, the building up of trust on both sides, the eventual return of entire populations to their homes, seem as if they will take an eternity.

And now 30,000 Croats who fled Baranja last summer are threatening to reclaim their homes, whether or not the UN thinks the time is right for the refugees to return. It is certainly not the time.

Although the federal army has pulled out and a Serb 'multi-purpose police brigade', with its police-blue armoured personnel carriers, has been half-disbanded, there are countless other 'police forces' armed with kalashnikovs and civilians with guns at home.

'Refugees must be able to come back in dignity with a proper legal system in place which does not exist now,' says Commander Jean-Marie Jockin, a Belgian.

No. A year ago the Serbian government in Krajina passed a law that enabled refugees to return provided they had not been involved on the enemy side or had relatives there.

The mayor of Beli Manastir, Borivoje Zivanovic, happily cites the law as proof of the government's tolerance towards Croats and Hungarians. He reserves the bulk of his hate for the local Belgian UN battalion. 'All they lack is a swastika badge on their sleeves,' rants Mr Zivanovic, a former tax inspector. 'They are only interested in uncovering organised Serbian terror against non-Serbs.'

He believes Croat emigrés in Belgium were among the first to join the Croat side in the war and concludes: 'Baranja will be Serb territory for at least the next 1,000 years. If need be we'll go to war again, and this time we will take Osijek.'

There are reasons why relations have turned so sour. While in no position to allow refugees back to their homes, the Belgians are far in advance of other battalions in their implementation of the peace plan.

There is also a good deal at stake here; Baranja is not a heap of rubble like Vukovar.

A year ago, the federal army took the area in only two days. If the Catholic churches are missing their steeples, the houses are still standing, and the land is still good and rich.

Cutting from THE OBSERVER *- 20/9/92*

Testimony from Croatian woman who remained in Baranja during the war

1. When the war started, I was confused, afraid, depressive. I hoped people would become reasonable and find peaceful solution very soon. Everything was unknown and strange: new sounds, like shooting and grenading, new people—changed in something wild and violent.

My family decided to stay because of opinion we have not done anything bad or evil. My father and I, both doctors, have always helped to the people. But, we could see very soon how violence and power of weapon have changed the people. Life become very dangerous. It was enough to say one 'wrong' word, to be 'on wrong place in the wrong time', to be a member of a 'wrong nation' or just to have nice house to lose everything, including the life. It was the time of silence—because of saving my own life I had to listen many lies, many bad things about my people without any comment but with terrible feeling of shame and anger. I have seen a lot of broken or forgotten friendships. Some people have become traitors—to save their own heads, to prove they were on 'right' side... The nights were the worst—no dreams, only waiting for bomb or killers. When I have heard sound of explosion in some other street, I thought 'Thank Goodness, that's not my home.' That time of darkness, fear violence has made us on one way selfish, with only one idea—to survive. We have had only basic needs—to sleep, to eat, to have some clothes and we have been satisfied with every new gifted day.

Shooting has become something usual for me—like part of my life. Sometimes I do not react on it. I was much more afraid of grenading and still I am. In the beginning I didn't know anything about weapons and dangers connected with them. Many times I was on very dangerous places, on so called 'front line' and I was thinking and doing first like a doctor. Because of my profession I was in possibility to see a lot of wounded and dead people—something what couldn't be forgotten until the end of life. My medical education has not prepared me on so much unhappiness on one place in so short time. My best sedative was my work. Whenever I was afraid, sad, depressive, I have tried to work more, because only with the helping to the other more afraid and sick people I was able to forget my own fear. My only idea was to stay honest in and to myself—to be sure I can watch (look at) myself in the mirror.

My family and friends were my main supports. My mother, sick and old, has shown me how strong and brave could be a woman. She has given me a power to stand and to go further in most difficult situations. I have learned from her that men have started wars and fighted but women are real heroes.

My friends were the light in all that darkness. I was disappointed in few, but most of them have not changed. Our little company has stayed close together helping each other to survive psychically and physically. We are the best proof that people of different nations can exist together. I will never forget the words: 'Don't go. My home will be yours. I will always protect you staying in front of you.' And it was so.

Finally, what have I learned from the war and violence? They destroy our lives terrible, making us stronger and hurt in the same time. They show us that everything in life is so relative and basic survival sometimes could be bigger satisfaction than money and many material things. They put the masks from people's faces down, so we can see exactly who is who—but the price is too expensive. They change some people so much waking the animal in themselves. The most important is to save humanity in ourselves, to stay honest. Real and good friends are the biggest richness. On the end, after everything I have gone through I can say: I am sad, angry, bittered, but I don't hate anybody.

2. When the communications were broken, in September 1991, I was horrified because the great part of my family—my brother, aunts, uncles were 'on the other side.' But we have found different ways to contact each other very soon. It was not possible to phone directly to Croatia but we have done it by choosing first the numbers of some towns in Bosnia and Serbia and then, immediately number in Croatia. Our friends in foreign countries were connections between us and our relatives and friends in Croatia. It was sad and funny at the same time—when I wanted to contact my brother in Zagreb, I called my friends in Sweden. They called then my brother. Sometimes I sent my letters with the help of my UN friends. It became easier when we were able to go to Hungary. It was possibility to call relatives and to meet with them.

3. Whole war we were able to watch and listen different TV and radio stations—Croatian, Serbian, Bosnian, Hungarian, American etc. Knowing the situation in the region, listening the news 'from the other side' on meetings with friends and relatives in Hungary, we had possibility to compare all informations and to choose probably truth.

and the provincial radio station broadcast regularly in Hungarian.

Situated geographically between Bosnia and Croatia, controlled by centralist government in Belgrade, and hugging the border of ethnic neighbour Hungary, the Vojvodina has held a myriad of conflict cross-points throughout the war. The rights of indigenous minorities with particular reference to cultural expression and military service, and the influx of huge refugee populations, have been particular areas of concern. 'Conflict resolution to me,' said S., a teacher in Novi Sad dismissed because of her vocal anti-war position after the fall of Vukovar, 'means how to live with my neighbours who call me a traitor, how to deal with disputes in the community and town, and how to talk to my own government about stopping the war it is conducting against my former countrymen.' For S. the pragmatic approach to her first two dilemmas has been to organise for 'Humanitarian aid', appealing largely to European ecumenical organisations for food and medicines for her city which suffers the additional complication of sanctions. Once a month she attended a multi-faith service 'for peace' in Novi Sad—often held in the synagogue.

The rise of Milosevic-style Serb nationalism prompted the formation of other 'identity' voices in Vojvodina from 1990. The Democratic Community of Vojvodina Hungarians (VMDK) was founded in Feb. 1990 in Novi Sad. Its initial programme aimed at equal participation in the political process, adequate representation in administrative and judicial organisations and the use of Hungarian in education. At its first party congress, the 400 delegates, representing the 20,000 or so VDMK members, decided to seek cultural autonomy in the Vojvodina (in response to Serbia's new constitution which virtually eliminated provincial self-government). The main Croatian political organisation is the Democratic Alliance of Croats in the Vojvodina (DSHV) with headquarters in Subotica. In May 1990 the Yugoslav Alliance of Rusyns and Ukrainians was founded in Novi Sad. This organisation disclaimed any political agenda and declared its purpose to be to preserve the national identity of the Rusyns and Ukrainians. All three organisations have been vehicles for the expression of collective grievance and concern. In addition the Civic League of Serbia (composed of opposition groups) has spoken on their behalf to authorities.

In a special report on the Vojvodina in 1993 the Minority Rights Group International documented the following:

1. 30 January 1992. The Democratic Alliance of Croats in Vojvodina issued an appeal to President Milosevic and foreign ambassadors. This alleged that houses in the Vojvodina belonging to Croats had been machine-gunned, their occupants threatened with eviction and terrorised by armed groups in collusion with local police. As a result Croats were fleeing the Vojvodina and their houses being taken over by Serbian refugees. For example about 1,000 Croats from Novi Slankamen in Srem were said to have been forced to leave.
2. In March, the VMDK said up to 12,000 Croats had fled the Vojvodina and that appeals to the Serbian authorities for protection had been futile, with police assisting in the expulsions in some cases.
3. Also in March, the Rusyn Social Parliament protested about rumours that the return of Rusyn families, who had been expelled or had fled from neighbouring Slavonija in Croatia, was 'not being considered as an option.' They pointed out that Rusyns had lived in the Vojvodina and the plain of Slavonia for 'no less than 250 years.'
4. By the beginning of April 1992 there were some 62,000 refugees in the Vojvodina including the latest influx from Bosnia-Herzegovina. The brutalities of the war in Bosnia spread to the Vojvodina. There were similar aims of 'cleansing' areas by expelling perceived 'foreign'—i.e. non-Serbian—elements. There were reports of Rusyns and Ukrainians being sent to Zagreb, and of Hungarians and Croat families receiving intimidation.
5. May 1992. The leader of the Vojvodina Social Democrats, Nenad Canak, warned of the threats to minorities, especially Rusyns and Ukrainians, living in the border zones with Croatia.
6. June 1992. The Civic League of Serbia, comprising a number of opposition groups, accused the authorities of complicity in attacks on Croats in the Vojvodina. They said that homes in the Srem villages of Hrtkovci, Platicevo, Nikinci and Ruma had been set on fire and attacked with explosives.[10]

As the throwing of hand-grenades into yards became a recognisable tactic, lists of 'undesirables' were compiled by 'hard-liners' such as the Serbian Radical Party and publicly read out in villages. Serious clashes and explosions in the courtyards of the 'unwanted' became commonplace. In the Bac area by the end of August five of the named were murdered in three weeks. The climate of intimidation localised conflict in the extreme.

The 1992 C.S.C.E. (now known as the O.S.C.E.) Mission to Kosovo, Sandzak and Vojvodina included a team of monitors in Subotica, Luf Havansson of Sweden, a diplomat, and Lech Marek Skibinski of Switzerland, a businessman seconded to this position. They described their mandate as:

1. the promotion of dialogue,
2. collection of information about human rights,
3. to establish contact points for problem solving,
4. to provide information about minority rights legislation, and precedent outside Serbia,
5. to convey in 'ombudsman' fashion, complaints from the local level to authorities in Belgrade. They saw themselves as 'a channel who can be used by anybody', and expressed a hope that they could encourage moderate voices. They also defined their objective as conflict prevention.[11]

The mandate for C.S.C.E. missions is given by the host country. Yugoslavia was active in the early 1980's in the formation of C.S.C.E. structures, so this was acceptable to Belgrade. (Not, however, to Zagreb at this time). Havansson and Skibinski took the view that violence was not part of the tradition in the Subotica region, but were concerned by one case of 'ethnic cleansing' to the south in a small town called Hrtkouci. The main complaints brought to them were excessive conscription, particularly of Hungarians, increasing intimidation of minorities, Serbian media control, and the fear of violent incidents just before the National election.[12]

Subotica

Before the war Subotica's population was approx. 150,000, over 40 per cent of whom are ethnic Hungarian, and some twenty other 'nationalities' and groups comprising the remainder (with Croatians the second largest group). The population rose with the influx of refugees—largely 'Serbian', who have fled from such places as Vukovar. Estimates as high as 200,000 refugees were suggested by C.S.C.E. observers. Hungarians fled north towards Budapest for two reasons:

1. The expulsion of Croatians and Hungarians from some villages in Vojvodina adding to a climate of fear in Subotica which was exploited by the Serbian Nationalist party there, and
2. a general trend for Hungarians to leave rather than serve for the Yugoslavian National Army.[13]

The name Subotica comes from Hungarian for 'free town'—*szabadka.* Education, the media, street signs, etc. were in both Hungarian and Serbo-Croatian languages. The Orthodox Church in the town was still insured in 1992 by a Croatian insurance company. The choir from the same church had sung several times for the Pope at the Vatican. Subotica's Catholic and Orthodox churches stand approximately 50 meters apart. The town square boasts a large, stately and impressive memorial to the population massacred by the Nazi army in the last war.

Although some trade continued in spite of sanctions, by and large the population felt their country's economic isolation. Shops were empty except for local goods, 80 per cent of manufacturing ceased, the bicycle factory closed because it lacked parts which were previously imported, and public soup kitchens fed the new unemployed. Petrol was expensive and rationed, with preference for farmers with tractors to sustain production for the area.

In 1992/3 local government was run by a coalition of the Democratic Union of Vojvodinan Hungarians and the Democratic Union of Vojvodian Croatians. The Subotica population faced the conscription and death of loved ones, the inability to communicate or travel across new borders, the loss of homes, health and livelihood, the loss of jobs and resources for those citizens otherwise not directly involved. Classic feelings of encirclement and isolation were heightened by news not only of possible armed intervention in Bosnia but also that N.A.T.O. had promised the Hungarian government assistance against 'any aggressor'.

4.4 Complexity in actors and processes

In both E. Slavonia and Vojvodina individuals experienced and articulated the difference between **manifest** and **latent** conflict. In the shadow of Vukovar (central to the overall region and the epitome of organised military and social violence against an urban settlement and population) they felt the tensions in their own divided communities and the propensity for this to spill over or explode into violence.

'Stages' of conflict and related processes and behaviour mechanisms have been described by Chris Mitchell, who particularly emphasises the linkages between situation, attitudes, and behaviour. (See Appendix I.) In his outline (which he stresses is not deterministic, as not all conflicts need pass through this complete process) parties may pass from a seemingly co-operative stage to circumstances in which certain interests, goals or objectives become mutually incompatible (even though this is not recognised immediately) and conditions of *incipient conflict* will then exist. When both parties recognise the existence of mutually incompatible goals between them, conditions change to those of *latent conflict,* while both parties consider what action (if any) to take in such circumstances. Finally, parties may initiate action in order to achieve their own particular goals, and make opponents abandon theirs, or give up objectives and search for a compromise settlement. If action is taken to openly claim, attack or respond, then conflict is manifest.

Mitchell's formulation is not unlike that of Fisher and Keashly (1991) who identify four stages of 'conflict escalation,' which move from low intensity to high intensity—discussion, segregation, polarisation, and destruction—based on the degree of communication and interaction taking place between the parties, their perceptions of each other, the tendency by either side to take unilateral action, or the willingness of the disputants to compromise on the issues.

By mid-1992 the fighting in Bosnia-Herzegovina was utterly 'manifest' and high intensity. **But other conflicts were ongoing in the region, at different levels, and at earlier stages in the escalation process.** As rival para-military groups jockeyed for position with gunfire at dusk in Osijek, and incidents of violent intimidation or thuggery were witnessed in Subotica, citizens felt the potential 'real life' slide (pictured on the theoretical graph above)—from incipient to open conflict—and back again. Questions arose in climates of fear and propaganda about ways to prevent the rise in hostilities.

In Osijek the moderate and non-reactive leadership demonstrated by Prof. Zlatko Kramavic (during war and siege) was counterpoised by the iron rule of Branimir Glavas. Misha Glenny refers to Glavas (in *The Fall of Yugoslavia*) as 'a serial killer in fatigues'. Glavas' method of influencing the population included occasional car bombs, the withholding of salaries and pensions, dismissal from employment, and personal threats: 'Adored by many Croats in eastern Slavonia, he was viewed nervously by Tudjman in Zagreb because of his ruthlessness, his ambition and his unpredictability' (Glenny, p. 104). Meanwhile, on the 'other side' of the new ethnic lines were the Serb White Eagles and Arkanovci, the latter boasting a training camp for prospective members of Raznjatovic's (Arkan's) terrorist units in the village of Erdut (formerly Centre of Territorial Defence of Croatia).[14]

Those of the population of Osijek who did not 'adore' Glavas needed ways to express their own values under his regime. Residents and the recent influx of the displaced needed ways to live with each other. Refugees eyed their former homes from both sides of the divide and questioned, sometimes demanded, the return 'home.' People in Baranja felt the sudden 'independent' isolation of SAO status, with new local Serb leadership enforcing some aspects of political life while a line to Knin was meant as the new central authority. Fear and suspicion became everyday commodities. S. speaking in 1996:

> 'We lived here in a war situation. No communications. These were assaults on some Croats and Hungarians who stayed, by gangs taking their goods if they looked "rich." Municipality leaders did not interfere.'

4.5 Local initiatives

Osijek

Several crisis groups emerged in Osijek (during its bombardment) which focused on particular themes of social work, civil protection, and non-violence. Representation from the Bund für soziale Verteidigung, Pax Christi and the Helsinki Civic Parliament visited during the war and assisted with communications, public discussions, and networking. Under the leadership of Katarina Kruhonja and Krunoslav Sukic a centre for Peace, Non-violence and Human Rights was formed in affiliation with the Croatian Anti-War Campaign. In the course of 1991/1992 'approximately 20 peace education workshops were held in Osijek, comprising themes: prejudice reduction, communication skills, peaceful mediation, non-violent action, education for work on human rights protection, and the Gospel and concern for peace.' (Center for Peace, Non-Violence and Human Rights 'Principles' May 1993)

Crisis groups and local government convened (in conjunction with ARK) major meetings in spring '92 to address specific 'post-war' reconstruction needs and social policy issues. Participants of one workshop produced the following questions they felt faced their community:

Questions raised at the May 1992 Osijek Workshop on Refugees and the Community.[15]

1. The need for shared experience and advice on returning to destroyed villages.
2. How do we psychologically prepare people for their return?
3. How do we deal with the hatred and fear which divide neighbourhoods, schools, hospitals etc.?
4. How do we address the question of identity for the next generation, including 'mixed' families?
5. How can the functioning of authorities be enhanced; civil protection, police, services such as water supply and public sanitation?
6. What practical steps will assist with recovery from trauma for children?
7. How do we help heal mental scars and provide new skills/livelihood for civilian and army invalids? (Jobs possible for those with artificial limbs, etc.)
8. How do we support the reuniting of families after the mass evacuation of Osijek and after separations due to military service?
9. What rituals or forms of expression are appropriate to help with collective grieving?

Testimony from a Macedonian JNA officer who deserted, as quoted by Glenny (1992)

"On 17 September, we were told we were going to Pirot (a military garrison in south-east Serbia near the Bulgarian border). But after seventeen hours we were disgorged on the front in Bobota near Osijek. We were then taken to the Laszlovo front (Laszlovo is a mixed Hungarian-Croat village south of Tenja and Bobota which was contested bitterly by both sides for the entire duration of the war). I refused to go to the Front and demanded to be released from my duties which was my legal right because we had been misinformed about our task. I was arrested and then taken to Bobota where a field prison had been set up. Here I was screamed at, spat at, racially abused, they called me a Bulgarian and VMRO fascist and then told me I was going to be killed. They did not actually touch me but they were on the verge of doing so when some colleagues from Stip, Serbs in the military police, intervened and prevented things from getting worse. They told me that I must either go to the front or they would have to leave me with the Chetniks in Bobota. They said they could do no more, so I returned to the front. We were under permanent attack there from the direction of Cepin (a village just south of Osijek on the main road into the city).

The army was badly equipped and totally unprepared for the type of war they were fighting. The Croat weaponry was invariably superior to ours. They had extraordinary German guns for their snipers which kept us almost permanently at bay. Both sides were constantly breaking the cease-fires which were a waste of time. However, there was a difference in motivation. Most of the JNA soldiers just wanted to go home alive, while the reservists who came mostly from Vojvodina, Hungarians and Serbs, rebelled in whole units, running away and mutinying. Croats were excused duty on the front line although I suspect this was because the commanders were afraid of treachery rather because of any respect they may have had for the Geneva Convention or anything like that.

I was there when one reserve unit arrived in the middle of the night. They had no idea where they were, they were forced to sleep in the wet and the cold open air. But worst of all, they had been sent to this bloody front without weapons!

There were a plethora of different uniforms on the Serb lines: Chetniks, who were kept at a distance from the JNA, and Arkanovci who were organized in special units to go into the villages when the defences had collapsed and clean up and take prisoners. There was tremendous tension between the JNA, the reservists, the non-Serbs in the JNA and the Serbs, the locals, the Arkanovci, and the Chetniks. For example, some Croats who stayed in Stara Tenja were killed by the Arkanovci provoking bitter protests from the local Serbs. But there was just as much tension on the Croat side between the Zengas (National Guard) and the MUP (special police), the latter being better paid., better organized and better fighters while the former were not only badly disciplined they were also on drugs and drinking a lot. If ever we took a Croat position, there was always evidence of much drug taking. Mutual slaughter occurred on both sides...

Another thing was that JNA soldiers informed the Croats. I was in Silas when a mortar attack began at 15.00. The attack failed miserably as the tanks were in hidden positions. At 18.00 four grenades fell precisely on one hidden tank killing the three occupants inside. No other grenades fell. An attack like this could only have been carried out with inside information and a military investigation later established who had done this but I don't know what happened to him.

As an officer, I was given the chance to visit home one weekend at the end of October and I simply didn't return, so I am now classified as a deserter...

Serbs and Croats in eastern Slavonia can never live together because too much blood has been spilt and the Serbs will never let go of any of this territory. As far as I could work out, the Croats had provoked a lot of the nastiness in the first place but searching for the one who started it is a waste of time. Once it had started the massacres were unstoppable. It will never end whether they have a cease-fire, peace-keeping troops or whatever. This is not a war, this is extermination."

10. Will returning soldiers need help with 'Vietnam syndrome'?
11. How will returning civilians deal with guilt after fleeing their city?
12. How do we best organise for more social responsibility after this war?
13. How can we address 'silent terror'—disappearances and arrests by our own authorities?
14. What about War Crimes of this war?

In the course of the following year practical projects were begun, largely targeted at the displaced and refugee community:

1. A programme on 'psychosocial adaptation' of 'expatriate' teachers and elementary school children which engaged now unemployed teachers in creative art, play and post-trauma work with children,
2. Training and materials for refugee women for sewing, embroidery and knitting as self-help and income-generation,
3. A restoration project in the destroyed village of Laslovo,
4. A greenhouse project for the refugee camp at Cepin to encourage renewed agricultural production.

Katarina Kruhonja was clear in her view then that co-operation was possible with local authorities 'due to overlaps between wishes of the Croatian government and the peace movement/crisis centre.' Both were concerned to rebuild, if possible to re-integrate areas eventually, and the government needed to send refugees back 'in order to reclaim territory.'

As it happened the plight of refugees remained a bargaining chip for years to come, and the Osijek peace group found itself concerned equally with human rights issues within Osijek itself, notably those of the now 6—7 per cent Serb minority. Human rights violations causing concern included coercive eviction from military and public apartments as well as private homes, violations of labour law, denial of citizenship papers, and non-payment of benefits. Their direct action to prevent evictions and forcible removals have been well documented by Adam Curle.[16]

Subotica

An initiative of local intellectuals (who felt isolated from or by Belgrade) backed by HCA, the European Civic Centre for Conflict Resolution began in the buildings of the Open University, formerly the Workers University (state run) and was dedicated to serving the needs of the local community for educational, vocational and cultural advancement. There were practical problems—no funds or fuel for heating, no toilet paper, no fax or printing paper, etc. As Vedran Vucic explained in December 1992, a newsletter could be produced only after a German Green MP to the European Parliament supplied paper, sent by car over the border, naturally, from Budapest.

Vucic saw the centre's aims as educational and cultural and worked 'on a knife edge', as to be openly and simplistically 'anti-war' would invite closure or worse. But he could enable communication and development for minority groups, work with refugees, and promote community relations and understanding. The centre organised a minority rights 'round table' series with representatives from Hungary, Rumania, Moldova, Czechoslovakia, Bulgaria, former Yugoslavia, Macedonia and the Romany cross-border community. Some of the participants had been imprisoned under former regimes, and the more contacts, dialogue and 'bridge building' made possible did feed back to their own communities. The centre hosted an inter-church programme for Subotica, and with help from the George Soros Foundation[17], sponsored summer camps for refugee children. One project was a huge popular/rock music festival 'Muzica Mira'(Music of Peace) held the weekend before Christmas in Subotica bringing together musicians and bands from Serbia, Slovenia, Italy, Macedonia, Hungary and Bosnia. UNICEF (Belgrade) sponsored travel and accommodation, live broadcasts throughout the region were planned, and all proceeds went for relief work. A 'listening project' was undertaken under the auspices of the Pancevo peace group to elicit community views, as opposed to official propaganda (see page 65).

The civic centre worked on points of hope: human relationships, dispelling rumours, enhancing participation and citizen action. 'Fear has wide eyes' is a Slavic saying: it notices everything... then let there be confidence building too. A 'telephone bridge' functioned, quietly organised by citizens. Three days a week, for a few hours each day, people in Serbia could ring Milano and give the operator there a number in Slovenia or Croatia. The Milano operator made a separate call to that number, then connected the two. In this way 800,000 calls were made which defied new government definitions of 'enemy' and enhanced hope, contact, and the renewal of human bonds. In Subotica the Civic Centre and the Open University co-operated on two distinct cultural ventures: an international film festival in which every film shown just happened, in a subtle way, to have an anti-war theme, and an 'Open Book' series of lectures by new authors. For the 'Open Book' evenings, writing was sought which promoted awareness, questioning, creativity and sensitivity to life. The local ministry for culture gave money to buy copies of each book presented and these were distributed to the audiences, between 50 and 100 copies per time. Another Slavic proverb has it that 'When flags are fluttering, the mind is in the Trumpet'. Such activities consciously sought to rescue the mind, and to keep it open.[18]

4.6 'Structural conduciveness' and local capacity building

Daniel Druckman writes (1987) that a priority social-psychological issue for conflict research is 'that of linkages between microprocesses (e.g. interpersonal relations, communication, and social learning) and macro phenomena (e.g. the structure of institutions or the structure of regional systems).' Condor and Brown (1988) suggest that a full understanding of inter-group conflict needs to take account of the way in which ingroup-outgroup imagery becomes associated symbolically with realistic inter-group conflict. They quote Sherif (1966):"The psychology of inter group attitudes and behavior must specify contemporary events within the framework of the past relationships between people and their future goals and designs," and add that such an approach must also be sensitive to the power available to social groups to define and to act upon particular situations of inter group conflict.

The 'power', ability or 'capacity' of individuals to affect collective behaviour is thus a determinant of both the course and outcome of a given conflict. The early Subotica and Osijek initiatives sought in their own ways to mobilise public awareness and resources for the recovery from and/or pre-emption of organised violence. With their emphasis on networking, attitudes, skills development and group formation they exemplified classic 'resource mobilisation' response.

Resource mobilisation

Resource mobilisation, as an approach, emphasises the ability of any given goal-oriented or discontented group to act rather than underlying motives or frustrations. To quote L. Kriesberg (1973) 'Rather than stress the discontent that people feel as the basis for revolutions, violence, and other forms of conflict behaviour and social movement activity, they stress...ability...to act. They argue that dissatisfaction is prevalent; whether or not people try to better their lot depends on their ability to do so rather than on their level of dissatisfaction...In examining interaction between adversaries, their relative mobilisation of resources is especially important.'

For Oberschall, mobilisation 'refers to the processes by which a discontented group assembles and invests resources for the pursuit of group goals'(quoted in Gamson, 1975, p. 137). The process-orientation of this approach is all important, and may be seen on varying levels or in stages; for Himes (1980) active power must be delivered and injected into a social relationship (to achieve goals) in two steps:

1. the identification, discovery and control of accessible resources; and
2. extracting and transforming potential power to active power.

In this study the defining feature is the attempt to mobilise *against war*. As such, emergent groups sought to separate out underlying 'objective conditions' (history, scarcity, power-struggle) from the <u>processes</u> which led to belief in incompatible goals, and corresponding action. **In trying to intercept (and make choices about their own participation in) levels of escalation they were attempting violence <u>prevention</u> (while often using the language of conflict <u>resolution</u>).** They fostered the belief that choice and behaviour could affect outcome; that de-escalation or alternative settlements were possible. The experiences—'We just watched in horror as everything happened and didn't know we could make any difference' (Jasenka, music student, Osijek.), 'We have descended into Dante's Inferno but cannot, must not let it happen again' (Karlo, classics teacher, Vukovar)—reflect graphically how events spiralled. Against conflict progression civic initiatives demonstrated the possibility of 'turning events around' (Kruno, philosophy teacher, Osijek).

Structural conduciveness

In the *Theory of Collective Behaviour*, Neil Smelser identified six categories of variables for analysing collective behaviour:[19] These may be seen as characteristics indicating conducivity for social violence or war.

1. structural conduciveness,
2. structural strain,
3. growth and spread of generalised belief,
4. precipitating factors,
5. mobilisation of participants for action, and
6. operation of social control.

Applied loosely to the situations in E. Slavonia and Vojvodina, these categories should shed light on factors lending themselves to the potential for organised violence:

A. <u>Structural Conduciveness</u>: Insecurity and scarcity due to economic decline in Yugoslavia prior to the outbreak of war. High degree of military readiness and preparation. What has been described as 'authoritarian' cultural dominance.1

MEASURES ADDRESSING STRUCTURAL CONDUCIVENESS TO WAR

INDICATORS OF SOCIAL VIOLENCE/WAR CONDUCIVITY	CAPACITY-BUILDING NEED	EARLY INITIATIVES TO REDUCE VULNERABILITY	
		E. Slavonia/Osijek	Vojvodina/Subotica
A) Structural Disparity: Insecurity and scarcity due to economic decline in Yugoslavia prior to the outbreak of war. High degree of military readiness and preparation. what has been described as 'authoritarian' cultural dominance.	**A) Fulfilment of basic human needs** in spite of economic insecurity (food, shelter, recognition, etc.).	**A)** Cepin Greenhouse Project, sewing/income generation programme for refugee women, work with teachers and children on 'non-authoritarian' modes of learning.	**A)** Round tables on alternatives to military solutions, churches meals programmes for refugees, anti-war film festival, co-operative learning/games for refugee children summer camps.
B) Structural strain: rise of 'ethno-nationalist' parties and ideologies.	**B) Resistance to/or balanced judgement of new ideologies** which demand 'them/us' divisions and mass support.	**B)** 'Public stand' on multi-culturalism, inclusion of all groups in activities, inter-church dialogue.	**B)** Round tables on minority rights, multi-cultural youth broadcasting, inter-church dialogue.
C) Growth and spread of generalised belief: the spread of majority/minority fear and threat due to the use of historical symbols and official media: Serbs feeling threatened in Croatia, Croatians feeling threatened in serbia (Vojvodina).	**C) Sufficient independent media and communications to counter dis-information**, constitutional and symbolic guarantees to minorities, avenues for safe participation.	**C)** Workshops on prejudice reduction, support for student journalism, E-mail facilities, citizens meetings.	**C)** 'Open Book' Programme, workshops on prejudice reduction. 'Telephone Bridge', E-mail.
D) Precipitating factors: incidents, rumour, reaction, such as Borovo Selo, 2 May.	**D) Rumour control,** enough information to check incitement, communication systems which make this possible.	**D)** Workshops on mediation and conflict resolution. Local Democracy Embassy..	**D)** 'Listening Project' workshops on mediation and conflict resolution, publishing, Local Democracy Embassy.
E) Mobilisation of participants for action: JNA recruitment, Croatian army recruitment, official conscription, emotional peer-pressure conscription, incitement of popular action, mass propaganda.	**E) Basic rights,** conscientious objection, alternative sources of service, media which counter-balance official propaganda, alternatives for disputes settlement/management and outcome.	**E)** Input from War Resistors International (via ARK), human rights awareness, legal advice.	**E)** 'Music of Peace' Festival, input from War resistors International (via CAA), human rights awareness.
F) Operation of social control: wages, pensions, employment conditional on 'ethnicity' and stated loyalty, neighbourhood/community values, new borders, financial limitations, basic needs.	**F) Allies 'outside' the system,** human rights mechanisms, functioning legal systems, support systems for minority rights.	**F)** Human rights monitoring, direct action, international networking.	**F)** Round tables on minority rights, international networking.
Each of the above generates specific vulnerabilities	***Capacity-building in wartime needs to address such issue-specific areas.***		

B. Structural strain: rise of 'ethno-nationalist' parties and ideologies.
C. Growth and spread of generalised belief: the spread of majority/minority fear and threat due to the use of historical symbols and official media: Serbs feeling threatened in Croatia, Croatians feeling threatened in Serbia (Vojvodina) 2
D. Precipitating factors: incidents, rumour, reaction, such as Borovo Selo, 2 May. 3
E. Mobilisation of participants for action: JNA recruitment, Croatian army recruitment, official conscription, emotional peer-pressure conscription, incitement of popular action, mass propaganda.
F. Operation of social control: wages, pensions, employment conditional on 'ethnicity' and stated loyalty, neighbourhood/community values, new borders, financial limitations, basic needs. 4

Each of the above generates specific vulnerabilities. Capacity building in war time will need to address such issue-specific areas:

A. Fulfilment of basic human needs in spite of economic insecurity (food, shelter, etc.)
B. Resistance to/or balanced judgement of new ideologies which demand 'them/us' divisions and mass support.
C. Sufficient independent media and communications to counter 'dis-information,' constitutional and symbolic guarantees to minorities, avenues for safe participation.
D. Rumour control, enough information to check incitement, communication systems which make this possible.
E. Basic rights, conscientious objection, alternative sources of service, media which counter-balance official propaganda, alternatives for dispute settlement/ management and outcome.
F. Allies 'outside' the system, human rights mechanisms, functioning legal systems, support systems for minority rights.

Mark Bradbury has observed that 'People are not passive in emergencies.'

> 'In all emergencies opportunities exist to support indigenous non-governmental forms of social organisation, and efforts should be made to promote alternative forms of representation to predatory military structures...
>
> In wars where the state has collapsed, identifying and working with legitimate civil or political structures must start during the conflict. But the crucial question is, how does one identify 'legitimate' political and civic structures to support and work with?
>
> The incorporation of developmental approaches to relief has seen an increase in 'capacity building' programmes in emergency situations. Behind this lies the idea that capacity and vulnerability are related. Development is seen as a process of increasing capacity and reducing vulnerability. Vulnerability is seen to arise as much from organisational, institutional and political weakness, as from lack of material or physical well-being' (Bradbury,1996).

Certainly the experience that 'the state has collapsed' in Yugoslavia from 1991 was replaced by competing claims to statehood, mini-statehood, and authority. Group building and community organisation (particularly in light of 'post-communist' structural changes) had to be done out of social chaos. Capacity building meant the creation of alternative forums for decision making. Philip Peirce, speaking from the 'coal face' in Bosnia would later describe capacity building as: 'Assisting or facilitating the creation of a coalition of interests for the provision of services to the community on a multi-ethnic basis—an alternative forum for community participation in decision making.'[20]

Notes for Chapter IV

1. See Smelser (1967), Chapter VI on 'The precipitating factor—that which transforms Anxiety into Fear.' Such a factor is like a 'spark'—an event which has the effect of transforming widespread anxiety into fear or panic. These emotions in turn lend themselves to subsequent action and reaction. Roger Brown (1965) considers that the calculated use of violence in incidents of intimidation and threat result when individuals feel it is worth their while to act in an anti-social way. The norms of 'social control' can alter dramatically. If the norm is not to attack another person aggressively, then such an action would be 'unsocialized' as opposed to civil, 'socialized behaviour.'

   > 'The outburst will occur because the total set of conditions produces a payoff matrix such that each person can act on his unsocialized impulse and be free of punishment or guilt. Potential participants in an aggressive or hostile outburst can never be as sure of the nature of the payoff matrix, as sure of what others will do as can potential participants in a panic. For this reason hostile and expressive outbursts usually require to be triggered. Someone must initiate action so that others can believe in the action-readiness of the mass' (Roger Brown, *Social Psychology*, New York: The Free Press, 1965, p.760.).

2. Smelser's study is classic in its exploration of conducivity. He speaks of 'social cleavages' (p. 231) which can in themselves contribute to the propensity for violence or outburst. Symbols were very important in the re-development of 'social cleavages' between Serbia and Croatia. National symbols and flags are a case in point. (See 4. below).

For the stages, dynamics and an understanding of conflict widening, see Mitchell (1981) Part 1 "The Structure of Conflict.'

> 'Tito left Yugoslvia with a foreign debt of $19 billion and by 1986 the average standard of living had fallen by a third and inflation was approaching 100%. By 1991 there was an internal trade war when Serbia banned imports from Slovenia and nationalized stores, factories and petrol stations belonging to Croatian firms, and Slovenia and Croatia countered by imposing taxes against Serb properties and blocking deliveries to Serb oil refineries.The ruling party, the League of Communists in Yugoslvia (LCY) lost authority, and in the wake of the 1981 attacks, when Albanians in Kosovo attacked Serbs, nationalism and federalism came to the front of the political agenda. The political agenda became framed in terms of centralism versus federalism, liberalism versus conservatism, and was increasingly dominated by economic concerns, often expressed in economic nationalistic terms' (*The Contingency Model of Mediation in the Yugoslavian Conflict* Keith Webb with Vassiliki Koutrakou and Mike Walters, University of Kent p.4).

To understand underlying general insecurity, and B.'s daughter's reference to the 'standard of living', see the study of economic decline in Yugoslavia in Christopher Bennett, *Yugoslavia's Bloody Collapse*, London: Hurst & Co. 1995, Chapter 5.

3. Gojko Susak was one of President Trudjman's closest advisors, whose personal fortune, from an Ottawa pizza company, helped fund Trudjman's 1990 election campaign.

4. Milan Kosuta's study (1993) of ' the coat of arms in use from 1941 to 1945..., and the one chosen by the Croatian democratically elected Parliament in 1990' concludes 'that the new coat of arms does bear a resemblance to the one in use between 1941 and 1945, but also resembles both that from before 1941 and after 1945..., all of which were accepted by the Serb population in Croatia. All the coats of arms include the red and white checkerboard pattern, which has been the basic element for at least 400 years continuously.'

The emotional message became 'The Croatian government is introducing the red and white checkerboard coat of arms which for the Serbian people is a reminder of tragic events during World War II, and we will never accept the symbol.'

> 'The following excerpts, one from a 1941 law and the other an amendment to the 1990 Croatian Constitution, are further examples of the same fear-evoking process. One of the first laws passed by the quisling regime in 1941 stated that:
>
> The use of the Cyrillic alphabet is forbidden in Croatia.
>
> The amendment to the Croatian Constitution of 1990 specifies:
>
> The Latin alphabet is the official alphabet in the republic of Croatia. In addition to the mandatory use of the Latin alphabet, in those administrative areas of Croatia where the majority of the population uses the Cyrillic or other types of alphabet, the use of such alphabets for official and other purposes is guaranteed [author's emphases].
>
> The message clearly conveyed to the Serb minority in Croatia was that the Croatian government was limiting the Serb's right to use the Cyrillic alphabet.
>
> As in the example of the Croatian coat of arms, these led to the Serbs' perception of the government as a recurrence of the quisling fascist Second World War regime, leaving to an ever-intensifying fear.'

5. Silber and Little (1995) document discussions between Milosevic and Tudjman ('secret talks') at Karadjordjevo on

1. the orchestration of Prime Minister Ante Markovic's removal
2. Tudjman's authority over the status (or resolution of this) of Croatia's Serbian minority, and
3. the participation of Bosnia-Herzegovina (p. 143).

Held in 1991, these 'secret talks' and their Machiavellian connotations seemed to be common knowledge by autumn 1992 in activist circles. I was told about them by quite different people in Subotica and Zagreb.

The question of leadership and 'chains of command' is a particularly fraught one in East Slavonia and Vojvodina. The Serbian autonomous area in Eastern Slavonia became an isolated enigma in many ways, leading to Novi Sad opinion (journalists, intellectuals, social workers, refugees from Croatia) in 1994 that it was 'uncontrollable by Belgrade.' (Personal discussions at 'Zena, Mir I Humanost' meeting and during a visit to Vukovar.) The Aspen Institute (Tindemans, 1996) Report of the International Commission on the Balkans notes the 'gangsterism and corruption on a huge scale' which was endemic in the region (p. 97).

On the other hand, evidence emerged in early 1997 that Serbian secret policemen 'under Milosevic's direct control co-ordinated a covert dirty war by arming thousands of convicts and sending them to fight in Croatia and Bosnia. From April 1991...to 1995 these paramilitary groups, such as the Serbian Cetnik Movement and Arken's Tigers, carried out a murderous campaign..' (Julian Borger, 'The President's Secret Henchmen' in The Guardian 3.2.97. Borger). Borger argues that a 'vojna linija' (military line) linked Arkan, etc. to a State Security Department group which answered to Milosevic. Charges and counter-charges fly in the light of possible indictments by the United war crimes tribunal in The Hague.

Similar accusations stand in Croatia, particularly with regard to Tudjman and 'Bosnian Croats' in Herzegovina. But in no sense did opinion (so far as I could gauge it) in Osijek 1991-1996 hold Glavas to be a puppet of Zagreb. On the contrary, it would be whispered that even Tudjman was afraid of him!

6. See Misha Glenny, 'Warlords rule in a Hobbesian World' in *The Observer*, 4 April 1993, p. 21. Glenny considers Arkan, Glavas, and Mr Kojic (of Vukovar):

> 'The warlords are nationalists, but their convictions are uninteresting. They are technicians of violence, rather than ideologues.

The Importance of Symbols

CROATIAN COATS OF ARMS

A Sixteenth century onwards
B 1941–45
C 1945–1990
D 1990 onwards
(checker pattern in red and white in originals)

From: Milan Kosuta (1993)

The Importance of Symbols

COAT OF ARMS OF SERB VOJVODINA FROM 1848

From P. Matic and P. Zivkovic <u>History of Serbs in Baranja</u> Beli Manastir 1995

Earlier than everybody else, they understood that ethnic nationalism had delivered the ordinary people of the Balkans straight back to Hobbes, to the pre-political state of nature where life is nasty, brutish and short. In the state of nature, the man with a Zastovo machine pistol and a Cherokee chief is king. For he can provide the two commodities everybody here craves: security and vengeance.

Once the Yugoslav Communist state began to spin apart into its constituent national particles, the key questions soon became: will the local Croat policemen protect me if I am a Serb? Will I keep my job in the soap factory if my new boss is a Serb or a Muslim? The answer to these questions was No, because no state remained to enforce the old inter-ethnic bargain. As a result, every individual rushed, pell-mell, to the next available source of protection—the warlord.'

7. Personal interview with Dr. Kramaric, Osijek, May 1992.

8. Report of the HCA fact-finding mission 10-15 March 1992.

9. Personal interview, May 1992

10. See 'The Hungarians, Croats, Slovaks, Romanians, and Rusyns/Ukrainians of the Vojvodina' by Hugh Poulton, in *Minorities in Central and Eastern Europe*, Minority Rights Group, London, 1993

11. Personal interview, Subotica, Dec. 1992.

12 The August 1992 Yugofax (War report) interviews with Vojvodina delegates to the 'other' London conference referred to incidents in 28 places of the republic where Croats were expelled from their homes. There were examples of peace activists wearing the yellow star to publicise these events and to show solidarity with minorities.

13. *The Budapest Post* of 10 Dec. 1992 estimated that 20,000 ethnic Hungarians had fled Vojvodina rather than serve with the JNA.

See also Marcus Tanner 'It isn't ethnic cleansing but they're leaving just the same' *Independent on Sunday* 28.11.93 p.11.

14. Raznjatovic (Arkan) personally led his units committing atrocities in Bijelina and near Sarajevo, according to Ana Diklic of 'Glas Slavonije' (*Guide Out of the War* '91/92. For evidence on the dubious composition of those units and complicity with criminalised police and the 'vojna linija' (military line) in Belgrade, see 'The president's secret henchmen' by Julian Borger, *The Guardian* G2 3 Feb. 1997.

15. Personal record.

16. Adam Curle presents a personal account in his 1995 book *Another Way*, London Jon Carpenter.

17. Later known as the Open Society Fund.

18. Conversations with Vedran Vucic and young Subotica journalists, December 1992 and Spring 1993.

19. See Smelser, as above and W. Gamson, *The Strategy of Social Protest*, Dorsey Press, London, 1975, p.137

He suggested a hierarchy of components strikingly comparable to Mitchell's ideas:

Mitchell		Smelser
1. attitudes	⟷	values and norms
2. behaviour	⟷	mobilisation into organised roles
3. situation	⟷	situational facilities

20. Personal conversation enroute to Mostar from Gorni Vakuf, Oct. 1996.

10 **EUROPEAN NEWS**

Hundreds of refugees defy warnings to march home

Peace troops stop Croatian clash

Ian Traynor in Zagreb

UNITED NATIONS troops, under orders to open fire if need be, blocked roads in the open countryside of eastern Croatia yesterday to prevent a confrontation between hundreds of Croatian refugees trying to return to their homes and Serb gunmen in control of the territory.

Defying warnings by UN peacekeepers that the attempt to reclaim their homes would end in a massacre, about 1,000 Croats marched from the eastern town of Osijek towards the village of Tenjski Antunovac on the other side of the Serb-Croat frontline.

The fertile triangle of land known as the Baranja, to the north of Osijek, was seized by the Serbs in last year's war, together with large tracts of land to the south and the east of Osijek.

Serbian snipers took up rooftop positions behind the UN checkpoint that separates the two sides, and other gunmen massed to the rear. The Russian contingent of UN troops placed lorries across the road to bar access.

But the Croats stopped short of the UN blockade, heeding appeals from Russian officers that the time was not yet ripe for them to reclaim their homes.

"It is the nastiest situation since we came here," said a senior UN official.

The UN forces started deploying in the Serb-held areas of Croatia in March, and they are now nominally UN-protected zones. But senior officials freely admit that their authority is limited, that Serbian "gangsters and hoodlums" are running the territories and that they are murdering about five non-Serbs every week.

The reign of terror in the Serb-held enclaves set back UN plans to facilitate the return of the thousands of Croats driven out last year.

The delay is generating mass anger in Croatia and causing problems for the Zagreb government.

Yesterday's confrontation featured a good deal of brinkmanship on all sides, but UN officials say tension is so high that events could easily spin out of control.

General Aleksandr Chromchenko, the Russian officer in command of eastern Croatia, said yesterday that the UN troops did not have the right to open fire.

"Those who might shoot are behind us," he said, referring to the heavily armed Serbs.

But senior UN sources said the Russian troops were under explicit orders to shoot if need be.

General Satish Nambiar, the UN commander in former Yugoslavia, had issued orders to the Russians three times this week that they should be braced to use force.

President Franjo Tudjman of Croatia has asked the UN to set up a four-party body to deal with the refugees' return, bringing together Croats, Serbs, UN peacekeepers and the UN High Commission for Refugees

The idea was believed to be under discussion in Geneva yesterday, where Mr Tudjman held talks with the president of rump Yugoslavia, Dobrica Cosic.

After their meeting the two leaders announced that the Yugoslav army would pull out of the strategic Prevlaka peninsula in Croatia by October 20 and pledged that their states would work towards mutual recognition.

Meanwhile relief workers in northern Bosnia waited apprehensively to see whether a scheduled evacuation of the Trnopolje detention camp would go ahead.

Militants Serbs have recently stepped up their violent campaign of evicting Slav Muslims from their homes in the area, and the Croats have all but sealed the borders, leaving the Muslims trapped and desperate to leave.

The International Red Cross is hoping to evacuate 1,400 Muslims from the camp today and ferry them into Croatia in 35 buses.

Cutting from THE GUARDIAN - 1/10/92

VERONA FORUM FOR PEACE AND RECONCILIATION IN FORMER YUGOSLAVIA

on Geneva peace talks about Bosnia-Herzegovina, January 6, 1993:

Prevent a 'Munich 1938' outcome; no partition of Bosnia- Herzegovina, no recognition of results of ethnic cleansing!

Increase European and international commitment in ending the war! Promote humanitarian assistance, war crime prevention, restoration of inter ethnic coexistence, of human and minority rights!

Stop talking to war-mongers. Different voices must be heard in Geneva.

The Steering Committee of the VERONA FORUM FOR PEACE AND RECONCILIATION IN FORMER YUGOSLAVIA discussed the on-going peace talks in Geneva at its conference January 5, 1993 and reached the following results:

There is a feeling that Geneva 1993 may become seen like Munich 1938: negotiations with alleged war criminals, blackmail under an already imposed fait accompli, *and in particular by putting the victims at the same level as the aggressor. The ethnic partition of Bosnia-Herzegovina seems to be pre-ordained; the proposed cantonization will inevitably lead to further ethnic cleansing and annexations.*

In Geneva all those not fitting into the nationalistic frames of Karadzic and Boban are conveniently swept into the 'Muslim party' of President Izetbegovic. What about those who, in the first place, feel they belong to the Bosnian entity that has resulted from a centuries-long process of fruitful interaction among three world civilizations (Western Christianity, Islam and Byzantium Orthodoxy)? Who is defending their rights at Geneva's negotiation table? Such a policy is not only destroying Bosnia-Herzegovina, but by the 'Palestinisation' of Bosnians it aggravates hostilities between Europe and the Islamic world and can only lead to further escalation of the conflict.

The dramatic failure of Yugoslav and international (especially European) politicians is evident. The solutions imposed on Bosnia will surely affect the future of the whole continent: the choice lies now between ethnic cleansing (which means the ominous emergence of still more racist states and further ethnic wars in Europe) and inter-ethnic coexistence with clear guarantees for minority and human rights. This choice concerns Bosnia-Herzegovina, the whole former Yugoslavia, the whole of Balkans, the whole of Europe...

The Verona Forum sought a hearing for voices other than nationalist government.

Chapter V

The intervenors

The Listening Project in Banski Brestovac

The Listening Project was the turning point for us. Concretely, it happened in the village of Banatski Brestovac which is located 30 km from Pancevo with Serbian majority and Moslem and Roma minorities. One hussle and mutual beating in a caffe bar between unemployed and hopeless guys who belong to different ethnic groups caused the conflict situation in the village. The two surpluses, surplus of the desperate powerlessness and surplus of energy in their hands, culminated tensions in the local community. The local population faced inter ethnic polarisation and distrust. The lack of communication was the first symptom which showed that something is wrong. Actually, communication and truth are the first victims of the conflicts. Because of that fact the rumours, lies were occurring every day in the local community and threatened the further escalation of the conflict. Such rumours in fact, expressed the very concrete FEELING OF FEAR in people. In the atmosphere of fear and distrust various aggressive extremist were using the opportunity to offer their radical solutions—physical elimination of 'others'.

We have done the 49 interviews in the village of Banatski Brestovac. We examined all demographic and social parts of the local community. Thus, we interviewed Serbs, Moslems, Roma people and among them peasants and workers by occupation, and both, women and men, old and young. During the exercise of interviewing we practised the Active Listening as Herb Walters have taught us to do so. Implementation of that method based on rules of new communication in the process of the conflict enabled us to reach attitudes which the interviewed people did not want previously to confess even to themselves. The results of such an opinion poll shows that for the people from Banski Brestovac the burning issues were poverty, ruined economy and decrease in the quality of life. Young people, including those involved in above mentioned hussle and beating, were complaining that they face the lack of any positive perspective in their life and corruption of the village authorities which do not worry about anything but their private interests. It is very interesting that the opinion poll shows that 'national problems' were on the bottom of the list of expressed problems. Additionally, we have discovered the relationship between the war and social crisis. Thus, approximately one third of all interviewed think that possible solution of the present crisis is stopping of clashings. The two thirds think that it is necessary to direct media in more objective and independent way in order to stop the fuelling of an inter ethnic hatred and war. Majority of answers express readiness of people from Banski Brestovac to resolve their problems by themselves.

Ildiko Erdei the Movement for Peace-Pancevo
in *Civic Conflict Resolution* 1992 Autumn No. 1.
Subotica: European Civic Centre for Conflict Resolution

V. The intervenors

5.1 Second track intervention

The idea of structural conduciveness lends itself to an intervention framework which differs from classic models of 'third party' involvement in conflict. Second track intervention in the conflict in ex-Yugoslavia is best understood in specific relation to the type of war which took place there. For a start there is no neat 'dyad' or two party polarity, to which an external actor adds a third. Chapter IV attempted to demonstrate the multiplicity of actors even in two regions; to extend the analysis to encompass Bosnia would further underline this point. Hence, the use of Bilder's definition of intervention as 'third party' is questionable. Bilder cites 'an individual or group that is external to a dispute between two or more other individuals or groups and that either tries to help the disputants reach a settlement or, in some cases, is authorised to determine a settlement (Lewer and Ramsbotham, 1993).

Secondly the notion of 'settlement' is not immediately applicable, as intervenors impacted not so much on belligerents as on affected populations. In other words, in a conflict configuration of two or more parties with assumed symmetry of power (as indeed Tudjman and Milosevic were perceived in official diplomacy) the idea of settlement has relevance, and the level of centralised decision-making is appropriate; hence the eventual Dayton Agreement (Izetbegovic added to the equation).

Affected populations are those mobilised for, affected by, divided by, and/or working against the use of collective violence. In complex political emergencies we witness primary and secondary bifurcation (forking or division). Slovenia separates from Yugoslavia. Croatia separates. Groups within each state separate. Primary social groups which resist war as policy are thus oppositional to, in conflict with their own governments (Diagram 1, Chapter I). This type of conflict configuration is asymmetrical, in that internal social movements generally lack the resources, coercive ability and influence of state governments.[1] They may also be representative of minority national opinion. Affected populations include many social actors who do not question, do not act, but feel 'acted upon', represented by the government or military in question, or locked into local para-military configurations.

Moreover, for affected populations a political settlement does not necessarily improve conditions in the local environment. Settlement may bring a cessation of formal war, but also a condition of negative peace. Curle (1990) observes that 'the no-war definition begins to break down in those places where there is...political oppression, economic exploitation, detention camps, arbitrary arrest and imprisonment without trial, persecution of minorities and other loathsome practices.' It is precisely this arena of social conditions and actors which has been the realm of second-track intervention.

Second track intervention, then, targets the social fabric itself; the conditions, agency and structure forms out of which manifest violence emerges. In their work on the international politics of ethnic conflict, Carment and James acknowledge that antecedents to a conflict are usually structural in nature' (Carment and James 1997, p.210). While Smelser pioneered with his ideas of structural conduciveness, Pruitt and Rubin (1986) developed what they call the structural change model of conflict escalation, suggesting that 'conflict, and the tactics used to pursue it, produce *residues* in the form of changes in the parties and communities to which the parties belong. These residues then encourage further contentious behaviour, at an equal or still more escalated level, and diminish efforts at conflict resolution' (Pruitt and Rubin, p.92). Three kinds of structural change are identified: psychological change (dehumanisation, demonisation, deindividuation, exaggerated fear of small losses etc.); changes in the groups (increased cohesiveness, emergence of militant leadership etc.); and changes in the community context of the parties (polarisation and third party intervention, demographic fluctuation). Their work, as well as that of Brockner and Rubin (1985) is representative of a body of rigorous study on conflict processes and dynamics. Structural indicators need not be limited to power parity (weapons, resources) or economic performance (Carment and James, Ibid.) but can include processes which become embedded in the social fabric rendering it conducive to war. Examples would include: the manipulation by elites of belief systems and ideology (Little and Smith, 1988); regime coercion (Gurr, 1970); militarisation (Rapaport, 1986, Ryan, 1990); heightened ethnocentrism (Kuper, 1971, Kellas, 1991); physical separation, residential segregation and a sharpening of territorial boundaries (Brown, 1993); psychological distancing, through stereotyping, scapegoating, dehumanisation and the creation of an enemy image (Mack, 1990, Horowitz, 1985, Spillmann and Spillmann, 1991); sanctification and demonisation (Kuper, 1989); entrapment and over-commitment (Janis and Mann, 1977, Mitchell, 1991); and economic decline or underdevelopment (Azar, 1990). There are then, a myriad of intersecting points and parts which contribute to the composition of the whole. [2]

If we accept the structural change model of escalation, second-track intervention may be seen as intercepting or even pre-empting cumulative tendencies towards violence. Paradoxically, in its aim of enabling conditions for positive peace, the second track approach also exhibits some of the same characteristics often ascribed to peace building. In its essence, however, it is informal engagement. It is horizontal linkage between internal and external groups.[3] Ryan (1990) reminds us of John Galtung's tripartite classification of conflict resolution strategies which he believed interacted with each other in a complex way. These were peacekeeping, peacemaking and peacebuilding. The first of these was concerned with keeping apart warring factions. The second was with third party interventions in the negotiation processes between decision makers, whilst the third was directed at the socio-economic environment and the negative attitudes that the parties to a conflict have of each other. Simply put, whereas peacekeeping is about building barriers between groups who want to fight each other, peacebuilding attempts to build bridges to allow for positive and creative interaction; whereas peacemaking is concerned with interventions at the elite, decision making level, peacebuilding is focused on the social, economic and psychological environments of ordinary people at the grass roots level.

5.2 The intervenors

There are two main difficulties in conducting any study of intervenors in the ex-Yugoslav context. One is a 'wheels within wheels' problem of language or parlance to do with 'intervention'; for example, the phrase 'levels of intervention[4], is used <u>within</u> the discourse of psycho-social project speech at the same time as 'psycho-social' approaches may themselves be seen as one type of intervention (Agger, 1993). (Similarly the phrase 'conflict resolution' appears on documentation and in conversations again and again, as does 'NGO.' These latter problems are dealt with at length below, in Chapters VI and VII.)

Secondly, the multiplicity—the *sheer numbers*—of actors is daunting in itself. This chapter can at best offer a typology of interventions and identify trends and themes which appear dominant or noteworthy. This will be done within the 'second track' context, and with Lederach's model (see Chapter II) in mind.

Intervenors came because they were drawn to the situation, they were asked to come, or thought they could help. In some cases all three conditions apply. Many individuals offered themselves, as per American, Canadian and British academics who considered they had something to offer[5]. More often than not it was networks and connections that were activated in a more collective manner.

In some instances the approach of the intervenors evolved, as in the case of WRI and BSV who collaborated with other initiatives to move away from 'workshops' to the formation and fielding of the Balkan Peace Teams (see below). In other cases intervention style has remained constant while recipient parties/partners have themselves evolved; as in CCCRTE offering 'facilitation' and 'workshops' over a five year period. In the latter case, as with 'Lebensgarten' Germany (see below) there is a facilitator/client relationship which also bears 'institution building' fruit—in the way of contacts, links with donors, publicity channels, etc.[6]

Institutions have also been designed and imported as an intervention. The 'local democracy embassy(s)' are a case in point.[7] Located in Osijek and Subotica, they encourage links 'on the ground,' being meeting places for young people, journalists, civic representatives, local initiatives, and also bring international cultural connections with at least three other European states. Their brief is literally to encourage local democracy.

Personalities who had pioneered their own human development or communications approaches gained followers in Croatia and Serbia. Examples would include Danaan Parry[8], founder of an organisation called Earthstewards which sponsors citizens diplomacy in conflict areas, and Marshall Rosenberg[9], founder of Non-violent Communication methods.

What follows then is an attempt at a typology of second-track interventions which aim to alter the course or effects of war towards more peaceable and just socio-political structures. Examples given are interventions which attempted precisely what Rosenau (1968) stipulates: <u>a deviation between an intervener and a target state which is aimed at altering the authority structure in the target state</u> (this study Chapter II), thus undermining war capability, promoting positive peace, and inducing structural change. It must be stressed that these are selective examples and not in any sense a comprehensive list. Categories examined are

1. aid
2. advocacy
3. communications
4. education and training
5. facilitation
6. mediation and negotiation
7. reconstruction
8. therapeutic work
9. witness.

A. Origins

The concept *"local democracy embassy"* was initiated (in co-operation with Médecins Sans Frontières (Belgium) & Amnesty International (Belgium)) and proposed by *Causes Communes Belgique*, supported by *Causes Communes Suisse*, discussed with the *Helsinki Citizens Assembly*, incorporated in the CLRAE's Resolution 251 and later worked over and clarified by the Monitoring Committee set up under CLRAE auspices.

B. Aims

The chief aims of a *local democracy embassy* are:

- to foster peaceful co-existence through mutual acquaintance and understanding developed by means of exchanges and intermunicipal co-operation;
- to strengthen the democratic process where it exists and to put in hand confidence-building measures (in accordance with the scheme devised by the Council of Europe) through intercultural activities, human rights and peace education;
- to combat racism, intolerance and xenophobia by implementing non-violent solutions;
- to encourage the development of unbiased and pluralistic information;
- in general, to promote dialogue and mediation.

2. Role

The role of *local democracy embassies* is to promote respect for human rights in general and to help implement and consolidate the democratic process in all sectors of local life. Particular attention will be given to:

- human rights and minority rights
- the working of local democracy
- cultural exchanges
- economic exchanges.

The duties of *local democracy embassies* may be described provisionally as follows:

- to serve as a temporary logistic base for humanitarian aid missions conducted by the founder municipalities;
- to facilitate two-way communication between the participating towns and their neighbouring regions;
- to compile a record of local, cultural and economic resources and transmit this information to the network of European municipalities as a means of forging micro-economic and intercultural links;
- to actively support various local activities that concord with the objectives of the permanent mission. Active support may consist in:
  - . helping with the practical organisation
  - . stimulating participation
  - . additional fundraising;
- to establish constructive contacts - in a spirit consistent with the aims of the *local democracy embassy* - with local political parties, local NGOs, the churches, the youth organisations and the independent media.

Extract from Discussion Paper on the Creation of Local Democracy Embassies, Secretariat of the Council of Europe, Strasburg, 28 June 1993

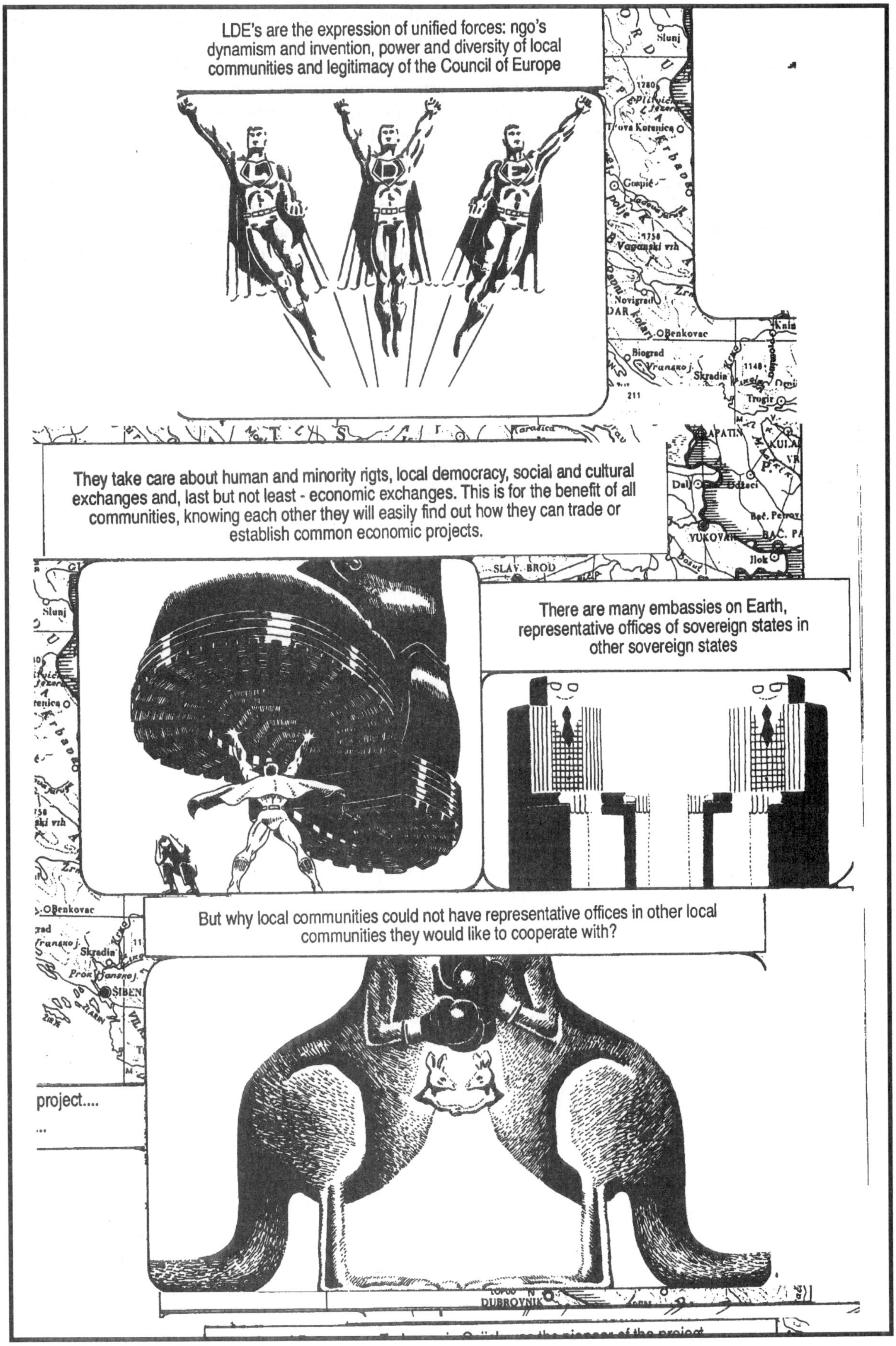

Local Democracy Embassy poster, distributed widely in Croatia and Serbia 1995

5.3 Aid

Aid is generally construed as material and foodstuffs, but in fact financial aid has played an enormous part in enabling projects to grow. The Osijek initiatives in Cepin and Laslovo, for example were funded by 'sister cities' Wageningen (Netherlands), Gödöllö (Hungary) and Marfelden-Waldorf (Germany). The question of funding is addressed in Chapters VII and VIII.

Vukovar and Borovo Selo were beneficiaries in 1994 of lorry loads from the British 'Oak Tree Trust' representative of a plethora (if not an explosion) of "Taking humanitarian aid to Eastern Europe' ventures to spring up in the early 1990s in the UK. It took comparable loads to Novi Sad and Zagreb, drawing on the charity of Bromwich Albion for footballs, as well as public donations for a new dental chair and equipment for Borovo, and sports equipment for the 'start of rebuilding the bombed gym' at Vukovar school.[10] 'Feed the children' founded in July 1990 assured its contributors in publicity promotion of winter 1993, that 'We build up trust not dependency! We work with local people not for them...We keep in contact by letter, phone, fax, telex and even radio.'[11] There can be few people in Britain who do not know of at least one local initiative to send goods to former-Yugoslavia; the same will be true of the Netherlands, Italy, Germany and Switzerland.

Women's Aid to Former Yugoslavia was founded in the UK in October 1992 with a particular mandate 'to meet refugee women and women involved in the anti-war movement to find out what their situation was, to bring out their messages and needs and to act upon them with what resources we have.'[12] Their philosophy was in keeping with the self-help and social-engagement themes described above in 'Responses to war':

> 'In writing about refugees, it is imperative to get away from portraying the strong as weak, the opinionated as vague, the healthy as sick, the active as passive. The conventional images of refugees presented as helpless, sorry, bloodied people, constructs a patronising mentality where refugees are seen somehow as children. From our experiences in collecting aid we found that people wanted to see refugees as children, and much more to give to children. We feel it important to portray people as individuals, how they really are and what they really say, even if sometimes, like the women who wanted the arms embargo on Bosnia lifted, it doesn't fit in with our own ideals about peace and non-violence.'

It was the WATFY view that a vast proportion of the medicines delivered as 'aid' to former-Yugoslavia were out of date, sometimes by years, and had to be thrown away as it arrived. 'TV dinners and old army rations are the other delights that refugees can look forward to, courtesy of Britain and the USA.' (Jones, 1993). WATFY talked directly to women living and working in refugee camps to assess needs, and also linked directly to CAA Belgrade, the anti-war centre and peace movement of Novi Sad, the European Civic Centre for Conflict Resolution in Subotica, plus ARK, activists in Karlovac (as well as Slovenia and Bosnia) to name a few. In turn they spoke directly to women back in Britain, to inform them of the situation on the ground as opposed to on the media. As such they were aid with a difference, even joining in Women in Black vigils. They are mentioned again below under 'Advocacy.'

European ecumenical church aid to Novi Sad assisted peace activists there in setting up their own distribution and income-generation centres, such as Panonija. German Baptists assisted a 'Hilfe zur Selbst-hilfe' (help for self-help) scheme in Novi Sad and responded to emergency shortages there of medicines, food and clothing, as well as finding sewing machines for the project.[13] Tilburg Zamir Netherlands offered an ingenious scheme of donated computers, modems and skills training in fax and E-mail communications.[14]

5.4 Advocacy

Advocacy refers here to taking up a cause and campaigning for it. When Drago Hedl, a journalist in Osijek received death threats from Glavas, a joint campaign was launched by the International Federation of Journalists and the Local Democracy Embassy (with European partners) who wrote letters to/and petitioned Glavas direct on Hedl's behalf. The threats were rescinded.[15]

In the early days of the war there was considerable concern about the detention without charge (in both Croatia and Serbia) of individuals who held opinions contrary to those of their government. Amnesty International[16] offered seminars on the subject of prisoners of conscience and campaigned for general human rights awareness. BSV/WRI did the same for the right to conscientious objection. Women's Organisations including WATFY campaigned on rape as a war crime. The International Helsinki Federation assisted initiatives to bring about the war crimes tribunal at The Hague, as called for in early statements of both CAA and ARK.

The meaning of human rights also had a strong domestic dimension. In Croatia, 'dismissals of people with the 'wrong' nationality, or of different political opinion, blackmail through withholding citizenship certificates (Domovnica), the suppression of reports on massacres carried out on Serb civilians, as well as the suppression of any media publishing them, are all unthinkable in democratic countries. But here such acts are shielded by silence' (Tagirov, 1995). *Arkzin*, the ARK newspaper publicised rights violations and stated in June 1993 that at least three 'removals' (of people from their flats) had been prevented or delayed by activists from the Zagreb centre and groups such as the Serbian Democratic forum.[17]

One of the greatest tragedies of the war has been the forced migration of peoples. (See Appendix 2) 'Otvorene Oci' (open eye) the Croatian Balkan Peace Team participated in direct action to prevent evictions in Zagreb, accompanied individuals seeking legal assistance in Split, and documented forced removals.[18] In Zagreb, journalist Vesna Bernardic went on hunger strike in front of the Sabor (Parliament) after she had almost been evicted from a flat her mother exchanged for one in Belgrade. Following adverse reactions from international organisations and a personal intervention from Cardinal Franjo Kuharic, the Constitutional Court brought the first decision postponing an eviction (Tagirov, 1995).

Oxfam UK, which intervened initially in an 'aid' capacity as above, was innovative in adapting to the human rights situation. They were instrumental in setting up a network of legal advice centres—Karlovac, Knin, Pula, Vukovar, and Zagreb—with communication systems and data development so that refugees on either side could have assistance with concrete information on the state of their former homes and conditions for possible return.

LEX of Zagreb and the CAA Committee for Monitoring and Raising Consciousness about Violations of Human Rights, Belgrade, worked through roundtables, petitioning constitutional courts, and publications. The latter undertook a study of 'hate speech' in the media, and published a Bulletin 'Voice.' They liaised with the UN Centre for Human Rights in Geneva, Mazowiecki's Country Mission and Helsinki Watch. 'Contra Bellum', published by the Movement for Peace Pancevo made its debut in September 1993 with an issue including a feature on the harassment of minorities and argued for their rights as citizens.

Kostic (1994) points to the phenomena of spontaneous ad hoc local initiatives such as the 'Spiritual Republic Zitzer' of Tresnjevac, a village not far from Senta, which campaigned for rights of conscientious objection, but (lacking wider networks and resources) either could not or did not pursue formal consolidated organisation.[19]

The area of 'advocacy' overlaps appropriately with that of communications, given the importance of independent media for campaigning, and in the ex-Yugoslav context the importance of advocacy for independent media, as well. The Independent Association of Journalists was founded in Novi Sad in 1990, attracting some four hundred members over the next four years. Trade Unions such as RTU Novi Sad, and 'Independence' Belgrade also campaigned for professional standards and help for colleagues who were fired. Assistance was given by Italian trade unions.

5.5 Communications

Communications refers to the imparting or transmitting of news, information or messages. The 'Telephone Bridge' which functioned via Serbia/Italy/Croatia was an innovative communication form which helped people who could access it stay in touch with friends and contacts officially deemed 'The Enemy.' There is no question that denying contact leads to a hardening of positions. If you cannot hear directly from someone on 'the other side' it is impossible to test or validate information given. Dephi STAR provided technical assistance and training in E-mail as well as help with computer/modem/printer outfits.[20] Tilburg Za Mir did the same. This meant that groups who could neither phone, write to or visit each other could have 'on line' conversation.

External support for more independent media was forthcoming for both Croatia and Serbia. The International Media Fund (based in Washington DC.) assisted with establishing media resource centres in Zagreb University Radio, provided equipment and training to B-92 and Radio Monitor, Belgrade. They supported television stations Studio B and TV Win, Belgrade, and TV Marjan in Croatia. (Split). Such publications as *Noviska Document* and *Erasmus* (Zagreb)[21], SVET of Novi Sad and Vreme, Belgrade received equipment and training.[22]

The importance of communications intervention is well illustrated by the cases of Beta and Borba in Belgrade. The state news agency Tanjug was effectively purged during the war with Croatia with 'blacklists' of hundreds of 'traitors' read out on state television between 1990 and 1993. By late 1994 government harassment of Borba culminated in legal proceedings claiming 'improper incorporation' (Markotich, 1995) and a government take-over. Staff of the independent paper reincorporated under the name of *Nasa Borba*. There was an undercover campaign waged against *Nasa Borba*, 'warning printers, frightening off advertisers and blocking supplies of newsprint' (McKay, 1995). The European Commission

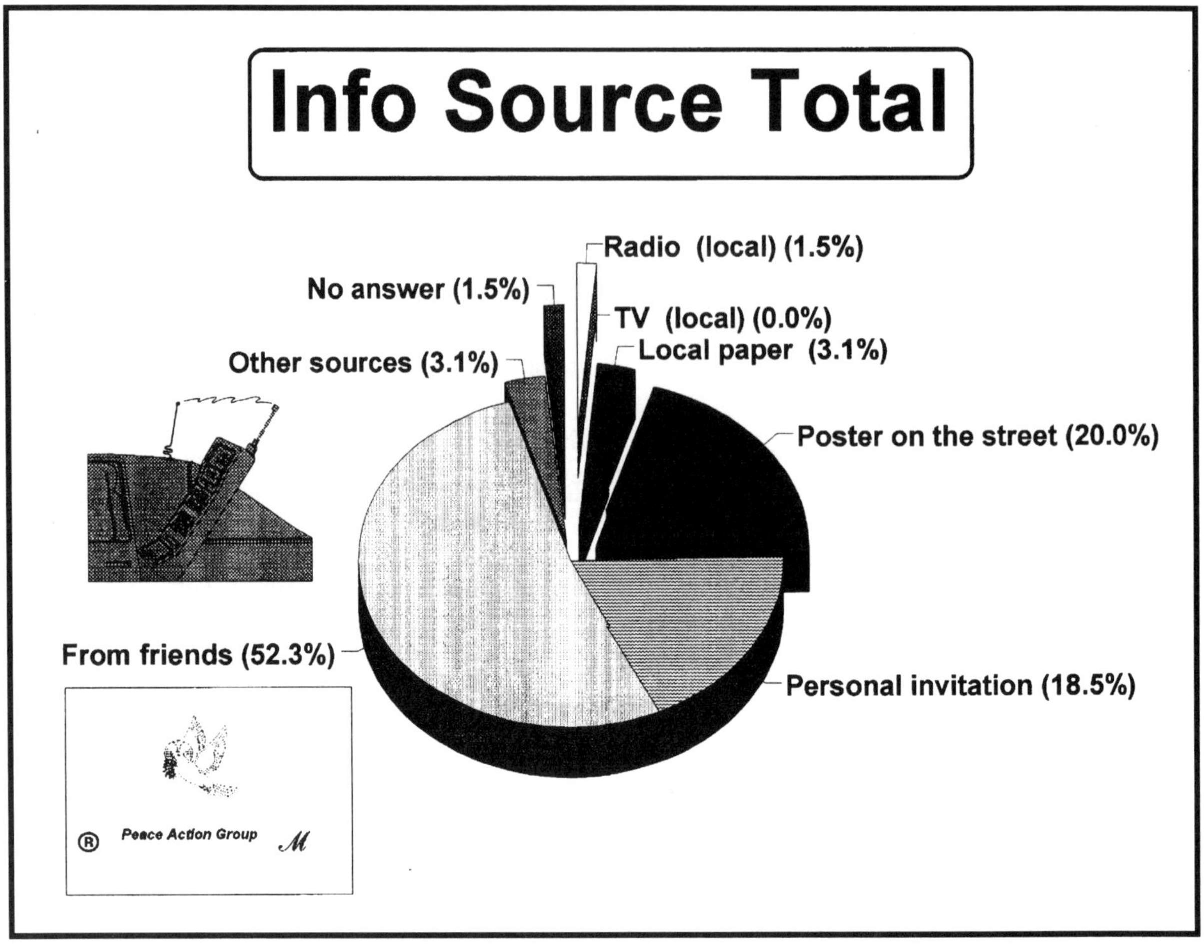

Courtesy of Mirko Mandrino 1996

Communications: Mandrino highlights problems and patterns in communication in his pie chart based on polling those who attended discussion evenings organised by his peace group throughout 1995/96.

donated 200 tonnes of newsprint and a contract was eventually signed with a small independent printer (Ibid.).

War Report London, *Press Now* Amsterdam, and the International Foundation of Journalists, Ljubljana and Novi Sad, continually campaigned for support of independent media. Viktor Ivancic, editor of the independent weekly *Feral Tribune* was quoted as saying that Croatian war reporting was Croatian lying, 'and it will take decades for the profession to recover from producing so many lies.'[23]

Dissecting lies also happens when people talk to each other. Herb Walters of Rural Southern Voice for Peace (USA) introduced the concept of neighbourhood surveys and door-stop discussion with his 'Listening Project,' training and assisting activists in Pancevo for a pilot programme in the village of Banatski Brestovac. Their account of findings, and their ideas about 'the relationship between war and social crisis' are shown on the first page of this chapter.

The vital importance of communications, and the relationship of information to power may be seen in the fact that a year 'into the peace' after Dayton, three postal and telecommunications services were still operating in Bosnia—the Serbian, Croatian and Bosnian BTT. Telecommunications was one of the most difficult reconstruction issues to unravel. Separate media space continued to define political space. Understandable then, that as early as 1992 UN special rapporteur Tadeusz Mazowiecki called for a TV and/or radio blitz on Serbia and Croatia. Ideas then ranged from compelling the regime to show responsible programming prepared outside to establishing out-of-country transmitters along the lines of the World Service and Voice of America.

Borden, Lukovic and Plesch (1993) even called for the jamming of military communication of anyone launching an armed offensive, stating that:

> 'Western electronic warfare capabilities can completely disrupt all military electronic systems without a shot being fired. This can be done selectively, targeting only the precise communications one wants to block. This option is rarely, if ever, mentioned by the 'Bomb Serbia' lobby—possibly because the military is shy of revealing how powerful these capabilities are.'

Communications interventions, then, are perhaps only in their infancy.[24]

5.6 Education and training

Education and training were key concerns of local groups from early days of the war. At the Bratislava meeting in '92 there were requests for training in non-violent conflict resolution and mediation. At the meeting with local authorities in Osijek later that spring, teachers and social workers asked if there were 'forms of education to help our children out of trauma and into a better future. Can we educate for a future without war?'[25]

'Training' as a term has been stretched with an elasticity of meaning to embrace everything from a theological approach to non-violence (Christian, Buddhist etc.), to experiential group work on self-development, to mediation[26], to direct action and more (see 'Dilemmas of training', next chapter). The International Fellowship of Reconciliation, WRI, BSV, CCCRTE, Lebensgarten were among the principal actors in training who used the terminology of conflict resolution.

Trainings in 'Non-violent Communication' under the auspices of Marshall Rosenberg had also drawn Croatian and Serbian participation as early as 1993. Largely due to the efforts of Nada Ignjatovic in Belgrade, NVC was accepted by the Ministry of Education for incorporation into the national curriculum for kindergartens in Serbia[27]. C-dur (Centre for Mental Development) Belgrade, affiliated with MOST, promoted non-violent communication trainings for young adult and adult groups in Vojvodina. It was adopted by youth trainers of ARK and Osijek, as well.

With assistance from intervenors such as Quaker Peace and Service (London) trainings for teachers from primary schools were initiated in 1993 in Osijek with particular emphasis on recovery from trauma (many of the affected children were refugees, displaced, or had immediate experience of war) and creative, co-operative approaches to difference. Many of the teachers were themselves displaced persons. Perhaps because of their 'post-war recovery' relevance, these programmes were given co-operation by local authorities. Workshops were held in schools. Curle (1995) estimated that in two years 720 workshops were given to over 1000 children in local schools in and around Osijek. Local trainees published[28] their own materials in 1994 and by 1996 it was estimated that 5000 children in Croatia had benefited from such sessions[29].

In Vojvodina the Soros Open Society Fund supported work with youth workers and children's summer camps in a similar vein. UNICEF trained 600 teachers and primary health workers in a comparable programme 'Self Esteem Enhancement Through Co-operative Communication' in 1993 alone, for implementation in schools and youth groups[30]. Alexander Weisner pioneered the 'Schools Without Violence' project in Pancevo, (see Chapter VI), also bringing out a translation of Mildred Masheder's *Let's Cooperate*.

If the above represent trainings for a type of peace education, there were others of a more technical or legal nature. E-mail trainings assisted basic communication between entities. Human Rights trainings by Amnesty, Helsinki Watch, and civil liberties groups from Europe led to solid work on legal aid, return, protection of minorities, employment and housing law. Finally, as early as September 1993, Zoran Ostric in his report on 'ARK Network, Member Organizations, Programs and Projects' (p. 5) announced the advent of 'education and training activities' on NGO strategy and management. This is a subject we will return to later in this study.

5.7 Facilitation

Facilitation refers to measures which enable or ease transactions which may be interpersonal, group, or even material as in goods or funds. The channelling of goods and funds will be to effectively by-pass corrupt or non-functional systems, as per Belgrade financial structures 1993-1996 when citizens were burying Deutsch marks in their gardens rather than touch banks. In the early days of the war the personal delivery of messages, documents, paper or ink across borders was a facilitation service international agencies and individuals could offer. An 'international' could carry messages or small parcels (from people in Croatia) into Vukovar, for example, with access from Novi Sad. Dutch printers in Holland made possible, *facilitated* the Pancevo 'Art for Peace' posters and promotion.

The Balkans Peace Project document (Gutlove, 1992) refers to its 'workshop facilitation team' as

Voices from Baranja

1. *I don't suffer violence [physical and psychic] to me, or to other people by me.*
In last 6 Year was many bad things.
I was chief and many time I had position to protect endangerment people, from dangerous, bad people.*
I need to be crafty and clever, and in such a way to win vulgarity and stupidity.
Now, I am tired about all of that.
I need peace and social class.

2. *At the beginning of the war, when was telephone line broken, we come to know about relatives from Croatia through family from Brcko.*
They are Croatian nationality, we are Serbia nationality.
When beginning the war in Bosnia they left Brcko.
Now, I don't know, where are this family.
I have wish to meet with them, or to be informed about them.
*Later, during the war I meet with my friends and relatives in Hungary.***
It was dangerously for both,
We meet each other during the all war times.
I am proud on this.

3. *During the war, I listened different information and watch different TV Serbian [government and non-government], Croatian, Musliman, Montenegrin.*
I listened radio Europe and radio America.
After that information I had possibly what happened in other part of side in conflict.
All of them had one-sided 'truth'.
I had better inspection in whole situation.

*'chief' would be literal translation to English, meaning local official.
**a reference to meeting at Mohac (see 'Facilitation').

offering a variety of approaches to conflict resolution. CCCRTE moved increasingly towards the language of facilitation and away from 'training'[31].

Peace Bridge Mohacs was an intriguing experiment in facilitation which centred on a meeting house in Mohacs, Hungary, almost equal-distance from Osijek and Baranja. Founded by Peace Bridge Basle (under the leadership of Louis Kung, formerly of PBI) and sustained with Dutch/Swiss collaborative support, this initiative organised summer camps in Holland and Hungary for young people from all the former republics, and hosted cross sectional meetings for literally thousands of civilians. Sometimes these were organised seminars on themes such as ecology or education. Othertimes it undertook the reunion of families and friends who could not otherwise meet each other until UNTAES border initiatives enabled such gatherings.

Oxfam facilitated a meeting between Croatian and Serbian representatives from E. Slavonia in Vukovar, June 1996. This took the form of a human rights and NGO development seminar, attended by 25 Croatians and 30 Serbs. A significant event in a volatile area, the assembly was threatened by local extremists. The participants were able to handle this (with assistance from UNTAES) and went on to assist with the founding of a human rights centre in Vukovar.

Local Democracy Embassies also assisted with facilitation designed to involve the population of E. Slavonia. US Ambassador Peter Galbraith talked to public meetings in Osijek and in Vukovar, following the Erdut decision on reintegration. With LDE backing the mayors of Osijek and Subotica were able to keep in contact in spite of extemist attempts to render this impossible.

5.8 Mediation/negotiation

'Mediation,' writes Curle (1995) 'of course requires two protagonists whom the mediator can try to bring together.' It was not, as he found many people had come to expect, 'the expected panacea.' If intervenors such as Curle, CCCRTE, and Lebensgarten brought the idea of mediation when they came to Croatia and Serbia, they could not immediately put it into practice. Curle continues:

> 'And there was no obvious way of mediating from a provincial base about an international matter. Anyway it was impossible practically; there was no contact between the people of Osijek and those of the surrounding UNPAs. The frontier was guarded by the UN and even if it had been possible to cross, it would have been extremely dangerous...But, in any case, the potential outcomes even from successful mediation were not really attractive to most people: either to resume hostilities, or to return to their old homes (provided they had not been taken over by Serbs) under continued UN protection in a country still Serb dominated. In fact hardly anyone, Croat or, I think, Serb, was willing to consider compromise, which is, of course, the prerequisite of mediation' (Curle, 1995, p. 117).

This is not to say that mediation was not taken up and practised by local actors, an issue which will be examined below. (See Chapter VI).

Curle (1990) defined mediation as 'a *psychological* effort to change perceptions both of the conflict and of the enemy to the extent that both protagonists gain some hope of a reasonable resolution and so are more prepared to negotiate seriously.' In a practical sense the international volunteers at the Pakrac Social Reconstruction Project (below, No. 5.9) attempted to do this in 'confidence building' mode. They were allowed to cross from the Croatian controlled sector into Serb controlled Pakrac and to return again. Nominally concerned with bricks and mortar reconstruction matters, they also carried news, messages, and personal accounts back and forth across a divided community. It was not, however, for the community to negotiate. The May 1 1995 Operation 'Lightning' (or 'Flash', the Croatian offensive) made the solution to division a military one.

Otvorene Oci, the Balkan Peace Team based in Croatia, attempted informal, low-key mediation between individuals and authorities, accompanying people to official proceedings or ministries in Zagreb and Split, particularly on issues of state documents or threats of eviction[32].

Mediation, as defined by the Lebensgarten 'Light in Conflicts' school was framed rather differently. Here it was part of 'professional further development'...to 'improve inter-personal relations'...'the mediator is a facilitator of the interpersonal who helps in finding a solution.'[33] This highly personalised model found its followers, and regular self-development sessions were held in Osijek.

The Peace Bridge Mohacs centre served as a meeting point for ARK and Most[34] activists involved in the Pakrac project. They, unlike their international peers, could not cross the divide. After the 1995 offensive they worked jointly, through Mohacs and E-mail, to exchange information on separated families, obtain lists of dead and wounded, and negotiate safer passage and aid for those deported to Belgrade.

Mohacs was also the site for an attempt by representatives of Die Schwelle (Germany) to bring together representatives from Baranja and Osijek the following autumn for a negotiation process parallel to that of Erdut. Area middle-range officials Goran Hadzic, Milan Milanovic and Slauk Dokmanovic sat at the negotiating table with UN representative Thorvald Stoltenberg and US ambassador Peter Galbraith to hammer out details on a transition period for Eastern Slavonia. It seemed to Dirk Heindriks of Die Schwelle that a people's agreement on behalf of local populations would be a good thing. The attempt was not successful.

5.9 Reconstruction

It could be said that the Pakrac Social Reconstruction Project was an experiment by UNOV/UNDP in using second-track entry points to social reconstruction in a divided area. UNOV and UNDP approached ARK in early 1993 for the provision of personnel and local expertise to run the project (including ex-*Suncokret* volunteers), hence PSRP's initial project status within ARK structure. UNOV/UNDP operated not merely as a source of funding and various other resources for PSRP, but also monitored the project with an eye to replication. It was thus a pilot project in the new developmental slant to UN thinking on approaches to complex 'post-war' situations[35]. ARK and PSRP deliberately played down this link, or stressed that they had no connection to UNPROFOR. UNPROFOR was perceived negatively by much of the population in Croatia because they patrolled

Extracts from KAKO, International Newsletter of the Pakrac Project No. 2 June 1994

In the first issue of Kako si we have described how the projects works: international volunteers working with local brigades to clean bricks, repair roofs, etc. Through this work they relate with people to establish normal, at least different human relations.

Besides this joint work with local brigade, a range of projects has been initiated: English lessons for all ages, community assistance work for social needy in co-operation with the local office for social work, the youth development project, culminating in the opening of the Youth Club, the women's group and the on-going work of building a playground, a park, etc. All this means a lot to the inhabitants who see that life is returning to their destroyed town. Various UN-branches and NGOs recognize the importance of the project and are making connections with it. The Project is growing in range, and also in perspective. Especially in the current situation where many believe that cease-fire agreements may finally lead to a normalisation processes, the focus will (or should?) gradually shift from peace-keeping and humanitarian aid to active engagement in reconstruction and development of social and economic conditions. Rebuilding infrastructure and restarting production in agriculture, construction, and industrial production are on the agenda. In Pakrac we find this too: houses have been supplied with natural gas, new telephone lines are laid. An important gift from Mensen in Nood (Dutch Caritas) of 200.000 DM worth of seeds has reached the Serbian side. Farmers there have taken the opportunity to work their land for the first time in three years, about 100 square kilometres have been ploughed and sown in! We could see people working on their plots of land, growing potatoes and vegetables. This is significant not just because they will have better food, but also because it means that the so much longed for normality of village and country life is returning to this area. Imagine the difference in taste between canned corned beef and roasted rabbit with home-grown onions and garlic.

But things are still far from normal in and around Pakrac. In the last few months five people were killed (2 by bullets, 3 by a mine) and shooting from both sides occurs every now and then. The negotiations between Zagreb and Knin about normalisation and re-integration of occupied territories seem to trigger new tensions and provocations from different directions. A good example was the visit on the 7th of April of the Christian-Orthodox patriarch Pavle from Belgrade to Pakrac, together with the bishop of Slavonia. They requested permission to visit the orthodox church and the bishop's house which both lie on the Croatian side, about 50 meters from the checkpoint (actually the Croatian guards use the bishop's house as their post). From the Serbian side this visit was presented as a sign of normalisation and reconciliation, in line with the negotiating process. For the Croatian side it was a provocation, an intrusion on their territory not with military but with ritual means. The whole affair ended without a clash, but it showed how easily tensions can pop up from completely unexpected sides. Another major incident took place at 30km distance from Pakrac on the 13th of May. Masked men killed five refugees from Bosnia and wounded another three. Although nobody is sure, of course most believe they were Serb terrorists. And of course this only hardens positions at the negotiating table.

So there is a light side and a dark side to the Pakrac picture. For the project the most important consequence of al this is at the end of April the Croatian authorities forbade any traffic across the cease-fire line. This meant that the work-camp on the Serbian side of Pakrac came to a halt. This was serious since the camp was just getting on the way. The seed program luckily didn't suffer from it, but the English lessons, the confidence building between volunteers and locals, as well as the development of plans for the kindergarten and the community centre to be built are impossible without good communication...

Children's Peace Wall, Pakrac 1994

Local and International Volunteers on Reconstruction Site, Pakrac 1994

enemy lines and kept secure territorial gains many felt were illegitimate, (a situation to be 'remedied' eventually by Operations Storm and Lightning or Flash). ARK worked to co-ordinate international volunteers who rebuilt houses, cleaned up rubble, and mended roofs. CARE (Austria) assisted on the Serb side with the regeneration of agriculture, and in rebuilding a community centre. Dutch Caritas contributed 200,000 DM worth of seeds for planting. Service Civil International assisted with recruitment of volunteers. Funds for working projects such as the laundrette were contributed by support groups such as Swissaid, Hulp an Pakrac (Netherlands), Gemeinde Gemeinsam, QPS and more.

There were attempts in E. Slavonia to regenerate the local economy; Swiss and Dutch initiatives, for example, which attempted partnerships in sunflower seed growing or chicken farms for export to north European markets. Success rates were low, as the area was not only undergoing transition from war to peace, but also from state agricultural and industrial enterprise to a new post-communist, post-Dayton market economy. A micro-loan credit bank was established in Osijek by Opportunity Trust, having 'in the order of $3.5 millions to loan at rates well below those exorbitant rates being charged by local banks, though no loans will be larger than $20,000 and the aim is to get the average below $5,000 on a one or two years repayment period. This is seen by UNTAES as essential work in its attempt to get the Serbian population to stay in the zone. There is about 70% unemployment here and officials are desperate to get small businesses pump primed and people back to work[36].'

In their twinning project with the ruined village of Laslovo the citizens of Wageningen, Netherlands, fund-raised for the rebuilding of the village primary school, reconstruction which by 1997 had not been realized due to saturation of the area by mines, and a high casualty rate as a result[37].

5.10 Therapeutic work

Not all therapeutic interventions are 'psycho-social', but the latter category represents an active area in ex-Yugoslavia deserving detailed study in

Dear Friends,

We are happy to invite you to apply for a three days workshop/training program in early March. the subject—IMPACT OF WORKING WITH WAR VICTIMS ON SERVICE PROVIDERS, including burnout and secondary trauma, The Program is sponsored by the Center for Psychology and Social Change (CPSC), an affiliate of Harvard Medical School.

The project was developed after a psycho-social needs assessment in Zagreb during the summer of 1993 by Nancy Roof, Ph.D., CPSC. and interviews with service providers from Croatia and Bosnia (professional and paraprofessionals) visiting in the United States. The Assessment indicated that there was a need for trainings in the impact of war on service providers, including burn out and secondary trauma. Persons working with trauma victims are susceptible to the symptoms of trauma themselves, often without realizing it. Burnout is also associated with working under war conditions. Funding from the International Rescue Committee has made it possible to develop a workshop to address these issues.

We have spent two months searching for the most qualified and caring team of experts from the Harvard University Community to develop a professional training program. The team members are affiliated with trauma, community crisis, and refugee program at Harvard Medical School, Harvard School of Public Health, and Harvard Divinity School. They will work in partnership with Anti-War Campaign, Vesna Terselic, National Coordinator as well as with participants, to develop a workshop that address the most significant problems encountered by service providers and one that creates a safe and supportive environment for sharing of knowledge, experience, and solutions as well as creating a sense of community and inspiration.

(extract from a letter to Croatian professionals,1993
re: Balkan Secondary Trauma Project, N.Y.C.)

itself. The introduction of the medical diagnosis of 'post traumatic stress disorder' (PTSD)[38] has radically influenced care provision and both psychology and social service thinking in the region. As a concept PTSD is not without controversy[39]. It has become so accepted that newly demilitarised Croatian soldiers cannot obtain a war pension without a diagnosis of PTSD, 'posing a dilemma for Croatian psychiatrists, because they know there are no job prospects for these men' (Summerfield, 1996).

While the majority of psycho-social interventions were instigated in UN agency (Belgrade) and EC (Zagreb) levels, there were also 'second track' initiatives. The Balkan Peace Project (above, Chapter III) used 'family therapy' approaches in their workshops in Croatia and Vojvodina (Gutlove et al, 1992). The Centre for Psychology and Social Change, an affiliate of the Harvard Medical School, offered workshops in 1994 on 'the impact of Working with War Victims on Service Providers, including burnout and secondary trauma.' Attending their courses in Zagreb meant a nominal possibility of follow-up courses in the USA, which some participants went on to do. MEDACT assisted with 'trauma intervention' programmes in Belgrade, and also devised 'caring for carers' inputs for staff at refugee centres in Serbia[40]. Norwegian People's Aid and the Association of Country Women (UK) supported 'psycho-social assistance' to refugee and displaced women relocated to Zagreb (Pecnic, 1995).

Like the term 'training', 'psycho-social' as a phrase has become all-embracing. With physical (building) reconstruction and the return of refugees so difficult, activity focus shifted to personal integration and livelihood, i.e. ways of coping in the new environment. The Osijek 'Assistance to the Psycho-social Adaptation of Refugee Women' project in 1993 focused on providing 'sewing, tailors and machine knitting courses.' (Much needed intervenors were people who could find overseas markets for the resultant products.) At the 'Days of Peace Culture' event organised by the Osijek centre that summer, these women, their families and friends were encouraged to bake traditional delicacies and exhibit crafts and goods in the central square. This affirmed not only their traditions, but also their skills, potentials, and lives. Pecnic explained comparable work with women from Bosnia and Vukovar in a Zagreb collective centre:

> 'We had begun our work in refugee camps with open groups for socialisation and making needlework (crochet, embroidery, lace, knitting) with the initial aim to encourage women to get to know each other., support each other, build community within the camp, as well as to enable programme users and professional programme workers to get to know each other and develop trust...
>
> This initial stage also allows for meeting strong cumulated aggression, bitterness and (self)destructiveness of displaced and refugee women who have, by that time, spent almost 2 years in the camps. Their pain was affirmed and their obsession with the past losses was used to construct new meanings in their coping with the current situation (talking about their way of life, sharing traditional skills, keeping customs and presenting them to others, etc.)...
>
> Group workers are perceived as representatives of the 'outside world' who do not share the experience of displacement and life in a refugee camp, but do share some of the other 'war experiences' (e.g. life under air-raids and black-outs, sons or husbands fighting in the army). They facilitate restoration of value system which was shattered by multiple losses that women experienced. For example, their salient value of devoting life to work and acquiring material goods, after having lost all possessions in war, is followed now by attributing more significance to some other values, like strengthening and deepening interpersonal/family relationships, preserving traditional skills, customs, songs. Upbringing of children and traditional power relations in the family also change and the group workers are the catalysts of that process' (Pecnic and Miskulin, 1995).

These local Croatian strategies were paralleled in Vojvodina, particularly by Panonija under the leadership of Danica Stefanovic, supported by Swiss and German peace and church groups. The groups here were Serbian women who had fled Croatia and Bosnia. Their new environment was constrained by sanctions, so dressmaking was undertaken with recycled cloth, and craft work devised out of local hemp and hessian. Young aspiring fashion designers joined refugee women in producing a fashion show for internationals attending the 'Zena, Mir, I Humanost' conference in June 1994[41].

Therapeutic intervention was not limited to the needs of women. Branka Drabek, Director of the state Rehabilitation Centre in Osijek, drew on Lebensgarten and the work of Danaan Perry experiences to devise a programme of 'psycho-social support for Military and Civil War Victims'[42]. This targeted veterans, disabled soldiers, former prisoners, members of the displaced community and their families. It included counselling, stress reduction workshops, self-help groups, re-training, massage and 'super learning.'

'Super learning' is a relaxation technique intended to enable better cognitive functioning. It was brought into the region, along with yoga, circle dancing, co-operative games, trust-building exercises, and personal development plans designed to make people feel better[43].

5.11 Witness

Witness by its very nature needs to be treated with understatement and tact. This refers to observation and documentation of events and deeds related to human rights abuse, atrocity or conduct of war. As Schuch (1995) points out, such reports 'are sometimes funnelled through emergency response networks, which are composed of thousands of people ready to send faxes, telexes, letters or make phone calls to protest against the violation and press for change.' Other times reports go to Amnesty or UN commissions for use in dealing with an offending state government or regime.

'Through Heart to Peace' was an initiative started by women from near Zagreb which organised international women's convoys to Bosnia and E. Slavonia and publicised their observations, while trying to bear 'witness' of their concern to host communities.

In fact 'witness' is probably three-pronged: there is witness *to* a community of wrongdoing, in the name of a higher, better ideal and so to remember those who suffer; there is witness *of* events in the interest of truth and accountability, and there is witness for others who are specific to a context and trying to both survive in it, and change this context.

1. *Witness to a community* would include Women in Black with their weekly Belgrade vigils, or the brick wall built in Zagreb to symbolise the

Compulsory mobilization in Yugoslavia

A CONSCRIPT HUNT

During the last week the Federal Republic of Yugoslavia (FRY) started a compulsory mobilization of the conscripts who ran away from the territories in Bosnia and Croatia under Serb control. A mass and well synchronized action was conducted jointly by the authorities and the Serbian and Montenegrin police, together with the police of the Bosnian and the Krajina Serbs.

The only official data on the number of moblilized people so far can be found in the UNHCR announcement issued in Geneva last Friday, June 23, in which a mobilization of 2,500 conscripts was claimed. There is no other official information on compulsory mobilization, but only indirect, obtained through hundreds of appeals received by various humanitarian and antiwar organizations in Belgrade. From them it is evident that the police summons the conscripts to interviews, but afterwards sends them to the military barracks.

According to sources close to the Bosnian and Krajina Serbs contacted by Beta, during the last seven days around 18,000 men were sent to Bosnia and Krajina. Sources close to the Yugoslav police claim that at least 20,000 men were transported by bus across the Drina River.

It is very difficult to establish the credibility of these claims according to which between 18,000 and 20,000 people were mobilized in a ten-day action. It is possible that the authorities attempted to use 'unofficial sources' to convince the public of the great success of this operation. Still, according to information coming from various parts of Yugoslavia, it is almost certain that at least 10,000 people were sent across the Drina.

Witness: Od: Rade Jovkovic Do: BETA Novinska Agencija
Jun. 29 1995 06:41PM

Human Rights

In the days following 'Operation Flash' the situation in the former Sector West was both unstable and dangerous. Some Serb citizens reported harassment by local Croats and by members of the armed forces. In the villages around Okucani, 76 houses were blown up between May 1 and 3. Looting of abandoned houses continued for several weeks, with little done to stop the persons exiting villages with stolen property. Once the Croatian army was withdrawn from former Sector West and civilian police control established, the threatening atmosphere for many remaining Serbs began to ease. However, with continuing nationalist sentiment, the recent 'Operation Storm', the influx of a refugee Bosnian Croat population, and the recent exhumation of a mass grave in Donji Caglic, tensions are on the rise, and with them, the number of reported cases of abuse.

Civilian Deaths

Current reports of large numbers of fresh graves in former Sector North and South recall a similar situation in Western Slavonia after 'Operation Flash.' During the action UN troops reported seeing as many as 30 civilian bodies lying along the road south to Bosnian Serb-held territory near Novi Varos. soon after, this area was completely clean and disinfected, although evidence of machine gun fire above scraps of clothing can still be seen on the wall under the bridge south of Novi Varos. Other eyewitnesses reported seeing soldiers enter villages and firing indiscriminately at fleeing civilians.

The Croatian government, in a statement on May 22, claimed that 188 Serbs had been killed during the action. Of these, it claimed, a possible total of 54 of those killed were civilians,

Whatever the truth, the fact is that large grave sites do exist, and many of the graves are unmarked. As an example, international observers found a large area of recently disturbed earth in the cemetery south of Okucani in the second week of May. Later, this site was altered to appear more as individual burial sites with the addition of 47 new wooden crosses. Only 15 of these had names on them. Today this site is overgrown with tall weeds, and many of the weather-worn crosses are leaning or falling over, To date, the Croatian government has still not provided international monitors with details as to the nature of the deaths of the people buried in this and other such cemeteries.

Witness. Extract from 'The Reintegration of Serb-held Areas of United Nations Protected Area West, six months after. A Comprehensive Report.' by Otvorene Oci, November 1995.

dead and missing of Vukovar. Internationals who joined 'Through Heart to Peace' caravans did so as witness to the futility of war and in solidarity with war's victims. Peaceful anti-war processions in Pancevo and the candle-lit vigil in Osijek following the murder of Police Chief Kir did the same.

2. *Witness of events* is more difficult for a local population if it renders them vulnerable to intimidation. The Balkan Peace Team with its emphasis on language skills and human rights training documented their findings on Operation Storm, the sudden take-over of Republika Srpska Krajina[45]. They published comprehensive reports on the reintegration of UNPA West into Croatia (see extract on 'Human Rights'). International volunteers in Pakrac assisted in establishing namelists of missing persons and taking testimonies for IRC[46]. ARK sponsored a public letter of protest to the Croatian government signed by activists and NGOs.

   Helsinki Watch Serbia spoke out publicly against the compulsory mobilisation in FRY of Bosnian and Krajina Serbs in June of 1995. CAA called for the protection of rights of these men (as did opposition parties) who had sought refuge in Serbia only to be sent back to the firing line to swell the ranks of Bosnian Serb forces. Beta News Agency provided rapid transmission of the reported actions and concerns.

3. *Witness for others* was taken by Amnesty International who published on human rights violations and wrote directly to the Croatian government in September 1995, as well as lobbying other governments to delay Croatia's

Adapting to crisis: the birth of Group 484

After the Croatian army's offensive in August 1995, and the mass exodus of the Serbs from Krajina, PAKRAC Project activists became involved in the emergency operation of helping men, women and children arriving in Serbia. They went to the border, to collective and individual private centers. In conjunction with humanitarian organizations, assistance was offered in the form of food, hygienic material for babies and adults, clothing and footwear. Information exchange continued with the Direct Protection of Human Rights initiative in Croatia regarding separated families, arrested and missing persons. In conjunction with several international and domestic non-governmental organizations, a project was developed to support a group of 484 refugee families who were to be provided long-term assistance. This gave rise to the 484 group and program.

Based in Belgrade the program was conceived in such a way as to enable maximum involvement of the refugees themselves. This also achieves the basic aims of the program: solving the problem of exile through integration in the local environment, voluntary repatriation or relocation to a third country. There were four basic activity designs:

1. *Social-psychological support to families and children to facilitate their adaptation to the new environment, including social, urban, educational and cultural life.*

2. *Legal aid and protection includes a service that provided: (1) all relevant information on refugee rights, (2) the conditions for voluntary repatriation, (3) the conditions to obtain citizenship in FR Yugoslavia, (4) property and other legal matters, and (5) information and assistance regarding relocation to a third country.*

3. *Information about and making contact with war-separated families in Serbia and Croatia.*

4. *Social-economic support including: (a) short-term, urgent humanitarian aid to the families most in need, and (b) long-term activities to qualify refugees to work on their own and earn their own living, including sponsorship for the most needy pupils and students.*

Members of the Co-ordinating Group participated at meetings in Mohac, PEACE BRIDGE DANUBE, where communication was maintained with Croatian peace centers. The Group Co-ordinator also attended the General Assembly of the Helsinki Citizens' Committee, in Tuzla.

Voice 9 Report

admission to the Council of Europe. When Croatia was admitted, November 1996, Amnesty continued to publicise concerns, which included the bombing of the home of Ivan Z. Cicak, President of the Croatian Helsinki Committee for Human Rights, attacks on the Urhovine advice centre (part of the Oxfam supported network mentioned above), and continuing intimidation of journalists and independent voices.

Amnesty also documented prisoners of conscience and political prisoners in Serbia, ill-treatment and torture in Kosovo, and the use of force by JNA and VRS forces for the displacement of populations[47].

The US organisation Physicians for Human Rights assisted with exhumation of mass graves near Vukovar[48].

Finally activists in Osijek and Pancevo have felt 'upheld' by international connections in the eyes of their often disapproving local authorities.

These are but a few general observations on the subject of witness.

Notes for Chapter V

1. For an excellent and early discussion of the symmetry—asymmetry dimension of conflict dynamics see Herman Schmid, 'Peace Research and Politics,' *Journal of Peace Research* 1968, pp. 217-232.

2. Systems theory, particularly the work of Fritjof Capra, was popular with leading antiwar activists. See Capra's *The Web of Life*, published by Harper Collins, 1996.

3. 'Individual human rights, a nation's financial welfare and other internal conditions were formally linked with external spheres of international jurisdiction, particularly peace and security, when the first summit meeting of the Security Council took account of the non-military sources of conflict. Boutros-Ghali presented proposals for strengthening the security capacity of the UN in June 1992 in his *Agenda for Peace*, which included the term "peace-building".' Quoted from Jarat Chopra's article, 'Peace-Maintenance: the last stage of Development' in Global Society Vol. 11, No., 1997.

4. Agger offers a 'pyramidal model' in which five levels are differentiated:

   '*1. Emotional and social interventions*
   Examples: Concrete services such as practical help with child care, tracing of disappeared family members, translation by interpreter.

   2. Task-oriented group interventions
   Examples: Educational activities, knitting groups for women, income-generating activities.

   3. Psychologically oriented group interventions
   Examples: Self-help groups, trauma-survivor groups, testimony groups.

   4. Counselling Interventions
   Examples: Individual, family or group counselling (with focus on the present and the problems which the clients are already aware of).

   5. Intensive Psychotherapy Interventions
   Examples: Individual, family or group therapy (with focus on the present in perspective of the past and of unconscious psychological dynamics).

   The strategies to enhance protective factors and diminish stressor factors can be combined with each level of psycho-social intervention'(Agger, 1993).

5. Some of these individuals were extremely welcome and spoken of with great affection by local people. In other instances groups felt 'lectured to' in inappropriate ways. Mirko Mandrino of Pancevo reckoned he had spent up to 59 'person hours' in Feb. and March of one year entertaining visiting professors who came with their own agendas.

6. Note: BSV and WRI are also supporting members of the CCCRTE, so these are overlaps which render distinctions tentative.

7. 'The creation of *local democracy embassies* is one of the measures proposed by the Standing Conference of Local and Regional Authorities of Europe in its Resolution 251 (1993) for encouraging the maintenance and/or development of the democratic process at local level, taking due account of material and institutional differences between one part of the territory of the former Federation of Yugoslavia and another' (Discussion Paper, Secretariat of the Council of Europe, Strasbourg, 28 June 1993).

8. See Danaan Parry's book *Warriors of the Heart*, UK edition by Findhorn Press, 1994. Parry founded citizen diplomacy programmes as an 'international network of people who are committed to positive change.'

9. *A Conversation with Marshall Rosenberg* by Guy Spiro (1992) is available from The Aspectarian, P.O. Box 1342 Morton Grove, Illinois 60053 USA. The Centre for Non-violent Communication founded by Marshall Rosenberg is on E-mail at 104360.1521@compuserv.com

10. 'Report trip to Vukovar/Loznica October 1994' The Oak Tree Trust, Walsall, 1 Nov. 1994.

11. 'Feed Back: Security Check List' Feed the Children Winter 1993, Reading Berkshire.

12. 'Women's Aid to Former Yugoslavia' Report Dec. 1992, WATFY, Southampton.

13. Interview with Gudrun Tappe-Freitag by Ute Caspers, Bückeburg 23 Feb. 1996.

14. In the Netherlands Tilburg ZaMir had contacts and co-operation with such groups as Pax Christi, Press Now, Amnesty International, Stop the Arms Race and Fatima Maria, and with many small local initiatives. Tilburg ZaMir, Press Now and Pax Christi combined efforts to publish the quarterly *Now Future*, a magazine reporting on civil society and its independent media and NGOs in the former Yugoslavia. Tilburg ZaMir P.O. Box 3164, 5003 DD Tilburg. Tel: 31 13 4561801, Fax: 31 13 5362147 E-mail: mermans@kub.nl

15. Glavas sent a personal message via an MP, to Hedl, threatening that he would be crushed and turned into smoke and ashes. 'The basis for this action was Hedl's writing in papers such as *Herald Tribune* and *Bumerang*. He was further accused of being a foreign agent—of going to Belgrade and co-operating with foreign journalists. In early 1994 they were making a TV film about the death of Paul Jenks, the British journalist who was killed on the front-line at Osijek when investigating the death of Christian Wurtemberg, who joined the Croatian Army in an attempt to write an undercover story. Glavas seemed to have been particularly infuriated with this film.' See 'Under Threat,' *War Report* September 1994, Issue No. 28.

16. Amnesty International published numerous reports documenting mass human rights violations in the region, and made recommendations to both government authorities in the region as well as to the international community for the investigation of such crimes and the prosecution of those responsible. In addition to its research and documentation on forcible expulsions, extra-judicial executions, 'disappeared' and missing persons, torture and ill-treatment, rape, and refugee concerns, the organisation also published widely on the subject of human rights protection in peacekeeping operations, the International Criminal Tribunal for the former Yugoslavia (ICTY) in The Hague, and the implementation of the civilian dimension of the Dayton Peace Agreement.

17. See the International edition of *ARKZIN*, No. 3 June 1993, Zagreb, 'Army Flats Third Part' by Zoran Ostric, p.6. Schweiz Ohne Armee sponsored an in depth study of Human Rights organisations in Croatia by Ostric in 1994 apo/Yugo/antiwar.

    Volunteers from the Osijek peace centre, sometimes accompanied by 'internationals', distinguished themselves by non-violent direct action, 'sit-ins,' to prevent the eviction of fellow citizens in Osijek at the risk of severe threats from Glavas. A formal 'Protection of Human Rights' project was developed after these successful personal demonstrations, with an office for counselling, legal assistance and mediation staffed by three lawyers and averaging (1996) 30 cases per month.

18. Balkan Peace Team Newsletter 1.3.94 No. 1 and subsequent issues. See also Lisa Shirch (1995) for selected references to BPT, particularly p. 64, and pp. 107-108.

19. Simendic, Nevena, 'Ime Kao greh' in Contra Bellum September, 1993 issue 1, p.7. 'A so called "Spiritual Republic-ZITZER" was declared in Tresnjevac, a village not far from Senta, on 26th June, 1992. The main reason for the formation of this informal, free association of citizens was delivering of 220 orders to report to military service. The first to react were local women, and then all the residents of the village reacted angrily during the meeting which gathered 700 people. They were protesting more than 62 days in the local club "Zitzer" and in that way established their "Spiritual Republic ZITZER".' (Kostic, 1994, p.12.)

20. STAR stands for 'Strategies, Training and Advocacy for Reconciliation', sponsored by Delphi International, Washington DC. This agency works with independent multi-ethnic women's organisations. They donated 40 greenhouses for Eastern Slavonia and funded the laundry in Pakrac. Soros both pioneered electronic communications beginning in Belgrade, and funded independent media initiatives.

21. The Erasmus Guild began its bimonthly Erasmus Journal for the Culture of Democracy in April 1993 and published books as well, including *The Rulers and Managers* by Vesna Pusic, *Liberalism and Democracy* by Norberto Bobbio, and Eric Hobsbawm's *Nations and Nationalism*. It also received support from the Westminster Foundation for Democracy, London and Press Now Amsterdam and others.

22. March 1994 project funding records document 'disbursement to date' funds for Croatia at $209,611 and for Serbia $12,942. Obligated project funding to Serbia was in fact far higher than to Croatia but must have proved harder to channel through (International Media Fund Final Report. April 1994).

23. Quoted by Mark Thompson in the Article 19 publication *Forging War; Media in Serbia, Croatia and Bosnia-Herzegovina*. See War Report June/July 1994 p. 7 of the special media insert.

24. The Verona Forum, in its statement of 7 November 1992 also called for the provision of satellite telephones to citizens of Bosnia-Herzegovina and the placing of telecommunications at the top of the Geneva Agenda. They advocated the unblocking of air waves, the supply of paper for newspapers, tapes for television, transmitters for radio, and the re-establishment of some types of postal service (Verona Forum, c/o European Parliament, BEL 3007 97-113, rue Belliard-Str. B1040 Brussels).

25. Personal notes.

26. Adam Curle offered sessions in Tibetan meditation at the Osijek Centre's Week of Peace Culture in summer 1993. The Schule fur Verstandigung und Mediation im Lebensgarten, Stegerberg, Germany made meditation a central tenant in its approach to mediation. In fact Curle has a poem on this very theme. See 'Mediation/Meditation' in A. Curle, *Recognition of Reality* (1987), Hawthorn Press, p. 29.

27. Rosenberg's 'giraffe and wolf' talk had to be adapted for use in Serbia. The wolf in Communication puppet play was originally typecast as a negative figure. In fact the wolf is an important positive symbol in Serbian folk mythology. It was duly replaced by the snake.

28. *Budimo Prijatelji* (Let's be Friends) by Maja Uzelac, Ladislav Boznar, and Aida Bazic, Zagreb 1994.

29. *ARK Activities Report Summary* 1997.

30. 'Sensitivity to Others' by Ljilana Cvekic, unpublished text on the UNICEF experiment, Novi Sad 1994.

31. 'We began the day on our own realities as trainers with a consideration of the role of workshop facilitator...to help or enable participants to discover new ways of doing things rather than to have theories or answers for everything.' Diana Francis, 'Beyond Training: Report of a Workshop Held in Croatia Feb. 24-28 1997' in CCCRTE *Newsletter* No. 5, p. 13 Spring 1997.

32. Perhaps inevitably they sometimes found it hard to

be 'in the middle' and not take sides. For the difficulties of being civilian intervenors see Lisa Schirch *Keeping the Peace*, 1995, Life and Peace Institute Uppsala (as above, Note 18).

33. 'Für Verständigung und Mediation' Streit-light Schule, Stegerberg, 1993/94. Introductory paper 'Hintergrund und Ziele Unserer Aus-und Weiterbildung in Mediation-Vermittlung im Konflikt.'

34. Most means 'bridge.' Most is a working project for social assistance and recovery under CAA Belgrade auspices.

35. See Jarat Chopra, 'Peace Maintenance: The Last Stage of Development' in *Global Society*, Vol. 11, No. 2, 1997.

36. Situation Report from Nic Street 20 Feb. 1997. Nic also wrote: 'I learn from the Bank that the first loan offered in the zone was to a woman who wanted to buy some cows so she could breed calves and sell them on—she did this before the war in a successful way. All was agreed but just before the day to sign the agreement the woman backed out, saying she dare not proceed as her neighbours had told her that if she did they would kill all the cattle she bought in. Intimidation and fear runs deep in this society.'

37. Personal correspondence with Bert van der Linde and Nic Street, July 1997.

38. Summerfield (1996) offers the following definition:

    'PTSD (Post Traumatic Stress Disorder)

    The successor to earlier formulations known as 'shell shock', 'concentration camp syndrome' and 'war neurosis', PTSD was officially classified around 1980 and applied to many US Vietnam war veterans. Criteria for a diagnosis of PTSD can be divided into three groups: liability to re-experience aspects of the original events (in sleep or during the day), avoidance of reminders of events (or diminished interest in things generally), and increased nervous system arousal (manifesting as sleep problems, irritability, poor concentration, excessive watchfulness, jumpiness etc.).'

39. See Summerfield (1996) and P. Bracken, Joan Griller, and D. Summerfield, (1995) 'Psychological Responses to War and Atrocity: the Limitations of Current Concepts' in *Soc. Sci. Med.* Vol. 40, No. 8, pp. 1073-1082, Elsevier Science Ltd.

40. See 'Former Yugoslavia: Helping War-traumatised Children' in *Global Security* No. 10, Spring 1995.

41. 'The Wonder of Weaving' by Zelko Kos is a paper describing traditional hemp, flax and wool textiles and their revival in Yugoslavia (a creative adaptation to sanctions' shortages), Gallery 'Hilandarske dveri', Novi Sad.

42. 'Programs of Psycho-social support for Military and Civil War Victims', paper by Branka Drabek Milekic.

43. The Life Foundation School of Therapeutics (UK) advertised its 'powerful self-help techniques'—'BHM (body, heart and mind technology) Really Works.' Books, tapes and videos.

44. Contact Hazlewood House, Loddiswell, Devon.

45. Note in particular the *BPT Newsletter* No. 8, 'The Storm and the Ship of Fools' by Dave Bekkering, Sept. 1995.

46. 6 May Report from Wam Kat, Gavrinica account, information from representative of CARE Austria, Austria C.O. project, UNOV and Pakrac project, APC/YUGO/ANTIWAR

47. See *Refuge: Europe, Who's living in my house?* A Report on obstacles to the safe return of refugees and internally displaced people, Amnesty International, London, March 1997.

48. See Amnesty, *Concerns in Europe July-Dec. 1996*, and Reuters report 'Croatian Grave Yields 200 Bodies' in the *International Herald Tribune* 8 Oct. 1996, p. 4.

Sample training intervention

Summary of the Non-Violent Conflict Resolution Seminar

June 9-12, 1994
Belgrade

This past weekend a four day long non-violent conflict resolution seminar, organized by the Group MOST for cooperation and mediation, was held at the Center for Antiwar Action. The leaders of the Seminar were Diana Francis and Clem McCartney from England and Ireland respectively. There were, in total, 21 participants in the seminar, ranging from psychologists,teachers, conflict resolution trainers, peace workers from different groups as well as interested individuals from various towns in Serbia and Vojvodina (Leskovac, Nis, Cacak, Vranje, Negotin, Sombor and Beograd)

The conversations touched upon many topics:

--sharing our experiences from our present work,
--sharing the challenges and obstacles we face in that work,
--how we can motivate people to work with us,
--judging people's needs and how to meet them,
--learning what methods to use to reach out to those in need,
--learning how to teach people the benefits of cooperation,
--exchanging our experiences on self-motivation and self-organization,
--support,
--the needs of a group; intergroup relations,
--communication,
--defining objectives and target groups,
--creating new groups,
--expanding the MOST network of mediation and conflict resolution
to different towns in Serbia and Vojvodina,
--the benefits and foreseeable difficulties of such a network,
--and learning various methods and games to be used in futureseminars.

At the end of the seminar all the partcipants had very positive comments about the usefulness of the seminar, each mentioning different aspects that they found especially fulfilling.

Michael Szporluk, BVS Volunteer
at the Anti-War Centre.

Chapter VI

Conflict resolution: contested concepts 1

Defining terms

Conflict management

A term used to describe any situation where a CONFLICT continues but where its worst excesses are avoided or mitigated. Conflict management would, in particular, seek to avoid or terminate violence between parties. Conflict management is normally achieved by strategies of mutual, general DETERRENCE. Traditionally conceived, the BALANCE OF POWER was a system of conflict management based upon these ideas. A situation of neither WAR nor PEACE under a REGIME of mutual and general deterrence can continue for relatively long periods of time. Normally relations between the putative adversaries will show signs of improving or deteriorating as the case may be. If deterioration spills over into violence then management can be restored through palliatives such as cease-fire and TRUCE agreements. PEACEMAKING should properly be regarded as the function of CONFLICT SETTLEMENT and CONFLICT RESOLUTION rather than management.

Conflict resolution

A somewhat esoteric form of CONFLICT termination. In order to achieve resolution the parties come to redefine their relationships in such a way as to perceive either that they can realize their goals without conflict or that they can redefine their relationship so that their goals no longer conflict. Unlike CONFLICT SETTLEMENT techniques, resolution tends to rely heavily upon academic, rather than diplomatic, modes of termination. Resolution techniques borrow heavily from sociology and social psychology and, in particular, from small group experimental studies. Resolution approaches to conflict have been strongly championed by 'controlled communication' advocates such as J.W. Burton. Experimental studies have particularly concentrated upon COMMUNAL CONFLICT situations where strong barriers often exist towards face-to-face communications and where it is held these techniques can be particularly effective. Although highly imaginative and provocative, conflict resolution is probably destined to remain an ideal type in the lexicon of conflict termination against which actual DIPLOMACY can be measured.

Conflict settlement

A portmanteau term for the ending or termination of CONFLICT. A conflict may be settled by one side prevailing over the other. Winning as a form of conflict settlement implies conquest, defeat and submission. Historically this has been the most significant form of settlement. There is evidence, both impressionistic and quantitative, that this is currently changing and that settlements short of outright victory are becoming more prevalent. Settlement of this latter type implies a willingness by parties to COMPROMISE. In a small number of instances ADJUDICATION and ARBITRATION may be used as techniques for settling differences.

From Evans and Newnham (1990) *The Dictionary of World Politics*

VI. Conflict resolution: contested concepts 1

6.1 Introduction

This study has thus far attempted to delineate levels of possible intervention in complex situations of war, in particular first track governmental and diplomatic approaches and second track non-official ones It has sketched out a range of responses from local populations in Croatia and Serbia, and looked at specific contexts in E. Slavonia and Vojvodina. Similarities in experience and features of conflict in these two areas (nominally 'different sides' in war) were identified which included structural disparities and strain, the spread of generalised belief and fear, intimidation through use of symbols and terror tactics, incidents and rumour, and the rise of new local power configurations often based on coercion. The idea of capacity building was introduced as the means by which resources and capability could be strengthened to enhance the responsiveness of local groups. Political violence has here been outlined as a feature of state and community disintegration, as much as a feature of military domain on clear battlefields. The term 'front line' has had many meanings for the population of ex-Yugoslavia since 1991; it can mean a demarcation of warlord controlled territory in your community, or a new entity border now patrolled by peacekeeping forces which runs through what was once an integrated neighbourhood; it could mean the area of most recent forced removal and clash of armies in Bosnia, not so far away. The multiplicity of divisions and cleavages rendered classic 'third party' role conceptions of intervention less useful than a multi-track view of intervenors who have complementarity in building up social structure and supporting local initiatives.[1]

Categories of second track intervention have been introduced for consideration: aid, advocacy, communications, education and training, facilitation, mediation and negotiation, reconstruction, therapeutic work, and witness. In practice many of these listings have overlapped, i.e. WATFY both delivered needed goods and took on an advocacy role for those they met, in particular women and children as victims of war, campaigning for rape to be seen as a war crime, etc. A reconstruction project, whether Pakrac, or a market garden scheme in E. Slavonia or later Gorni Vakuf[2] in Travnik canton Bosnia needs continual mediation and negotiation, communications and facilitation. It may also require aid of sorts, for bricks and mortar, for seeds or tools. Education and training may be closely related to therapeutic work and so forth.

Some, but by no means all intervenors came bearing goods marked 'conflict resolution'. Visiting academics talked about it. Trainers offered problem solving or 'sculpting'[3] (BPP), role plays (CCCRTE), meditation (Lebensgarten) and even organisational development principles under the heading of conflict resolution. This latter suggestion will be examined in more detail under 'dilemmas of training' below. As such, and because many training principles have been lifted from either a Fisher and Ury 'win-win' approach to negotiation or a Burtonian 'human needs' approach to conflict[4] there is a growing literature which critiques and judges conflict resolution on an attitudinal base line. That is, an attempt at social engineering *rather than* the generation of choices. Moreover, the discourse which now claims conflict resolution for debate is that of NGO and donor efficiency. Consider the following quotation from Duffield:

> 'The different undertakings that fall within conflict resolution represent an important growth area for aid agencies (Voutira and Brown, 1995). Aspects of conflict resolution, however, have a long pedigree. For example, in relation to resolving labour and business disputes in the West. What marks the present departure, however, is the extension of this type of approach to the larger and more complex field of political processes within countries. Conflict resolution is nothing if not the promise of social engineering on a grand scale. It is also a good example of the manner in which the theory and practice of development has radically changed over the past couple of decades...
>
> Inequality, economic growth and resource redistribution *per se* are no longer the main issues within the new 'human development' paradigm (UNDP, 1992). It is how people cope with their situation and the means by which they can be supported in mitigating the risks and stresses involved. Development has been increasingly redefined as a series of measures, which, rather than the international system, are intended to change the behaviour and attitudes of institutions, groups and individuals within the countries concerned' (Duffield, 1997).

Whereas social development was once seen as one aspect of conflict resolution, (Curle, 1971, 1990; Kumar, 1997; Chopra, 1997) in public policy and development debates the latter has become internalised in the former.

Conflict resolution, then, has become a contested concept. This is also true of the often accompanying term 'civil society'. Note Paul Stubbs:

'Genuine grassroots social welfare organisations, based on broader social movements, have developed in Croatia. Many of these derive from independent women's initiatives which were founded in the late 1980s or from a network of peace, human rights, and anti-war groups which grew up in 1991 in response to the aggression against Slovenia and Croatia. The attempt to maintain a "peace culture" has been fraught with difficulties in the context of globalisation and, indeed, of a misplaced faith in "civil society" as the panacea. The achievements of the Anti-War Campaign Croatia (or ARK), which derive from its flexibility, sensitivity to local concerns, and refusal to bureaucratise, should not be understated. However, there is an underlying ideology to the approach of ARK which reflects a general anti-political stance and, further, an emphasis on what is in danger of becoming a new orthodoxy, namely "non-violent conflict resolution" ' (Stubbs, 1995b).

This chapter will seek to probe meanings of 'conflict resolution' as they are used in discourse pertaining to international relations and/or to domestic situations. It will look at levels of application in theory and practice, the emphasis on 'problem solving' and questions surrounding methods and efficacy of training.

6.2 Conflict resolution: theory and practice

Conflict resolution theory and practice is neither coherent, nor unified as a body of thought and action. The very term is all-embracing, divergent, and open to continual reinterpretation: 'Everything and Nothing' in the words of a Zagreb activist, some years on from initial idealism. 'An enigma of Variations' observes a music professor in Novi Sad, who attended seminars in Belgrade. We begin then, with some basic definitions, and comment on the confusion of semantics and all-inclusive terminology. The definitions offered by Evans and Newnham in themselves reveal irony for the term. John Burton, cited as a founder/champion of the approach, was in fact very clear about a prevailing lack of clarity:

'Any conceptual development necessarily creates problems of language. The sharp differences that are present and which need to be articulated, are not readily communicated because the same terms are often used in the two distinctive thought systems. For example, the term *conflict resolution* is still used even when conventional enforced settlement is being discussed. *Mediation* is used to mean both third-party interventions designed to impose a settlement, and those that seek to facilitate direct interactions between parties. *Negotiation* is used to cover not only bargaining, but also problem-solving outside any power framework. When a new paradigm emerges a new language is required to describe the new conceptual notions requiring a special jargon. It is more convenient to use existing terms, while giving them special meanings. This is why we make a distinction between "settlement" and "resolution", two terms that have mostly been used interchangeably' (Burton, in Light and Groom, 1985).

Duffield (1997) appears to demonstrate the confusion between 'settlement' and 'resolution' when he states that:

'Rather than conflict resolution being implemented by governments and seen as effective in some circumstances, it has increasingly become a form of commercial product, packaged and sold to donors as fit for general application.'

What is open to question is whether conflict resolution can be 'implemented by governments', as indeed settlement sometimes can. Less contentious is Duffield's concern about training packages; a concern Burton shared and anticipated when writing in 1987 under the heading 'current confusion':

'Definitions of the field of conflict resolution range from deterrent strategies and star wars, through power-bargaining techniques, normative and legal approaches, to psychological attempts to change attitudes of participants in simulation groups to something vaguely termed 'problem solving', which itself can be interpreted to mean any of the above. When the focus is on peace making as distinct from peace keeping, it tends to be on some particular economic, psychological or other aspect of this complex a-disciplinary subject.

Alternatively the focus is on process, as though all that need be known is how to manage a meeting between conflicting parties. There are profitable enterprises that train persons in the art of mediating discussions...

In determining which approach to conflict resolution might be adopted in teaching, in research or in practice, there is a comfortable liberal attitude which is to encourage all flowers to bloom. However, some may be weeds with quite poisonous consequences. Conflict resolution as a subject deals with interventions in relations between states and peoples. There are ethical considerations that require professionalism of a high order, and in particular an adequate theoretical framework on which to base tested processes. Some of the above approaches could well do more harm than good' (Azar and Burton, pp 40-41).

One source of linkage between 'international'[5] conflict (i.e. the conduct of war) and intergroup or interpersonal conflict was Burton's controversial introduction of human needs theory into the international relations discipline. He argued (in Light and Groom, 1985, p51) that the concept of human needs and especially the need for identity, leads to a different explanation of events. 'The notion of power as the controlling element in world society is not discarded, but its location is change. Effective power does not reside in the state itself but in identity groups.' (ibid.). Burton discounts neither power nor structure in his views, stating clearly that with deep-rooted conflicts analysis must include institutional sources... 'With the exception of conflicts that are the result of some misperception or misunderstanding, the remedies must be, therefore, structural, institutional and environmental' (Burton, 1990, p153) He allows for specialist areas as per Fisher (negotiation) and Kelman (problem-solving) as divergent approaches.[6]

'Conflict resolution' has implications different from those of judicial settlement or of one side subduing the other by superior violence. At its most basic, resolution attempts to deal with the issues in dispute at source, rather than looking to 'impartial' authority structures or resorting to a fight. Hence the reticence of one commentator on South Africa even to use the term, given the comprehensive levels of change implied, preferring the semantics of 'accommodation' or 'management'.[7] In resolution, the 'source' of a dispute is taken to lie in attitudes as much as in structures or institutions. This is a tall order, as anyone dealing with interpersonal or domestic violence will realise. It is in the personal sphere that resolution was first attempted—in counselling, affirmative action groups, non-adversarial divorce proceedings, or neighbourhood mediation schemes.

In this view, values must change in order to tackle the diverse structural sources of any given violent dispute. Violence itself cannot bring about change without generating emotions of hostility, even if it can shake up the structures involved. The same applies to the coercive halting of violence. The domestic initiatives mentioned above were taken during and after the 1960s, a decade of social upheaval in much of the North, manifested in many anti-authoritarian demonstrations, and in the rise of the new feminist movement.

Whether Burtonian and political science ideas (Burton, 1990; Azar and Burton, 1986; Deutsch, 1973; Banks, 1984; Kriesberg, 1973; Volkan, 1988) have been watered *down* to the level of groupwork and training, as exported to ex-Yugoslav recipients, or whether 'conflict resolution' ideas have been elevated *up* to international dimensions is not the topic or realm of this study. Our key areas of concern may be identified as levels of application, problem solving as a dominant theme and dilemmas of training.

6.3 Levels of application

Herbert Kelman summarises the wide usage of levels for application:

> 'Practitioners of conflict resolution work at different levels, ranging from the interpersonal to the international. They operate in different domains, such as the court system, public policy, labor-management relations, inter-ethnic relations, or international diplomacy. They derive their ideas from a variety of sources, such as law, psychotherapy, management theories, group dynamics, peace research, decision theory, the study of conflict resolution in traditional societies, and theoretical models based in the entire range of social-science disciplines. Despite the diversity in level, domain, and intellectual origin that characterizes the work in this field, there are certain common threads—shared insights and approaches to practice—that run through all of its manifestations. Thus, it can probably be said that, with different degrees of emphasis, all of them call for a non-adversarial framework for conflict resolution, an analytic approach, a problem-solving orientation, direct participation by the parties in conflict in jointly shaping a solution, and facilitation by a third party trained in the process of conflict resolution.
>
> Agreement of these general principles still leaves considerable room for differences in theoretical assumptions and in philosophy and style of practice. Moreover, the level at which and the domain in which practitioners operate inevitably influence their goals, methods, and overall approach' (in Sandole and van der Merwe, 1993).

Sandole (ibid.) draws on Walz (1959) to suggest these levels as a) individual, b) societal/national, c) trans-societal/international, and d) global. Recall the very specific levels of tension and dispute identified in the E. Slavonian context, Chapter IV:

1. Personal—in crises of loyalty and allegiance, in unemployment or housing situations, and in

families and friendships according to now pronounced 'ethnic' difference. For example, the Croatian wife following (or not) her Serbian husband into exodus in Baranja, or conversely the Croatian family in Osijek hiding their daughter's Serb fiancé from neighbours and authorities.

2. Group—tensions between citizens who had stayed during the war and citizens who had fled and were now returning.
3. Community—the Displaced and an influx of refugees from Bosnia versus professionals attempting to help them and local authorities, as the lack of resources and poor communications complicated tense uncertainty about the future.
4. Political—emergent organisations of the displaced on both sides of the Sava, local elected officials versus Glavas, peace activists versus militant patriots and nationalist leaders.
5. National/international – dictates (or not) from Zagreb and the new Croatian army, international UNPROFOR forces occupying the region.
   (Dayton and UNTAES were forthcoming)

It must be said that when conflict resolution and mediation training were requested for Croatia (at the Bratislava conference) this was with personal, group and community level in mind. No one imagined for a moment that there would be, for example, any attempt to mediate with Arkan. Rather there was urgent concern at the flare-ups possible because of personal anxiety (Levitt, 1968), overcrowded collective centres, expressions of retribution and revenge, etc. Ambitious schemes were mooted in Osijek as early as 1992 to accompany the displaced back to their homes, to mediate with new ('enemy') occupants, and to solve community reintegration problems. As Subotica, Pancevo and Novi Sad experienced their first waves of refugees (and watched local special reserve troops return from first Vukovar and then the Bosnian front), the aim was also community based and preventative in nature. There was no way of knowing then that the questions of return and repatriation would still be largely unsolved five full years later, or that the full theatre of war would spread to the nightmare proportions which it did.

As it happened, the majority of individuals did not have the opportunity directly to deal with 'the other' in their experience of national cleavage and displacement. They had to deal with themselves.

'They had to deal with themselves': application

In the field or in 'real life' the transitions and transactions in levels from personal to social change are evident and discernible if we have the focus to trace them. The realm of 'second track' conflict resolution intervention may thus encompass an initiative for a singing group of women from four camps (for refugees and the displaced) in Zagreb. Initiated by Zagreb women, funded by Norwegian People's Aid and the Association of Country Women, the group drew on women aged 30—75 years coming from acute war-affected backgrounds. Initially singing was an outlet for personal questions of emotion, trauma, or self-confidence, then for identity, i.e. traditional local patriotic pieces such as 'Hymn of Vukovar', 'Song about Ilok', 'We are Babskans'. After eight months the group had collectively transcended these needs and toured with a universal repertoire 'Shalom', Gospel and Black spirituals, Verdi's 'Refugee Choir' from 'Nabucco', Beethoven's 'Ode to Joy'. Writing on these developments, Nina Pecnik and Mira Miskulin made the following observation:

> 'Besides strong group cohesion, group leaders noticed increasing confidence and readiness to respond to needs of other people and communities. Their self-esteem and identity are affirmed through appearances in public ... Public appearances also prepare them and make them feel co-responsible to contribute in creating positive psycho-social climate in current and future environment in which they plan to return. It is our impression that by participating in the singing group and its appearances in public displaced women "raised their voice" individually and collectively, and that the singing group has acquired some characteristic of a group for social action, or a peace group' (Pesnic and Miskulin, 1995).

These were not incidental changes—they were consciously worked for in a framework which allowed for the expression of loss, fear, pain and next steps. Choice of repertoire as well as the choir name 'Messengers (female) of Peace' were made by the participants themselves. If there was a 'conflict resolution' framework held by the facilitators of this project it was on a personal level, but with a belief that personal > affects social > affects wider 'national' dimensions. The time line of intervention, then, is not a closed determinant, but an extremely open variable. If and when these women are able to 'return' to their home localities it remains to be seen how they transfer values to the next stage of community life and identity.

This was a local initiative, and a long-term one. Seemingly simple (but profound), it required a minimum of outside resources. Using artistic engagement to meet social needs, this initiative prepared part of the affected population to face their future.

Other examples of the internal application of conflict resolution would include:

1. issues of co-ordination within anti-war movements themselves, as networks grew and diversified, with changing fortunes according to resources and political climate,
2. clashes with local authorities over questions of eviction and minority rights,
3. differences with central government; in Zagreb with Tudjmans NGO legislation, discriminatory citizenship legislation, operations 'Storm' and 'Flash', and policy in Bosnia; in Belgrade over forcible conscription of refugees, clampdowns on media and Open Society fund, economic policy and support to Bosnian Serbs.

If anything, the groups targeted by outside intervenors and facilitators for work on 'conflict resolution' needed to know how to creatively wage their own campaigns and push conflict further towards desired change. While BSV, BPP and CCCRTE all used facilitation as a mode of delivery, their style and content in training was in the *empowerment* tradition of conflict resolution.

The nature of empowerment

Empowerment may be defined as the activity of conferring power (or the ability to influence) on the weaker party in a conflict which is asymmetric. In their pivotal essay 'Injustice, Empowerment and Facilitation in Conflict' Groom and Webb (1987) observe that as an idea, empowerment is persuasive and seductive and plays a role in many community mediation services both in the United States and Britain. It is not unusual for organisations specialising in conflict resolution to train their initiates in the techniques of empowerment: 'While the idea is much older, and is indeed embedded in a tradition within peace research, empowerment as a technique came to the fore during the era of the United States Civil Rights campaigns, particularly with respect to educating minorities about their civil and democratic rights, aiding their organization, and providing legal resources for the oppressed and unrepresented. The apparent success of this movement lent credibility to the technique, and hence gave encouragement to those wanting to use it under wholly different circumstances.' (Groom and Webb, ibid.)

The central tenet to such an approach is far from the alleged 'harmony' of Duffield (ibid.), Small, 1996, Voutira and Brown, 1995. It is far more likely, on the basis of accumulated evidence and data from groups and workshops in Croatia and Serbia between 1991 and 1995, to be *active problem solving*.[8] Individuals interviewed were representative of twenty-five events (or series of workshops) sponsored by eighteen foundations or organisations during this time period. Eighty percent of interviewees stated that communication skills and problem-solving were the resultant focal points of their 'training'. Twenty percent, interestingly, claimed 'self-knowledge' as an outcome.

6.4 Active problem solving

Kelman, above, refers to 'a non-adversarial framework for conflict resolution, an analytic approach, a *problem-solving orientation*, direct participation by the parties in conflict in jointly shaping a solution, and facilitation by a third party trained in the process of conflict resolution'. (in Sandole and van der Merwe, 1993) Tillet (1991) defines conflict resolution as 'a multi-disciplinary, analytical, *problem-solving approach...*' Kelman is one of several scholar-practitioners who have brought together leaders and middle-range decision makers from opposing sides in crisis situations in order to decrease polarisation and improve communication. There is an established genre of research and literature on such 'problem solving workshops'.[9] Tillet writes for organisations and groups, possibly more akin to another genre from organisational development or 'managing change' literature aimed at businesses and voluntary associations.[10] The key point here is that in both genres (or levels) problem-solving is a non-hierarchical collaborative activity which involves adversaries who are encouraged to see their dispute as a shared dilemma, exchange perceptions, and 'disaggregate' the broad conflict to see if there are any areas of agreement.

In identifying the empowerment tradition used in second track interventions in former Yugoslavia, we must then necessarily ask in this context 'problem-solving by whom, and for whom?' We have established (above) that the method has been utilised as a form of group building rather than for reconciling opposing sides. This has led to some disquiet, as voiced in the following personal communication:

> 'I speak for myself when I say that here in Croatia this type of work is being done in the wrong manner. All those people who teach democratic ways of thinking do so only to people who already have an affinity for this kind of thinking. Nothing is done with all those other people. Even newspapers such as *Feral Tribune* and similar carry other opinions, even calling for lynching without teaching people how to think. This must change.'[11]

By 'democratic ways of thinking' the writer above refers to the willingness to listen to other points of view, share perspectives, work towards positive outcomes. This she holds to be a departure from her previous experience of party hierarchy and directives from rigid authority.

The organisational development approach to problem-solving (see note 10) calls for the creative breaking down of a problem as a whole into its parts, to make it more manageable, to enable working steps towards an outcome. This is also the case in approaches to community mediation (Crawley, 1992; Ackland, 1990) and political negotiation (Zartman and Berman, 1982). It is not without its critics.

Lewis (1991), in his study of *Negotiating across Cultures* places problem-solving firmly in an Anglo-Saxon adversarial legal tradition which relies on reason and logic: 'Out of the interplay of opposing arguments a formula will emerge that is satisfactory to both sides. In the problem-solving *erabi* paradigm, therefore, reason is seen as the vehicle of progress.' He questions whether this assumption is shared across cultures. Folger and Bush (1994) go further in a critique entitled 'ideology, orientations and discourse':

> 'The question remains, why is the problem-solving orientation so influential, what explains its appeal and its power for those in the dispute resolution and mediation fields? To explain this, we must identify the broader ideological premises on which it rests. These premises explain why problem-solving is so entrenched as an orientation to conflict and why alternatives are often unseen, untried, or overtly resisted.
>
> The strength of the problem-solving orientation derives from... ideology that is central to the mainstream culture of the United States. This framework, which applies not only to conflict but to every arena of social life, views the human world as made up of radically separate individual beings, of equal worth but with different desires (i.e., perceived needs), whose nature is to seek satisfaction of those individual needs and desires.[12]
>
> Problem-solving is essentially aligned with Individualistic assumptions about human nature and social interaction. As an orientation to conflict it embodies the view that conflicts represent problems faced by autonomous individuals in achieving mutual needs satisfaction. Further, it reflects the view that conflict resolution can and should involve finding solutions that maximize the satisfaction of every individual involved.'

Väyrynen goes further, observing that the problem-solving approach often considers prevailing power relations and institutions given. 'In that sense it is non-structural and ahistorical, and is more concerned with tactics than with strategy'. (Väyrynen, 1991) Mirko Mandrino of Pancevo expressed a similar opinion during a conversation in early 1996: 'I have people coming here telling me how to solve conflicts when they do not understand at all the system we live under. We need strategies for mobilizing non-violently. We need to change the very structures of violence which we inherited.'

Mandrino's frustration, his emphasis on 'structures of violence' further anticipates Väyrynen's argument. For the latter stresses that trying to understand the functions of violence leads to questions on the nature of the social order in which this occurs. 'The consideration of social orders and their proneness to violence, internal and external, hints at the existence of alternatives of which some are better than others. Thus consideration of the functions of violence injects, in contrast to problem-solving theory and conflict management, a normative element into the effort to resolve conflicts. In so doing conflict resolution is better equipped to avoid the pitfalls of political engineering and the neglect of the structural context of violence.' (ibid.).[13]

Weisner and colleagues, also of Pancevo, echo this in their argument that *collective violence cannot be separated from social structures and their transformations.* This philosophy underpins their 'Schools without Violence' project, their own attempt to begin that transformation process in the educational system. It calls into question the assertion by Lewe and Ramsbotham (1993) that 'there is a common set of individual and group skills which can facilitate and enable mediation and 'mediaction'[14] processes and thus promote peace formation'. It is this belief in transferable skills which underlies the popularity of 'conflict resolution training'.

6.5 Dilemmas of training

'Conflict resolution training' is one particular Western phenomenon, a specific cultural form intended to enable individuals to better deal with disputes or prevent escalation (through anger and fear at a personal level) to violence[15]. Conflict resolution mechanisms, that is cultural institutionalised forms intended to assist groups in dispute-handling, and to regulate or prevent violence, are to be found world wide. Writers on such traditions and the question of culture include Auruch and Black (1991), Augsburger (1992), Goverde (1990), Kirkbride and Tang (1990). Bradbury (1993, 1996) and Qleibo (1993) consider the efficacy of custom and traditional approaches, as do Nader (1988), Comatroff and Roberts (1981) and Schapera (1938).

> Education *is defined as 'activities which aim at developing the knowledge, skills, moral values and understanding required in all aspects of life rather than a knowledge and skill relating to only a limited field of activity. The purpose of education is to provide the conditions essential to young people and adults to develop an understanding of the traditions and ideas influencing the society in which they live and to enable them to make a contribution to it...'*
>
> Training *is 'a planned process to modify attitude, knowledge... and to satisfy the current and future needs of the organisation.'*
>
> *Both education and training are achieved by creating conditions in which the necessary attitudes, skill and knowledge can be effectively acquired by a learner who, as a result, becomes relatively confident of his or her abilities to apply them...*
>
> *People's learning is typically classified as either education or training; education is 'for life', while training is for work. It all sounds logical, and fairly easy to remember.*
>
> *We are, however, in danger of ignoring our early words of warning. Our definition remains based on generalised concepts. The reality is situation-specified.'*
>
> Reid, Barrington and Kenney, 1992

The transfer of learning skills

The idea of transferable skill sets, or more recently 'tools'[16] is evident in recent production of training guides and handbooks, some of which are intended to bridge potential cultural divides.[17] A Bradford University peace studies document lists a 'skill set' as:

information finding/sharing
reflective listening
assertion
bridging
constructing integrative solutions.[18]

This list is characteristic of findings in other materials, of which the following are representative:

conflict analysis
human needs theory
perception and cognition
listening
empathy
self-disclosure
mediation
negotiation
problem-solving
evaluation of outcome.

As Duffield (1997) suggests, 'training groups of people in conflict resolution techniques, for example, is one thing. Whether such activity can mollify societal instability or entrenched group hostility, however, is another.'

Vucic, having experienced a western European training package given at Subotica which included 'the oil price game' (negotiation skills) and 'being assertive' (communication skills) expressed serious misgivings about the new import of 'skills'. 'Actually,' wrote Vucic, 'people who are engaged in conflict resolution, as far as I see and understand... have not properly assessed the situation in the region.[19]

Vucic saw possibilities, however, that he thought relevant to his situation: Concerted work on symbols and the power they held to arouse emotion (particularly fear and hatred) were one priority area; 'Self-assessment' exercises to understand attitudes, position, and choices; wider social communication areas such as E-mail and media; and strategy design. 'Skills must be firmly rooted in the context of the conflict,' suggests N. Babic, an educationalist from Split. 'Otherwise you end up with self-development, group development and organizational development. But the war still goes on.' (Mari Fitzduff's *Community Conflict Skills* was cited as a good example of training material geared to a particular setting, in this case Northern Ireland).

Quite apart from situations involving armed intimidation and war, the 'transfer of learning debate' is controversial in other settings. One example of a developmental scheme for learning is that of Boydell and Leary (1993):

1) acquisition of specific knowledge, attitudes, and skills;
2) transfer of knowledge attitudes and skills to the work/life situation;

Pancevo Project of education for peace:

SCHOOL WITHOUT VIOLENCE

Author: **Aleksandar Weisner**, teacher, student of special pedagogy for prevention and resocalisation

AIMS: The aims of this project is to develop and satisfy social/creative needs of adolescents, develop a spirit of peace and tolerence, deal with primary prevention of psychopathological and behavioral desorders (destructivness, violence against oneself and others, delinquency...)

EXPLANATION: A long-lasting influence of mass-media, strongly marked with *PREJUDICE, CENSORSHIP* and *KITSCH,* along with a scholing system caracterised by *REPRESSION, OBEDIENCE, IDOLATRY* and *DOGMATISM,...* have reduced education to indoctrination, information to propaganda and art to mere kitsch. Such an atmosphere, full of primitivisme and chauvinisme, has produced many generations of submissive, illiterate and passive citizens. This has formed an ideal foundation for a totalitarian way of thinking easly misused by the regime to serve its military and political goals.

Violence present in political institutions can be considered asa consequence and a reflexion of violent behaviour common in our family, school and social groups. School manuals encourage hatred against peoples of former Yugoslavia, chauvinism and submissiveness to the autrorities. A totalitarian way of thinking is introduced into our schools as a violence that the regime performs through the teaching stuff - in the end, it becomes a way of living. Teachers are the most responsible for the repressive character of our school; they are, at the same time, in the best position to protect children and elleviate the consequences of violence performed through institutions, authoritarian attitudes and indoctrination. Unfortunately, aour teachers do not know for an "open" school programme, school without walls, Dewey's, Decroly's or Frainet's method, nor do they realise that their work provokes with children a series of psychological desorders, such as phobiae, intellectual inhibitions, dislexy...Yet, the school, along with some positive influence that the family still can have, are almost the only factors capable of orienting children towards real crativeness. Outbutsts of aggressivness are common with such children since they take almost any occasion to release these unbearable psychological tensons. Totalitarian regimes abuse of these problems - either by not helping adolescents to overcome them or even by imposing some - in order to make young people serve political and other goals of the state.

PARTICIPANTS AND TRAINERS: This project covers different activities with teachers, pedagogues, psychologists, adolescents and parents.

FORMS: Education of teaching staff will assume the following activities: reading of books/publications related with their line of work, analysis of school programmes/manuals, lectures, research, panel discussions, workshops with children, publication of reviews/books, cooperation with international institutions and organisations. The activities to be carried out with adolescents are: round tables/panel discussions on the following subjects: authority, discipline, loneliness, love, punishment, confidence, civic and moral education according to school programmes in Great Britain, France... Leaflets, posters and discussions will be the basic forms of psychological/pedagogical education of parents.

METHODS: The expected change in behaviour of the participants in this project is based on the application of the following methods: free participation, free choice, personal expression, open character of the process, active and authentic attitude towards others/world.

...ТЕМА ВАШЕГ РАДА НА ЧАСУ ЛИКОВНОГ ЈЕ "ЈЕСЕН У МОМ КРАЈУ"!
МОГУ ЛИ ДА НАЦРТАМ КЛЕМПАВОГ КЛОВНА?
НЕ!
ЈЕН'... ДВА... ЈЕН'... ДВА...
ЈЕН'. ЈЕН'.
ЈА БИХ ДА ИГРАМО ФУДБАЛ НА МАЛЕ ГОЛИЋЕ!
НЕ!
...ВАШ ПИСМЕНИ ЗАДАТАК БИЋЕ НАСЛОВЉЕН "КАКО САМ ПРОВЕО ЛЕТЊИ РАСПУСТ"!
ЈА ЖЕЛИМ ДА ПИШЕМ О СЕСТРИЋИМА ПАЈЕ ПАТКА! МОГУ ЛИ?
НЕ!
ДЕСЕТ ГОДИНА КАСНИЈЕ...
DIPLOMA
ДВАДЕСЕТ ГОДИНА КАСНИЈЕ...
ТАТА, МОГУ ЛИ ДА СЕ ВОЗИМ НА РИНГИШПИ-ЛУ?!
НЕ!
НЕ!
НЕ!??
"У ДЕЦИ ЈЕ СВЕТА КЛИЦА
НОВА МОЋ СЕ У ЊОЈ КРИЈЕ
БОЉИ СВЕТ БИ МОГО НИЋИ
КАД БИ ЗНАЛИ РАЗВИТИ ЈЕ"
Ј.Ј. ЗМАЈ
ЦРТЕЖ: АЛЕКСАНДАР ЗОГРАФ ◆ СЦЕНАРИО: ALEKSANDAR WEISNER
ИЗДАВАЧ: - ИНСТИТУТ ЗА ПРЕВЕНЦИЈУ НАСИЉА, ПАНЧЕВО

3) becoming competent in using knowledge, attitude and skills;; and
4) continuous improvement of competencies.

But social/cultural and political structures will filter any imported training inputs. Trainees must return to their original settings when the training is over. Hence the comments of one participant (Vojvodina resident) returning from a UK organised training event held abroad, 'I felt the techniques were artificial. The problem with us is that arguments are honest. We like quarrel. You are alive if you argue. We don't like compromise. We like winning.' Alexander Weisner felt that conflict resolution training was not useful without understanding group dynamics, social dynamics, psychology – 'underlying factors, not just symptoms'. On the other hand, Branka Kaselj of Osijek felt that it was training in stress reduction, 'super-learning' and relaxation, which helped her cope: 'I can do my job better. I can cope with the situations and attitudes here.'

Conflict Resolution Training: Sample Format, Belgrade 1993

The program of the training included:

First day: Introductions; What is the group MOST about from your point of view? (one sentence); Listing of different aspects of the work; What is going well and what isn't?; What shall we focus on these days?. After the lunch break: What are my motivations and resources to a. engage in this type of work; b. to sustain with it? (making a drawing or diagram); What would give me greater strength, sensitivity, hope and conviction; What gets in the way? (small groups); Round of: actions I can take to begin to address my own deeper needs; things I can offer to others. Game: reduction of tension exercise.

Second day: Name and gesture; Assertiveness (Speak Out) exercise (three stage model of assertiveness); Developing scenarios for role plays on mediation (Call situations of which you felt: here could mediation do something); Decide on two (1. Parents, living separately, on visiting their child; 2. Hungarian village in Vojvodine, with conflict about a road between Roman Catholic and Protestant villagers); Mapping needs and fears (in three groups); Providing the detailed mediation plan.
After the lunch break: Prepare the role play; play it; feed back in groups (hand out feedback sheet); plenary feedback; evaluation of the day; game: Mrs Mumble.

Third day: Game: How to reach out for the second party in mediation; Professor-student conflict; in 3's: play the meeting with the 2nd party; change the 2nd party; feedback in groups; plenary feedback; Brainstorm on; What could we do to overcome prejudice barriers? Hand-push - game in hassle-lines; Input on Goal setting and agenda-building for seminars.
After the lunch break: Hand out Stages in Conflict Sheet; Mapping of needs and fears in own internal group conflict (in 4 small groups); Discuss: 1. In which stage would you say the conflict is? 2. What would be the appropriate next step to take? 3. What could you do to forward the process?; Plenary feedback; Brainstorm on what would be needed to become more a mutual support-group?; Evaluation: learnings and how do I see the future of the group?; Texas Hug.

It was made very clear in the evaluation round, that this follow-up training came at the right moment for the group M.O.S.T. It provided them an opportunity to look at themselves as a group, they have been strengthened in practising mediation, I could give them a number of suggestions to improve group-coherence and group-decision-taking, and the assertiveness exercise was experienced as very useful in everyday-life. The Monday-afternoon session evoked lots of feelings of depressiveness because of the situation in Belgrade nowadays (empty shops, almost no public transportation; lots of time needed to provide your daily necessities, no perspective on any change; fear of war coming to Serbia, etc.). I think it was useful to share these feelings of suppression (sic), even when you can't provide an alternative perspective, it is good to hear that you are not the only one having those feelings, and that sharing them can also provide a certain strength to cope with them together!

(Ted Ages, October 1993)

Frequently, in peace movements there are people who are definitely against war and violence, but they are not capable to avoid sided attitudes and behaviour Because of that, conflict resolution including third party intervention cannot be effective or even worse, it is counterproductive.
Sometimes, people who are willing to be involved in training others about conflict resolution want just to provide for themselves references and to improve carrier to get more money or to convince trainees by any means that their conception is the right one.
In addition, people who are engaged in conflict resolution are coming mainly from the West Europe and they are not familiar with the following characteristics of people in Eastern Europe:
- agricultural mentality (such a mentality should be analysed in order to understand why individuals identify themselves so fastly with groups (influence of internalised patriarchal father as a representative of a common morality in the process of forming personality), why ther identify groups with ethnicity (despair and unsuccesfull searching of individual identity is compensated by compulsive enforcing a group identity which is characterized by the commonly recognized symbols-ethnic or religious symbols and finally, why such ethnic groups identify ethnicity with territory on which they live (agricultural mentality which is still predominat in the former Yugoslavia, the Balkans and Easten Europe is based on direct connection between land-soil and those who live on it; agriculture is the main source of life, thus the land has an ancient and saint character in atavistic relationship with an identity of individuals and groups-ethnicity is therefore confused with teritorry on which the certain ethnic group lives).
- internalisation and somatisation of outside opression (during the communist regime it was not possible to openly express disagreement and dissent with ruling authorities. Even worse, to be silent and internalisation were the on ways to survive. Such a process is present now as well. But, there are some aggravating circumstances as well. Actually, in many parts of Eastern Europe and the Balkans and some parts of the former Yugoslavia people can express what they feel, but what they feel is confusion of fears and conceptual contradictions of their opinions (There is a lot of illiteracy and political illiteracy particulary in the region). For that reason, a variety of self-assesment exercise should be very useful.
Somatisation of political and individual pain is always present when people a not able to process political and individual pain in their mind and emotions. Then, political and individual (by individual i think private pain, pain which derives from familly, childhood etc.) pain is somatised and pain is identified with body. Furthermore, any disagreement is understood as a potential attack body; that's why people easily are becoming conflictual and violent.
One of the consequences of that behaviour is identification groups, ethnicity and territory with body. Everything which could be understood as attack on person's respective group, ethnicity, religion or territorry perceived as a part of ethnicity is therefore understood and perceived as attack on his/her or their own body. Therefore, exercise which involve full involvement of body are from my point of view highly recommended.
- role of symbols (In Eastern Europe, the Balkans and the former Yugoslavia respect and acceptance of the communist symbols was a key point of existence, social certainty and security. Meaning of that fact is at least twofold. Firstly, the commonly accepted symbols are commonly accepted as a way of social communication, perception and order. The common symbols should be dominating people frequently think, or at least symbols of minorities should be present but much less than of majority. Since communication is mainly concentrated on symbols other sorts of political responsiveness are less present, but problem and crisis are still going on which increases somatisation, internalisation and other social-pathological processes. Furtherly, because of lack of communication presence of different symbols have been mutually understood as...

Comments on Conflict Resolution Training - Vedran Vucic 1993

Language

Almost without exception conflict resolution training sessions were initially conducted in English or German language in the cases surveyed. This meant either simultaneous translation or limiting session intake to those competent in a second language. Problems of meaning, nuance, and concepts ensue frequently in such situations, A word like 'feedback' (meaning response to information) may seem meaningless. An English phrase like 'Let's not throw the baby out with the bath water' evokes bewilderment. Even a word in itself ('territory', 'politics', 'history', etc.) can have multiple meanings and associations for participants.

6.6 Training the trainers

I met people in Autumn '95 (particularly in Belgrade and environs) who were scathing at the thought that a 3-day workshop could train trainers then prepared to run similar events. ('That is pyramid selling, not making for peace', was one comment). During the previous year an American foundation had been doing this with three day sessions on conflict resolution and management training. (This criticism seems reasonable, depending on particular objectives of the training, i.e., it might work in the case of learning to use E-mail because specific technical skills are easy to transfer systematically.)

It remains that many individuals took the new ideas and ran with them, adapting methodology, using their own language. CCCRTE gave particular emphasis continually to building local capacity in training and leadership. They also took a huge step in participative evaluation in October 1993, inviting 25 trainers and activists from former Yugoslavia plus 15 people of western non-violence or training backgrounds to a five day meeting in Budapest. The creative adaptation of method was obvious at this gathering. The following observations are from the CCCRTE report on this event:

> 'The report from a group of those in former-Yugoslavia on problems created during the training process listed the following:
>
> 1. A lot of information in a short time at the beginning
>
> 2. A different way of learning and different knowledge than we have been used to
>
> 3. Inner conflicts and prejudices which were created by the outside situation (war, violence)
>
> 4. Resistance to outside people who were offering something different from what we knew
>
> 5. We expected identification and we were offered empathy (people from outside)
>
> 6. Lack of coordination and communication between all the similar groups and initiatives
>
> 7. Lack of educated people for further steps
>
> Additional criticisms made were that certain workshops had not been systematically presented, and that the spiritual element of the concept of nonviolence did not gain much attention in most training...
>
> Point 2 was widely discussed. The concept of experiential learning was new to most of the participants from former-Yugoslavia, and was not always fully appreciated. To some extent, training methodology can be perceived as 'anti-intellectual': it does not rely so heavily on analytical reasoning or linear argumentation. A 'brainstorm', for instance, asks people to call out half-formed ideas with the intention of stimulating other ideas which only become structured later. A role-play (simulation exercise) often seeks to explore a situation by acting out a simplified scenario in the safe atmosphere of a group: this helps to develop insights into behaviour and possible responses, or illustrates the course a conflict might run. Other exercises use imagery or non-verbal expression, and then facilitators often suggest games, songs or even physical exercises as a way of reviving the energy in the group. People involved in conventional political or intellectual work quite often have a resistance to these ways of working...'

Participants were encouraged to develop their own regional networks and approaches. Particularly noteworthy examples of subsequent local training developments would be MIRAMIDA (Zagreb and Pakrac) and the work of Group 484 as well as MOST (Belgrade).

6.7 Attitudes

If the transfer of skills as techniques is problematic, the transformation of attitudes is more so. Writing in reference to training interventions for organisation learning Reid, et al (1992) observe that:

> 'Attitudinal aspects of training are extremely important as they predispose learners to action. The relationship between attitudes and action is, however, by no means a simple one: in

AGENDA FOR SEPTEMBER 1992
NONVIOLENCE WORKSHOP
EUROPEAN CIVIC CENTRE FOR CONFLICT RESOLUTION

Note: The education process used in this workshop will involve presentation, large and small group discussions, and activities.

FIRST DAY (8 hrs.)

I. Philosophy and Principles of Nonviolence

II. Brief history of Nonviolence

III. Developing a Grassroots Organisation

1. Principle of organisational development

2. Process of organisational development
a. forming organising committee
b. developing initial goals
c. outreach to build membership
d. analysis of issue
e. organisational structure/leadership/financing

IV. Developing a nonviolent campaign

1. Developing Strategy
a. definition of long term, immediate and short term goals
b. principles for setting goals
c. identifying change agents
d. process for setting your goals

2. Six Steps in Nonviolent Campaign Development

3. Analysis of opponents and change agents

4. Developing a strategy for change

SECOND DAY (3-6 hrs.)

The agenda for this day will partially be determined by what occurs the first day. It will remain flexible so we can go into more depth in areas of particular interest to workshop participants. This day will include more in-depth discussion and practice of methods of nonviolent direct action.

outline, we would state that attitudes are formed through our relationships with other people and are notoriously difficult to change'[20].

Initial dilemmas of training then include the identification of types of skills and learning to be conveyed, the appropriate targeting of these with an understanding of context, and consideration of prevailing attitudes. An alternative to the 'tool kit' approach is workshop design (see sample from Ted Ages) more akin to process consultation.

6.8 Process consultation

> 'In process consultation the guiding principle for the consultant is the collaborative working with the client in a manner that enables the client to develop his/her own diagnosis of the situation and the skills to act on it...
>
> The tasks of the consultant are to gather valid information, help create the conditions for the client to make free and informed choices and be internally committed to the choices he/she has made' (Maybe and Mayon-White, 1993).

In an internal report to CCCRTE in June of 1994 Diana Francis and Clem McCartney observed the importance of 'a maintenance function of psychological and emotional support, with someone else carrying some of the responsibility for a short while and holding the process.'

Process consultation can take groups beyond 'skills delivery' to situational analysis and needs identification. If it looks even beyond attitudes to the very foundations of these, it will lead us to the consideration of values, norms, and culture. Here is the very nub of the dilemma of 'changing society': *The question of social learning and its relation to aggression and violence as social action.*

6.9 Social learning

Our model of 'structural conduciveness' has in part a human needs dimension which suggests that society becomes more prone to violence when disparity results in frustration; when power to manipulate goes unchecked, and when people do not have the capacity for choice and alternatives amid highly armed and tense environments. Aggression and violence are sometimes viewed as 'instinctive', even normal (as in the power politics

On 'Social modelling'

I remember my initial shock when I first saw Chetnik insignia on bearded young thugs in the center of Belgrade peddling chauvinist tape cassettes and blood-curdling pamphlets. They looked like caricatures of the Chetniks from the Second World War. The only models the young had were from the war movies that glorified the Communist Partisans and treated the Chetniks as collaborators, rapists, looters, and killers. That was precisely what had made them attractive to the new converts! It was a Serbian folk version of the skinheads and neo-nazis in the West. Similar cultural blends in the Croatian paramilitaries mixed Ustasha symbols with heavy metal music and skinhead and Rambo images, sometimes topped off with Catholic prayer beads and a cross. These were the groups that would do some of the fighting and commit most of atrocities in the wars that summer.

Bogdan Denitch, 1993

Modeling and reinforcement influences operate jointly in the social learning of aggression in everyday life. Styles of aggression are largely learned through observation and refined through reinforced practice. The powerful effects that these two determinants have on the form and incidence of aggression are most strikingly revealed in ethnographic reports of societies that pursue a warlike way of life and those that display a pacific style of behavior. In cultures where interpersonal aggression is discouraged and devalued, people live peaceably (Alland, 1972; Levy, 1969). In other societies that provide extensive training in aggression and make it an index of manliness or personal worth, people spend a great deal of time threatening, fighting, maiming, and killing each other.

Bandura, 1976

You say to me that educating myself will not change wider society, and I tell you that it already had. For wider society can no longer intimidate me. Wider society no longer rules me. If it is death and madness then this no longer engulfs me. And I can look at my brother's killer in the eye to say 'I do not need to kill you in return. You must live with your own deed.'

from 'Talking to the Elders' by Irena Pavlovic
(unpublished manuscript

or realism school considered in Chapter II). This argument is countered by Mead (1968) and Hinde (1990) and by the *Seville Statement on Violence* (UNESCO, 1991). The Seville Statement was issued by a working party of scientists and scholars. It argues that the technology of modern war has exaggerated traits associated with violence both in the training of combatants and the conditioning of general populations. There is no genetic disposition towards warfare; it is not a feature of every society. Yet we take organised political aggression as given. The critical view does not deny severe conflicts of interest, nor opposing goals, but argues for a transformation of process away from destruction. Particularly in the post-cold-war context of increasing socio-political disintegration and the emergence of questions of ethnicity and identity, the utility of war must be sharply questioned.

Albert Bandura (1973) has developed a theory of *social learning*. He argues that not only does frustration contribute (in some personalities) to aggression, but the use of violence can also be taught, *modelled* as behaviour:

> 'What appears irrational and pathological to onlookers, and to the targets of aggression, often serves the aggressor as a method for getting what he wants when other options have failed or remain unavailable. Human aggression is activated by anticipated positive consequences as well as by aversive experiences (Bandura, 1976).

(See the diagram below of alternative motivations for aggression.)

Bandura argues for *observational learning, reinforced performance and structural determinants* as origins of aggression (ibid., p.123). The evidence for his theory in ex-Yugoslavia is strong. Consider for example the testimony of Borislav Herak, a self-confessed murderer and rapist, about how he 'learned' to hate and kill his Muslim neighbours.[22]

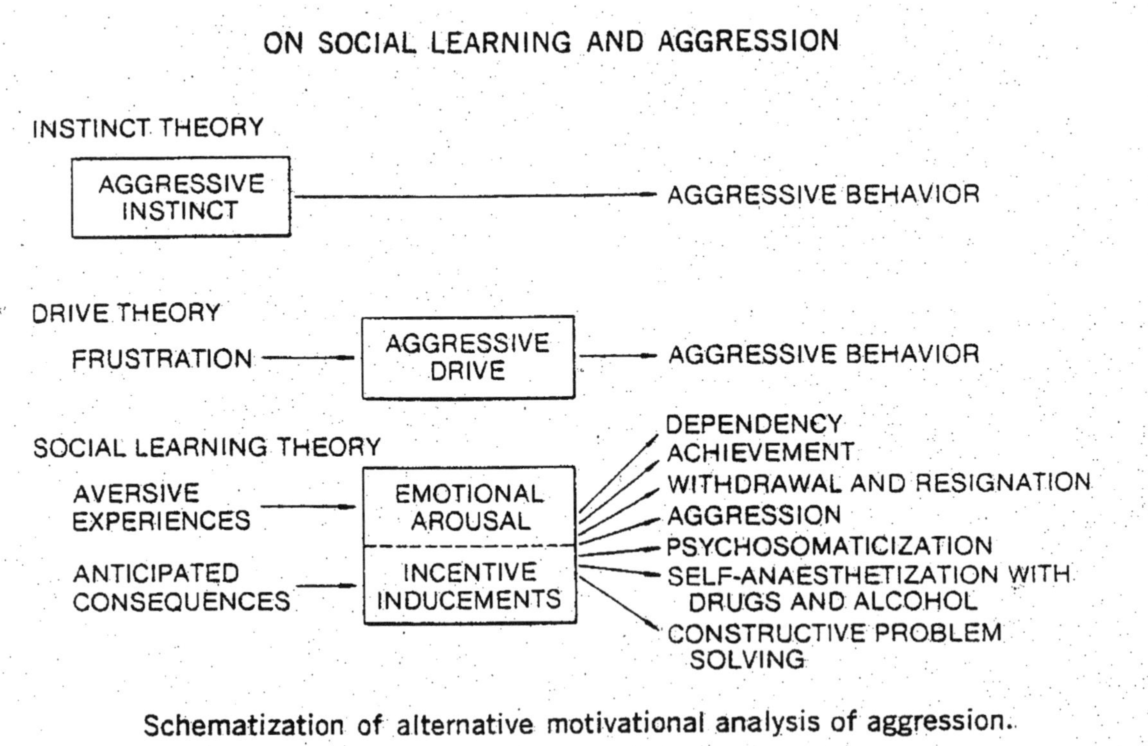

Schematization of alternative motivational analysis of aggression.

From: Albert Bandura, "On Social Learning and Aggression" in E.Hollander and R. Hunt, eds CURRENT PERSPECTIVES IN SOCIAL PSYCHOLOGY (1976) Oxford U. Press

Thoughts on training

My observation is that conflict resolution training internationally has been dominated by three characteristics:

1. *It is prescriptive in nature and transfer-based, with the transfer movement going from North to South, and more recently, from West to East. Training is, or has become in many instances, the packaging and selling of social knowledge.*

2. *Training is event driven, where evaluation of success lies with the effectiveness of a particular event, thus keeping attention on a short term focus.*

3, *Training is dominated by a technique orientation, where the key is the transfer of models presented in the form of technology.*

These three of course come back to the crisis I experienced in gringo story, where not only was it clear that the model, even if translated, was embedded with cultural assumptions from one setting now being suggested as an answer to another, but the methodology was imperial, that is the resource and answer lay outside the setting. In other words, I raise here the question of whether we approach people in a given setting as* recipients *of our expertise or as* resources *in developing approaches to their situation/context. This raises key questions we may wish to grapple with in this seminar:*

To what extent does training method turn attention toward resources from outside or toward building on resources inside?

To what degree is the transfer of conflict technique possible, desired, and/or appropriate from a cultural and relational point of view?

1. *We have not adequately nor explicitly enough identified the cultural assumptions and ideological biases of the models we propose in conflict resolution, communication, and mediation. We must be careful not to simply rely on an explanation of values as a replacement for the more difficult work of looking at the roots of our approaches.*

2. *We need to more fully critique our training methodologies, and have relied too much on a transfer based approach. In this we have much to learn from the sustainable development and appropriate technology fields.*

3. *We have done, I think, a somewhat superficial job of clarifying how training relates to the needs at various levels across an affected population in a protracted, violent conflict. We must not rely on an event oriented approach that tends not to undertake a comprehensive view of the place of training and/or a given event.*

4. *Finally, we must better address this issue of how short and long term agendas are linked. We are too much dominated by a short term view that inadequately addresses relationship, context, culture, and sustainability.*

John Paul Ledenach
Outline for Comments:
Intercultural Issues in Conflict and Training
Gernika, April 1993

** The Gringo story involved a training conducted by Guatemalans in fluent Spanish who were told by their host group that they looked and sounded like 'Gringos', this reflecting the cultural tone of the content they were delivering.*

A SAMPLE SPECTRUM OF CONFLICT RESOLUTION TRAINING/ACTIVITY INTERVENTIONS.

Training + Resources + Responsibility + Action = Capacity Building

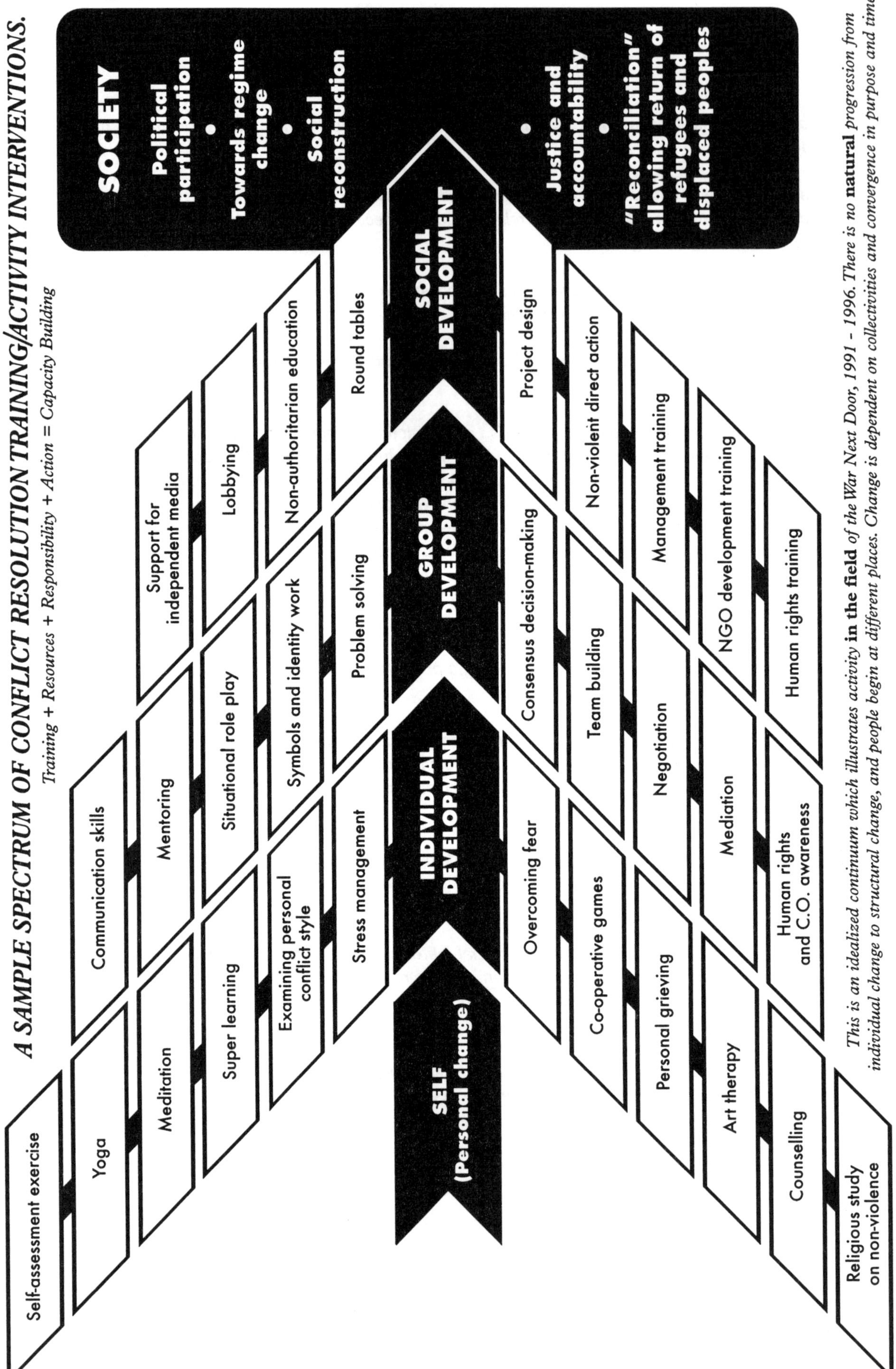

This is an idealized continuum which illustrates activity **in the field** *of the War Next Door, 1991 - 1996. There is no* **natural** *progression from individual change to structural change, and people begin at different places. Change is dependent on collectivities and convergence in purpose and time.*

This brings us to the crux of the entire debate on conflict resolution training: if murder and rape can be learned, is the inverse also true: can they be *unlearned*? Will different conditions produce different learnings: Can a 'culture of peace' be learned? What are the methods and time frame of such behavioural change?

Approximately 2/3 of the interviewees for this study suggested that it was not the content or skills of early trainings that proved valuable to them but the contacts they made, the networking and external support the trainings led to. Early skills-based workshops did indeed 'preach to the converted' albeit with new 'experiential' modes of learning. But a primary function of the trainings was to enable groups to form and address the questions they themselves identified for long term work. By 1993 the dominant training theme was no longer 'conflict resolution' but 'NGO development'. The paucity of early content based on 'getting to yes' had been filtered by old ex-Yugoslav structures and imbedded values (militarised power and hierarchy in authority). The new training claimed on one level to change those structures, to a pluralist 'NGO' mode of society. Where early conflict resolution trainings had been wedded to a conviction of non-violence[23], the new theme was also one of peace culture. Both prongs were to claim an overarching title: Civil Society.

Notes for Chapter VI

1. In fact intervening third parties may have any of a number of roles. Mediation may be one of these, or a strategy of direct help to one or other of the parties in conflict, or a decision to remain studiously neutral while letting the conflict run its course.

   'These options were posited some years ago by Oran Young (1967) when he attempted to throw light upon the nature of intermediaries in general by examining the behaviour of third parties at the time of the June 1967 War in the Middle East. "Third parties" according to Young, were "all those actors which became significantly involved in the crisis without becoming totally identified with either the Arab or Israeli forces..." He then identified outsiders enacting the role of *intermediaries* as "those third parties adopting a (more) impartial stance with regard to the opposing sides in the crisis" and went on to contrast them with another type of outsider which he called an *interventionist*, a third party "motivated by some combination of independent interests and partisan interests favouring either of the opposing sides" (Young, 1967, p. 52). Young's analysis implied the existence of three types of third party in situations of conflict, namely, intermediaries, intervenors, and those "totally identified with either party to a conflict" ' (Mitchell, 'The Motives for Mediation' p. 48 in Mitchell and Webb (1988)).

2. Gorni Vakuf, a town severely hit by war in central Bosnia, was officially divided (as per Mostar) after Dayton into Bosniac (Muslim) and Croatian sides. UNDP and UNOV supported a reconstruction project along the lines of Pakrac with outreach through building courses and materials, the reconstruction of houses (again alongside international volunteers), a children's club, Youth Club, school, women's sewing and knitting collective, and mobile clinic.

3. 'Sculpting is a tool used both in psychodrama and family therapy to explore intra-group or family dynamics.' Lynne Jones in Gutlove (1992).

   According to Gutlove, problem-solving workshop theory and technique was developed primarily by H. C. Kelman, and used by him to promote collaborative problem-solving between Israelis and Palestinians, A problem-solving workshop usually refers to a multi-day meeting of two adversarial parties in which they have an opportunity to discuss their interests and to engage in collaborative solving. For more information see: H. C. Kelman, 'Applying a Human Needs Perspective to the Practice of Conflict Resolution: The Israeli-Palestinian Case,' in J. Burton (ed.), *Conflict: Human Needs Theory* (New York: St. Martin's Press, 1990), pages 283-297.

   As a technique, 'problem-solving' is now a tenet of mainstream western management, and may be found in such books as H. Kindler, *Managing Disagreement Constructively* (Kogan Page, 1988), and U. Markham (1996) *Managing Conflict: How to deal with Difficult Situations at Work*.

4. 'Military interventions, by themselves, will not resolve the underlying strategic, political, and perceptual problems that propel ethnic conflicts. The key to true conflict resolution is the development of civil societies in genuine political communities. That, however, is something about which the international community still has much to learn—and not just in conjunction with ethnic conflict' Michael E. Brown *Ethnic Conflict and International Security*, Princeton 1993.

   Human needs, in a Burtonian sense (and drawing on the work of Abraham Maslow) could be seen as needs for: response, security, recognition, stimulation, a sense of distributive justice, meaning, and some measure of control of immediate environment or involvement/responsibility (Burton, 1990).

5. For a study of 'international' as not only relations between nation-states but also between peoples, as in a 'nation' of people in collective identity/heritage, see Waever, Buzan, et al, *Identity, Migration, and the New Security Agenda in Europe*, 1993, Pinter Publishers, London.

6. 'Fisher, for example, adopting a legal approach, seeks to improve bargaining techniques, believing that settlement and resolution can be combined in processes by which parties amend draft agreements which are sometimes prepared by a third party or mediator. Others, like Kelman, adopt a problem-solving approach which is analytical, in which the third party assists in analysis without putting proposals forward and in which options that satisfy both parties are explored. These two approaches have been divergent. The distinction between conflicts of interest and conflicts over needs clarifies the separate roles of each approach. It must be emphasized, however, that conflicts of interests are likely to have underlying deeper

issues that do not appear in a bargaining or negotiating situation' (Burton in Light and Groom, 1985).

7. See the reservations of H. W. van der Merwe, South African Initiatives, in Mitchell and Webb (eds.), *New Approaches to International Mediation*, Greenwood, 1988, New York, p.184.

8. Interviewees reflected training under the auspices of a variety of programmes including Responding to Conflict (UK), Lebensgarten (Germany), Balkans Peace Project (USA.), CARTE (UK), BSV (Germany), Swedish Ecumenical Council (Sweden), Oxfam (UK), Transnational Foundation for Peace and Future Research (Sweden), International Fellowship of Reconciliation (Netherlands), the Austrian Study Centre for Peace and Conflict Resolution, Stadtschlaining (Austria), and the Centre for Applied Studies in International Negotiations (Switzerland).

   For a comprehensive guide to the field (and other institutions in it) see *Prevention and Management of Conflicts—An International Directory*, Dutch Centre for Conflict Preventions, 1996, Amsterdam.

9. A number of scholar-practitioners have written on the subject of problem-solving workshops. See for example,

   J. Burton, 1969, *Conflict and Communication*, Macmillan, London.

   C. R. Mitchell, 1981, *Peacemaking and the Consultant's Role*, Nichols, New York.

   A. Smith, 'Conflict and Collective Identity: Class, Ethnic and Nation' in Azar and Burton (1986).

   M. Light, 'Problem-Solving Workshops: the Role of Scholarship in Conflict Resolution' in M. Banks (1984).

   A. J. R. Groom, 'Problem-Solving in International Relations' in Azar and Burton (1986).

   L. Doob, 1984, *Resolving Conflict in Africa: the Fermeda Workshop*, Jossey-Bass, London

10. See for example, *Systems Management and Change* by R. Carter et al, 1984, The Open University and Paul Chapman Publishing Ltd., *Managing Change*, ed. C. Mabey and B. Mayon-White, (1993), The Open University and Paul Chapman Publishing Ltd.

11. Letter from Dr. Biserka Tompak of Zagreb, 5 April 1997.

12. 'This Individualist view of the human world has dominated Western culture in some form for roughly the last 250 years. It can be traced from the writings of Hobbes and Locke to present-day philosophers like Dworkin (1977), Nozick (1974), Rawls (1971), and others. It underlies and informs modern political economy, from Adam Smith to Karl Marx. It has driven, in recent history, the civil rights, women's rights, and human rights movement—and their antecedents in the previous century. It underlies Western democratic theory and institutions. In all of these areas, the Individualist vision has been seen as heralding the liberation of all individuals, each to achieve full satisfaction in his or her own terms.' (Folger and Bush, 1994, p.15)

13. 'In a vertical social structure violence is a means of maintaining and challenging power. If the prevailing social order, assuring the prerogatives of the power elite, starts crumbling, violence becomes an instrument of both repression and empowerment. In that sense violence is secondary, and the political objectives and organization of the contending groups are primary. The distinction between repression by the strong and the empowerment of the weak is related to the distinction between reactive and proactive collective action which may be both violent and non-violent.' (Väyrynen, 1991)

14. 'Mediaction' is a term coined by T. Woodhouse to mean early measures which anticipate and prevent further disintegration in relations. This is seen as early intervention utilising many of the skills and techniques used in mediation.

15. According to Kevin Clements, from the George Mason University's Institute for Conflict Analysis and Resolution, the beginning of peace and conflict studies as a distinctive field in the 1950s and 1960 was in the USA, where pioneers intended to create an abstract, theoretical and quantitatively oriented science which would be relevant to policy makers – much along the lines of economics. With the advent of Alternative Dispute Resolution (ADR) in the 1970s and 1980s, a turn towards practice occurred.

    See Guus Meijer 'Empowerment and Training at the European Conference on Conflict Preventions' in CCCRTE Newsletter No. 5, Spring 1997.

    An interesting discussion on the possible 'macro' functions of such an approach was held at a Conference on Conflict Resolution in Cyprus in 1993, where it was suggested that all successful empires develop an inherent interest (and sometimes ideology) in peace, whereas empire-building (or breaking) can involve conflict, bellicosity, and sometimes violence. Discussion was inspired by a paper on 'Cross-Cultural Perspectives: Thoughts on Western Conflict Resolution in an Arab Context' presented by Paul Salem.

16. See even a 'toolbox' approach, Search for Common Ground Newsletter, Winter 1995.

17. See International Alert's *Resource pack for Conflict Transformation*, London, 1996; Bradford University's Diploma/MA Peace Studies course outline (1993) *Conflict Resolution and Peacemaking Skills*; Nic Fine and Fiona Macbeth, *Playing with Fire* (1992) Youth Work Press, Leicester; Quaker Peace and Service *Mediation Skills Course*; Chris Klug and George John, (1993) *Five Day Workshop Guide on Conflict Resolution Through Creativity*, Orissa, India. Under UNICEF auspices a guide book to 'Peace Kids International Peace Clubs' (1989, San Francisco) was introduced into Serbia and Vojvodina.

18. Bradford publications as above, p.9, with a citation for adaptation from P. Wallensteen, ed. *Peace Research: Achievement and Challenges*, Westview Press 1988.

19. Letter to Jill Sternberg of CCCRTE from Vedran Vucic, dated Subotica September 15, 1993. Vucic also gave me a copy of these comments, expressing concern that some trainings could be facile and dangerous, depending on the situation in which they were injected.

20. Reid et al elaborate on attitudinal change. Cognitive dissonance for example, is a concept

    'based on the premise that we normally like our attitudes to be in harmony with each other. Admiring a superior who actively supports an organisational practice of which I strongly disapprove, I am left in an uncomfortable and dissonant state of internal inconsistency, in that someone whom I admire is supporting something I dislike. The problem can be resolved by modifying my attitude about my superior, or about the organisational practice, or by a decision that the practice is not very important anyway. Whatever the outcome, I shall have altered my attitude in some way. In a training situation, cognitive dissonance can occur in role playing...

    Group discussion has been found to be one of the effective ways of attempting to modify attitudes. Examples may be found in Study Groups, and other forms of social skills and leadership training. Another method of attitude change is by providing new information' (1992, p.96).

21. Curle, writing in *The Friend* 28 August 1992, put it this way:

    But who are you or I to claim the ability to 'teach' others how to be more human? We need to be ourselves as much as, and often more than, the others. The answer is that we set up a situation in which we can share our experiences and help each other, for the first lesson is that we all have something to give and something to learn.

22. See 'Slaughter in the name of Serbia' by John F. Burns in *The Guardian* December 3, 1992. Extract below:

    'The Pofalici neighbourhood of Sarajevo where Borilav Herak grew up is a mixed community of Serbs, Croats and Muslims. Residents say there have never been nationalist frictions. During two interviews at the prison, the younger Herak spoke warmly of Muslims, in particular of Jankovic, his brother-in-law, whom he described as exceptionally kind and a good husband to his sister.

    Speaking of the couple's daughter, Indijana, who like tens of thousands of people in Sarajevo has a mixture of Serb, Muslim and Croat forebears, he says, 'I love her more than anything else in my life.'

    Herak had had nothing but good relations with Muslim neighbours in Pofalici, who had invited the Herak family into their homes for Bajram, the principal Muslim festival, and had been invited each year into the Herak home to celebrate the Serbian Orthodox Christmas. 'They helped me, Muslims. They were very good to me as people. Everywhere I went, Muslims helped me. They are a very correct people.'

    But Herak says that after he went to the bridge across the Milijacka River in late May, carrying a loaf of bread as a pre-arranged signal to Serbian fighters waiting for him on the other side, he began to get a different view of Muslims.

    From Serbian radio and television and in gatherings with other Serbian fighters, particularly the older generation steeped in Serbian folklore going back to Serbian defeats by the Ottoman Turks in the Middle Ages, he said that he learned that Muslims posed a threat to Serbs.

    Serbian political leaders and commanders told fighters that Muslims, who accounted for 44 per cent of Bosnia's pre-war population of 4.4 million, were planning to declare 'an Islamic republic' in Bosnia, which became independent of Yugoslavia under a Muslim-led government in April, just as the Sarajevo siege began.

    According to these accounts, Herak says, Muslims would also require Serbian children to wear Muslim clothing. 'We are told we would have to cleanse out whole population of Muslims. That's what we have been told. That's why it has been necessary to do all this.' The young fighter was also motivated by the urge to have things he never had before the war, including women, and goods like television sets and videos that Serbian fighters were encouraged to loot from Muslim's homes.'

23. See Douglas Bond, 'The Nature and Meanings of Nonviolent Direct Action: An Exploratory Study' in *Journal of Peace Research*, Vol. 25 No. 1, March 1988.

Under no illusions

The front page of Friday 21 August 1992's edition of The Independent *ran a full headline: 'UN force thwarts armed Serbs'. With a byline from Marcus Tanner in Belgrade, the article described how a group of 25 Serbian militia men in full combat gear had surrounded a small UN Force from Belgium guarding the bridge between Croatia and Serbia on the river Danube and ordered them to dismantle the checkpoint. Armed personnel carriers rolled through the 'supposedly demilitarized UN-controlled zone towards Batina, in what seemed like a preparation to attack Belgian forces':*

> *Mr Thornberry said that 'resolute attempts' by the Belgian peace-keepers to disarm local Serbian irregulars had triggered the crisis. The situation in the UN-controlled Baranja region in eastern Croatia is likely to worsen. A group of 20,000 Croats from Baranja, expelled by Serbian militants last year in the first big case of 'ethnic cleansing', threatened on Tuesday to walk across UN lines and go home.*
>
> *The UN closed the two checkpoints between Baranja and Croatian-held territory, to stop them crossing. But the Croatian refugees say more that 18,000 are still preparing to march back home to Baranja in 10 days.*
>
> *The biggest problem is the UN's failure to disarm a force of 16,000 well-armed Serbian irregulars operating in the UN zones in Croatia, posing as local policemen. Mr Thornberry said they 'are responsible for many outrages, expelling Croatians who refuse to leave, and they are suspected of killing people… Disarming these special police is the real problem'.*
>
> *He added: 'There is no way we can allow any refugees to return home until we have taken real control'.*

Approximately a fortnight after this incident Dr Katarina Kruhonja of the Osijek peace group was asked how she would categorize the work of the group. Under no illusions about the nature of volatility and militarized factions in her city and region, she answered 'Education'. Adam Curle, who was to become a mentor to the Osijek Centre, elaborates on the basis of his conversations with her:

'Education'. Education about the nature of the trauma inflicted by violence; education in the rights of human beings now being abused because they had become foreigners – no longer fellow Yugoslavs, but hated Serbs; education in the psychological and social problems of refugees; education in what they might encounter if they tried to return to their homes in occupied country; education for the police in how to help in this process without dangerous confrontation, education in how to negotiate with the Serb authorities who would also be involved; education in the nature and effects of violence; education in values other than the prevailing vengeful militarism; education of themselves in playing this difficult, embarrassing and even dangerous part in a community to much of which peace is a dirty word.'

(See 'Small Circles: work for peace in ex-Yugoslavia'
by A. Curle, in *The Friend*, 2 October, 1992)

Chapter VII

'Civil society': contested concepts 2

'It is in conducting the affairs of civil society, that mankind find the exercise of their best talents,as well as the object of their best affections. It is in being grafted on the advantages of civil society, that the art of war is brought to perfection; that the resources of armies, and the complicated springs to be touched in their conduct, are best understood...

But there is no peace in the absence of justice. It may subsist with divisions, disputes, and contrary opinions; but not with the commission of wrongs. The injurious, and the injured, are, as implied in the very meaning of the terms, in a state of hostility.'

Adam Ferguson *Essay on the History of Civil Society* 1767. (Edinburgh U.P.,1966). p. 155

'If Ferguson in 1767, or later French revolutionaries, romantics and others did not use the words NGO they did think of CIVIL SOCIETY as the "consequence of civilization and in contrast to Oriental Despotism".

...people who write using this last key term in a much developed version, with knowledge about Hegel's, Marx's, Gramsci's, Althussers's, and others arguments about ***civic culture*** *as political culture...think that civic culture "is a vital ingredient of stable democracies"... In that sense I have to look for the definition of such a claim also in terms of an individual's political stance... So that now it is taken for granted that an individual believes both in acceptance and respect for political authority and the detachment and independence from it.*

I should ...express my protest against this type of "speak" which is unsustainable in the former socialist countries. For instance, in the Serbian version "gradjansko drustvo znaci aktivno gradjanstvo" (civil society means active citizenship) would mean that a former "proletarian" or "worker" has now become a citizen within the same political rhetoric of the past.'

From notes by Vanda Krajihovic, 1992

'It is not at all the case that individual civil society actors, who can, of course, assert their wish to 'do their own thing' and who can make a plausible argument for the vital need for what they have chosen to devote their energies to, are the major problem. Rather, foreign donors, in directing the majority of their funding to particular kinds of activities, justified through the concept of 'civil society', reproduce a particular distortion of priorities and approaches which are politicised (whilst pretending to be non-political) and unrelated to real social need.'

Stubbs, 1995b

VII. 'Civil sociey': contested concepts 2

7.1 Debates on civil society: 'The people themselves'

'Civil society' has become a contested concept because for donors and implementing agencies it can be prescriptive— 'a mono-theory applied across continents regardless of conditions, institutions or history' (Duffield 1997). For N., speaking in London in early 1994, it had been a desperately vital ideal in her activist days with CAA, Centre for Anti-War Activities, Sarajevo. 'We were 60 to 100 members when Bosnia was recognized in April 1992. Most of us have been forced by the aggression to flee. Some of us are dead.' To N. it is important that the context of the ideal be remembered, and that its meaning can somehow be revived.

To understand what the term may mean in practice, what it meant to primary social actors in the early days of the war, and to contrast this with the term as an implementing guideline for the Dayton agreement, it must be placed firmly again against the earlier setting of conditions, institutions, and even recent history. This means 'unpacking' a contested concept, a concept that has not gone unnoticed in the study of international relations.

Robert Cox (1989)suggested that 'there has been little attempt within the bounds of international relations theory to consider the state/society complex as the basic entity of international relations. As a consequence, the prospect that there exists a plurality of forms of state, expressing different configurations of state/society complexes, remains very largely unexplored, at least in connection with the study of international relations.'

In *practice* the plurality of form is much experienced and explored. For example, the 're-integration' of a self-declared SAO (failed) 'state' into another self-declared viable state (Croatia) involves complex re-working of such different configurations.

This chapter will consider such an example and examine the background, history of meaning and use of the term 'civil society' in the ex-Yugoslav context. A brief general overview of debates on the term will be offered. The chapter will attempt to shed light on particularly formative Yugoslavian antecedents: 1) a 'culture' of militarism, 2) penal restrictions on free speech and their implications for public participation, and 3) control and use of the media.

Understanding these areas is essential for gauging the impact of second track interventions. In the activities of primary anti-war groups, they become focus themes and aims known as peace culture, civic participation, and new communications.

Debates on civil society

In mid-May 1996 the mood among UN civil affairs officials in what had been known as 'Sector East' (Baranja, East Slavonia and West Srijem) was positive, particularly in Beli Monastir, Baranja.

From mosquito spraying to sanctions policy or Council of Europe membership, peacemaking interventions after, and during the war in former Yugoslavia have operated on a myriad of levels. While media and public attention focuses on high level summits and tribunals, the words of a UNTAES official resonate; surveying the detailed projects, accompanied and escorted meetings and incentives to rebuild a torn society he observed of the farmers, teachers, builders, shopkeepers, and local people of all generations, 'at the end of the day, it is all up to the people themselves.'

7.2 Historical interpretations

In the popular traditions and publicised protocols[1] of much of North American and Western European thought 'the people themselves' constitute what is sometimes called 'civil society'. The phrase denoted for many the popular movements and interest groups which developed in Europe as monarchies were either thrown off or gradually outgrown by new religious and economic development. Eisenstadt (1973, p.5) suggests that European 'civil society' was characterised by its relative autonomy with regard to the state, having its base in newly emerging strata, especially the bourgeoisie, the intellectual and professional groups. These groups evinced an independent and yet highly committed attitude to the social and political order, trying 'both to participate in it and to shape it.' They often claimed their rights and autonomy in the formation of political order by citing liberty, rationality and progress.

In his major study, *Media beyond Socialism* (Splichal, 1994, p.8) Slavko Splichal cites the importance of civil society as 'certainly one of the central issues of democratisation of both capitalist societies and societies in transition, although for different reasons:

> 'Is it possible to claim that civil society does exist in post-socialist countries? Is the concept of civil society even useful and valid? Do clear-cut boundaries between state and civil society exist, and should they exist? These questions are legitimate for several reasons. First, the modern

'Plurality of Form': Reintegrating Baranja 1996

The main thrust of all UNTAES civil operations was to prevent panic among the Serb communities, thereby preventing an attempted mass exodus. On the question of the proposed policy of the Croatian Government towards its responsibilities and obligations to the UNTAES area under the Dayton Accord, a statement was expected from Zagreb. It was clear that the Croatian Government remained reluctant to agree to the return of Serbian refugees to their homes in Croatia. The attitude towards Serbs remaining in Baranja was also unknown. Croatia had been given three years by the Council of Europe to comply fully with the provisions of that organisation in respect of human rights etc. Some 1600 police from both ethnic sides would be engaged as the new police force for the sector -applicants to be cleared by both sides before engagement. 400 of these new police were to be trained in human rights issues at the Police Academy in Budapest.

All internal police/militia posts in Baranja had now been removed. On the military side, the Pakistanis were based in Darda and deployed in the middle sector, with the Belgians working in the northern sector. Demilitarisation had de facto *already occurred—even though not planned to be officially started by the Security Council until June—there were only five tanks left in the UNTAES area (two of these at the Bilje crossing and another two in a car park just on the northern side of Darda).** The heavy snows of the winter together with the lack of pumping of water channels meant that some anti-personnel mines were floating in the waterways and flooded area of the sector and had entered the River Danav itself. Plans for specialist de-mining of fields and roadsides were being discussed with central Serbian and Croatian military authorities.*

Specific practical steps ranged from negotiating back payment of pensions to Baranja citizens (from the Croatian government), mosquito spraying, re-connecting telephone exchanges, de-mining railway lines and agricultural land, repairing the electricity grid, planning for postal exchange with Osijek, and enabling gradual refugee 'visitations' to prepare for return.

Such are the fine points of the 'social micro-surgery' necessary to re-unite a scarred and divided population.

Meanwhile in an independent civic initiative Mayor Zlatko Kramaric of Osijek and his deputy had visited counterparts in Subotica the previous week, 'over the line' and under the nose of hard-liner regional commander Glavas.

Report from Nic Street May 1996 (See Appendix 3).

history of the idea of democracy is closely related to the idea of civil society, from which the state should be clearly delimited... Second, technological developments and the growing productivity of productive forces, the restructuring of capitalism, and the fall of sovietism (rather than socialism) also challenge traditional conceptions of the capitalist system and bourgeois democracy' (Splichal, 1994, p.4).

Splichal argues that in industrialised Western societies discussions are intensified as a result of the rise of 'invisible power' in the hands of capital and non-representative institutions and the decline in the power of democratic institutions. In less developed, and particularly in the (former) socialist countries, the ideas of civil society and impersonal rules of democracy became popular with the fall of 'scientific' socialist utopia and the decline of the socialist state.

In the 'great dichotomy' (civil society/the state) the former is taken as that part of social relations that enjoys a degree or form of autonomy from the latter. Norberto Bobbio[2] suggests a 'non-state' approach:

1. Civil society as the *prestate* is defined as the historical precondition of the state.
2. Civil society as the *antistate* is defined as the antithesis or alternative to the already existing state.
3. Civil society as the *poststate* is defined as the positive negation and dissolution of the state. (Bobbio, 1989, p. 24)

Hegel (1981) defined civil society as the *antistate* (i.e., the state was excluded from civil society) but also as a moment in the process of the formation of the state. While Hegel pioneered in defining civil society as the sphere of social relations not controlled directly by state authorities, Antonio Gramsci (1971) introduced a distinction between economic life and civil society by shifting civil society from the sphere of economic necessity to the sphere of social superstructure. As intermediary between economic realm and the state it was also a terrain of struggle. Struggle is what the term represented in the late 80's in eastern Europe, and in Yugoslavia at the beginning of the war. To quote Splichal (1994, p. 19) again,

> 'Specifically, the state as political system regulates the use of coercive power to prevent disintegration; we can consider it a "coercive order." In a systemic perspective, the contrast between civil society and the state might be also defined as the contrast between the formation of demands aimed at the political (sub)system (the state) and the capacity of state institutions to supply answers to these demands (Bobbio 1989, pp. 25, 51)... if the lower-level opposing ends of civil society and the state are transformed into conflicting means that imply an interaction between, and a higher-level objective shared by, the state and civil society, we can speak of a dialectic rather than a dichotomy.'

The 'lower-level opposing ends' might in Western parlance be called 'grass roots' actors or movements.

7.3 Contemporary meanings

Miroslav Samardzic[3] considers how (or whether) the term 'civil society' translates into what was once called the Serbo-Croat language: 'Civilno Drustvo would probably refer,' he says, 'to those living in the town, or to something not from the military.' There is nothing to imply participative, much less democratic involvement, or any particular relation to state authority. 'Grass Roots', or 'Korjenje Trave' has no meaning on its own except one to do with fields and growing grass. Semardzic would prefer 'Organizaciva obicnih Lzvoi' or the 'organizing of the ordinary people.' Nina Pecnik expands on the English words in extending meaning to activism. To her 'grass roots' is a

> '...word/concept that does not exist in the Croatian language so no one is quite sure what it means. For us "grassroots" has to do with values rather than fixed models. It reflects our philosophy about how to put a human rights perspective into practice in changing circumstances. Above all, our values concern transformation rather than imposed interventions. We are aiming for change from below, with the agricultural metaphor being useful in terms of our commitment to organic processes in which we grow and emerge rather than transplant models from elsewhere' (Pecnik and Stubbs, 1995).

Pecnik echoes Havel's philosophy of 'Politics from "below". Politics of the people, not of the apparatus'[4]. The idea is central to a definition of civil society offered by Herbert Fröhlich[5], a Catholic priest and member of Pax Christi: 'Civil society is a society that presents (gestaltet) itself in a variety of formations, not through the state or through the powers of economy; not from above but from below. *People or groups that don't primarily share in power but who live their relations be it of neighbourhood, cultural , sportive or political kind.*'

In his study of unofficial peace activism in the former Soviet Union and east/central Europe Vladimir Tismaneau (1990) points to 'political uniformization and atomization, all-pervading controls, and ideological manipulation' as classic means of repression of civil society in Eastern bloc countries, pre-1990. 'Limited to fractious rivalries at the top, politics as such appears to the ruled as a sterile exercise in conformity. For a long time, because of police repression and widespread scepticism, autonomous political activities seemed to be inconceivable...For many citizens the only way to repudiate the ubiquitous mendacity propagated by the system was the complete avoidance of politics—the de-politicization of human discourse and the emancipation of social communication from the ideological burden imposed by the ruling power.' Regaining power was regarded as a struggle against the frozen figure of *Realpolitik*. The universalization of politics, as professed by Leninists, discouraged many citizens from weighing the possibility of devising a counter-culture rooted in a renewed sense of community, non-institutional forms of communication, and the refusal of the alienated symbols of power, including the language of domination' (p.4).

Tismaneau states that civil society is institutional pluralism in *statu nascendi*. It includes autonomous unions, the independent professional associations , independent religious associations, human rights, ecological and pacifist movements, as well as other groups committed to rescuing the individual from the all-embracing official ideology..'(p.182). The notion is not without its critics. It has been pointed out that Karadzic once engaged in 'green movement' activity. Church members in Rwanda participated in the 1994 genocide there.

As John Keane suggests, an institutionalised distinction between state and civil society is normally viewed as a fundamental precondition of pluralistic, parliamentary democracies in modern complex societies (Keane, 1988, p.25).

But Paul Stubbs (1995) argues that an over-emphasis on civil society fails to challenge nationalist frameworks and meanings : 'Few words have been seen as more resonant with meaning in the post-socialist or post-communist societies of Central and Eastern Europe than that of "civil society"...Yet it is always under-theorised, insufficiently concretised in terms of specific practices, and rarely subjected to critical scrutiny.'

In the context of post-socialist transition, the so-called decline of the 'great powers', and a new north or western dominated world order, the ideological construct of 'civil society' is convenient if it tends to focus on individual or human rights, perhaps somewhat on minority rights. 'In this way, the concept of oppression, referring to class, gender, ethnicity and other forms of social relations are conveniently by-passed...Democracy is found... wherever USAID supports "civil society." Questions of poverty, of the rights of workers, young people and so on, belong to the "old regime" and are passé at best, and subversive at worst' (Stubbs ibid.). It may well be, as Stubbs concludes, that 'the political nature of civil society is contingent.' **As a banner for emergent anti-nationalist and anti-war groupings in ex-Yugoslavia the term embraced participation and response.**

Tismaneau, drawing on his own experience in the former Soviet Union, describes such motivation:

> 'Civil society has been a major vehicle to recreate the conditions of a normal social life. It has been within its emerging nuclei that citizens have learned the rules of democratic dialogue and the virtues of the common endeavour to recreate a genuine body politic. For theorists and practitioners, civil society is not a disruptive undertaking. On the contrary, its major aim is to construct and reshape the broken bonds of human solidarity, to rehabilitate the notion that human beings have the right to hold their rulers accountable for acts supposedly carried out on their nation's behalf' (p.182).

Tismaneau hints thus at the need to reclaim 'civility' itself, in the face of depersonalised or harsh authoritarian structures; the (re-)forming of human relationships. Civil Society can mean 'the opposition not only to the barbarian state of nature, but also, and particularly, the opposition to all forms of despotism, feudalism, and political interference in personal, family, and business life in general' (Splichal, 1994, p.8).

7.4 Culture and militarism: the need for non-military alternatives

'After Tito, Tito' is a phrase one heard throughout the former republics from 1991. B., a classics professor, formerly at the University of Osijek, explains the saying: 'When Tito died we lost a strong father-figure leader with military associations. Now we have them everywhere.' A former soldier himself and now in his sixties, B. describes his interest in 'anti-authoritarian education' and its promotion in the late 1970s and early '80s. 'The further west we went in our own country the more interest there was. Teachers in Slovenia, by virtue of geography and maybe more western lifestyles were very interested. In Croatia less so. In Serbia not at all. Maybe levels of wealth and opportunity also made a difference. I don't know any more.' Biserka, a woman scientist of the same generation, observes 'It is as though the very thing that saved us in 1941 completely destroyed us in 1991—the cult of the soldier.' Professor B. draws on literature to quote Rousseau in saying that citizens should be soldiers 'by duty, none by profession. Such was the military system of the Romans; such is that of the Swiss today; such ought to be that of every free state...' (Rousseau, 1782) Biserka disagrees, stating that blind duty to authority is more damaging for society than military organisation itself. She was brought up in a German-speaking east Slavonian family in Osijek. She remembers Nuremberg.

As a once leading advocate of 'non-alignment' Yugoslavia cultivated a form of well-armed independence based on high levels of preparedness against external attack.

'The Center represents an embryo of a peace movement in a country and a region that have never been known for their pacifism and have never developed a culture of peaceful negotiation and conflict resolution. With this in mind, the Center's activities have been aimed at both short and long-term objectives. The former include immediate antiwar and peace actions, while the latter relate to the construction of civil society, respect for human life, individual and minority rights, and democratic institutions.'

Statement of the Centre for Anti-War Action Belgrade, September 1993

'Croatian civil society is weak, but in strong development. In former communistic regime a lot of quasi-NGOs (QUANGO) existed; only a few of them still existed and make efforts to continue work in new circumstances. Some new QUANGO and GONGO are founded. Many of former dissident and alternative organisation also stop work in new regime. Political activities and public attention are concentrated inside political parties and into state structures. The political regime is strongly authoritarian, power is concentrated inside ruler party and especially in hands of President Franjo Tudjman personally.

However, many new grassroots organisations, citizens initiatives and NGOs have been founded during the last three years. People who work in them actually work to create institutions and structure of independent civil society from beginning. Development of people activities is of key importancy for preserving democracy in Croatia.'

Statement of the Anti-War Campaign Croatia, Zagreb, September 1993

7.5 War preparedness

For Paul Rogers writing in *The Guardian* 17 August 1992, it was clear that one of the remarkable aspects of the war was 'the sheer quantity of armaments and the ability of a wide range of irregular forces and militias to wreak havoc on civilian populations. The widespread use of mortars, machine guns, mines, light artillery and sniper rifles, and the ability of ground troops to conduct high-mobility operations, is a continuing shock to many outside observers...' Based partly on the wartime experience of the partisans, Yugoslavia developed a particular kind of strategy based very largely on territorial defence through partisan operations. It was this strategy which, by terrible irony, produced large numbers of irregular forces who adapted these tactics, and their own training, for use in civil war and intervention.

By the early 1980s, 15 years after the Czechoslovak experience, Yugoslavia had established armed forces numbering about 250,000 with 60 per cent made up of conscripts serving for 15 months. The air force and navy were professional services with a small minority of conscripts, but three-quarters of the army were conscripts, with mainly Serbian officers.

> 'It was never believed that the regular armed forces could defend Yugoslav frontiers successfully in the event of war with the Soviet Union. Their function would be to "buy time" for the mobilisation of army reserves amounting to 500,000 people and, crucially, the much larger Territorial Defence Force, numbering in excess of two million and dispersed throughout the country. The regular army, reserves and the Territorial Defence Force together made up one fifth of the entire adult population' (Rogers, 1992).

The Territorial Defence Force itself mainly comprised former conscripts who knew their local areas well and many of whom were trained and equipped in the use of small arms, mortars, light artillery, portable anti-tank and anti-aircraft missiles, and the various technologies of sabotage. In the event of a full-scale invasion, and once these reserve forces had been mobilised, the regular army would fall back from the frontiers and merge with local units to establish a state-wide process of guerrilla warfare, making life well-nigh impossible for an occupying force.

To back up this strategy, weapons and munitions were dispersed throughout Yugoslavia and a major arms industry was developed which made the country largely self-sufficient. It comprised a markedly militarised society, with the strongest forces located in Serbia and Serbian-controlled areas, and included large numbers of adults, mainly, but not entirely, men trained in partisan warfare and able to adapt those tactics. 'You must understand,' says Biserka, 'we had a culture of being ready to fight.'

Survival and security were tied (for those of the Tito generation) to a concept near to that of the 'garrison state' described by Lasswell in his writings during the second world war (1941):

> 'In the garrison state all organized social activity will be governmentalized; hence, the role of independent associations will disappear, with the exception of secret societies. (Specifically, there will be no organized economic, religious, or cultural life outside of the duly constituted agencies of government.) Government will be highly centralized, though devolution may be practiced in order to mitigate 'bureaucratism...' Not only will the administrative structure be centralized, but at every level it will tend to integrate authority in a few hands. The leadership principle will be relied upon; responsibility as a rule will be focused upon individual "heads" ' (Quoted in Bramson and Goethals, 1968,p.323).

Lasswell made key distinctions between 'instrumental' and 'mystic' democracy. He suggested that instrumental democracy is found wherever authority and control are widely dispersed among members of a state. Mystic 'democracy' is not, strictly speaking, democracy at all, because it may be found where authority and control are highly concentrated yet where part of the established practice is to speak in the name of the people as a whole. Any dictatorship may celebrate its 'democracy' and speak with contempt of such 'mechanical' devices as majority rule at elections or in legislatures.

7.6 The idea of culture

Slavko Splichal argues that 'civil' society through the voices of intellectuals succeeded in destroying and de-legitimising the one party 'garrison' type state in the late '80s. (Splichal, 1994, p. 143). Leadership principles and social structures were left in some ways, however, intact. Authoritarian and hierarchical forms are seen as incompatible with the wider realisation of civil society[6]. New values were required.

In *Building a Global Civic Culture* Elsie Boulding postulates conditions of behaviour and value interaction conducive to violence reduction:

> 'If we want to describe what is involved in coming to know, we need to distinguish among the actual learning process, learning settings, and agents of learning. This will give us a clearer sense of what needs to be done about learning. One way to talk about the whole learning system is to talk about socialization, which involves all the influences that come to bear on the individual in the process of becoming the kind of person "society" wants. Society, of course, consists of all the individuals and groups and institutions that are involved in that becoming' (Boulding. 1990, p.89).

Boulding draws on a tradition of sociologists and anthropologists who believe that the conduct of war is acquired learning rather than inherent behaviour[7]. She emphasises that socialisation processes are not simply externally imposed—that the individual, the 'choosing self' must make something of influences from outside. Similarly, John Keane in his chapter 'Uncivil Wars' (who cites Arkan and Tiger paramilitary activity) draws on Hannah Arendt's concept of 'radical loss of self' in trying to explain (if not understand) contemporary unrestrained killing: 'They are often no-hopers who believe in nothing but their own private fantasies. Their senses are attuned only to violence...They vandalize the threefold division of government, army and civilians once enforced by conventional warfare...' (Keane, 1996, p.141) Ideals of civil society are meant to bolster the latter element in this ideal triangular configuration. It is significant that the Helsinki Citizens Association promotes dialogue and round-table themes on 'The Politics of Demilitarization' alongside 'Developing Civil Society.'

Moreover, taking Splichal's point about leadership principles and social structures, 'culture' itself must be seen as 'entire processing context where values, norms, feelings and beliefs interact with individual and collective actions, and with institutions' (Demertzis, 1985). The Osijek centre with its focus on 'peace culture' and the Panchevo Schools without violence programme were not behaviourist in approach. They sought a type of social transformation which would creatively counteract (in the long term) old structures. In the words of Nicholas Demertzis (ibid.):

> 'Political culture therefore cannot simply denote psychological orientations in concurrence with the politics of the elite, but must include a spectrum of values, needs and practices that not only react against given political structures but also posit the "political" itself. Thus the actors' point of view is essential in an alternative conception of political culture that represents the way people actually make politics and the way politics is understood by them.'

New social movements and the banner of 'civil society' were a major departure from experience and precedent in 'the actors' point of view.' 'Peace culture became a viable standpoint and objective.

7.7 Penal code vs. participation: The legacy of dissidence

V. aged 40 is a lawyer who has been unemployed since his jailing in the early 80s for his involvement with communist 'praxis' groups. 'We criticised from the left', he says. 'We were liberal Marxists whose dissidence was for human rights, anti-Stalinists advocating socialism with a human face, using free university approaches and the Friday talks in Belgrade.' He explains that under the Yugoslavian penal code it was a criminal offence to make any 'verbal attack' on government, including jokes or criticism. Specific legal code articles dealing with counter-revolutionary activity carried up to eight years imprisonment for wrongful speech. V. recalls the examples of 'enemy propaganda' he experienced as a young man—the chemistry professor in Vojvodina who said in the classroom that Bulgarian heavy industry was better than Yugoslavia's, and got five years in prison for his opinion. An economist who thought foreign loans were too heavy and said so got two years. A Latin teacher who suggested that the school system was not perfect, two years. 'When the public became too opinionated, proportional witch hunts began. Someone from each sector would be tried simultaneously—a farmer, an engineer, a peasant, an intellectual. You could say we Yugoslavs had total equality in criminal charges and trials participation. This way we were reminded as a population of the risks of thinking out loud.'

There was also the spectre of ghosts from the past. 'It was a legal secret, the crime of a teacher who disappeared from my school', says V. 'The legal secret was a word kept hushed in our house, and that word was **politics**. In the second half of 1984, the beginning of '85, 114 cases were pending for something called 'counter-revolutionary plot'. When I qualified as a lawyer I read Amnesty literature about cases in my own town which I would otherwise not have heard of, such was our climate of fear. The message in all of this to the population was quite simply that politics is bad, criminal, and not to be engaged with unless you are using party structure and party language. Names of the victims were whispered; Vlado Dapcevic, kidnapped and killed in Bucharest, his corpse brought back to Vojvodina. Radoir Radovic, tortured and killed. Official 'suicides' or car accidents in Croatia.'

Amnesty International's records indicate that fears of imprisonment were well-founded. A.I.'s Yugoslavia report of 1985 documents... 'the contentious use of Article 133 in cases of what are commonly referred to in Yugoslavia as "verbal offences". Besides Article 133, there are a number of other legal provisions which penalize "verbal offences", among them Article 157 of the federal criminal code which deals with "damaging the reputation of the SFRJ". Other offences such as "spreading false rumours" or "damaging the reputation of a socialist republic or socialist autonomous province", are penalized under sections of the criminal codes of the republics and autonomous provinces dealing with "offences against public order" and "offences against honour and reputation"'. Cases are listed of people convicted and imprisoned solely on the basis of private conversations considered 'hostile propaganda' under Article 133, sometimes in connection with other legal provisions, such as Article 157, which penalise 'verbal offences'.

Amnesty International also noted an increase in the number of cases of people 'imprisoned on charges based solely on the alleged contents of their private conversations, which have been regarded as "hostile propaganda".' Writers and intellectuals were targeted particularly in the early 1980s.'[8]

B. a doctor in a provincial town in Vojvodina agrees. 'For me as a woman,' she says, 'the western feminist phrase that the "personal is political" was completely incomprehensible. When I first heard it I felt it was madness. I guess we saw ourselves in the 80s free-speech movement as anti-politics. I know friends in Slovenia who became "punk" saw themselves as the same.' K., a young clerical worker in Belgrade is also clear: 'We liked the message of Miroslav Krieza, Croatian dissident, about opposing the "two lorries" of the church and nationalism. We also said to the older generation, don't tell us about Croatian culture or Serbian heroism. We want to talk about music and the environment and a future in a wider world. Somehow events totally overtook us.'

V.'s father was beaten several times for his son's beliefs. Yet father and son share a carefully articulated view that politics should be about the People, not the party. One of the original founder members of MOST, V. left because the group became 'mostly psychologists not prepared to deal with structures'. He cites the 15 May 1996 government dismissal of Dragoslav Auramovic as National Bank Governor. Auramovic had by January 1994 been credited with halting the country's hyper-inflation by bringing in the 'super-dinar' (exchange rate 1:1 to the DM). Spontaneous protests erupted as news of his firing spread: in Nicé 10,000 workers were reported wandering in the streets. 'How do we organize action and be heard?' asks V. 'We need training in direct action and we need the belief in ourselves that we can do it.'

> *'In Yugoslavia, you have people growing up from the very beginning thinking that the state is something that is unnatural, it's always against you. What you do for yourself and your family and your friends is always something that is played by common rules. You never break the rules of the common society, but you always break the rules of the official society because they are something that is far away from you. In Yugoslavia, nobody fooled us into thinking that our government was okay, democratically elected, doing things for our benefit. We all knew they were just fuckers who were doing things for themselves. If you say that to ordinary people here, say, "Look, all these politicians are just making money for themselves—they don't give a fuck about you", they'll say, "No, no, we have democracy". But government rules are stupid rules always: they don't have anything to do with common sense. Common sense is that every single person will want to take maximum out of the possibilities that we have, so you just try to see possibilities around you and get them so you can exploit them. That is the whole story.'*
>
> Quote from Goran in Linda Grant.'Citizens of the World'
> *The Guardian Weekend* 13 April 96

For V. the central question is how to motivate people. He sees his past and present as a 'culture of confrontation, with positional (national) parties and an authoritarian regime.' Instead of confronting each other on a regular inter-personal basis, the majority must organise to confront their own rulers. 'Without a culture of participation in a meaningful sense, democracy will mean nothing or the wrong things in this country.'

The 'high politics' legacy

The lamenting of a lack of tradition in participative citizenship, an intrinsic factor to any real 'voluntary sector', is echoed in Croatia. An ERASMUS supporter speaks of the 'mystification of very high politics...We still admire the King, but have no sense of the citizen.' Nostalgic though for a past, earlier outburst of expression, (as is K. above) he adds 'Remember we had Sting in Zagreb in '89, and The Rolling Stones were here in the 70s.'

Franjo Tudjman, of course, was himself sentenced and jailed under the Communists in the early 1980s for a pro-nationalist interview with a group of foreign journalists. The dysfunctional leap from entrenched communist party leadership to extreme nationalist/charismatic ('After Tito, Tito) heads of state in Croatia and Serbia is explained in part by Vedran Vucic[9]:

> *'Although there was some kind of worker's participation in the decision-making process it was impossible to practise genuine participation, since participation is a state of mind and not just behavioural skill. More politically, participation usually means more than just taking parts or taking action.*

It implies active involvement in the taking of decision or the formulating of a policy in a full and fair discussion in which all sides of the question are examined and everyone with anything to contribute has been allowed to have a say. In the communist system any kind of above defined participation is forbidden, and people who tried to truly participate in political process were punished or jailed. So-called self-management was not participation. It was de-concentration of power, rather than decentralization since all laws are (were) passed in the centers.

Presidencies which exercised power of the Central Committees of Communist Party were witnessing inefficiency of their economies which were periodically blocked because of political bottlenecks. Contradictions of the state and political order caused tensions in population. (Namely, inefficiency, corruption of politicians and members of nomenclatura, and privileges irritated the population.)...Furthermore, although political opponents have always been punished, in fact, inefficiency and increasing of oppression strengthened opposition. Unfortunately, depersonalized population was not able to find new alternatives. Moreover, personalized territory, culture, national symbols and nationality became the basis for nationalist tendencies.'

7.8 Control and use of the media: the need for independent journalism and new communications

'The Constitution of the SFRJ of 1974 guaranteed freedom of thought (Article 166) and "freedom of the press, freedom of association, speech and public expression, and freedom of assembly" (Article 167).

'Several days ago—though it is hard to remember dates amidst this endless chaos—national communications ceased. You can no longer telephone from Belgrade to the West; you cannot obtain Zagreb or Ljubljana. Roads have been disrupted and it has become almost impossible to travel. Traffic has ceased.

This breakdown has left communications entirely up to the media. Through Croatian and Belgrade radio and TV, our own Big Brothers create and demonise an enemy, tell us that all others are to be called Ustashi, Chetniks, blood-thirsty murderers, pyromaniacs, monsters. The threat of being blackmailed as a national traitor is raised for those who will not go along. People working in the media know very well that with a short period of intensive propaganda you can incite any group of people. This has been done...

We must not say that the people are at war. The evil has been manufactured. Though war has been taken up, hatred is not stronger than love. Still, we can't be sure. As they sing at the end of 1984: "Under the spreading chestnut tree, I sold you and you sold me."'

Borka Pavicevic, Belgrade, Sept. 1991 (Yugofax 21)

However, the Constitution also contains important restrictions on these, and other fundamental rights, among which are the following: "No one may use the freedoms and rights established by the present constitution in order to disrupt the foundations of the socialist self-management democratic order established by the present Constitution" (from Article 203). This clause of the Constitution provides the theoretical justification for a number of legal provisions which make it possible to imprison individuals for exercising their right to freedom of expression when this freedom is used to oppose or even merely to criticize the established political order.

<u>Freedom of expression and censorship: under the provisions of the law on preventing abuse of freedom of the press and public information</u> (1977) "no one may use the information media to subvert the foundations of the socialist self-management democratic order established by the Constitution of the SFRJ or to jeopardize the independence of the country or to jeopardize peace and egalitarian international co-operation" '(A.I. 1981).

New 'legality': new repression

Croatia held its first multi-party elections in April and May of 1990, while still one of the constituent republics of Yugoslavia. The Milosevic regime in Serbia, bowing to mounting popular pressure, finally legalised alternative political parties in August 1990 and allowed elections in December of that year...

HDZ took over from the ruling communists in Croatia and began its own systematic control and purge of the media. One target area was the Istrian peninsula (Pula, Rijeka) where almost all municipal governments were formed by opposition politicians who defeated HDZ candidates in the 1990 elections. As part of the HDZ's effort to weaken its opponents, it used control of government ministries to shut down alternative sources of information in the area. One of the most striking examples of this occurred in August 1990 when the Croatian Ministry of Information dismissed the director of Pula's radio and television station and suspended the station's operating license (Andrejevich, 1990, A).

Mark Thompson records that within two months of the elections, the Croatian Radio-Television Act was rushed through parliament. The name Radio-Televizija Zagreb was changed to Hrtvatska Radio-Televizija (HRT), making clear its intended role as the media flagship of the nation-state. As a public broadcasting organization, its ownership status did not change: it remained 'state-owned.'

> 'The new law gave parliament the power to appoint and dismiss the director general of HRT; directors of radio and television would be appointed by the government, at the director general's proposal. The incumbent director-general, a Serb by nationality, was quickly replaced by a prominent member of the ruling Croatian Democratic Union (HDZ). The editor-in-chief of new programmes was also replaced. Trade union investigations indicate that about 970 of HRT's 3,500 staff were removed over the next three years' (Thompson, 1994).

Independent Journalism:
The Feral Tribune takes a satirical view of the Dayton Peace Talks, November 1995

KRAMBIN I BRMBIN

FAN CLUB

Kako su dvije najzanimljivije političke figure grada Osijeka, pa i cijele regije, nedvojbeno osječki gradonačelnik Zlatko Kramarić i župan osječko-baranjske županije Branimir Glavaš, imali smo namjeru predložiti im otvaranje na zapadu (a tome težimo, zar ne!?!) vrlo popularnih Fan Clubova. Kako je prvi od njih doktorirao makedonsku književnost, i bavi se književnom kritikom, a ističe da ne zazire od čitanja tekstova različitih žanrova i kvaliteta, čitanje pisama obožavatelja ne bi mu trebao biti veliki problem. A druga navedena osoba toliko je sklona druženju sa širokim narodnim masama (od prognanika do stanovnika Šljivoševaca), tako da smo skloni vjerovati kako bi i on ovakva pisma vrlo rado prihvatio. Fan Club je ideja koja je tek trebala biti predložena, ali kada su neki Osječani čuli za nju jednostavno joj nisu mogli odoljeti. Na njihovu zamolbu objavljujemo ova pisma.

The satirical tone of the text suggests that local leaders Zlatko Kramaric (Mayor) and Branimir Glavas (Sheriff) enjoy such popularity that western-style 'fan clubs' could surely be established in their honour. It also implies, and this is reinforced with the play on the heroes' names to include the word 'bin', that all letters would immediately go into the bin if sent to authority figures!

From the Student Magazine "Unbearable Lightness of Being from Osijek" October 1995, no. 7

Top party officials in Serbia and Croatia were put in charge of the most influential news media and influential independent or semi-independent news media put out of business or taken over in both countries (Danas in Croatia and NIN in Serbia). The director general of Radio-Television Serbia sat on the executive committee of the ruling Socialist Party of Serbia (SPS). A leading HDZ official, Antun Vrdoljak, was director of Croatian Radio and Television at the same time that he was the fourth candidate on the HDZ's election list for parliament. Another HDZ leader Milovan Sibl, was director of the national news agency. In 1992 and 1993 the HDZ imposed its people and general editorial line on several important news media which had struggled to maintain some independence, such as the newspapers *Vecernji list*, *Vjesnik*, and *Slobodan Dalmacija* (Basom, 1996).

Milosevic had taken over Belgrade TV and *Politika* publishing house (an influential group of three daily papers and ten magazines) before making his decisive move to the leadership of the League of Communists of Serbia in 1987. By 1989 he controlled the vast majority of the news media in Serbia and had tightened his control dramatically by extensive purges of editors and reporters in Belgrade TV and in the most influential newspapers and news magazines. The day after the Berlin Wall fell, the top story in the state-run newspapers was that a small town in southern Serbia had made Milosevic an honorary citizen. The Milosevic regime twice banned the opposition newspaper Srpska Rec, allowing only one issue to appear between its founding in May 1990 and the promulgation of the new Serbian constitution on September 28,1990 (Andrejevich, 1990 B).

The largest anti-communist protest in post-Second World War Yugoslavia occurred March 9-13, 1991 when 80,000 to 100,000 demonstrators in downtown Belgrade demanded more airing of opposition views at the state-controlled Serbian media and the dismissal of the Director of Belgrade television (who was a close Milosevic associate) and four other television officials. JNA troops were called in. After two days of violence, the protest was allowed to continue peacefully for three days. The government agreed to meet all the protesters' demands, but it retained most of its control over the major news media. By the summer of 1992, Milorad Vucelic, the director for Radio-TV of Serbia was removing several employees for broadcasting an anti-war song or in other ways deviating too far from SPS-approved policies. The independent news weekly *Vreme* is one of the few alternative sources of information and opinion in Serbia that survived the government onslaught against independent journalism. However, its circulation of under 30,000 is no match in terms of influence among the population for the government's television audience of approximately three million (Basom, 1996).

In his book *Media Beyond Socialism* (1994) Slavko Splichal cites Yugoslavia as an 'exception' to the east-central European late 1980s' 'authoritarian model' of broadcasting. He cites the emergent 'right to publish opinions' which began to feature (particularly in Slovenia) at the end of that decade of political and economic transition. The turn-around by both new regimes (Zagreb and Belgrade) meant regressive measures.*

Free expression—cultural or political—was strangled at birth. In June 1992 in an appeal to journalists' associations world-wide, the Association of Reporters of Croatia claimed that over 100 journalists, both Serbian and Croatian, had recently left Croatia because they were unable to work normally and feared physical abuse; that eight reporters had been fired from Radio Rijeka, 17 from Radio Osijek, and 55 from the Zagreb daily *Vjesnik*. According to the appeal, 'reporters of Croatian nationality who refuse blind obedience to the authorities are exposed to the most drastic persecution'. 650 employees had been dismissed from *Croatian Television*, and the Belgrade dailies *Politika* and *Borba*, the news agency *Tanjug*, and the Skopje daily *Nova Makedonija*, had all been forced to close down their offices in Zagreb, Split, Osijek and Rijeka. By February 1993 journalists at the radio station *B—92 Belgrade* were receiving death threats (*Index on Censorship* 5 & 6, 1993)

In Vojvodina 76 Novi Sad TV employees were sent on 'paid leave'. They included writer Laszlo Vegel (a member of the Supervisory Committee in the recent elections), and the Vojvodina Minister for Minority Issues, Ferenc Deak. It was reported that the Serbian authorities had banned the use of Hungarian place-names by Novi Sad radio, and that staff using them were being dismissed.

By 1994 Splichal (p.144) would write that while the traditional paternalistic or even authoritarian model of broadcasting favours the interests of elites in power and enables them to transmit their ideas, attitudes, and instructions to the people, a similar position was taken by the new anti-communist ideologies and groupings in power. If one compared Serbia, where the former Communist Party (now Socialist Party) was still in power, and Croatia, with the straight anti-communist government of the HDZ, one would find hardly any difference in terms of media regulation. In both countries, which

* Slovenia, for its own part, went through its own independent way—in terms of press and information technology freedom as well.

did not obviously share common ideals and objectives, the media were subject to a similar form of political control and censorship. Croatian and Serbian television were comparable in how biased their reporting was when related to 'national interests' (e.g., the war). Alternative 'civil' voices had no official entry points[10].

In Forging War (1994) Mark Thompson is scathing and direct in his views on the shaping of society for an (un)civil war:

> 'National consensuses had to be formed, and the media were a crucial tool. Media "campaigns" served as the forerunner of military campaigns; verbal violence engendered physical violation. The task was not easy. Many media were purged of independence and dissent, in brutal ways that anticipated the purging ("cleansing") of territories. It was the fruit of several years' labour by government, which used its power to marshal media workers who either volunteered for nationalist service (through conviction) or were press-ganged (by economic pressure, fear of professional isolation, reprisals, or ingrained habits of obedience). Journalists who opposed the government faced marginalisation or, in government-controlled media, demotion and sacking, while others departed in the face of government pressure' (p.2).

7.9 From social movement to NGOs

> *'Professionalization led to passivization'*
>
> J. K., Vojvodinan peace activist, referring to 'NGO' forms emerging from the anti-war movement.

'A true movement,' says Jasenka K. aged 28 of Pancevo, ' must encompass people of different backgrounds. At the beginning of this war the peace movement was a successor of the green movement, but it also drew on the dissident tradition, on religious and ecumenical groups, and on what I would call the emotional people; the people who didn't want to kill or be killed.' From Nov. '91 to Aug. '94 Jasenka attended candle-lit vigils (against the war) in her town's main square every day. After that for a year she managed every weekend. She and a handful of other women overcame both extremes of freezing winter weather and hot mosquito-ridden humidity in summer. 'We stopped when we realized we had no effect.'

Jasenka says that the local Authority were co-operative at first. 'Very often policemen were visibly kind' in giving permits for special organised demonstrations. "We had a passive local government which knew there was no "critical mass" of protest, but which continually monitored the situation.' Later, as sanctions began to bite into the local economy, she was openly called a 'traitor' by colleagues at work. Eventually a silent 'boycott' drove her to leave her job. Regarding the war, Jasenka now says bluntly 'We didn't do anything. Tomorrow it will happen again.' Today she works for a major British relief charity distributing food and blankets, 'always blankets', to refugees from Western Slavonia who have settled in makeshift camps and requisitioned buildings nearby.

The rite of metamorphosis or mutation from 'grass roots' organisation or 'social movement' to 'NGO' is a subject of much private soul-searching and little debate in Croatia and Serbia; perhaps even less among external donors, intervenors, or interested observers. Suncokret, which began in 1992 with students and peace activists responding as volunteers to the needs of refugees, had in its origins both social radicalism and an anti-war stance[11]. By 1995 it was sufficiently well organised, UNHCR affiliated, and established to refuse public opposition to Operations 'Lightning' and 'Storm'[12] The Centre for Peace in Osijek had pause in autumn 1995 to reconsider its altered role and status. While lamenting the loss of a community/volunteer support base, they could boast USAID funding and centre members having received training in NGO development and management in the USA, Sweden and Germany. Across 'the line' from Osijek to Baranja, the fledgling peace office based at the Agricultural College at Darda had in its library a Yugoslav government publication listing NGOs in Belgrade. Called "Guide Book for Refugees' it is an English version, published in 1995. It lists everything from Mother and Baby health groups to the Humanitarian Law Centre and even ECHO offices.

In the words of Mirko Mandrino, peace activist and engineer, of Pancevo, 'When we started[13], the term NGO was known only from Western UN documents. Now it means anything not connected to government. Pilot clubs, church groups, women's groups, spiritual groups, psychology groups, peace groups. From nothing we have gone to everything.'[14] In Mandrino's view, there was a progression during the war from the time when Belgrade peace leaders proclaimed direct action ('street manifestation') to the time of 'The Project'. It is The Project which commands respect from Western European donors. It is The Project which will have its own experts, budgets, and core planning.

Paul Stubbs (1996) points out that: '...there is terminological confusion about what is meant by Non Governmental Organisations, and an increasingly polarised, debate about their role. There is a real disjunction between US and UK terminology: the former emphasising "non-profit organisations" and the latter "non-governmental organisations". NGO's in Western Europe have tended to be studied by sociologists, in Central and Eastern Europe by political scientists, and in the South (Africa, Latin America, and so on) by specialists in developmental studies. There is little common ground or agreement between these disciplines and, of course, huge questions about whether one term can encompass such a range of different cultural, economic and political contexts. Alternatives which have been offered: "the independent sector", "the third sector", "the voluntary sector", contain as many, if not more, problems.'

By using the term NGO, the biggest problem is that when defining organisations as 'not government', there is an implicit pull to the nation state as level of analysis, rather than a comparative or globalised context. The term 'NGO' includes organisations which work throughout the world—Oxfam, for example, (whose mandate includes 'the relief of suffering arising as a result of war or any other cause in any part of the world'[15], now works in some 65 countries in Africa, Asia, the Middle East, Latin America and the Caribbean, and Eastern Europe and the former Soviet Union[16],) as well as small associations of citizens working, for example, to prevent crime on a housing estate in Inner London. Any group of persons with a task or objective not overtly governmental may seemingly qualify. And yet funding links for the same may well trace back to governments.

In a major study on complex emergencies undertaken for UNICEF in 1994, Mark Duffield wrote that compared to the Horn of Africa, there were relatively few NGOs in the Former Yugoslavia: 'most have arrived since the beginning of 1993. NGO geographical distribution is uneven. While there are exceptions, especially the established French relief agencies, as a rule of thumb NGOs are concentrated in the physically secure and less politically sensitive regions. The majority therefore are in Croatia while there are very few in Serbia and Bosnian Serb areas' (Duffield, 1994).

Of Bosnia Duffield wrote that there were around 65 NGOs but only about 40 of these could be said to be operational. Most confined their operations to the relatively secure areas. There were consequently few or none in places like Sarajevo, Zenica and Mostar East.

'It is difficult to make general conclusions about NGOs in Voivodina, but NGOs which were formed as a reaction to the war (except the humanitarian one), have been extremely active in both wars (Croatia and Bosnia and Herzegovina), but their current activities are few or with changed contents. In the same time, the enormous influence they had in the country and abroad, is now reduced to participation in some international seminars. Most of them, being isolated, is seeking for the forms of future activities. The government and its media have turned to peaceful option, thus accepting the attitudes which the NGOs had been pleading and suffered repression for. What we have to bear in mind is the fact that they were striving not only for cessation of the war, but for conscientious objection, for international co-operation and tolerance too. The actual regime has never supported these principles and consequently paves the way of the future activities of NGOs. We mustn't forget the war still goes on. But the influence of these NGOs have been reduced and their future is uncertain. Regarded the conditions of their formation, we simply hope there won't be reasons for the activities they were carrying out during the war.

So far, the influence of the NGOs has been limited to certain social circles of educated young people. Other citizens are, in one way or another, acquainted with their work, but only a few of them know exactly what their aims are and how they function. In other words, these organizations haven't succeeded to impose their attitudes to public. Moreover they haven't managed to use their independent magazine "The Independent" to promote their activities in the best possible way. Some new initiatives, such as new magazines, radio stations or joint manifestations would certainly help their promotion. Their influence would be more extensive, if they achieved actual advances on the local level. Undoubtedly, their influence is obvious, but limited in the circles of their followers and sympathizers (in some cases on the international level). The NGOs are not the only ones to be blamed for their limited influence. In the situation when the middle class has been going through the process of marginalisation and pauperization, when national, rather than civil option has been prevailing, when access to media is limited, without supportive institutions, financial or professional help, it can hardly be expected to achieve more.'

Kostic, 1994

There was a distinct new generation of small NGOs, some formed specifically for the crisis in the Balkans. French and British agencies were well-represented in this trend, such NGOs including Sans Limites, British Direct Aid, Intervener, Bosnia Aid, Atlas, Edinburgh Direct Aid, The Serious Road Trip and Children in Crisis. Initially most of the new NGOs operated outside of the UNHCR system.

Duffield's report observed and anticipated problems distinct to the ex-Yugoslavia area:

> 'NGOs wishing to establish projects have to get clearance from the political authorities. Conditions vary however. In Croatia NGOs have to get authorization from the government's Office of Displaced Persons and Refugees (ODPR) for all activity. This is in addition to any local agreements. Food aid, however, is subject to few restrictions. Shelter and health is different. ODPR retains allocation rights in any shelter programme and there are also restrictions in health... In contrast, probably because needs are greater and fewer agencies operate, Bosnia is relatively free of controls. In the main agreements are with individual civil authorities on a project by project basis.
>
> Owing to the emergence of new NGOs, a characteristic of the Former Yugoslavia which contrasts with Africa is that many agencies have arrived with no funding. In Croatia, the EU is an important source of funds. Indeed, on the grounds of neutrality the EU operates a policy of only channelling its considerable support through European NGOs. This is another factor which has shaped geographical concentration. Indeed, some fear that there may be too many NGOs operating in Croatia. Since they tend to take over direct responsibility for individual camps or areas there is a danger of both undermining civil capacity and fragmenting service delivery...'(Duffield, 1994).

Branislava Kostic is precise about the emergence of NGOs in Yugoslavia:

> 'NGOs in Voivodina were formed and registered for the first time in 1990, in the form of associations of citizens, where legal conditions in our country were created (27th of July, 1990). This particular Law/Act does not recognize the term "NGO". Instead, the terms, such as "associations of citizens and social organizations" were used, without a precise distinction between them. It is interesting that, the formation of the political organizations was allowed by the same law and regulations. An important effect was achieved: not using the term "NGO" created an impression of continuity of "social organizing" which had been existing in times of communists, and the work of associations of citizens was treated as political organizing. The Law/Act regulates, very precisely, the aspects of organizing, necessary documents for work or cessation of work of an organization. The precise demands of these regulations, thus, define elements of internal structure of organizations (article 2 of the Act).'

Kostic points out that such legislation was a kind of invitation for the 'social organisations' which had been existing in times of communists to re-register. Most of them (trade unions, ecological movements, humanitarian organisations, Young researchers of Voivodina) did so. Although only a few NGOs in Voivodina originate from former social organisations, the tradition of social organising had an influence on certain NGOs. The most important characteristics of the former social organisations were:

- budget financing
- hierarchical internal structure
- precisely defined place in the socio-political system.

She refers to 'forms of recidivism of the past': those organisations which are carrying out the same activities the former organisations used to deal with (ecological groups and 'independent' trade unions). Most of these keep clear internal hierarchy and insist upon formal connections with authorities, regional or local.

Both writing in 1994, Duffield recorded 65 NGOs in Croatia and Kostic listed 51 in Vojvodina. The latter was an internal study and included many small localised groups as well as independent trade unions.

By 1996 the International Council of Voluntary Agencies had published its own directory of agencies operating in ex-Yugoslavia[18]. A rough count of their data indicates the following number of NGO's:

Serbia (Yugoslavia) 61
Croatia 243
Bosnia/Herzegovina 300+

7.10 From protest to proposal writing

Primary social groups early in the war linked with outsiders (or second track intervenors) who brought an anti-war or alternative society impetus with them—BSV, WRI, BPP, CCCRTE trainers and activists, for example, came with ideas for campaigning, for group work, for training or organising in an empowered way. As a rule initially such incomers came freely to groups which functioned voluntarily. If there was a 'voluntary

Quotations on the NGO question

'Far from "democratising development", NGOs are often the providers of palliatives to competing factions in conflict... Rather than promoting accountability, NGOs are perhaps "dancing to the tune of the prince", whether the prince is a government, an insurgency movement, or a local war lord. We should scrutinise and challenge the assumptions underpinning the mythology about NGOs; and donors should base their actions on a realistic assessment of NGOs capabilities, rather than on the suppositions of "NGO lore".' (Goodhand and Chamberlain, 1996).

'I cannot understand how the voluntary sector suddenly found itself co-opted into obligatory importing terminology which incorporates the baggage of neo-Hegelianism. Words become reified, and take on constructed meanings unrepresentative of what we are doing...' (Alan Pleydell, re. 'NGOs' and Civil Society, personal conversation, 3 July, 1996).

'The basic assumption is that support for such activities and for local civil society will promote pluralism and that transition will come from within or from below. However, although many NGOs certainly meet a need, and individuals benefit from some of their work, they cannot change deep structural factors. Additionally, NGOs can be described as private bodies working on public functions, but without accountability or responsibility to the public. In the former Yugoslavia, some NGOs are taking over services which should be provided by the state.'

Jens Stillhoff Sorensen, 1997

sector' in ex-Yugoslavia it existed briefly in 1991 and 1992. As the war moved 'Next Door', as indeed for post-Dayton Bosnia BiH (where newly partitioned entities eyed each other nervously as 'next door') the emphasis shifted to social reconstruction; self chosen or donor led.

Whereas early contacts for resources might have meant small grants, a fax machine or paper, volunteers for Suncokret, etc. , the new 'NGO development training' meant project design and proposal writing on a major scale. Given the correct theme or emphasis, projects usually consisted of financial assistance for offices, equipment or project running costs; legal or psycho-social assistance; and training seminars, workshops; and materials, brochures, leaflets and so on.

A degree of conformity was necessary to submit project proposals: English or German languages were needed, as was formal registration with the state. An influx of funding inevitably changed the face of what aspired-for 'civil society' might look like.

A well known peace centre in Croatia, for example, organised a weeks events on the theme of peace culture and civil society in 1993 working on a 'shoe string budget'. Local displaced and refugee communities were involved, an women given the ingredients to bake traditional festive cakes and pastries. Children were involved in pavement art and co-operative games. Townspeople of all ages joined (if shyly) in circle dancing and music events. even the Croatian army loaned huge cooking pots and observed in a non-threatening way. Two years later a similar event was repeated.

This time peace group participants had resources at their disposal, grants from USAID, from the Royal Netherlands Embassy Zagreb, and up to 20 other European donors. The proposal writing had been good. Activists were now professionals, budgeting for their time, claiming for their roles as translators, as hosts to international quests, as organisers. What had been a peace group was now a fully fledged NGO. But their format and constituency for the week had changed. Now events looked more to talks by religious leaders, to holistic spiritual approaches, counselling, dialogue, meditation and panel discussions. It left the impression that Sorenson is correct when he suggests that

> 'The local NGO sector is primarily the creation of an urban middle class, which has been squeezed in the social transformation in the new republics. With polarisation increasing as the privatisation process in the newly-created ethnic states rewards supporters of the ruling party, what remains of the politicised middle class can find a new niche in NGOs' (Sorensen, 1997).

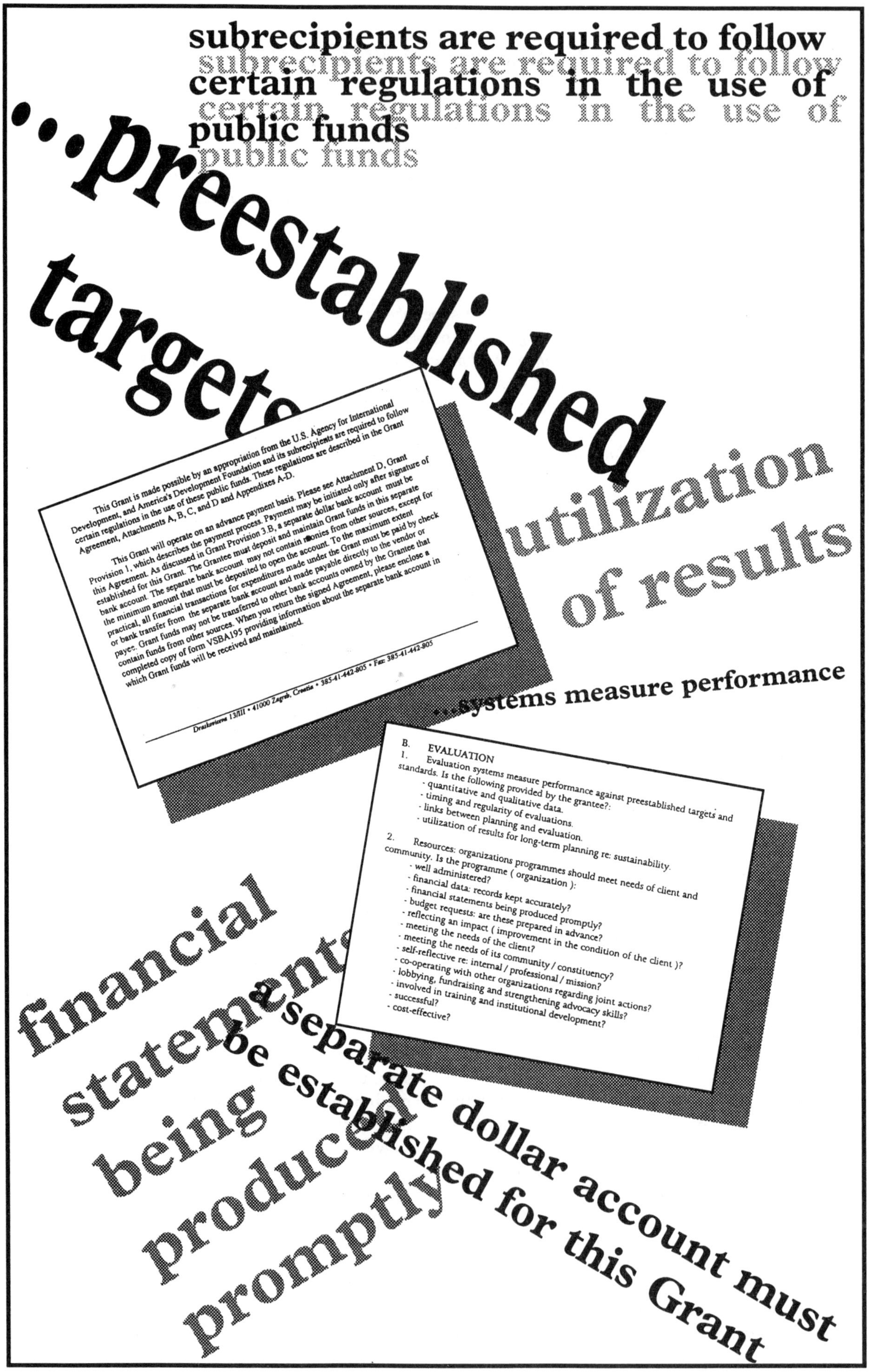
subrecipients are required to follow certain regulations in the use of public funds
subrecipients are required to follow certain regulations in the use of public funds
...preestablished targets
This Grant is made possible by an appropriation from the U.S. Agency for International Development, and America's Development Foundation and its subrecipients are required to follow certain regulations in the use of these public funds. These regulations are described in the Grant Agreement, Attachments A, B, C, and D and Appendixes A-D.
This Grant will operate on an advance payment basis. Please see Attachment D, Grant Provision 1, which describes the payment process. Payment may be initiated only after signature of this Agreement. As discussed in Grant Provision 3.B, a separate dollar bank account must be established for this Grant. The Grantee must deposit and maintain Grant funds in this separate bank account. The separate bank account may not contain monies from other sources, except for the minimum amount that must be deposited to open the account. To the maximum extent practical, all financial transactions for expenditures made under the Grant must be paid by check or bank transfer from the separate bank account and made payable directly to the vendor or payee. Grant funds may not be transferred to other bank accounts owned by the Grantee that contain funds from other sources. When you return the signed Agreement, please enclose a completed copy of form VSBA195 providing information about the separate bank account in which Grant funds will be received and maintained.
Draskoviceva 13/III • 41000 Zagreb, Croatia • 385-41-442-805 • Fax: 385-41-442-805
utilization of results
...systems measure performance
B. EVALUATION
1. Evaluation systems measure performance against preestablished targets and standards. Is the following provided by the grantee?:
- quantitative and qualitative data.
- timing and regularity of evaluations.
- links between planning and evaluation.
- utilization of results for long-term planning re: sustainability.
2. Resources: organizations programmes should meet needs of client and community. Is the programme (organization):
- well administered?
- financial data: records kept accurately?
- financial statements being produced promptly?
- budget requests: are these prepared in advance?
- reflecting an impact (improvement in the condition of the client)?
- meeting the needs of the client?
- meeting the needs of its community / constituency?
- self-reflective re: internal / professional / mission?
- co-operating with other organizations regarding joint actions?
- lobbying, fundraising and strengthening advocacy skills?
- involved in training and institutional development?
- successful?
- cost-effective?
financial statements being produced promptly
a separate dollar account must be established for this Grant

It was not only 'privatisation' squeezing the middle classes, or the entire population, but in the case of Serbia the Embargo. Milos Vasi (1995) states that sanctions achieved their usual result: redistribution of social wealth: 'There is no more middle class in Serbia. Five percent of the population is exceedingly rich; 95 % barely survives.' Indeed, it was former television broadcasters, teachers, economists, scientists, lawyers etc. who co-operated in Novi Sad with Hungarian Interchurch Aid and the Ecumenical Forum of European Christian women (and others) to form humanitarian NGOs. An independently formed pharmacy using basic donated medications (aspirin, pain-killers, antiseptic cream, anti-seizure tablets, etc.) saw over 1,000 people during a one week visit I had to Novi Sad in 1994. State run pharmacies were simply bankrupt.

(The impact of the Embargo on the population of sanctioned Serbia is a subject fully deserving study in itself. For brief additional notes on this, see Appendix 4 and Maricic, 'A visit to Serbia' at the end of this chapter.)

Sorensen also points out that NGO's which attract more funds can become 'top dog in relation to other NGOs, and either take them under their wing or crowd them out of the competition.' (ibid.) Less well financed NGOs are usually found outside the capital, in rural or less accessible areas, markedly as per Crepaja, Zrenjanin and Kikinda in Vojvodina. The ability to attract funds is not necessarily connected to validity of purpose or capability. There is thus almost a 'centre-periphery' problem in NGO formation. As provincial capitals both Osijek and Subotica served as major focus points for some donors, as have ARK Zagreb and CAA Belgrade. Small initiatives need an affiliation to larger ones if they are to survive in 'NGO' form[19].

Form and Content

Zoran Ostric writing in 1994 created some categories and abbreviations for NGOs :

- ICSO—Independent Civil Society Organisation
- OCPP—Organisation Connected with Political Party
- OMG—Organisation Manipulated by Government
- GONGO—Governmental NGO (or false NGO)

Notes from Jane Longville

'Social Reconstruction and Social Development: An Agenda for Change?'

International Conference, Zagreb, Croatia 21 May 1996

Evident at the conference were the valuable attempts made by the formation of local non-government organisations at the outbreak of war and their endeavours to address the needs of the flood of displaced people and refugees in Croatia. They shared languages, cultural understanding and kinship with their despairing communities and in this way generated trust and hope. But, their voice was unanimous in their feelings of restriction by their lack of 'status' and recognition by the international organisations working in Croatia.

It became clear from the outset that the scale of the situation would necessitate an international response from both government and non-government agencies. As Dr. Vesna Bosnak, UNICEF, so rightly expressed, the unfortunate label of the involvement of international organisations, is that they are seen to have the capacity to rectify all situations by their influence and resources. Hence, pressure was exerted on the international humanitarian aid agencies to utilise their expertise, training and seemingly unlimited material resources to respond in a timely and effective manner. These 'elite' agencies were then seen by the operating local organisations as disempowering local potential by their ability to override and flood the aid market.

'ARK operates first and foremost in a civil society, aiming to eliminate tensions and intolerance in inter-personal (and especially in inter-ethnic) relations... All ARK's actions are strictly neutral in a party political sense. ARK does not promote any particular political program, but rather the principles of peace-loving, democratic and just resolutions of conflicts, tensions and social problems in general.'

ARK, 1994, 3, Zagreb

'The battle to build a civil society is a priority for CAA. This includes not only teaching the standards of conduct in a civil society, but also the education of non-violent crisis resolution, the development of a spirit of tolerance and forming a civil conscience.'

CAA Bulletin, Bulletin 10. 1996, Belgrade

'For almost half a century, politics had been a sham and had bred a bone-deep cynicism...'

'The decades-long experiment in workers' self-management was not merely a sham. It did substantially limit the powers of managers and it did involve large numbers of workers, over prolonged periods of time, in managing their own enterprises. The basic weakness was that all these experiments, good and bad, were brought in from the top down by the party. They thus provided no genuine sense of empowerment and responsibility that victories gained in prolonged political and economic struggles bring to the mass of the people.

The League's systematic repression of a normal development of responsible opposition groups, journals, and parties created an intellectual and moral desert. That human-made desert became a happy hunting ground for charlatans, adventurers, and demagogues who came to prominence overnight as the system collapsed. There had been no time to develop alternate views an politics to be tested in debate and mutual criticism.'

Denitch, 1993

He cites ARK as an ICSO. For an OMG one thinks of the eventual fate of SOS Telefon Osijek, whose lines were disconnected in August 1995, only to be reinstated when the initiative was co-opted by local (Glavas) government. Pupavac (1997) cites Friends of the Children of Serbia, formerly part of the young Pioneers organisation, as an example of a state organisation becoming an internationally funded NGO. An NGO form tells us nothing about its actual content. Croatia, Serbia and BiH all levy fees (taxes) on local NGOs for registration which makes them into an income generating project for each state. The Tudjman government attempted legislation in 1996 to make it mandatory for a government representative to sit on each NGO board. As yet this has not been enacted, largely because of the opposition this generated.

The very form of proposals and a strong dependence on project-based funding puts pressure on NGOs to legitimise their projects and present them as successful in self-evaluation and reporting[20]. Thus the critical assessments which can be made in the field rarely take place, learning from experience is not a driving force, and the exercise becomes one of justification and self-perpetuation[21].

Finally, given the cycle of proposals, budgets, funding sources and donor led relationships, the form of 'local NGOs' may be foreign in that it does not relate to the local economy for viability or support.

7.11 The problems with NGOs

This study of second track intervention sits in tandem with a time frame which is also claimed as a 'relief to development' continuum in emergent schools of social policy and conflict reduction thinking. (See Chapter I). 'Civilian Implementation' of the Dayton Agreement (Annex 10) has in practice used NGO development as a means for building local capacity and civil society, as evidenced in OSCE democratisation programmes[22] and the co-operation of UNHCR with the Independent Bureau for Humanitarian Issues (IBHI) which conducts training programmes in NGO development, co-ordination, management and networking[23]. OSCE documentation (ibid.) even states that 'such a local network of civic initiatives throughout the whole country provides the strongest local support in the long run for the bottom-up democratization process when all the international organisations leave BiH.' Such programmes may be seen alongside Croatian and Serbian counterparts with sponsorship from international agencies including Soros funds, the National Democratic Institute (Washington D.C.) USAID, and others. UNDP strongly supports what it calls 'preventative development':

> 'Post-conflict reconstruction indeed amounts to establishing new governance structures which duly reflect the broad and diverse concerns of civil society as a whole, based on the will of the people to reconcile and to address and redress the problems which caused the very conflict.' [24]

Positive as this is in intention, and indeed a welcome departure for many from 'top down' peace settlement enforcement ideas, there are nevertheless problems inherent in this approach in the *experience* of primary social groups in ex-Yugoslavia. Firstly, you cannot programme reconciliation. Secondly, 'the problems which caused the very conflict' included personalities intent on the abuse of power and heavily militarised conditions for exactly this. Many of these personalities are still in office, still moving about freely, and may be seen as enjoying the rewards of their enterprises. Arkan in Belgrade and Dario Kordic in Zagreb are cases in point at time of writing[25]. Thirdly the work of Smillie (1996), Duffield (1996, 1997), the work of Paul Stubbs and the Leeds Metropolitan University Social Policy Research Unit (1996), the survey conducted by Dave Bekkering of Gorni Vakuf, Sorensen's reflections (1997) conversations with activists and indeed MIRAMIDA 'brainstorms' *all call into question the danger of equating civil society with service delivery or functional form only*. Kostic (1994) commented on both the service niche and competitiveness problem in her study, stating that 'If such circumstances last long enough, NGOs as a form of articulation of future civil society and democratic option could meet a failure in this region.'

7.12 Conclusion

Even in post-war or 'war next door' situations development projects are neither designed nor implemented in a vacuum nor purely because people ask for them. They are part of a broader context of which they form an integral part. Within that context are four broad categories of constraint and influence: donor foreign policy, national politics, macro-economic policy and the local environment. (Gow and Morse 1988) Development assistance through its ensuing programmes and projects is thus 'quintessentially political' (ibid.) since it deals with the allocation of scarce resources among competing groups and because it articulates certain goals and objectives. Donor governments will have long term diplomatic goals (i.e. in this case they would prefer a peaceful ex-Yugoslav region, the reduction of threat of hostility to the surrounding areas, Kosovo, Macedonia, Albania, Greece, etc. normalcy in relations and trade, and so forth). They also have short term goals to alleviate suffering (altruism plus the desire for a quiet life vis a vis the electorate who know so much via CNN these days) and to enable post communist economic restructuring of the region. Seen in this light, all development assistance becomes a tool of foreign policy, and the divide between development studies and international relations has perhaps always been a manufactured and slightly artificial one.

At point of delivery of aid, projects and funding will be of interest to various groups, and can also be politicised in the host country. An economically successful local group may be viewed with envy or hostility and cease to do what it does in a successful manner. Or it may cultivate a manner of operating which uses the language of 'democracy' but in fact functions as a client of the donor, and\or of the donor state. The deliverers of some projects will also be affected. Types of conflict training groups, for example, which began as a voluntary network, sought funding as a training body, and now ensure full payment for trainers. So there is mixed interest and gain all along the way.

In a society influenced by heavily militarised structures, the penalising of free speech and systematic attacks on independent media, 'civil society' was an ideal, an aspiration towards something representing less authoritarianism, more participation, free speech and independent media. As an ideal it informed actions and aspirations. It has become caught up in the restructuring of ex-Yugoslavia less as an ideal than as a project in itself to be implemented. Perhaps ideals are better nurtured over time than "operationalized' as project outputs. If 'civil society' is a contested concept, the essence of the debate should be not the term itself, but its reification and application by a donor community in a hurry to put things right.

Notes for Chapter VII

1. Helsinki Final Act 1975

2. 'As a first approximation we can say that civil society is the place where economic, social, ideological and religious conflicts originate and occur and that state institutions have the task of solving them either by mediating or preventing or repressing them. The agents of these conflicts and therefore of civil society proper...are social classes (or, more broadly, the groups, movements, associations and organizations that represent them or declare themselves their representatives); as well as class organizations there are interest groups, associations of various types with social and indirectly political ends, ethnic emancipation movements, civil rights groups, women's liberation, youth movement and so on. Parties...in reality do not entirely belong either in civil society or the state' (N. Bobbio. 1989. *Democracy and Dictatorship: The Nature and Limits of State Power* p. 25).

3. Interview with Miroslav Samardzic in Zrenjanin, May 1996.

4. 'Yes, anti-political politics is possible. Politics from "below." Politics of the people, not of the apparatus.

   Politics growing from the heart, not from a thesis. It is no accident that this hopeful experiment has to be lived just here, on this grim battlefield. In conditions of humdrum "everydayness" we have to descend to the very bottom of the well before we can see the stars' (Vaclav Havel, 1988. 'Anti-Political Politics'. In *Civil Society and the State*, edited by John Keane, p. 398. London and New York: Verso).

5. Interview with Ute Caspers, Heidelberg, February 1996.

6. 'From this perspective, and in contrast to stable Western democracies, disintegration of the political state could be countered, perhaps paradoxically in terms of traditional conceptions, by societal reintegration stemming from civil society—from educational, scientific, and cultural institutions; churches; communications media; professional organizations; and interest groups. As I argued earlier, the specific importance of civil society in post socialist countries is based on the fact that political (r)evolutions and the inauguration of parliamentary democracy resulted from "intellectual opposition" developed within civil society. Autonomous groups of civil society succeeded in destroying and delegitimizing the former one-party political system in the late 1980s, but the new system is still in the process of formation. The moral power of civil society seems to be strong enough to re-integrate society beyond political institutions, following the patterns of previous transformations initiated by civil society, especially by defining "key issues" to be discussed and institutionally resolved. Certainly, the formation of the new system also depends on the behavior of other actors affecting the system state' (Splichal, 1994, p. 143).

7. See 'Warfare is only an Invention—Not a Biological Necessity,' Margaret Mead's classic essay in *War: Studies form Psychology, Sociology and Anthropology*, edited by L. Bramson and G. Goethals, 1968 New York and London: Basic Books. From the same volume, Mark May, "War, Peace, and Social Learning.' A more recent contribution to the debate is Robert Hinde, 'Human Aggression: Biological Propensities and Social Forces' in *A Reader in Peace Studies*, edited by P. Smoker, R. Davies and B. Munske (1990). Oxford: Pergamon Press. See also *The Seville Statement on Violence*, UNESCO 1991.

8. One of the most important 'show trials' of the decade (still cited frequently by interviewees in Serbia) in 1995 was the trial of six Belgrade intellectuals: Vladimir Mijanovic (previously sentenced in 1971 and 1973); Miodrag Milic, Dragomir Olujic; Gordan Janovic; Pavlusko Imsirovic and Milan Nikolic (the last two were former prisoners of conscience sentenced in 1972).

   'Their trials followed a police raid in April 1984 on a private apartment in Belgrade where 28 people had assembled to hear a talk by Milovan Djilas. This was a meeting of the so-called "Open University"—one of the unofficial discussion groups which, with the knowledge of the authorities, had been meeting in similar circumstances for at least seven years without any official harassment. In the indictment the six were accused, among other things, of having formed a group which aimed to change the social and political system and get rid of the present government, and of holding meetings at which, both orally and in writing, they had attacked "the heritage of the liberation struggle, the building of socialism and the character and acts of Tito."'

   The trial began on 5 November 1984 and finished on 4 February 1985 after considerable world press coverage. Support for the defendants was widespread, both internally and externally, and over 30 petitions on their behalf, 18 of them originating in Yugoslavia, were sent to the authorities.

   See: *Yugoslavia: prisoners of conscience—An Amnesty International Report* A.I. Publications UK. 1985

9. Personal communication, December 1992.

10. 'Sarajevo was a site of conflict, but the daily bombardment of the city by Serb forces was not mentioned for two months. The fact of a siege was not denied, it was turned inside out. "The Muslim authorities are holding Sarajevo under siege from within," said reporter Rada Djokic, adding, "The Serbs continue to defend their centuries-old hills around Sarajevo." According to Petar Lukovic of the Belgrade independent weekly Vreme, it was not until 31 May 1992, four days after the bread-queue massacre in Sarajevo, that Serbian television first revealed that Serb forces were bombarding Sarajevo— "broadcast[ing] the statement of the Serbian government denouncing the 'bombardment of Sarajevo by the Serbian forces,'" according to Lukovic, in a desperate effort to forestall the imposition of UN sanctions against Serbia' (*The Media in Serbia, Croatia and Bosnia-Herzegovina* by Mark Thompson p. 5. An Article 19 Publication adapted by I.W.P.R. Insert in Balkan War Report June/July 1994, No. 27).

11. See 'Suncokret Update' 15 May 1993 on beginnings and grassroots relief orientation, Marusevacka 8, 41000 Zagreb.

12. 'What Now?', paper by Vesna Terselic ARK circulated with a list of Croatian organisations speaking out against the offensives. Sept., 1995.

13. This refers to anti-war demonstrations in 1991.

14. Personal interview, May 1996.

15. Whittaker B (1983) *A Bridge of People: a personal view of Oxfam's first forty years.* Heinemann.

16. Oxfam Supporter Services(1995) *Oxfam at Work Overseas 1994-5.* Oxford

    See Deacon B, with Stubbs P and Hulse M (1996) *Globalism and Social Policy Ch. 6: Non-Governmental Organisations and Global Social Policy in Conditions of Conflict* Sage, forthcoming.

17. Popular parlance now sometimes includes MANGOs and BUNGOs. MANGOs are Mafia-affiliated NGOs. BUNGOs are agencies which 'bungi-jump' in and out of emergencies.

18. The ICVA Directory Sarajevo, Sept. 1996. (International Council of Voluntary Agencies).

19. Kostic, 1994: 'For example, Banat Forum and Crepaja for Peace have no developed international contacts, while NGOs affiliated to Open University do. Organizations, such as peace groups, which were formed as a reaction to actual social situation, are now disappearing or looking for new orientations, due to changed circumstances. Although the war still continues, a certain stagnation in their work, specially in small towns, has already been noticed.'

20. See 'Recent Changes in the International Relief System.' ODI Briefing Paper. January 1993, London.

21. Papavac (1997) makes the following wry observation:

    'Local organisations which receive foreign funding seem to be very conscious of not biting the hand that feeds them. For example, the Centre for Anti-War Action in Belgrade, unlike practically everybody else, including UN officials and European politicians, has not wanted to criticise the UN and European policies in the region. Its publication *Warfare, Patriotism, Patriarchy,* sponsored by the international NGOs CARE, Causes Commune and the Soros Foundation, not only attacked the nationalist content of school history textbooks in Serbia, but also the textbooks' criticism of European Union and UN policies in the Balkans. Its reluctance to criticise is perhaps not surprising considering that it used to be just a small marginalised peace group but despite this, thanks to foreign funding, today they boast an impressive number of computers and faxes. When I first visited their offices, they looked like most offices in Belgrade—shabby and in need of repair. However when I went back there in September 1994, workmen were busy installing marble flooring!'

22. See 'An OSCE invitation to potential donors: an introduction to the Civil Society in Bosnia' (1996) OSCE Sarajevo.

23. See 'Strengthening Local Capacity' in UNHCR *Information Notes on Former Yugoslavia* No. 11 Nov. 1995 p. v (Zagreb).

24. Quotation from *Post Conflict Reconstruction Strategies* UN Dept. for Development Support and Management Services and UN Industrial Development Organization Colloquium, Stadtschlaining 23—24 June, 1995.

25. See 'War Criminals left free to walk the Streets' by Ed Vulliamy *The Observer,* 17 Aug. 1997.

    Also, 'Three Tasks That Remain in Bosnia' by Kemal Kurspahic in *The International Herald Tribune* 19—20 Oct. 1996.

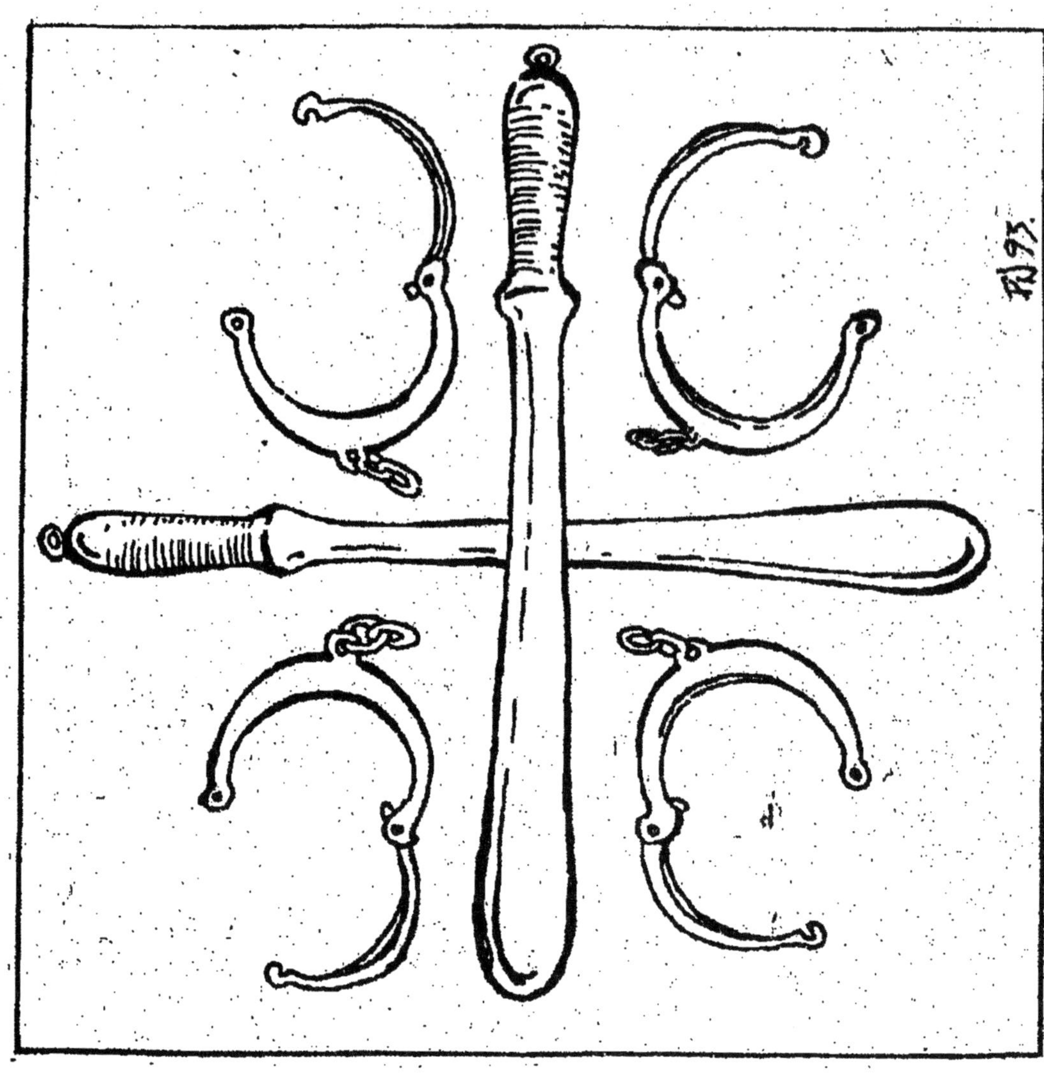

Independent media:* <u>*Contra Bellum*</u> *makes its own point about overly nationalist symbols. September 1993. Cartoon by: Nikola Petkov

REPORT from

'A VISIT TO SERBIA' by Vladimir Maricic

'The new anti-hero is Arkan who now owns a five floor villa overlooking the Red Star football stadium. He also owns the Hotel Majestic and the adjoining fashionable shopping centre.' 'Ruthless accumulation of riches is still described in the Socialist press as prvobitna akumulacija kapitala *(the primary accumulation of capital); a terminology which smacks of my Belgradian school years.*

*The first impression of Belgrade is hundreds of street sellers of car fuel. Containers of variously coloured petrol perched on the tops of cars with signs displaying 3.5, 3.7 or 4, representing Deutsche Marks per litre, (the ongoing rate was 3.3 dinars per mark). When I bought petrol I realized that these "primary capitalists" are university educated fellows. Small businesses have popped up across Belgrade and New Belgrade in their thousands. Virtually all vacant space in housing estates has been converted into business space. The rule for a successful business is to declare around 25% of turnover, with the rest run according to black market principles. Since the times of 30% per day inflation, businesses have had to declare their revenue every two weeks to the SDK (*Sluzba drzavnog Knjigovodstva*—equivalent of the Inland Revenue), such taxes as are paid are usually fixed sums (*pausal*).*

*'A kilogram of the best veal costs 12DM and its price is set by the director of the biggest chain of state owned supermarkets who is at the same time the deputy prime minister of the Serbian government. Many other Socialists from the government are at the same time directors of social, private or State companies. It is not easily verifiable how many and what ranks they hold in the reserve military and police force. The government has allocated 73.5% of the State budget to the army. The police budget is not given in the daily papers but I assume it forms a significant portion as councils (*opstine*) have increased the police ranks considerably. Knic village council in central Sumadija, which had one policeman in 1939, now has 70. The same village has 10 council workers in charge of highways, rubbish, etc., considered as incompetents except when stealing village property.*

Travelling on the Serbian motorway one is struck by the desolation of the roads. The few buses, trucks and Serbian made cars seen on the roads are often stopped by one of the vast number of traffic police. I was told that since the war started most of the towns have control checkpoints on their outskirts. Some people see these as necessary safety controls, while others view this as State authoritarianism...

A feeling of resignation regarding Serbian politics is noticeable. Everyone knows the elections in Kragujevac were rigged as the election boxes disappeared for days. Among the farmers in Raca some 50% still do not have running water or toilets in their homes. The person considered to hold the strings to people's destinies and future, is baba Julka *(or grandmother Yulka). She is Mirjana Markovic, wife of the Serbian President and herself President of JUL—Yugoslav United Left. This party consists of people whose sole responsibility seems to be the juggling of considerable wealth accumulated by the former Communist Alliance and the former Socialist Alliance in the form of social and State property. The best building sites in Belgrade and new shopping centres are theirs.*

If, along with the number of policemen, the number of television channels is seen as an indicator of potential social conflict, then the potential is high in Serbia. Belgrade now has 11 channels, Kragujevic 8, Nis 9, etc. The "private" channels are supposedly subsidized by advertising but this is highly doubtful. Why would a private individual provide this service for nothing? Somebody must be paying for this. And it is not Soros! The new BK Channel is provided by the richest men in Serbia, the four brothers Karic, whose main capital investment seems to be in Russia... Studio B has become the channel of the Democratic opposition parties. However it can be viewed only within a radius of approximately 150 km from Belgrade. This is the only channel for which the Bosnian Serbs are still of news value.

If I were not particularly interested in non-governmental organizations, I surely would not have found out about a conference of human rights and anti-war groups held in the Hotel Metropol. These socially marginal groups have been busy leaving written proof of their existence and opposition to war. The non-governmental organizations (NGO) in Serbia apparently do not seek broad support; this is perhaps because their fund-raising is mainly done in the West...

From *The South Slav Journal* Issue 63/64 Vol. 17. 1996. (With permission of the author).

HOW TO STAY SANE DURING AN INSANE WAR

As you obviously need to be informed, listen only to the absolute minimum of news. When doing so, try to choose the sources which can be at least a bit trusted, (maybe B92 or Studio B radio-programmes). As we live in the conditions of an absolute control over media, try to draw your own conclusions; the best thing would be if you could hear 'the other side' in order to compare. Try to avoid the top news, especially TV Belgrade, TV Novi Sad or the news at 3 PM of Radio Belgrade 1.

Whenever you hear a terrifying piece of information or see a horrible picture on TV, take a deep breath and slowly breathe out. Repeat it several times until you feel better. Try to avoid TV news, especially when they are showing the horrifying scenes of massacres.

Try to listen to all arguments that someone is bringing to you; do not confront them directly because you will only enforce their own beliefs by doing so. Try to make them doubt their own arguments. Your answer could be that war can only make things worse and not better. Show them that there is a possibility to choose. War is not a choice, only peace can be a choice. No conflicts can be resolved by force. The force activates the resistance and everything is only becoming worse.

Whenever you hear a general remark like 'Croats are genocidal people!', try to remember somebody who belongs to that nation and their good qualities. Keep in touch with the people of different nationalities, You can find out something about the problems of the other side by talking to them openly.

Show your solidarity to other people everywhere: in the house where you live, among the people who are with you on the same bus (public transport). That way you will not only feel better, but you will also be encouraging the people around you.

Keep in mind that there is a huge media war going on, a war which is difficult to resist and which keeps destroying your personality. The ultimate goals of this war are to make people accept their ideas, to make them frightened in order to stop all forms of organized resistance. It is better for you to go for a walk or to talk o your friends than to sit in front of the TV as you are used to.

Choose cheerful, bright colours for your clothes. Try to spend at least one hour every day thinking about the positive solution of the situation you are in. This will encourage your optimism and it will be good for people around you.

There is always 'the other side' of the problem. If you know nothing about the others' point of view, you cannot expect them to understand you. There is no such thing as the one and only truth.

Your positive action represents a possible way out. Talk as much as you can about the possibilities for peace. Many people are against the war but they do not think that peace stands a chance. If you manage to encourage them and to explain why it is important that they personally do something against the war, our chances for peace are getting gradually bigger. It is now that these chances are greatest. Have a peace slogan on you, on a badge for example.

WE REFUSE TO BE MISERABLE BECAUSE THAT IS NOT WHAT WE ARE

If you are a man, do not let others demoralize you by calling you a coward if you use your own head, want to survive, do not want to become a killer and if you do not agree with the reason or the need to make war. You have the right to defend your ideas; including the one saying war is unnecessary, that nothing is accomplished by it and that it will not bring any good to anybody!

If you have your own ideas about the peace actions; try to gather the people who share your opinion and start the work together.

Belgrade, 05/10/1991 Centar za antiratne akcije
Prote Mateje 6, 11000 BEOGRAD

APPEAL FOR CITIZENS DIGNITY

FREEDOM AND DIGNITY OF EACH CITIZEN START WITH HIMSELF

The whole of citizens relations and behaving fell in Croatia in last years on tragically level...

Citizens and human dignity starts with every citizen of this country, and it is their right, and their citizens duty to plead for them.

Citizens and human dignity, especially respecting of your own and other people's citizens' and human rights starts in your home, in place where you work, in your everyday surrounding.

Have you in last few several years witnessed somebody being discriminated, threatened or attacked only because of his belonging to different ethnic or confessional group, different opinions or some details from his previous life.

Turning your head away and staying silent are the worst possible way of citizen and human being should react.

What to do, how to act? One man himself cannot do a thing, they say...These are such times, they say...It will all be settled with time...But, maybe then you will ask yourself: what I was doing then, where I was, why did not I then raise my voice.

You do not have to stay silent and tolerate primitivism. React!

In school react if your son or daughter has to listen to professors' primitive outbursts. In your office react if reason for somebody's maltreatment is anything but doing his job lousy. Object publicly if your member of parliament, speaking for you too, in parliament or else in public speaks something which is against your education, citizen's culture, laws of this state. Insist publicly that writers, actors, journalists' associations etc. react if any of their members gives statements in public which are above any civilized level, or worse.

There are public mechanisms for that. Functioning of the legal state depends on you indirectly, but functioning of the civic society depends on each of us directly.

If you did not react as a citizen yesterday, if you fail to do it today, ask yourself: in what kind of state and society will you live tomorrow. Because, nobody and under any excuse has the right to represent and do things under basic civilized level, except if you let him do it.

1995 Group for Direct Protection of Human Rights in AntiWar Campaign Croatia, ## CrossPoint v3.02 ##

Chapter VIII

The question of impact

'In traditional volunteerism the concern is with a particular individual or group with a problem. The problematic situation is identified at a concrete level and practical help is prescribed. The helping intervention ignores the social structure both as a cause of the problem and as an approach to solving it. The perspective is individualistic and atomistic rather than social or global...'

Alexander Abdennur *The Conflict Resolution Syndrome* 1987

'In linear systems, small changes produce small effects, and large effects are due either to large changes or to a sum of many small changes. In nonlinear systems, by contrast, small changes may have dramatic effects because they may be amplified repeatedly by self-reinforcing feedback. Such nonlinear feedback processes are the basis of the instabilities and the sudden emergence of new forms of order that are so characteristic of self-organization.'

Capra, *The Web of Life*, 1997

'Since the agent, being an outsider, may perceive things significantly differently from the people concerned, the course of any changes provoked by his presence and influence may well be unpredictable. The fundamental problem could be stated in the following terms: if external agents of "disruption" are necessary for changes to take place, who should those agents be and how should they behave in order to overcome the danger implicit in these differences of perception?

There seemed no satisfactory solution to the problem. Adequate training of the agents was apparently the only answer, but it seemed a poor one. After all, no matter what was attempted, the agent was always a cultural outsider. I finally proposed a radically different approach. The "disruption effect", I suggested, should come from the...(people)...themselves, through a process of "horizontal "confrontation" and awareness ...'

M. Max Neef (1982)

'According to structuration theory, action at the level of process is viewed as producing or reproducing context or structure, and context is viewed as conditioning action. Thus process and context are inextricably interlinked and should be viewed together as different aspects of the same reality. Linkage between the two levels, in stucturation theory, is provided by three dimensions which can be loosely described as meaning, power and morality. Actors draw on schemes of meaning, sources of power and standards of morality or norms to get others to carry out actions. In so doing, they produce new structures or reproduce old structures of signification, domination and legitimation.'

Mabey and Mayon-White (1993)

'Looking back, without what you call "the intervenors", we would have been very much alone. We just had to learn how to handle them, and how to discern our own needs and what to continue and what not...

Peace Activist, Zagreb, Oct. 1996

'At best we felt part of a big vibrant international network, instead of being only local odd people. At worst we thought (just sometimes) "who the hell do these guys think they are?" "

Peace Activist, Belgrade, Nov. 1996 (re.: intervenors)

VIII. The question of impact

8.1 Impact analysis; preliminary thoughts

The question of impact is different in kind to that of evaluation. It is more to do with aftermath than event, with effects more than with method or intent. Whereas evaluation may be event-driven or geared to specific operations or delivery (of goods or training in a specific time and place) impact analysis is cumulative and must include grey areas such as 'knock-on effects' or 'unforeseen consequences'. Above all it attempts to deal with the 'whole' picture, within designated parameters.

> '**impact**...n., the impulse resulting from a new idea or theory, strong effect, influence...'
>
> '**analysis**...n., a resolving or separating of a thing into its elements or component parts: ascertainment of those parts...the tracing of things to their source, and to so discovering the general principles underlying individual phenomena...' (*Chambers 20th Century Dictionary* 1983 Edinburgh).

Both evaluation, considered below, and impact analysis can attempt to deal with the link between the activities of a group and the apparent outcome of those activities. Both are determined by the questions we choose to ask, the questions we choose not to ask, and how we deal with information.

So an international NGO moving into Zagreb to commence operations in 1993/4 might evaluate staff performance and delivery functions after one year according to its project mandate and find specific indicators to measure success. Meanwhile a significant number of citizens in Zagreb may be saying, unheard, (as was the case by 1995) that property prices in the city have soared, that local professionals are leaving their posts in droves to work for foreign NGOs, that there are divisions in NGOs over staff payments, and that the local economy is distorted because of what internationals can pay taxi drivers as opposed to what the state can pay teachers or nurses. These disparities, these questions, will be familiar to anyone working in the development field during the past three decades. At time of writing they are relevant (if not acute) issues for Sarajevo.

The most impressive combined impact and evaluation study I have seen to date is the Joint Evaluation of Emergency Assistance to Rwanda[1]. A five volume (including the synthesis report) study conducted as a multinational, multi-donor effort, the study has already influenced rethinking on the part of relief and development agencies. Policy, codes of conduct (see Appendix 5) and possible need for regulation or 'quality control' of intervenors are areas of ongoing debate and discussion. They are relevant to Bosnia, where Larry Hollingsworth of UNHCR estimates that during his tour of duty UNHCR 'rescued' at least one broken down or stranded voluntary van or truck *every week* which had found its way into Bosnian mountains with untrained drivers and ill fitted vehicles[2]. With regard to handling, responding to or even 'servicing' complex emergencies, debates are at least underway regarding intervention efficacy and even morality[3]. When it comes to the broader, related question of preventing these same emergencies, of non-military intervention to reduce violence, to stop war or to enhance just outcomes, modern debates are in their infancy[4].

McDonald (1991) argues that track two diplomacy is in itself a form of conflict resolution that is 'non-governmental, informal, and unofficial. It is interaction between private citizens or groups of people from different countries, who are outside the formal governmental power structure.' This statement could be taken as the broadest possible view of actors, processes, and intersecting points of systemic change. (Czempiel, 1989). McDonald postulates a ground swell of citizen initiatives which can influence either leadership or structures, (as per east/west engagement and the end of the cold war). He postulates multi-track intervention. It is the contention of this study that **second track intervention during the war in ex-Yugoslavia recognised and responded to those civic and anti-war voices in the former republics which traditional statecraft and diplomatic relations could not**, given the latter's fixation on protocol and political as opposed to moral positions. Statesmen respond in summit form or treaty to other statesmen, or women (as currently with Mrs. Plavsic in Banja Luka)[5]. This is traditional form. Second track entry points were identified as aid, advocacy, communications, education and training, facilitation, mediation and negotiation, reconstruction, therapeutic work and witness. They linked in with and attempted to legitimise and strengthen the range of responses from primary social groups opposed to destructive violence.

It is the central paradox of the War Next Door study that whereas these combined efforts need viewing as a 'big picture' in a systems sense in understanding change, 'conflict resolution' has itself come to be viewed (and evaluated) as a training form in a reductionist sense. There are many reasons for this, not least because it has indeed been 'packaged' as techniques. It is the 'little picture' that is sometimes evaluated, or that we have paid lip-service to evaluating. Hence from early records of meetings in crisis situations... 'participants felt the session had been beneficial', and so forth. Hence the 1993 Budapest evaluation meeting and its attempt at a regional overview, or the Congress of Trainers in Nürnberg organised by Frankisches Bildungswerk für Friedensarbeit in May 1994 which was concerned with the 'clear professional image and working profile'[6] and professional development of trainers, and the meeting in London two years later organised by CCCRTE on 'Conflict Resolution: Dilemmas of Training'[7].

More recently, Mark Duffield has written a paper for the Chr. Michelsen Institute of Bergen, Norway, on 'Evaluating Conflict Resolution', 1997.

Duffield is also attempting a 'big picture', arguing on his first page that, 'Impact can only be imputed through critical sociological analysis'. On p.3 however, the preoccupation with packages and delivery is signalled: 'Since the stakes can be high for the aid agency involved, evaluation has also become a sensitive and often controversial undertaking' (as above). (The stakes are surely no less 'high' for local populations. It is their environment the agencies enter.)

Focus and actors

This chapter will draw on participative analysis, interviews, testimony, compiled evidence and observation in its attempt at a critical overview. It will also offer particular focus on E. Slavonia as a case study before putting forth tentative conclusions as to the limitations and possibilities of second track intervention.

In terms of 'high stakes' then, the first focus is on representatives of local affected populations. None of the initial primary intervenors here considered were actually aid agencies, and an update on their activities is appropriate here, some five years on. BSV (Germany) concentrated efforts on co-ordinating training, fielding and support of Balkan Peace Teams which are still active in the field. The Balkan Peace Project (USA) diversified into preventative work in Macedonia with a particular focus on teachers and the education system[8]. Representatives of the BPP have also been instrumental in OSCE policy shifts towards co-operation with NGO actors in the security field[9]. CCCRTE retained contact with particular individuals and groups in what might be characterised a 'moral support' fashion (which has looked less and less like training) and has facilitated exchange visits with Northern Ireland. CCCRTE has also branched out to do training work in the Caucuses, and affiliated individuals are working in a preventative fashion with the non-violent opposition in Kosovo/va. All of these agencies have obviously had to be accountable to justify their institutional existence to donors or otherwise, and have needed some sort of internal evaluations to do this.

The difficulty in gauging 'impact' includes the interrelationships between actors in society, and the nature of change itself. Here I have a fundamental conceptual difference with Duffield on approach. Duffield argues that there is a new paradigm which 'internalises' war, which holds the subjective realm of population and scarcity to be the central problem, thus rendering this a developmental rather than a political dimension. He states that 'conflict resolution is based on a socio-psychological model which regards internal war as a cyclical and relatively autonomous phenomenon having irrational and localized beginnings' (ibid. p. 27). I fundamentally disagree, while I acknowledge that he may be representing a view held by particular people in policy. There is no single model. There is always a need for informed analysis. Granted there is a danger in 'internalising' war if this effectively 'blames the victims' and disallows external responsibility or the power machinations of leadership. The framework of structural conduciveness developed in this study looks not only at strain (which could indeed be scarcity) but also at responses to it; not only at emotions, but also at the manipulation of these by power interests. I see no 'mechanistic connection between such social factors and internal war' (ibid.). On the contrary agency and structure are held to be of equal importance in this study; power, design, the construction of hatred, and arsenals of arms are also recognised. So is the international system, itself.

To take the example of conscientious objection then, which is recognised and allowed in Croatia today to a far greater degree than in 1992[10], we may choose to say that WRI had an impact on this particular situation, as did ARK, as did conscientious objectors who fled, as did the Council of Europe when it imposed human rights conditionality for membership on Croatia, or Amnesty International which continues its own campaign on this issue. **In any policy decision, where issues pose varying costs and benefits to different actors in the equation (both within the institutional social and political system and without) it will be several factors which prove decisive. It may not be the actions of one particular challenging group. Change will happen at convergence points of interest and actions.**

> *'To date we have no social science equivalent to chaos theory, no concepts or models that help us to discriminate between incremental and discontinuous changes. Incremental or large-scale change can thus be interpreted only after the fact. But once our hunch tells us that we are living in a period of relative normalcy or great turbulence, something that we must judge ourselves, then we can make contingent generalizations about systems, actors, rules, and interactions'*
>
> Katzenstein in Czempiel, 1989

To take a composite view is an important acknowledgement of complexity rather than causation. WRI and BSV did not 'cause' change in policy directly, but their intervention in response to localised concerns helped set a chain of events in motion.

8.2 The need for evaluation

Given the wider view necessary for analysing longer term impact, there is still a need for the evaluation of any serious intervention input. Critical evaluation attempts assist in learning, test mutuality, and provide a basis for either completion (exit) or continuation of work. It is extremely problematic in days of crisis or war. For a start there is a 'fools rush in' tendency when concerned groups and individuals feel they need to respond rapidly. (This is observation rather than criticism: urgency and 'solidarity' are valid forces in themselves.)

Secondly, recipient parties are often too appreciative of attention and allies (or too polite) to really say what they think. Herein lies the most simple of major flaws in evaluation, particularly if 'on the spot.' 'We were so grateful to have outside attention,' admits B. in Osijek, 'and to be honest in those days my English wasn't very good. Half the time we didn't even understand what they were saying.' She refers to a plethora of 'one off' visits and 'trainings' from internationals between 1992 and 1995.

This said, a framework is offered for consideration, (with full credit to Barry Baker and Martin Large[11] who provided the working paper on which it is based). It is set out in 'first person' for accessibility, and may be found in full in Appendix 6.

What is meant by evaluation?

In the training context it is any attempt to obtain information and feedback on the effects or outcomes of 'training' and to assess the value of that training in the light of the information gained.

In essence evaluation can be a large, complexly designed study on one hand, or simply asking 'what did you think of 'X' on the other hand.

So evaluation is a generic term which can mean many things to many people.

It is:
- an assessment process
- a process of judgement
- an information generating and gathering process
- a control process
- a problem and decision-making process

Why bother to evaluate?

It is possible to identify five reasons for evaluating:

Feedback:

Did I achieve what I set out to achieve?
Were there any unintended outcomes?
Was I effective in my trainer role?
What might I need to change next time?
Has the Department/Organisation benefited?
Can I do better?

Control (Monitoring):

How efficiently are resources being used?
Was training the right solution to the expressed need?
What still needs to be done?
Can we justify this training exercise and expenditure?
Is what is supposed to be happening actually happening?
Could I redirect resources to better ends?

Research:

Let me see which of these two training approaches produces the best results?
Which is the best approach for team development?

Intervention:

I want to introduce 'y' but I need to know what is currently happening
I want to influence the direction we take so I had better be involved in the process

Power Games:

To prove I was right—there you are!
To raise one's visibility in the organisation.
To establish evidence in support of a pre-determined solution!
To be seen to be doing something (tokenism).
To ensure only what you want to be. evaluated is evaluated, to ensure you are able to define what is success and failure; and so on.

None of the five are mutually exclusive in that a person may be evaluating for a declared reason e.g. feedback, but may also have a hidden agenda re intervention or exercising power. The last two should start to give you the idea that whatever else evaluation is, it is also a highly political process; people evaluate for a variety of reasons.

Probably, central to all the reasons for evaluating are the following: information gathering, analysis and decision-making.

8.3 The dangers of obsession with evaluation: the value of learning

The current obsession with evaluation, the 'audit explosion'[12] in the West is fine if there are clear goals and 'success' criteria or indicators, but potentially obsessive if it amounts to constant monitoring for the sake of monitoring. The latter tendency is indicative of either gross insecurity or the need for control. If we accept that evaluation is a highly political process, then the learning 'loop' described above (8.2)—information gathering, analysis and decision-making—must be central to the exercise. On these components will rest learning and application. Finally, even the most efficient evaluation exercise is no substitute for relationship building, engagement and long term commitment to change.

Increasingly groups and agencies working in the field are seeking new parameters and indicators for evaluation. Particularly in conflict situations it is vital to seek qualitative interpretation as much as quantitative measurement. So, *for example* (hypothetically) eight people were trained in word-processing and two computers were donated (quantitative report). Who actually has subsequent access to the equipment and how they use it would be a qualitative issue. Or, a certain number of people are trained in direct action (quantitative) but half of them are imprisoned and the groups' headquarters are firebombed as a result. The risks of any type of 'empowerment' are then a qualitative issue. To use a concrete example, an agency which sponsored a very successful cross-sectional meeting in Vukovar on community action and NGO development found they had unwittingly unleashed subsequent weekly demonstrations against reintegration into Croatia. The so-called 'hard-liners' had new methods in voicing their opposition.

In a post-war or 'interim peace' context intervenors may think in both structural and social terms for reflection on outcome and impact. A new clinic may be built, visible and operational; hence a positive 'output' in the structural sense. If one or several minority groups in the community are not allowed or too intimidated to use the clinic, this is a social challenge yet to be met which must also be taken into account. Does it call for political mediation? Has one party been assisted at the expense of the other? 'Structural' refers here to the creation of activities, institutions, and physical infrastructure and 'social' to relationships, attitudes, and values. This means embodying principles of peace-building in the work of the intervenors:

1) political peace building will be agreements and legal arrangements,
2) structural peace building is about activities which contribute to economic and institutional renewal, and
3) social peace building is about relationships, beliefs, values, skills and the renewal of community[13].

8.4 Participatory appraisal

Participatory appraisal denotes designed settings for individuals to reflect on, attempt to make sense of, and gain an over-view of experience. It may take the form of an event, of sustained group work, one-to-one meetings, or even the keeping of personal journals for scrutiny at particular junctures. Slim and Thompson marked the importance of listening to oral testimony in their 1993 publication of *Listening for a Change*. Written in a development context, *Listening* underscored the importance of validating and hearing the perspective of primary actors otherwise designated only 'recipients'. It stresses the importance of finding the right questions, ... 'imaginative listening and sensitive, but probing questions' (p.76). As the consolidation of experience, engaging in such a listening as appraisal exercise *is in itself an intervention.* Moreover, there are no 'fixed points' of reference save those agreed upon. 'You are trying to catch so many moving objects,' said a wise woman to me in Sombor, 'while you yourself are moving'. Krystyna Weinstein refers to 'taking time to question and reflect...in order to gain insights and consider how to act in the future' as *action learning.*'[14]

It has been intended that the War Next Door as a

project be an exercise in the reflective stage of action learning. I found continually that whereas I was interested in opinions and impressions about the efficacy of interventions, people I spoke with wanted to talk about their recent history and their very specific context. The way things were in 1989 versus the way they were in 1996, in particular. There was a tolerance for the intervenor's luxury of coming and going. And time and time again the key areas of concern were those voiced in the chapter on civil society: the legacy of a highly militarised culture which needed transformation, the need for independent media and new communications, and the desire for more participation and new non-authoritarian values.

My own categories of 'intervenors' then, are subsumed under the theme areas most prominent in what people have said. The outcomes below are a composite of recorded opinion and collected evidence.

8.5 Thoughts on the big picture; second track intervention, communications and facilitation

The following observations are offered as findings in this particular exercise in participative appraisal. As a study it has been perhaps overly ambitious (to take on such big questions), sometimes unwieldy and/or necessarily informal, and above all diverse.

Perhaps the most visible impact of second track intervention in the war in ex-Yugoslavia has been in the areas of communications and facilitation, and in the allocation of resources to enable local initiatives. (The latter category is somehow to be factored separately from the delivery of humanitarian 'aid', which has proved retrospectively controversial.) *Second track interventions in conjunction with local actors have enabled major breakthroughs in the control of/and access to information.*

Communications can make the difference between open and closed minds, and between open and closed societies. I can think of an intelligent professional woman in Zagreb, daughter of a partisan, a believer in all that was 'Yugoslavian', who came from a typically mixed marriage urban background (Serbian, Croatian, Orthodox, Catholic and touch of Macedonian antecedents) and spoke three European languages fluently. Denied access to her former closest friend (who moved to Belgrade on marriage two decades ago) --no letters, no phone calls--for five years, listening to state radio and television during that same time, she now harbours suspicion of that very friend as an enemy. On the other side, I think of G. in Belgrade, the restaurant owner described in Chapter III who hid Bosnian refugee men who were fleeing from

The impact of Soros sponsored (and other) communications, education and training: a (shared) despised enemy for Tudjman and Milosovich

Since the authorities are unable to control the Soros foundation, (see Poitika, *12 March 1995) they have resorted to outrageous libel in an effort to discredit its work. In government-fabricated press reports, the state-run* Borba *described the foundation as 'poison in the guise of humanitarian words' on 14 March and 'a politico-spy organisation' on 9 March. In another obvious effort to discredit the work of the foundation in the public mind, the state-run* Borba *also reported on 14 March that the foundation's real mission is to subvert impressionable young minds and in the process assail the very fabric of 'Serbian identity.' Mid-March* Borba *headlines went so far as to proclaim that 'Soros is Turning Our Youth Into Janissaries ' (forced conscripts under the Ottoman Empire), and that it is time to 'Ban the Soros Foundation '.*

(Stan Markotitch, *Transition*, p.36, 28 April 1995)

In his broadcast, Tudjman parades Feral Tribune as the main enemy of the state, a nest of 'Yugo-communism' and a refuge of Chetnik bandits. It is, he alleges, part of a dark conspiracy against the free, independent and democratic state of Croatia.... First, he says, the magazine receives financial support from 'the number one enemy of an independent Croat state'—US philanthropist George Soros' Open Society Institute. Second, every year Feral *receives an important international award. This, says the president, is obvious proof of a global conspiracy against Croatia.*

Drago Hedl, *War Report*, p.11, June/July 1997

Positive impact: facilitation in Subotica

On the political level, Subotica city is governed by a coalition of the Hungarian and Croatian parties. The coming of refugees however was considered to be organised on the national level, where the SPS (Serbian Socialist Party) is in power. Many people think, that the coming of refugees was a deliberate policy in order to increase the number of Serbs in the multi-cultural local society of Subotica, where no group has the majority. This created new tensions, amongst other political tensions. Two different concepts were propagated: the municipality should protect the non-Serb population and the second concept was the approach to protect all of the refugees and create a human situation for all of them. Because of a lack of consensus amongst the local political parties, an initiative was undertaken by the Open University and the Agency for Local Democracy in Subotica in order to create consensus. By the way, the lack of consensus existed amongst local politicians as well as local NGO's, local media and citizens.

Therefore the Open University and the Agency for Local Democracy in Subotica organised a meeting which was attended by representatives of all the main local political parties, representatives from NGO's, representatives of local media and interested inhabitants of the city (the meeting was publicly announced beforehand). Nearly a 100 people showed up.

After six hours of discussion, all the present people (so also the representatives of the political parties - amongst which the mayor of the city, the chairman of the city council, representatives of the Hungarian, Croatian and Serbian socialist political parties) agreed on the necessary interlinking of the following points: the humanitarian receptions of the new refugees, the protection of all non-Serb inhabitants of Subotica and the active maintenance of Subotica as a multi-ethnic, open society.

At the meeting, it was especially the contributions of the citizens that were of importance. Initially, the political parties' representatives could not bridge their differences. The citizens expressed their commitment to the cause of both the maintenance of the character of Subotica and the need to do whatever possible to provide the refugees with shelter and perspectives for a normal life. While expressing this commitment, the citizens enabled the political representatives to overcome their differences and unite on the combination of the points mentioned above.

Extract from 'The situation of refugees in Subotica, Vojvodina, Yugoslavia' COS, October 1995

forced conscription. G's closest friend lived on the Dalmatian coast and was Croatian and they had also not communicated for five years. 'I could not talk to her now' says G. 'The pain is too deep, and the walls are too great.' Listening to these women, so many miles apart, I fantasise about reams of small compact mobile phone devices being parachuted into both areas early enough to allow 'ordinary people' to keep in touch, to gain their own information, to counter demonizing media inputs.

For those who could access the 'Telephone Bridge' linking Serbia with Croatia via Milan then, there were profound personal benefits. For the hundreds of groups assisted by Tilburg Zamir or Soros in obtaining and using e-mail, there has been a communications revolution.

In both Croatia and Serbia the struggle for an independent media is a critical pressure point for de-militarising society and breaking authoritarian political pressure. After the 29 October 1995 elections in Croatia the election issue of Globus (3 Nov., Zagreb) proclaimed Tudjman's local defeat: 'HDZ Lost Authority in Zagreb but convincingly Won in Zepca, Siroki Brijeg and New Zealand.' (The headline refers to the widely denounced electoral role practices including the vote abroad of 'the diaspora' who had only HDZ on their voting papers)[15]. Just over a year later the population had had the opportunity of watching the televised BBC production of 'The Death ofYugoslavia' courtesy of Austrian television. 'Some 100,000 Croats took to the streets'[16] after the government moved to stifle Radio 101, the sole independent radio station in Zagreb, in late October 1996.

By September 1997 the *Feral Tribune* newspaper was no longer subject only to the strong arm tactics and threats of previous repression. Now there were new American style lawsuits and heavy fines. Nevertheless the paper revealed details of atrocities perpetrated against Serb civilians and opposition Croats (including women and children) during the war of 1991. A former paramilitary claimed that his special police unit had murdered on political orders to ethnically cleanse southwest and central Croatia, particularly citing Pakracka Poljana and Gospic. These revelations rocked a population continually fed on purist patriotic images and a diet of accounts where atrocity was all the doing of the 'other side'[17].

By January of 1997, in response to Milosevic's government rejection of election results (in towns where the opposition had won) the universities in Belgrade, Nic, Novi Sad and Kragujevac were on strike. Belgrade had seen three months of street demonstrations in favour of the opposition coalition Zajedno[18]. Tens of thousands of students, professors, professionals and journalists connected their computers to Internet web sites abroad when the government closed independent radio station B-92 for two days. The station made digital broadcasts in Serbo-Croatian and English using audio Internet links, and using its web site, continued reporting on the protests. The attempt at closure was foiled in a 'vibrant web of new technology.'[19]

In late February the government bowed to popular pressure, installing the Zajedno candidate Zoran Djindjic as mayor of Belgrade.

We must be cognisant of the widening however of a development gap when charting the communications revolution, and hope for responsible use of the new technologies internally and for the eventual closing of the gap. I refer to the huge urban/rural economic and cultural disparities which are still a feature in the new configuration of states and entities. The gap between a south Serbian village which has no electricity and a communal water supply and Belgrade; the gaps between the poverty pockets of rural Republilka Srpska and Sarajevo, or Herzegovina semi-ruined mountain villages and Zagreb are enormous.

As for communications and facilitation, it can be no coincidence that almost immediately on signing of the Erdut agreement the mayor of Osijek went to visit the mayor of Subotica. An elderly Osijek citizen laughed out loud when he heard and commented to me 'Right under the nose of Glavas!' It was an important, visible move for the populations of both cities. No coincidence, because of the careful network of town and city links in place which the LDE system enabled, so that systems and networks were in place. Similarly, in the wake of Dayton, and as the dazed survivors in Bosnia began to pick up pieces and resume civic forms, such as the Citizens Alternative Parliament which had its constituent assembly meeting in Tuzla in August of 1996, networks were in place to swing into action for co-operation with ARK and with the Belgrade circle.

8.6 The allocation of resources

The allocation of resources in itself is a form of facilitation, some say 'development'. The Osijek centre, for example, has achieved almost mythic status for some external observers[20], probably commands the largest budget of any action group in Croatia and has achieved a high profile with donors abroad. There appear to be several reasons for this. The city has been seen as sitting on a 'front line' of sorts since 1991/92 and has thus been of strategic importance to peacemakers. It is equa-distant to Hungary and Vojvodina, thus rendering external meeting points for otherwise estranged populations possible. The Mohacs experiment has been highly valued as a venue for the reunion of friends and families split by political divides. It must also be pointed out that citizens from 'both sides' took it on themselves as soon as it was possible to bus into Pecs or other Hungarian market towns to meet each other. There have thus been fine informal but sophisticated routes for the passing of messages, news, and small discreet parcels. Osijek has been in a similar strategic position vis à vis west Slavonia. thus attracting funds for people to assist with the first and second phases of the Pakrac project.

Centre members have at time been targeted by other locals as 'traitors' or 'Serb-lovers', particularly in times of tension, as in pre-Erdut days when the city was again sandbagged in full preparation for attack, and it was not known whether the last stage of the war would be fought bitterly again on the banks of the Drava. The cultivation of external links and friendships has been important (see page 145).

8.7 Advocacy and witness

In a striking external 'second track' communications move, a US based web site called 'Whereabouts' publishes information on the whereabouts of war criminals and lobbies for human rights and war crimes conditionality for IMF and World Bank loans to Croatia. (See *The Observer* article 'Website' page 161). The self-styled 'Coalition for International Justice' is a two person advocacy operation working from an office in Washington DC. This initiative began with work on return from Bosnia of fieldworker John Hefferman, in conjunction with Human Rights Watch. The coalition compiles the whereabouts of accused war crimes suspects on the basis of data from the field, demonstrating how NATO forces could do the same were there 'political will'. It also bears witness to the need for troops to stay in BiH until indicted war criminals no longer hold sway over local populations.

In a report to the UN (Economic and Social Council) Commission on Human Rights of 5 July 1995 Special Rapporteur Mazowieki cites independent data

Related learning

Communications and facilitation

High resources do not equal high impact

A strong link was made between the Osijek Centre and a Swedish ecumenical group which had in 1990 designed its own plan for a 'global peace service'; in other words, its own agenda. On successful negotiation of the peaceful reintegration of eastern Slavonia back into Croatia, it appeared that the peace service idea might take a pilot form in assisting with 'peace building' in Baranja, with a complicated plan for locals and internationals to train in Sweden and then work to help refugees return.

High profile, low impact?

However well intended, the initiative described above is one of many examples of an intervenor bringing its own agenda. It was compounded by the high budgets proposed, the need to organise a relevant residential course in Sweden, and the fact that after Erdut any attempt from Osijek to assist with refugee return was open to interpretation as the promotion of smooth political reintegration for a victorious Croatian state. *Meanwhile UNTAES busied itself with mass reunions on the border, providing tents, transport and security; with enabling a market at Klisa on Saturdays, to which thousands of people from either side poured in the interest of renewing commercial and social links. Other independent, low-profile and low-cost initiatives worked locally to help Vukovar develop a youth group and to assist the embryonic women's group there (in the face of extremist opposition). The peace service-resettlement scheme took a very long time to get off the ground. Meanwhile a comparable scheme for volunteers to assist in peace building in E. Slavonia was devised in an Austrian institute, without awareness of the Swedish plan.*

Low profile, high impact?

A contrasting experience would be Group 484 Belgrade. In the two day assault in early August 1995 on the self-proclaimed Republic of Serbian Krajina, Croatia expelled some 200,000 Serbs. Some 120,000 of these entered Vojvodina ( ) and many others fled to Belgrade or to the south (some reportedly sent on sealed trains from Belgrade to Kosovo to alter the demographic balance there). They received an uneasy, sometimes hostile welcome and were denied opportunities for immediate citizenship by Miosevic (perhaps because they would not be prone ever to vote for him in light of the betrayal they must have felt?) Group 484 named itself after the 484 refugee families it organised with and for in late summer 1995 in Belgrade. Initiated by activists who had seemingly 'broken away' from CAA, they assisted with housing questions, sought basic provisions, organised crèches and medical care, and after Erdut took it on themselves to liaise with the Serbian population in E. Slavonia. Many of these refugees felt they had fled in blind panic and fear, prematurely; that they had left behind homes and heritages that they should have held to even if this meant returning to the Croatian state. This was the message they tried to bring to people in Vukovar, in Ilok, in Borovo. With a low budget, and low profile, going as volunteers every weekend, they tried to help the fearful make up their minds about what was possible, about what choices they might have in the face of political change and personal realities.

>>>Moving forward>>>

Co-operative intervention

Group 484, Oxfam, and representatives from Osijek co-operated with citizens in Vukovar for the opening and running of a legal advice centre there. In its first (Sept. '96) two weeks the centre was visited by 197 people needing help and information on whether to stay or leave the area. Training for volunteers was funded by Die Schwelle. The advice centre could link in with the UNHCR data base directly, and liaises with other regions on conditions of former homes, documents, etc.

GROUP "484" REPORT
JUNE (1.- 10.) 1996.

During the first 10 days of June the Group "484" volunteers have been in the field 9 times (Vukovar, Ilok, Markušica, Sotin, Mikluševci and Tovarnik) and held 22 workshops: 7 with youths, 5 workshops with women, 3 mixed ones and 9 workshops with pre-schoolers and school children from lower grades.

In Ilok we were at Nedelka Vidić family's home, a self-supporting mother of 5 minor children (one is still a baby) who are in very difficult lodging, hygienic and health conditions. The mother is not completely mobile, the eldest daughter (14 years old) works in a factory and the son, instead of being in the 5th grade he is in the 3rd grade. Help to this family is urgent.

In Tovarnik five children were found without parents. Three children live with their grandparents but two are completely alone (they are refugees and their mother is in Kosovo in Serbia).

In Vukovar and Ilok the youth directed a warning concerning the alcohol and drug problem among the high school youth population.

Positive examples: The woman group from Mikluševci participated in the UNHCR BAZAAR in Borovo and reached an agreement concerning further cooperation in the handicraft project/knitted pocket handkerchiefs.

At the end of May a Croatian family who had moved out from Ilok in 1991 returned home. They returned to their own house from which they were forced to move out by a Serbian family who now had left to Serbia. The previous lodgers took with them almost everything from the house but together the neighbors succeeded to collect the most indispensable possessions and kept them until they came back. We will visit the family.

In Markušica we bought the magazine "Bumerang", the Osijek peace groups' magazine. The natives, although confused, read and gave comments to it looking for our judgment. The uncomfortable feeling is surmounted by our claim that only informed correctly and in time we can give adequate decisions. We had an exclusively useful conversation with Radenka Nikolić, the secretary of the local community. We can count on receiving help for everything and we have to include that in our work. In this village, which is situated on the first separation-line (Vinkovci - Osijek) we held three mixed workshops on the theme: "To leave or to Stay". The dominant feeling is to stay as long as possible.

Belgrade the 10th of June 1996 **For GROUP 484**

Spomenka Žarković

provided by civilian second track intervenors. In its section on Western Slavonia the report notes that 'a significant contribution to the restoration of confidence in Western Slavonia has been made by a coalition of 11 Croatian NGOs, under the name of the Co-ordination of Organizations for Human Rights. This group has opened an office in Gavrinica in which complaints on human rights matters are received and free legal advice offered.'[21]

Gavrinica is a suburb of Pakrac. The Croatian offensive on Western Slavonia was a sudden attack with now documented indiscriminate attacks on civilians and mass killings at Okucani. RSK (Republika Srpska Krajina) forces retaliated with a series of artillery and rocket attacks on several Croatian cities, including Karlovac and Sisak, which were carried out on 2-3 May 1995. More than 10 Orkan rockets packed with cluster bombs were fired during the mid-day hours into the Croatian capital of Zagreb, killing 6 civilians and wounding more than 100 others. One rocket struck a children's hospital in the city centre. For activists and international volunteers it was a nightmare returned, not least because of popular patriotic glee at military conquest and retribution.

Related learning

Patterns of aid and the privatisation of war

The Pakrac reconstruction project was financed in part (according to conversations with project workers) by UNDP and by USAID. There was some disquiet at the beginning of the project as to 'local ownership' of the idea—was it 'owned' or imposed in a well-meaning way? It was hard work trying to kindle any sort of community spirit or cross-line co-operation. In the event of attack volunteers stayed as long as they could and did whatever was possible for the vulnerable in the area. At the time of the offensive Charlotte Eager wrote from Zagreb for The Observer: *'America is in this one up to its neck. The transformation of the Croatian army from a disorderly rabble to efficient fighting force is no accident. For the past six months, Washington has been engaged in the "democratisation" of the Croatian army.'*[22] *In a subsequent article she revealed that the US embassy in Zagreb had admitted that Virginia-based military consultancy Military Professional Resources Inc. (MPRI) had been training the Croats 'on licence from the US government, but says that it concentrates on "democratization"...'*[23] *Subsequently a US State Department spokesman John Dinger stated that MPRI had helped the Croatian army 'avoid excesses or atrocities in military operations'*[24]*. Roger Charles, a retired Marine lieutenant colonel and researcher puts it slightly differently: 'The Croatians did a good job of co-ordinating armour, artillery and infantry. That's not something you learn while being instructed about democratic values'*[25]

In an article for The Guardian 8 Sept. 1997 Darius Bazargan documents the proliferation of similar training and 'manpower' (mercenary) firms in London. In 'High Risk Business' he lists Control Risks Group, Defence Systems Ltd., Integrated Security Systems, Sandline International and Saladin Security. 'Private armies...' states Bazargan, 'are a growth industry; the world's increasing number of civil wars spell big business...'

For the American government the privatisation of military assistance offers advantages. It provides an element of deniability about overseas entanglements, it allows the scaling down of military personnel while simultaneously retaining the capacity to influence and direct huge missions. Firms on contract can train an entire foreign army.

We may say then that there is also a pattern of aid which is a militarised 'second track'? There are implications here for 'witness' in western societies.

>>>Moving forward>>>

The outcome of the army offensive to retake Pakrac did not so much destroy as disperse the social reconstruction and peace building initiative. Local activists and international volunteers moved on, in large part even more convinced of their ideals and values. The MIRAMIDA and Centre for Peace Studies initiatives were subsequently founded by Croatian Pakrac project leaders. 'Internationals' from the first reconstruction phase may now be found in responsible positions throughout the region still working for human rights and in social reconstruction. Meanwhile the advice centre for human rights and legal assistance (mentioned above) remains fully functioning.

Notes on Crisis and Co-ordination: May—August 1997

The conventional wisdom that, in essence, the Croatian military action which began on 1 May 1995 to retake Western Slavonia demonstrates the failure of the work on reconciliation in Pakrac, is challenged by evidence of the vital work which Volunteer Project members, and colleagues from other volunteer organisations, performed in the immediate aftermath of the action. Having decided to leave the area on the evening before the attack began, a number of foreigners, from the Project, from a volunteer human rights organisation, Otvorene Oci, and from other projects, returned to the area soon afterwards.

*They performed invaluable work of direct protection and monitoring of human rights, together with a highly efficient and effective system of disseminating information about the situation by E-mail (cf E-mail news group APC/YUGO/ANTIWAR). The presence of these individuals, plus the broad context of NGO involvement in the area, may well have been a contributory factor to the action in Western Slavonia leading to fewer abuses of human rights than subsequent actions in 'Krajina' where such a network was not in place**. The effectiveness of these volunteers stands in sharp contrast, I would argue, to the work of UN and, particularly, EC monitors who had, of course, considerably greater resources at their disposal...*

*** Other factors also played a part: the historical context; the actions of military and politicians on both sides; and, perhaps, agreements between the Croatian authorities and key international agencies. That abuses were far worse closer to the border with Bosnia, around the town of Okucani, where volunteers were less present, tends to support this hypothesis.*

Extract from 'Social Reconstruction and Social Development in Croatia and Slovenia: the role of the NGO sector.' Abstract and a summary of research findings by Dr. Paul Stubbs to the ODA, June 1996, pp. 23-25

8.8 Humanitarian aid—mixed findings

With the exception of atrocity and death, the most emotive and bitterly debated topic in these findings has been 'humanitarian aid'. In 1993/94 I quite inadvertently became caught up in heated arguments (as a bystander, not as an interviewer) between government officials and new NGOs, once in Zagreb, and once in Novi Sad. The Croatian official accused the representative of a London based relief organisation of undermining the Croatian state capacity to deal with its own problems. (The newcomer had been questioning distribution policy.) (On the other hand I can think of a local (UK.) relief worker who has been personally honoured by the Tudjman government and presumably does not ask many questions.) In Novi Sad authorities chastised newly formed medical and social groups for 'bypassing legitimate organs of the state' and accused them of no respect for authority.

The subject is most divisive in Serbia, where sanctions levelled the majority of the population to being needy, and where activists were torn between dealing with 'victims or causes'. J., Pancevo. 1994: 'We are held as collectively guilty for the war so we are punished so we are ourselves victims. But victimhood is not the real problem. The real problem is the invalid use of power which has brought us to this. I will not distribute blankets if it makes me forget the centre of this misery which is in weapons and minds and war.' Some peace activists felt that humanitarian work, reaching out to 'social cases' was a valid expression of positive values. Others, as J. expresses it, felt it a dangerous distraction from the real job of changing policy and stopping war. Interestingly, discussions in Temerin in 1996 with Krajina Serbs (who arrived with nothing as refugees) indicated their expressed preference for political answers and return rather than 'charity and hand-outs'. More than one international agency in Vojvodina (as in parts of central Bosnia) had clothing bundles and wool for knitting thrown back quite literally in their faces.

In fact these comments are not directed in any sense at the small scale initiatives mentioned in chapter V, and WATFY comments (see page 70) highlighted the problems of inappropriate engagement. The broader view is best described in Dumamic's comments. See 'Questionable impact.'

Questionable impact: the dilemma of humanitarian aid

Events on the economic plane in the areas of the former Yugoslavia require us to differentiate between the situation in Croatia and Serbia and that in Bosnia-Herzegovina. In Croatia and Serbia the war, which was transferred to Bosnia, was regarded as a framework within which production resources assume a deciding role, and there is a transition from a society which did not manage to achieve the principle of equality (although this principle was elevated to the top of social values), into a 'new society' based on inequality. In practice a Latin-American type of society has been created: on the one hand you have a mass of poor and disinherited, while on the other hand there is a small number of rich people (in Belgrade they are referred to as 'Mafia', while in Zagreb they are called 'war profiteers'). Added onto this social stratification is a political-ideological and legal division of society on the basis of an ethnic principle, so that the lowest place on the hierarchy is occupied by the Bosnians (of all ethnic/religious traditions), Albanians, and—traditionally—Gypsies.

Humanitarian assistance helps the process of getting rid of this social and economic wilderness in two ways. First, it helps the part of the population that has rapidly become impoverished to survive. Second, it contributes to maintaining the illusion of a market world, the illusion that it is possible to achieve material well-being ('right after the war, as soon as we defeat the enemy'), something which should not be underestimated.

In other words, humanitarian assistance as a form of investment in Croatia and Serbia serves to maintain social stability (and, whether this was their intent or not, the donors help to maintain the existing regimes in power). The recent strike of railway workers in Serbia ended with an agreement that the government would distribute some of the most essential food items to the strikers (cooking oil, sugar, etc.) (see Vreme, Jan. 1994). In Croatia, the number of people with social-assistance cards has already come close to the number of those who have refugee-assistance cards, and all of them are fed from humanitarian aid.

Finally, the most important thing is to see the way in which the relative social balance contributes to the politics of war and regime-maintenance in Zagreb and Belgrade. Humanitarian aid is under the control of government, and is treated as goods free from import duty. In this way the government is in a position to regulate the distribution of aid: it formulates criteria for the distribution and decides which bodies are competent to deal with it. It is the rare organisation that can avoid this problem, and which act in accord with different criteria. If they do try to be autonomous they become the target for attacks, for all kinds of insinuations, and control...

Behind the mask of humanitarian aid a network of organisations has grown up which are financed by international government sources, or which operate under their patronage. The span of their activities extends from the movement of people to courses in cutting out and sewing and foreign languages that are offered for people endangered by the war.

Second, the misuse of the authentic humanitarian sentiment of the donors who identify with the recipients and the 'selling of unhappiness ' with the goal of attracting donations (in this sense one should regard the entire TV publicity aimed at gathering aid as repulsive). This pathology is above that which brought the war—and, it has to be noted, social restructuring—to the former Yugoslavia. This theme undoubtedly requires a deeper ethical analysis (in as much as among other things it is a valuable theme for helping programs aimed at establishing alternative criteria for ethics and solidarity).

Therefore, the use of humanitarian aid for maintaining the social peace, and thus the criminal form of the capitalisation of property, confronts us with a large question: 'Does it make sense to support such a government in a way which enables it to keep its own voters?' Or, a better way of putting the question would be to ask how to help the population without at the same time helping the regimes?

Sura Dumamic 'Ave Europa, Moriture Te Salutant', 1995

Pecnic and Stubbs (1995) suggest that 'humanitarian aid projects', 'psycho-social projects' and 'development projects' are 'discourses which allow for particular ways of seeing conflict, of identifying the population affected by the conflict, as well as determining possible responses. While they point out the dangers of over-stereotyping ideal types, their framework for 'Contrasting features' is a useful guide to the experience of impact.

In fact Pecnic and Stubbs presented their framework in a study which focused on the growth of Sunkocret as an organisation which emerged in a post-communist society, and the ways of thinking encountered during institutional growth. The framework resonates with comments I received on the subject of types of aid as intervention. 'Trauma counselling' had its place, certainly, and the concept of trauma was found to be useful by people previously not familiar with it. But in some cases it has been felt that it can 'promote dependency rather than self-help, growth and empowerment'. (Ibid.) (There are excellent examples, such as the work of Vive Zene, Tuzla, with women from Srebrenica, of integrated approaches which assist individuals out of trauma into supported situations and eventually to healthy self- sufficiency.)

Both action learning and participative appraisal were evidenced in a July 1997 event organised by the Society for Psychological Assistance in Zagreb. The international conference for professionals, practitioners, and educators was described as a 'forum for reflecting on individual, group. community and professional challenges brought about by the war in Croatia and Bosnia-Herzegovina...' (Book of Abstracts) The meeting allowed for diversity and controversy in the proceedings and findings. Lessons compiled (see 'Trauma Recovery Training') included the need for intervenors to understand local context and culture; the realities of competition and the mirroring of political interests in relations between different sectors; and that expatriates were most valuable when they came as peers and collaborators.

One paper presented at the above forum was on 'inter-ethnic prejudices' as a public health issue. The abstract introduces Suzana Kulovic's argument thus:

> 'Specificity of social context where such faulty and inflexible generalisations like negative ethnic prejudices are directing the development of community is the obstruction of democratisation. Their consequences on political life, human rights, health policy, efficiency of the work of health professionals and the health of the people are generally disastrous.'

Contrasting features of 'humanitarian aid' 'psycho-social projects' and development projects

Humanitarian aid	*Psycho-social project*	*Development project*
Dependency	Expert	Flexible
Patronising	Pathologising	Empowering
Demeaning	Medicalising	Engaged / social movement
Distorting of national economy	Distanced	Community based / localised
Needs of donors not recipients	Professionalising	Integrating
Divisive	Inflexible	Transformative
Disrespectful	Prestigious for workers not users	Links/connects different levels
Emergency	Needs defined by experts not communities	Human rights
Undermining local communities	Disconnected from community needs	Develops skills
Distributive effects –? reinforcing inequalities	Self-maintaining	Democratic
Unaccountable	Disempowering	Civil society
Self-maintaining business	Labelling e.g. PTSD	Political
Part of a war game	Creates elite	Action-research
reproduces war	foreign experts – unaccountable	
unjust	local experts – accelerated promotion and salary	
fosters mistrust	Self-fulfilling evaluation – narrow, quantitative	Long-term planning
prevents local solidarity actions	Unco-ordinated	
	Temporary	
	Duplicating	

THE RURAL EXTENSION BULLETIN 8 DECEMBER 1995

Trauma Recovery Training ...Lessons Learned

(Extracts from International Conference Book of Abstracts, Zagreb July 1997)

D. Ajdukovic, ed., Society for Psychological Assistance

from 'Challenges of Training for Trauma Recovery':

'...The international experts had to learn how to present their knowledge to an audience which had very high expectations and pressing needs. Some of the examples that were presented did not correspond to the extent of massive traumatization that some of the local trainees had experienced. The lesson is that true experts should study the situation and the culture in which they are to work with local colleagues. ..It is essential to be humble and respectful to colleagues form another culture who operate in the realities of their constraints. This is also true for international relief agencies....

Helping traumatized populations has been a challenging task for the national and international communities. As resources were always limited, competition became evident at all levels: among international relief agencies, among local non-governmental organizations, between NGOs and the government sector, between different interest groups. Political interests were mirrored in these relations. However an important lesson learned is that compassionate, professional, committed work, with the needs of the beneficiaries as the priority is the right path This is bound to be recognized once these values prevail.'

Dean Ajdukovic

from 'Lessons we learned and Lessons we Failed to Learn'

'...Although US and Western European mental health systems evolved from the same historical antecedents, there were some fundamental differences in the two systems ....As expatriate professionals entered Croatia and Bosnia and Herzegovina, their impact was limited by this disparity as well as by the ongoing political and social variables at work in the region...During the war there was no mechanism for dealing with the multitude of US and Western European psycho-social and mental health models brought by expatriates. Diversity of ideas can enrich, but it can also confuse if the diverse models are presented as competitive or incompatible...

The author proposes that more important than the lessons learned are the lessons which we have failed to learn. This is most critical for planning future directions for care providers who will be working under war conditions. Some lessons which we may have recognised but failed to integrate into our thinking for similar work in the future include: (1)Indigenous professionals working under war conditions were after the real experts , but there was no mechanism until relatively late in the war to make their expertise available throughout the region; 2) Throughout the war, the importance of co-ordinated effort existed more in the abstract than in reality. Co-ordination must be more than rhetoric; (3) Expatriates were most valuable when they came as peers and collaborators.

Daniel L. Creson

Related learning

Zagreb and Belgrade had feminist movements focused on violence against women which evolved naturally into their work with women victims of war. In Bosnia and Herzegovina no such tradition existed. In spite of a tendency for the concepts of psychology and therapy to be stigmatised, local women have provided this kind of support. Zena BiH (Women of Bosnia and Herzegovina), was established first in Zagreb by Bosnian refugees who chose mutual support among friends over international hand-outs as anonymous refugees. On return to Mostar, Azra Hasanbegovic, a founding member of Zena BiH, re-established the group following a needs assessment which determined income-generation as the principle concern of women in the area, most of whom were displaced. A scheme was set up which encompassed knitting and psychological counselling. 'The counselling was almost an ancillary activity, for the predominant cause of stress was the lack of both an income and a regular routine which the knitting project provided.'

Moreover, 'according to Hasanbegovic, it was difficult to find international funding for income-generating and employment schemes, while there was money available for work therapy programmes. This raises important questions as to assumptions made by international donors which reify dominant victim stereotypes' (Walsh, 1996).

>>>Moving forward>>>

Questions about inducing dependency and 'victimhood' are being raised increasingly by donors and field workers. In the aftermath of war there are development principles which do apply, i.e. 'do things with, rather than for, the population.' Consultation and inclusion of 'target groups' by the majority of intervening agencies, however, still have a long way to go. Standard evaluation methodology will not reveal these problems.

Kulovic is concerned about the institutionalising of prejudice.... 'inter-ethnic antagonisms should be considered at least as dangerous for public health as nuclear pollution is for the vitality of humanity.' Kulovic expresses the view that rehabilitation of victims can be achieved only if there are social and political conditions which militate against past hatreds. Severe prejudices are not good for community health. This argument, a sharp departure from medical models, brings us back to the reality of the 'social fabric'; the values, forms and relationships people experience in daily life. Herein are the elements of social control, peer pressure, growth and spread of generalised belief, and structural strain as outlined in Chapter IV.

Kulovic seems to suggest, as a specialist in 'psychotrauma', that it is not enough to target the individual disorder without examining (even addressing) social context as well.

8.9 Focus on East Slavonia

For a focus on the interrelated, interwoven nature of second track intervention we return then from the overview—in which communications and facilitation efforts seemed most evident as impact, and aid problematic —to the specific case study of E. Slavonia. As a cross-roads for the co-operative initiatives of local actors and intervenors, as the region of both Borovo Selo and Vukovar, (see chapter four) it is a major experiment in peace building and in 'peaceful reintegration'.

Unlike West Slavonia, where Tudjman chose to prove a point, and Milosevic not to respond (much to the bitterness and confusion of the ensuing refugees), it appears that there was a tacit agreement between Belgrade and Zagreb over the transfer of E. Slavonia. Beta News agency and Vreme of 3 November 1995 reported such an agreement, adding that 'in case the local Serbs fail to accept the reintegration, Belgrade would refrain from responding to a possible Croatian attack'. Vreme predicted that the majority of Serbs in the area—should fighting fail—would flee the area. Glavas proceeded to announce on local television that all Serbs in medical or teaching jobs in Baranja would be replaced by Croats. (As late as February 1997 the intransigence of Glavas was noted in dispatches from the region by Drago Hedl to the Institute of War and Peace Reporting.) The desperation of uncertainty took many forms, including a sharp increase in the suicide rate and the gradual transporting of valuables over the border. Questions of urgency included: What revenge would returning Croats visit upon former neighbours? Would all men of military age be arrested as traitors to the Croatian state? What would happen to currency, to documents, to the exchanges of houses?

Eastern Slavonia was regarded as a potentially dangerous flash point for a renewed war between Croats and Serbs, and a much feared repeat-performance by the Croatian government of its operations 'Flash' (West Slavonia) and 'Storm' (Krajina) in summer of 1995. Mediators hoped that the Erdut agreement would allow the return of almost 100,000 Croatian refugees driven out in 1991, let Eastern Slavonia's Serbs remain and avoid the fate of 150,000 Serbs who fled their homes in Western Slavonia and Krajina when the Croatian army attacked. There was no mention of a Serbian demand for a referendum at the end of the transition period to settle whether Eastern Slavonia should be Croatian or Serbian.

Three months later a public meeting attended by four hundred citizens in Beli Manastir would listen in incredulity as U.S. officials explained the fine print of the agreement to them, and enquire 'Who signed that?' in disbelief. The U.S. representative replied by simply pointing to a photograph of Milosevic. Having fallen for, and risked all for the idea of seceding within secession, (leaving Croatia after Croatia left Yugoslavia) the residents of 'Sector East' felt they were to be handed back to their enemy on a plate. Even those individuals who had attempted to maintain contact with family, friends, or 'cells' of anti-war activists on the 'other side' had reservations about the implementation of such an agreement, yet they had consistently met each other in Hungary, informally for reunions at the Pec marketplace, or formally for meetings at a "neutral" conference centre in Mohacs. For people on both sides, Osijek or Baranja, this has been a war of layers like those of the proverbial onion; layers of manipulation, loyalty, identity, and insecurity. The consistent wedge between those layers has been fear.

Here was a situation where local groups and clusters of individuals, however small and at times non-representative, had in Osijek, Vojvodina, Baranja, Backa Palanka ('Society for Peace and Tolerance') taken steady steps towards *reducing the structural conduciveness to war.* Whereas on p.66 of this study a structural change model of escalation was described, what was undertaken in this region was an attempt at conscious *de-escalation* over a period of five years, in fits and starts, with differing combinations of actors. Those involved reached as far as Zagreb(ARK), Belgrade(484), international volunteers and allies and such disparate voices as the associations for the displaced on either side.

It has been multi-level work, with co-operation from UN., US. and UNTAES officials, notably Thorvald Stoltenberg, Peter Galbraith, Gen. J. Jaques Klein, Graham Day and others. It has been a focus area for second track intervention since 1992. The different entry points of intervenors and their possible contribution to de-escalation are suggested in the grid overleaf.

At times quiet, tricky, and effective mediation was undertaken by members of the Osijek Peace Centre with representatives from other groups in the interest of returnees or the vulnerable in need of legal advice. Moreover, a network of related activities took hold over this period. If we note the rough model or grid on capacity building and interventions it is possible to place activities on the scale according to indicators. Below are the basic indicators of 'structural conduciveness', and the types of capacity building undertaken to counter escalation of violence.

A. Structural disparity

The greenhouse projects and small scale enterprises, the women's sewing initiatives and veteran rehabilitation programme fit next to A. as human needs focus addressing structural disparity. Also here we could think of the work with hundreds of teachers and children on creative expression (recovery from trauma, co-operative games, art as communication).

B. Structural strain

Dialogue, roundtables with religious leaders, communications between activists from either side of the line, public meetings and the 'peace culture' events attempted to work creatively against extreme nationalist positions and ideology, as in B. 'balanced judgement' of new ideologies. LDE presence helped here, by broadening perspective to other cities and civic links.

C. Growth and spread of generalised belief and
D. Precipitating factors

Personal development work, meditation, student journalism, lecture series, meetings at Mohacs and Pecs, youth exchange visits and shared camps (in Netherlands, in Hungary, in Vojvodina, organised by the Youth Action group) assisted in C and D, that is communications and the means to counter disinformation. The women's group organising in Vukovar was a major step in this direction as well.

E. Mobilisation of participants for action

Campaigning and direct action tactics on human rights, housing law, rights of minorities, presentations on the peaceful settlement of disputes, and the establishment of legal advice centres in Osijek and Baranja helped to reclaim basic rights, as in E. Non-violence training offered alternative strategies for belief and change.

If we return to the structural conduciveness model of chapter four, it is possible to hypothesize as to where intervenors fit into a wider picture of capacity building. A rough model, which will need testing against subsequent developments, might look like this:

INDICATORS OF SOCIAL VIOLENCE/WAR CONDUCIVITY	CAPACITY-BUILDING NEED	SECOND-TRACK INTERVENTIONS
A) Structural Disparity: Insecurity and scarcity due to economic decline in Yugoslavia prior to the outbreak of war. High degree of military readiness and preparation. what has been described as 'authoritarian' cultural dominance.	**A) Fulfilment of basic human needs** in spite of economic insecurity (food, shelter, recognition, etc.).	Aid, therapeutic work, reconstruction, (attempts at economic regeneration) education and training.
B) Structural strain: rise of 'ethno-nationalist' parties and ideologies.	**B) Resistance to/or balanced judgement of new ideologies** which demand 'them/us' divisions and mass support.	Communications, facilitation, mediation/negotiation.
C) Growth and spread of generalised belief: the spread of majority/minority fear and threat due to the use of historical symbols and official media: Serbs feeling threatened in Croatia, Croatians feeling threatened in serbia (Vojvodina).	**C) Sufficient independent media and communications to counter dis-information**, constitutional and symbolic guarantees to minorities, avenues for safe participation.	Advocacy, witness, communications, education and training.
D) Precipitating factors: incidents, rumour, reaction, such as Borovo Selo, 2 May.	**D) Rumour control,** enough information to check incitement, communication systems which make this possible.	Communication, facilitation.
E) Mobilisation of participants for action: JNA recruitment, Croatian army recruitment, official conscription, emotional peer-pressure conscription, incitement of popular action, mass propaganda.	**E) Basic rights,** conscientious objection, alternative sources of service, media which counter-balance official propaganda, alternatives for disputes settlement/management and outcome.	Advocacy, communications, education and training, mediation/negotiation, witness.
F) Operation of social control: wages, pensions, employment conditional on 'ethnicity' and stated loyalty, neighbourhood/community values, new borders, financial limitations, basic needs.	**F) Allies 'outside' the system,** human rights mechanisms, functioning legal systems, support systems for minority rights.	Witness, advocacy, communications.
Each of the above generates specific vulnerabilities	***Capacity-building in wartime needs to address such issue-specific areas.***	

F *Operation of social control*
Support from 'Allies' from outside (F) has been visible through regular visits, through diplomatic pressure in Zagreb, through the vital presence of international volunteers (organised through the International Volunteer Project). Among these, long term volunteers from the Austrian Peace Service, young people attending work camps to assist with physical reconstruction, and the 'open' house of Peace Witness Volunteers. In attempting support to those experiencing the 'operation of social control' volunteers have 1) assisted in accompanying individuals to court or government offices, 2) befriended and backed citizens denied pensions or subject to threats because of their minority status or indeed their peace activism, and 3) communicated to the outside world about the realities of the situation., and 4) provided transport across borders and checkpoints which locally registered vehicles could not cross.

It is a kaleidoscope of activities. At time of writing there is cautious optimism that the peace will hold. The critical incident, the thrown petrol bomb, the assault rifle out of control, the crazed killing, has not happened. It still could. The question then would be whether it would tip the balance completely, or whether local communities have the capacity to weather such an event without becoming heavily embroiled in a collective frenzy of hostility. As this study goes to press the latest update is as follows:

'Return of confidence? Yes, to a certain extent confidence has returned.

A great majority of the people have stayed so far or just moved their things to Serbia and are waiting for things to come. Just yesterday Croatia and Yugoslavia announced smoother border traffic and a possibility of double citizenship which might make things easier for everybody. Schools have started with the regular Croatian programmes but with hours for Serbian language and culture. This was a great test case because many feared children and parents would leave, but most did not. Of course the economic life is low and there is a lot of unemployment, but things can only get better from now on since investments are being made.

The International Volunteer Project succeeded in establishing a very active and dynamic meeting house /youth centre in Vukovar since January with a lot of activities...contact between youth has also increased and the first ever issue of the youth magazine Seva (made by youth from Osijek and Vukovar together) has been presented during our summer camp. International Volunteers keep an important role as facilitators, drivers, monitors, etc.

All together I am convinced that this has made a difference, due to the fact that before the peace process in the UNTAES zone started, youth from all sides already met and became friends during camps and exchanges abroad....' Personal correspondence from Bert van der Linde 17.9 97.

Van der Linde comments on how different the UNTAES zone now feels, with many houses being cleaned up and rebuilt, rubble cleared, habitation resumed. 'You can see people working day and night and in a matter of three or four months complete villages have been rebuilt. Reconciliation will take longer...but good conditions are here...'

8.10 Conclusions

'You are trying to catch so many moving objects while you yourself are moving'

Any conclusions offered here on the impact of second track interventions must be cautious and tentative. Every localised example is unique, as is each initiative. It is important to note that peace-building work on 'both sides' in E. Slavonia began in earnest *before* the political agreement on re-integration into Croatia. Even when there was a new border, a 'front line', individuals sought ways to address social cleavages, to renew contact, and to find viable means of renewing relationship. Intervention from outside may have contributed in a small way to the reduction of polarisation, and to confidence building for local actors. It is local actors themselves who have taken major steps for their own (non-political) re-integration.

The work of Mary Anderson, of Minnear and Weiss, and of Lewer and Ramsbotham (Appendix 5) has been excellent in looking to practical and ethical parameters for 'humanitarian' intervention into situations of war and/or complex emergencies. The War Next Door study has tried to push the debate on intervention further, to the realm of violence reduction and 'peace-building from below.'

Second track intervention cannot broker or negotiate international agreements, but it can assist in testing their viability and enabling local populations to improve conditions and take 'ownership' of outcomes.

Second track intervention cannot demilitarise a region or zone in thirty days, but it may help with the demilitarisation of 'mind sets' over a longer period to make a difference as to whether or not arms are used. It cannot apprehend or punish the perpetrators of war crimes but it can bear witness to atrocity and alert appropriate bodies to further developments. It can lobby for, and contribute to strategies for response.

> *'If states were no longer to be treated as the single set of primary actors in the world society, then multiple sets would have to take their place. These would have to be political parties, business firms, ethnic communities, ideological groups, and many others - some fully politicised, others apparently less so. If the behaviour of all these groups was to be understood, then their values would have to be analysed. Value analysis would therefore cease to focus on international stability, national security, and other items associated only with states, and instead shift to human needs and other basic concerns... Interactions between groups would have to be analysed comprehensively, covering all forms of conflict and of cooperation, so that power politics would become one category, but only one, within the new scheme.'*
>
> Banks, 1984

Second track intervention cannot provide complete physical security or be a substitute for effective policing and basic protection. It can assist in reducing climates of fear after cessation of hostilities, and enable local populations to take their first steps towards recovery.

Second track intervention can recognise, legitimise and raise the profile of local constituencies and leadership which favour non-militaristic outcomes.

Particular findings from this exercise regarding second track intervention and the resolution of conflict are:

- Intervenors have the potential of positive impact when enabling communication between groups who have been cut off for political reasons, when the motivation and intent of those groups is the healing and ending of situations of war.
- Independent media, new technology communications and the facilitation of face to face meetings has high impact, and can draw in or persuade other opinion sectors.
- Sustained, visible, long term commitment aids impact. (The population in Osijek and East Slavonia frequently referred to the ever-changing EU monitors as 'ice cream men' because only the uniform was consistent).
- Trainings in group development, team building, problem-solving and 'democracy' may be utilised to promote peace-building or to enhance systems of war and more efficient use of violence. (See p.147) For true conflict transformation, the infusion of principles of non-violence in such trainings is a prerequisite.
- While second track intervenors have more flexibility and a lower profile than formal first track networks, the levels need each other and benefit from understanding differing style but overlap of purpose. Education in the political and military sector would benefit both. (Van der Linde points out that while UNTAES Civil Affairs section was of help to internationals working in E. Slavonia and Osijek, UNTAES military often unwittingly obstructed or prevented movement 'partly blocking the peace process they were there for'.
- The replication of NGO forms can have negative or positive impact, depending on how confining and restrictive those forms are, and whether the groups taking them on can remain

State control

An NGO in Kosovo cannot be legally registered if the ten names of the founders (that are required for registration) are Albanian. If they are half Albanian and half Serbian, this hypothetical NGO might be able to register, but then people ask who this NGO is supposed to serve. The Serbian regime has restored apartheid and does not permit Serbs and Albanians to mix in state institutions, so that Albanians do not feel secure knowing that Serbs will be coming into the organisation. That would mean that this NGO which could legally be registered would be an empty assembly that would serve no one. Of course, if the NGO had ten Serb names on the list of founders it could be registered. The only problem is that we still would not have found a solution to the problem of the need of the 2 million Albanians for their own NGOs.

Notes from Jim Satterwhite CPT and BPT, Belgrade July, 1997

true to their original purpose and still recognisable to the local community. Sudden visible disparity in funding and equipment can mean new conflicts, new cleavages.

- The NGO culture of 'the project' may be an artificial constraint which can detract from the issues at hand and narrow focus. Consultation and reflection on purpose and form of work is central to the integrity of intervention.

- Intervenors are most effective when they enable indigenous leadership and activity rather than importing either expectations or packaged solutions. The inclusion of grassroots constituencies and community development is essential to long term outcome. It is also a determinant in whether interventions contribute to the creation of new elites or new vanguards for social and political change.

- Linkage between *processes* (educational, therapeutic, training, activity or exchanges) and *context* for visible impact on structure takes time, time we need to allow for[26]. I can cite cases in Bosnia-Herzegovina and Republika Srpska where 'hard-liner' authorities have banned inter-active learning, human development training and even youth groups. This says something about the potency of such processes and their potential impact on rigid ideology and power formations.

- Intervenors may organise joint events and meetings external to a conflict, but it is exploitative to impose unexpected agendas. There have been cases of people from 'both sides' being invited to meetings on topics like 'ecology' at a neutral venue. On arrival they have found a different, politicised agenda. The intervenor is attempting to put issues 'on the table.' Without prior consultation with participants this can badly backfire; with their subsequent feelings being resentment and betrayal. 'Don't do things *for* us,' says Lydia of Osijek. 'Do things *with* us.' Sensitive handling of a coherent time frame is of utmost importance.

- At appropriate stages in post-war reconstruction and peace building activity, community forums for reflection and participative appraisal may assist in 'fine tuning' interventions and assist in co-ordination, thus cutting down on the potential for duplication or cross-purpose activity. Such forums offer the opportunity to learn from success and failure!

These thoughts are given as a type of 'snapshot' at a given time, as an effort to appraise the impact of intervention activity, local strategies, and change. There are no fixed certainties. Glavas remains an unknown factor[27], although like Arkan he may opt for retirement in luxury rather than more violent exciting forms of intimidation. There are still literally thousands of unsettled futures in any equation offered here, as those in exile hope for return and those in residence ponder their prospects. One dimension (with many strands) of building a hoped-for peace has been explored. For activists in Croatia, Serbia, and in Bosnia-Herzegovina there are continuing challenges. There are also grim realities.

Surviving the peace: thoughts from Dave Bekkering's field survey 1997

'Local NGO assistance has.. become a very popular area of work amongst international organisations operating in Bosnia. The reaction to this activity is not only positive. During conversations with representatives of the world of Bosnian NGO development, the phenomenon of NGO development was referred to as a strategy of international organisations to survive, or as attempts to create an NGO world similar to that of the country of their origin, or as activity by donor-lead so called NGOs with political agenda's suddenly aiming at capacity building. The suggestion was put forward that it is time for international organisations to let this new world of local NGOs develop more by itself instead of the international community coming in with fixed ideas about how to run an NGO.

In his recently published report 'Service Delivery or Civil Society' Ian Smillie states that the efforts of international organisations assisting local NGOs are even causes of the current bad state that the local NGO community is in. 'The domestic NGO community in B&H is in serious trouble. It is weak and fragmented, and is largely the creation of external donors and international NGOs in a hurry'

Smillie, 1996

Taking Stock...

Circumstances have changed since we, women from every region of former Yugoslavia and women coming from abroad, first started meeting together in 1992. It is our hope that a process of decontamination from an authoritarian, militaristic and nationalistic consciousness is under way, but this will take much time. We continue our visible resistance because we have no illusions that a change of regime will alter the dominant cultural mentality. We will consider peace to be real in this regime only when all refugees have the possibility to live in dignity and when, in all the newly created states, the right to be other and different - and the right to express this Others and difference - is recognised. In this climate, it is crucial that we continue to broaden and strengthen our network, it is only by sharing our experiences and learning will we support and create women's initiatives for peace.

Women In Black, 4 June 1997 Statement

I am not going to describe horrors, now. (Croatia 1991, 1995. Bosnia 1992—1995). What I am stressing is that out of those horrors some good things had happened. In this letter I am talking about tens — hundreds local grassroots peace activists (women, human rights, media...). From Serbia and Croatia first. Unfortunately from Bosnia, too.
Sombor, Pancevo, Beograd, Nis, Zagreb, Split, Osijek, Darda, Pakrac, Karlovac, Zupanja, Porec, Zenica, Gornji Vakuf, Tuzla, Sarajevo, Mostar,...just to mention some locations these people work and live...
What I am saying there are large (large?, yes) number of extraordinary individuals who were/are involved in hopeless issue of actively opposing the war. I am not underestimating work of people who were doing 'direct relief work' i.e. humanitarian assistance. This is not letter about them. I'm talking about individuals, groups who were opposing hatred, national divisions, increase of rude primitivism (as unsocial behaviour not as lack of education), promoting tolerance, rights of minorities, women as humans not 'machines for making children=soldiers'.

These people, mostly not aware that they could be called 'peace activists', to stress again, have very little previous knowledge. GOOD NEWS is that there are number of journalists, researchers, competent observers, visitors—who are saving this knowledge for future (wars). Conferences, too.
So, there is further use of heavy work done.
The role of ARK way of thinking and doing, is (as I see it) to preserve human resources.
Even more—to go more public profile.
The role of Centre for Peace Studies is that one too.
Thru Miramida, Miramida advance, Zagreb discussions, Peace Studies etc. Between Miramida support, visits, etc.
Giving activists chance to test their work in front of public, to articulate their experiences—and keep using it in future.
Am I an optimist?
Yes, cause this cease-fire (called:peace) break I see as welcomed opportunity to do more in and out of country rather than 'no more war means no more anti-war activism.'

Public in Croatia is now more open to issues of civil society, NGO lobbying, civil disobedience, conscientious objection, freedom of speech,...
Let's respond to the needs of public before new peace-makers (yesterday's warlords) start to do it. Actually they started already.

Zagreb, February 2, 1997. Brainstorming letter written by Goran Bozicevic
(reproduced with permission)

If the practice and theory of conflict resolution is to merge into the broader field of peace-building and social reconstruction, what role can research play? It will either be crucial in the advancement of the field, or become increasingly irrelevant to it. Researchers may choose to play a relatively uninvolved and distant role in the practice-change sense. They may prefer to validate data for their own needs rather than for practice needs, giving theory an external research perspective only. But we need operational ideas about change which come from the field itself[28].It is not enough to focus on first track measures. It is not enough to ask (from outside) how NGOs can function better. Enquiry must extend to the experience of primary social actors; 'What works?' in their efforts to reduce violence? We need ways of learning that are valuable to all parties involved.

Traditional first track measures (armed response, the brokering of international treaties, deployment of troops or peace keeping forces) have a very particular but limited role to play in the cessation of war. The rest, as the UNTAES observer put it 'is up to the people themselves'. In the long term the condition of the affected population is of the utmost importance. The potential for grievance and renewed hostility may be high. Or a climate may be created for self-generated social renewal: the inclusion of minorities; acceptance of returnees; the healing of deep-seated division; capacity and mechanisms for the non-violent settlement of disputes; and resistance to inflammatory and exploitative interests. These factors contribute to the viability of physical reconstruction. They are as important as the restoration of infrastructure and services.

Second track intervention has significant impact on local levels. It can contribute to improving conditions: enabling communications; building partnerships, introducing resources in ideas, skills and goods; and by raising the profile of local actors who are working against coercion or incitement to violence (in such a way as to not endanger them). The findings in this study confirm the thesis of Norbert Ropers on approaches for 'constructive conflict management of ethno-political disputes' as portrayed in his model on p. 162.

The work of intervenors and local partners which has proved effective to date resembles the 'world of societies' approaches outlined by Ropers.

Hugh Miall, writing in his 1992 publication *The Peacemakers* (Macmillan, p.35) points out that 'Coercive power can compel, but positive forms of power can move individuals, and unleash the collective power in whole communities and societies...There are, therefore, other avenues for the interplay of power than armed force. Force is not necessarily the ultimate arbiter of conflict. It depends on context and circumstances.' This study has attempted an overview of second track intervention in very particular circumstances and context. It is offered in a spirit of learning from experience: experience of the war next door.

Notes for Chapter VIII

1. *The International Response to Conflict and Genocide: Lessons from the Rwanda Experience. Joint Evaluation of Emergency Assistance to Rwanda* 1996 in five volumes, Overseas Development Institute, London.

2. Personal conversation during a joint presentation at Taplow Court, 21 August 1997.

3. See Hugo Slim, 'Doing the Right Thing; relief agencies, moral dilemmas and moral responsibility in political emergencies and war' 1997 Nordidska Afrikainstituet. Available from Centre for Development and Emergency Planning, Oxford Brookes University.

4. For a positive example of the stirrings of this debate, see *Conflict Prevention: Strategies to Sustain Peace in the Post Cold-War World* 1997. Report of the Aspen Institute Conference July 30-August 3, 1996.

5. At time of writing Mrs. Plavsic (once considered to be more extreme in her views than Karadic) is being actively courted for her new stance on Dayton implementation, the rule of law and a campaign against corruption. According to a BBC World Service broadcast (midnight 5 Sept. 1997) Plavsic has called on NATO and the USA to train the Bosnian Serb army.

   The fate of war time leadership is a source of deep division in Croatia and Serbia, validating just war for some, and incomprehensible to others. 'The man once considered most responsible for stirring the post of ethnic animosity—President Slobodan Milosevic—has been embraced by the world as a peacemaker. Once described as the "butcher of the Balkans"...he is now presented as the region's guardian angel, shaking hands with PRESIDENT Clinton...'(Dean Murphey 'Bosnia shuns soul searching...' in The Guardian 18 December 1995.) Murphey points to Tudjman's 'violent ethnic cleansing' in Krajina done with advice and tacit consent from the USA...and quotes Mr. Dilas, historian: 'All the villains of this war have survived.'

6. Invitation via *Peace News*, 9 March 1997

7. See the CCCRTE newsletter report, 'Conflict Resolution Training: Dilemmas of Evaluation' *CCCRTE* No. 4 summer 1996.

8. Personal correspondence from Paula Gutlove 18 August 1997.

9. Ibid. See also article by Gutlove and Thompson in the *Helsinki Monitor* Vol. 6 No. 3 1995.

10. These observations are based on personal conversations with student recruits (in Karlovac) granted alternative service for the Croatian military.

Such service is still problematic and riddled with ambiguity. For an up-to-date detailed report on conscription in Croatia, FRY, Bosnia-Herzegovina and elsewhere in Europe see 'Out of the margins: The right to conscientious objection to military service in Europe' by Amnesty International, April 1997 London.

11. Baker and Large draw in turn on: Hamblin 1974 *Evaluation and Control of Training* McGraw Hill, Warr et al, *Evaluation of Management Training* 1970 Gower, and M. Easterby-Smith 1988 *Evaluation of Management Education, Training and Development* Gower.

12. See 'The Audit Explosion' by Michael Powers in G. Mulgan, ed. *Life after Politics* 1997 (Demos) Fontana Press, London.

13. 'Peacebuilding through Collaborative Action' is available from the Institute for Multi-Track Diplomacy, 1819 H Street N.W. Washington DC.

14. See Weinstein, K. (1995) *Action Learning* Harper Collins, London. Note: the Danish Agency for International Development Cooperation (Danida) has produced a manual for participatory development, *Logical Framework Approach* (1996).

15. My thanks to Boris Savic for his translation of this issue.

16. See 'End of an Era?' *The Economist* 3 November 1996.

17. For an English account, 'Torturers Confessions rock Croatia' by Ian Traynor in *The Guardian* 8 September 1997, p. 5.

18. 'Since 17th of November every day at 3pm people gather on the central city square and then march through the city (3 hours). It is cold weather but it is always between 100,000—200,000 people protesting. On 22nd of November the students of Belgrade University decided to protest too, and to see them activated again was really something that warmed my heart deeply. They were protesting several times since 1991 (the beginning of war) without any effect, so that they have lost faith in the efficiency of this kind of civil disobedience. Now, again thousands of students are together, first at Academic square at noon, and then marching the streets of Belgrade for 2 hours.' Fax from Nada Ignjatovic-Savio, 2 December 1996.

19. 'Milosevic caught in vibrant web of new technology' by Chris Hedges, *The Guardian*, 10 December 1996.

20. See for example *Sign of Hope* by Sr. Mary Evelyn Jegen (Life and Peace Institute Uppsala, 1996).

21. Commission on Human Rights, Fifty-second session, item 10: 'Situation of human rights in the territory of the former Yugoslavia' Period report submitted by Mr. Tadeusz Mazowiecki.

22. See 'Croatian army success made in America' *The Observer* 7 May 1995. p.17.

23. 'Invisible US Army defeats Serbs' in *The Observer*, 5th November, 1995, p. 25.

24. Ken Silverstein, 'Privatizing War' in *The Nation* July 28—August 4 1997.

25. Ibid. Silverstein states that in 1996

> 'the Bosnian government picked MPRI—over competing bids from SAIC and BDM—to train its armed forces. The $400 million program is being paid for largely by Saudi Arabia, Kuwait, Brunei and Malaysia. The stated aim of the training effort, which is being supplemented with large-scale shipments of US weapons to the Bosnian Army, is to deter Serbia's better-armed military. But with Serbia's army in disarray, many observers of the region increasingly worry that a newly trained and equipped Bosnian Army will be emboldened to attack Serbian forces after international forces withdraw, as they are scheduled to do next year' (p. 14)

26. Bunty Biggs worked as a Quaker volunteer in post-war Germany from July 1945 to March 1948. She went as a non-official international presence (in a small group) to assist with clearing, reconstruction, and in re-establishing contact with civilians. The comments she recorded ring many chords with ex-Yugoslavia today. For example, in my conversations with the early 20's age group particularly in Serbia there is scant belief that democracy would ever work in Serbia. Bunty found the same in Germany. She can cite youth (then) who are now elected officials and leaders in a fully fledged western European democracy—some fifty years later. The following comment dated 1946 would be appropriate for some parts of Croatia and Serbia (and other places!) today:

> 'A number of people who are just those who might be able to make a valuable contribution in a democracy, are sick of politics because it enters into local govt. administration and results in officers being appointed because of their party colour rather than on merit' (personal letter home from Köln, 1946).

While the phrase 'second-track intervention' was unknown then, conversations with Bunty point to her conviction in the value of personal links, quiet international contribution, and low-key, long term engagement. In her experience it might be twenty-five years before one sees concrete and visible 'results' of change.

27. See Drago Hedl, 'A Pleasant Surprise' in *War Report*, Jan./Feb. 1997.

28. For a valuable contribution based on practical experience in training, see John Paul Lederach, *Preparing for Peace: Conflict transformation Across Cultures*, 1995, Syracuse Press. Lederach stresses the importance of culture and context as a 'resource.'

A poignant visual record of a community moving from a peaceful multi-ethnic status quo to war is caught in 'We are all neighbours', Granada TV 1993. Anthropologist Tone Bringa revisits the Bosnian village she knows well, and traces the gradual erosion of trust through fear, rumour, and incident, and the eventual outbreak of violence.

The Observer 17 August 1997

Website that has tightened the net on 66 hunted men

'OF COURSE we're mocking Nato,' says John Heffernan with a mischievous smile. 'That's the whole point, to mock and embarrass everyone who either knows where they are and pretends not to, or who really does not know.'

Heffernan, who compiles the 'Whereabouts' Internet website, is executive director of the Coalition for International Justice, *primus inter pares* of a two-person operation working out of an office in downtown Washington.

He is also a thorn in the side of those in authority in the United States and Bosnia who continue to act out the tragi-comic farce of leaving 66 fugitives accused of war crimes at liberty.

Heffernan set up the coalition two years ago, after returning from the Balkans as a field worker for the International Rescue Committee, processing the wretched survivors of the Omarska, Kereterm and Trnopolje camps, and resettling them in a scattered diaspora. It was to be an international legal pressure group, but, he says, 'we have become attached to one issue — this one'.

The idea of setting up and updating a website which would tell the world where the fugitives were came late into programme which was primarily laid out to lobby for a linkage between economic aid and compliance with the Dayton agreement.

US threats to Croatia that World Bank and IMF loans would be vetoed unless Zagreb co-operated with The Hague was largely the result of meetings by the coalition with senior financial officials, at which they laid bare Croatia's record on shielding war crimes suspects.

Meanwhile, they showed a film about Camp Omarska, *The Calling of the Ghosts*, in order to draw attention to research by the group Human Rights Watch showing that Prijedor police chief Simo Drljaca, shot by British troops last month, was embezzling large amounts of aid money from Britain and distributing it among his local mafia syndicates. That was part of the groundswell that led to the War Crimes Prosecution Facilitation Act currently before Congress, which seeks to link all reconstruction funds to the apprehension of war criminals.

'Whereabouts' site: 'This is all happening under Nato's nose.'

Then came the idea for a website. 'It was a matter of assembling it all together,' says Heffernan. 'Press reports, word of mouth, our own calls and research — just getting it all in one place where everyone could see how ridiculous it is that all this is happening under Nato's nose.'

Much of the information has come from an indefatigable journalist from the *Boston Globe*, Elizabeth Neuffer, who simply took a copy of a 'Wanted' poster which is displayed on the wall of every I-For building in Bosnia showing photographs of the accused and their addresses. She visited the addresses, and at a large number of homes found the indicted suspects or members of their families.

The latest scheme from the coalition has been to harvest a vast arc of American Jewish, Christian, Muslim and human rights groups — probably the biggest of its kind assembled for the purpose to date — to sign a letter to President Clinton published in the *New York Times*, warning of the 'mockery of justice' entailed in a departure of American troops from Bosnia before all the suspects had been arrested.

Follow the war criminals' progress on the Web
http://www.wcw.org/ictty/whereabouts.html

Approaches for Constructive Conflict Management of Ethno-political Disputes in the World of States and Societies

	World of States	**World of Societies**
Micro-political Approaches	• Crisis interventions • Affirmative actions • Ad-hoc-programmes for improving the situation of disadvantaged groups • Establishment of minority-bodies with mainly symbolic powers • Enhancement of minority rights with individual reference → **Negotiations**	• Empowerment of disadvantaged groups • Improving multi-ethnic living conditions • Exchange and encounter programmes • Encouragement of multiple identities • Transnational networking of human rights NGOs → **Round tables, pre-negotiations**
Macro-political Approaches	• Institutional reforms in favour of more democratic and rule-of-law-structures • Enhancement of minority rights with collective reference • Non-territorial autonomy • Territorial autonomy • Other concepts of power-sharing (grand coalitions, proportionality, minority veto, condominions, etc.) • Secession → **Constitutional reforms**	• Codes-of-conduct for conflict-relevant groups and institutions (journalists, teachers) • Establishment of legitimate arenas for constitutional disputes • Mobilising social actors in favour of peace constituencies • Institutional strengthening of transnational loyalities → **Conflict transformation**

Appendices

Appendix 1

Chris Mitchell's 1981 exposition on the conflict structure and processes remains one of the clearest analytical frameworks available. He summarizes his 'Basic Conflict Structure' triangular model (below) with the following simple propositions:

> (a) *Situations affect behaviour* (goals, especially salient goals, being frustrated call forth intense efforts to achieve those goals).
> (b) Situations affect attitudes (goal incompatibility is likely to increase suspicion and mistrust).
> (c) Behaviour affects situations (success may bring more issues into the dispute as demands escalate).
> (d) Behaviour affects attitudes (destruction increases anger, success can affect the sense of in-group solidarity).
> (e) Attitudes affect behaviour (expectations that ... 'Our traditional enemies the X's are up to no good again' will affect defensive preparations and contingency plans).
> (f) Attitudes affect situations (More issues will be perceived to be in dispute with an adversary, so that a long drawn-out confrontation may develop).

His model of conflict structure is meant to illustrate inter-dependencies among the components, and the ways in which change in one feeds back to affect others. 'The model helps to emphasise the existence of such linkages, although it does not suggest the complexity of many of the feedback processes involved, the difficulties of tracing out the linkages, and the differential time lags almost certainly involved in one component bring about changes in others.' (Mitchell, 1981, p.55)

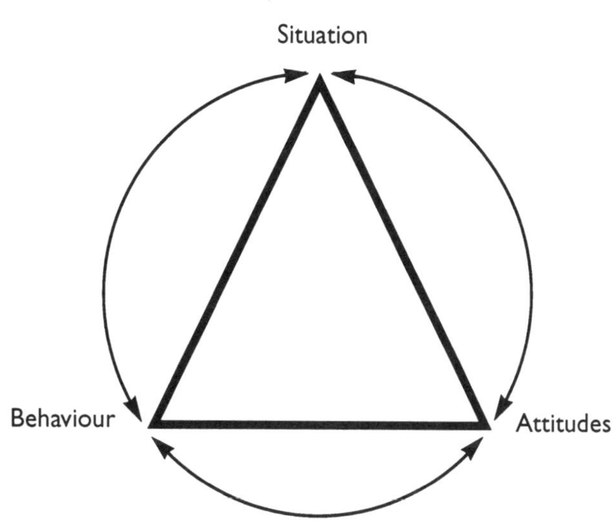

Basic conflict structure

Appendix 2
The politics of transfer

> *'...Resettlement—or population transfer—initially began out of fear of the war and nationalist extremism. Croats from the autonomous region of Krajina, and Serbs from parts of Eastern Slavonia, were both affected. In the next phase of the war the transfer was not the spontaneous result of fear, but became policy enforced by all sides. Examples of this are Western Slavonia and Baranja, and evidence is now emerging which shows that resettlement has been the consequence of premeditated political acts.*
>
> *Firstly, the politicians who started the war did not undertake military action to save the Serbs in Western Slavonia and the Croats in Baranja and Eastern Slavonia. Quite the opposite; people were actually advised to withdraw from these territories.*
>
> *Secondly, wherever possible, Croat refugees moved into apartments and houses abandoned by the Serbs who were forced, in the parts of Croatia where they constituted a small minority, to leave. Interestingly, there was no attempt to stop the forced displacement of Serbs from Western Slavonia and the Federal Army even helped them to move. Immediately after the first column of 15,000 refugees left from there, the government of the autonomous region of Slavonia, Baranja and Western Srem decided to repopulate Baranja. By some miraculous coincidence—or more likely a deliberate act—15,000 Hungarians and Croats had departed from this territory.*
>
> *...The Croatian government has a strict policy on this issue; territories have to be reclaimed and refugees returned to their homes. But nobody knows how or when this can happen'*
>
> 'Politics of transfer' by Zarko Paunovic Yugofax 3 Feb. 1992, page 3

Doing interviews for this study it was striking how many people had fled Baranja from sheer fear, rather than factual warnings of any advancing army. 'My parents had their own memories of terror from the last war,' says J., 'and were not going to wait to see this one.' Others felt now that panic had cost them their homes, their gardens, their neighbourhoods. The fact that so many left with a sense of incredulity, and as almost pre-emptive action probably influenced the unrealistic optimism in Osijek 1992 that they would soon be returning home.

Purely domestic transfer was enforced, as well. Tatjana Tagitou, Arkzin journalist, wrote in 1995 that no one knew exactly how many Croatian citizens had been evicted from their homes, citing estimates of over 14,000:

> 'Many Serbs were bullied into leaving through suspensions, threats by neighbours, or the government's refusal to grant them citizenship. Then their flats were broken into and given to whoever could present the most convincing claim. An estimated 3,600 evictions involved flats previously owned by the Yugoslav's People's Army (JNA), carried out by uniformed men at gun point. Vladimir Seks, vice-president of Sabor, called the evictions a product of just anger—justified by the war situation—for the benefit of homeless families of fallen heroes and the war invalids. It soon emerged that they never profited. In fact, the main beneficiaries were top military commanders, their friends and relatives. The Ministry of Defence has been issuing its favourites with so-called permits to use the flats of unlawfully evicted tenants temporarily, although the law is clear—these can only be issued for homes empty of people and furniture. Defying an agreement with the departing JNA, there is no legal basis for the evictions, although it is argued that they have been carried out under court warrants' ('The Short Arm of the Law,' War Report March 1995, p.35).

Finally, no one will ever know how many people organised their own transfers: the swap of houses, of flats, of holiday homes, according to new parameters of geography and ethnicity, was willingly negotiated by many families and friends. If you were a Croat living in the suburbs of Belgrade, it made sense to agree to exchange accommodation with a Serb friend who had been resident south of Zagreb. I have seen no documentation of such agreements, but the anecdotal evidence is substantial.

Appendix 3
UNTAES work, former Sector East

Post-Dayton UNTAES work was for a critical mass of action to ensure that the 're-integration process' continued at an accelerating speed. The following specific projects were central as of late May, 1996.

1. The Croatian government through UNTAES pressure has agreed to pay all pensions due to people in Baranja (as citizens of Croatia) from 1 July 1996. This will include back payments due, from the start of the war where appropriate—amounting up to 20,000 DEM in appropriate cases. It is not clear if the back payment lump sum will be paid in full or in part and some other arrangement made over the balance. It appears that payment will be in Kuna—arrangements are to be made for this 'foreign' money to be readily convertible into DEM or Dinars at the point of payment.

2. The mosquito spraying programme is going ahead in the next few days. Three crop spraying aircraft will be used with Croat and Serbian pilots in each and with an escort of UNTAES helicopters. Some 10,500 hectares are to be treated.

3. Direct connections to the Croatian telephone exchange in Osijek would be available from Tuesday 21 May. (Just dial 031) Presumably users pay two phone bills, one to Croatia and the other to Serbia for use of the Sombor exchange.

4. The railway line from Osijek to Mohacs (Hungary) is to be opened soon. The track is currently being de-mined.

5. Both sides have checked their electricity grid supply lines on their own sides and made necessary repairs. Joint teams are soon to go and check lines across the zone of separation—presumably after the area round the towers and the access to these have been de-mined.

6. A deal has been struck between UNTAES and Croatia for UNTAES to supply agricultural fuel oil for tractors in Baranja—this apparently to start flowing very shortly—presumably this to be paid for from credits given by other sources.

7. UNTAES has negotiated a deal where seeds and fertilisers are supplied by them and 'swapped' (bartered) with corn of equivalent monetary value to be supplied by the recipients after harvest.

8. Croatian refugees from Hungary were taken over the Udvar crossing on 16 May and shown round their own villages. This is the first of such visits planned though nobody was officially allowed to actually inspect their own homes and make contact with the families living in them. There was no trouble. Remaining neighbours actually came out to wave and greet their visitors, and there were moving family reunions. The dreaded single incident—the thrown brick or shouted insult did not happen.

9. A US AID office is to be set up in Baranja soon and will be offering loans from $500 to $25,000 for approved business projects. There are bi-weekly meetings between UNTAES and local business leaders to discuss ways of getting the local economy moving again—local people are still suspicious and very cautious. The rate of loan repayment will be based on the profitability of the firm concerned—all sums repaid will be available for reinvestment on a revolving fund basis.

10. $1 million has been made available from Scandinavian sources for house repair and rebuilding for the UNTAES area. A 'standard' two storied house with cellar can be built on the self-build system in the area for about 20,000 DEM.

11. Shortly an exchange of mail will be made across the line from both sides 3 days a week.

12. Several meetings of people from the two sides but from the same villages have already taken place at the tent specially erected at the Bilje crossing for this purpose. This process of community meetings is to be speeded up.

13. There are now exchanges of 'experts' from both sides regularly taking place with UNTAES help. Serb and Croat Experts also meet together in the specific Commissions (e.g. health, agriculture etc.) hosted by UNTAES.

14. The greenhouse project for women in Baranja is proceeding well—directed by Tanja Serbic from Osijek. Also Peter Fankhauser's project on bio-farming has attracted some interest and a pilot project of some 15 ha of sunflower seeds, to be grown organically, has started, with potential markets in Switzerland.

15. UNTAES are to set up legal advisory offices in Beli Monastir and Vukovar, staffed with international as well as ethnic Serb and Croat lawyers. These are to open this month and will deal with all the paperwork in connection with registration of citizenship, identity and property rights. Legally they will work under the Croatian Constitution.

The Guardian Wednesday October 4 1995

Deal reached on Serb-held territory in Croatia

Steps to peace in Eastern Slavonia

Julian Borger in Zagreb

INTERNATIONAL mediators claimed a breakthrough yesterday in the Balkan peace initiative, announcing a preliminary agreement on the future of the last Serb-controlled enclave in Croatia.

Thorvald Stoltenberg, the United Nations special envoy to former Yugoslavia, said Croatian and Serb minority representatives at a meeting in the border town of Erdut had agreed "guiding principles" for a settlement for Eastern Slavonia — a slice of territory at the eastern extremity of Croatia on the border with Serbia.

Few details were available yesterday evening, but it is believed that the Serbs accepted that Eastern Slavonia would remain part of Croatia, with guaranteed minority rights.

Western observers in Zagreb, however, said the agreement did not entirely eliminate the risk of a military clash over the oil-rich, fertile region. They pointed out that negotiators from the United States thought they had achieved a diplomatic breakthrough on the eve of the Croatian army's offensive against the breakaway Serb "republic" of Krajina.

Since that offensive overran Serb defences in early August, Eastern Slavonia has been the only part of Croatia still under Serb control.

At the UN headquarters in New York last week, Croatia threatened to retake Eastern Slavonia if the Serbs did not accept Croatian sovereignty, giving rise to fears that the dispute might derail US-led negotiations on an overall Balkan peace deal.

An official in Croatia's foreign ministry said yesterday that the groundwork for the agreement had been laid in earlier contacts between the two sides. "In a number of talks prior to this, at Geneva and New York, the Serbs resigned themselves to the fact that the area would come under Croatian sovereignty," he said.

The two sides agreed that the region and its 65,000 mostly-Serb inhabitants should have an interim administration, under the auspices of the UN, the European Union or the Organisation for

Co-operation and Security in Europe (OSCE), before a transition to full Croatian control, but there was no agreement on how long the transition should last.

There were also disagreements over the degree of Eastern Slavonia's autonomy and how extensive its links should be with the rump Yugoslavia (Serbia and Montenegro).

Eastern Slavonia has been the focus of a significant military build-up on both sides of the border. The local Serbs have a force of 8,000, backed up by a 10,000-strong division of regular Serbian troops. The Croatian army had deployed about 12,000 soldiers along the region's western periphery.

Before war broke out in 1991, Croats were the largest ethnic group in Eastern Slavonia, accounting for 44 per cent of the region's population. The main city, Vukovar, was predominantly Croat. The return of Croat refugees to Vukovar and the surrounding area is the most emotive issue in Croatian politics.

"I would have thought President Franjo Tudjman [of Croatia] wants to see people going back to Vukovar before he stands for re-election next year," said a diplomat based in the Croatian capital, Zagreb.

As one obstacle to a global peace settlement appeared to recede, fighting erupted near Sarajevo and Bosnian government forces fired artillery from the city, violating the Nato- and UN-enforced heavy weapons ban.

Marcia Nash, a spokeswoman for the UN rapid reaction force, said Bosnian government and Serb artillery exchanged fire near the small town of Trnovo, south of Sarajevo. "It appears that the Bosnian government began firing in response to an attack on them around 8 o'clock this morning," she said.

Possibly in support of their positions around Trnovo, government forces fired four heavy mortars from inside the 12-mile exclusion zone around Sarajevo agreed with the Serb rebels last month.

Nato action against Bosnian government positions is seen as extremely unlikely, but the UN officials were furious at the violation. "We will be protesting to the Bosnian government at the highest level," said Alexander Ivanko, a UN spokesman in Sarajevo.

Appendix 4
The Embargo

No study of this nature would be complete without due reference to the use of sanctions against FRY and in particular, their effect on the population itself. It is a subject deserving of extended research in itself. This appendix offers historical reminders and opinions on a much debated policy.

In September 1992 'the UN General Assembly voted that the new Yugoslavia must reapply for membership, whereupon it was readmitted as the FRY but excluded from the General Assembly and membership of the International Monetary Fund (IMF) was revoked in December and conditions established for the FRY and its former republics to succeed to membership. Political life and international relationships were dominated by Serbia's involvement in and primary responsibility for continuing the war in Bosnia-Herzegovina. Comprehensive UN sanctions and a European Community (EC) trade embargo were imposed in May in an attempt to force an end to the war, and were enforced from November by the North Atlantic Treaty Organization (NATO) and the Western European Union (WEU); by the end of November these sanctions had reportedly halved the FRY's exports and doubled its foreign trade deficit.

In mid-year a power struggle developed between Serbian President, Milosevic, and FRY Prime Minister, Panic, who sought an end to the war. Serbian police, in September, occupied and remained in the Interior Ministry buildings in Belgrade. Following his defeat by Milosevic in elections to the Serbian presidency in December, Panic also lost as vote of confidence in the Federal Assembly; his official position at first remained unclear as he refused to resign; Deputy Prime Minister Radoje Kontic was appointed to replace him and in February was mandated to form a new government.'

...'By January 1992 the FRY's foreign currency reserves were virtually exhausted and the foreign debt stood at $6,000 million. According to the Federal Statistical Office on Dec. 28, inflation reached an average annualized rate of 19,810 per cent in 1992.'

From Keesing's Record of World Events, Volume 39, Reference Supplement, page R129:

Aids

The answer to question why Serbs don't have AIDS used to be—because it is a disease of the 20th century. Now this phenomenon can be explained differently: in an article published by three American researchers and published in the London-based medical journal AIDS, the World Bank and the International Monetary Fund are accused of spreading this horrible disease. The authors claim that these two financial institutions often undermine the social structures of developing countries and that the 'behaviour of the populations changes, putting them at greater risk of contracting the virus.'

This could mean that Serbia and Montenegro are protected in a way, because thanks to a certain set of unfortunate circumstances they don't have any contact with the World Bank and the IMF.

If we look after sanctions, sanctions will look after us.

NEWS DIGEST AGENCY, VREME, 29th MAY 1995, page 5

'Croatia, Slovenia and Bosnia-Herzegovina were accepted as members of the UN on May 22, 1992 by decision of the General Assembly.
Resolution 757 of the UN Security Council imposed comprehensive sanctions on the FRY on May 30. These included (I) severing trade links;(ii) freezing government assets abroad; (iii) an oil embargo; (iv) a sporting and cultural ban; and (v) cutting air links (already severed by Canada, Germany, Italy and the USA).'

From Keesing's *Record of World Events, News Digest for May 1992*, page 38918:

'Budget - devaluation of dinar

On June 25 1993 the Federal Assembly approved a budget for 1993 amounting to 1,277,756,000 million dinars (the government having the previous day reduced the total by 50,000,000 million dinars from the original draft published on June 15); 76.6 per cent of the total would be for defence.

On June 16 a new rate for the dinar had been set of 1,100,000 to the US dollar and 700,000 to the German deutschmark.

Inflation between May and June amounted to 366.7 per cent. The Yugoslav economy continued to be severely affected by UN sanctions imposed at the end of May 1992, which had been intensified through joint Western Europe Union and Romanian enforcement operation on the Danube. The first full year of sanctions was officially stated to have cost Yugoslavia about US$20,000 million as well as causing economic damage to neighbouring countries of US$35,000 million, and gross domestic product had fallen by about US$12,000 million.

As the value of the currency was destroyed by spiralling hyper-inflation (the official monthly inflation rate increased from 430 per cent in July to 1,800 per cent in August), a 500 million dinar bank note came into circulation on Aug. 13.'

From Keesing's *Record of World Events, News Digest for June 1993*, page 39518

'...In an effort to limit the conflict, the Committee of Senior Officials of the CSCE agreed to impose an arms embargo on Yugoslavia. The United Nations Security Council unanimously adopted the embargo on September 25, 1991. This and later efforts would have little effect on the ability of the Serbian/JNA forces to wage war, however. They controlled considerable stockpiles of material established by the old regime. Some of these arms caches would come under the control of Croatian forces, improving their fighting capacity. In addition, both the Croats and the Serbs continued to receive considerable supplies from international arms merchants. Only Bosnian government forces, surrounded on all sides by either Croatian or Serbian opponents, felt the effects of the embargo. Eventually, however, Bosnian government forces, too, would secure access to the international arms market. Thus, in Yugoslavia as elsewhere, embargoes and, later, sanctions proved to have little effect.'

From: *International Organizations and Ethnic Conflict.* Edited by Milton J Esman and Shibley Telhami. Cornell University Press 1995. Ithaca and London

Chapter 9 'The International Community and the Yugoslav Crisis', Steven L Burg, page 244

THE EMBARGO AGAINST YUGOSLAVIA HAS GIVEN RISE TO THE BALKAN MAFIA

by Nikola Kitsevski, commentator on international matters for the independent daily, **Trud**, *Sofia*

If the financial sanctions imposed two years ago on Belgrade have had any effect at all, it is this: the Yugo-embargo has given rise to the Balkan Mafia.

The one-time prohibition of alcohol in the United States did not deprive the Yanks of their drink, it simply brought about a network of organized crime in America. Today the prohibition of free trade with a country in a state of war, desperately in need of its imports, has 'achieved' the following:

First, the establishment of local outlaw gangs, which have developed close links with powerful economic groups and masterminds in their own country.

Second, the foundation of a powerful Mafia-style network in the Balkans.

This illegal network has been created and developed as a consequence of the immutable laws of financial interest. The union of forces and co-ordination of the efforts of all the parties concerned was unavoidable for the very simple reason that it has always been impossible for one side on its own to overcome obstacles and barriers imposed by the UN. The result is clear: Several 'loopholes' have been found (or created) in the blockade, so that fuel, metal and weapons may pass freely and easily.

Furthermore, in a brazen 'display of strength', the Balkan Mafiosi delivered a slap in the face of the international community in the form of the hijacking, on 4 March 1994, of the Bulgarian ship 'Kian Kumbrat' with its load of 6,000 tonnes of oil, which finally ended up in the Serbian port of Lunavi Prachovo. As later became known, this criminal undertaking was carried out with the participation of Bulgarians, Serbs, Russians, Ukrainians, Romanians, Greeks...

When the Berlin Wall collapsed in 1989, I do not believe that Bulgarians, Romanians, or Albanians were aware that organized crime would figure among the 'goods' that democracy would bring to their countries.

But the series of tragedies has not omitted the Balkans this time either—the dissolution of the old system, including the instruments for fighting crime, coincided chronologically with the Yugo-embargo.

Inevitably, the sanctions will sooner or later be lifted, economic damage to neighbouring countries (for Bulgaria alone these losses already amount to 3.5 billion US dollars) will be noted in the 'Irretrievable losses' paragraph, and the only thing remaining will be its international Balkan Mafia.

As for the basic objective of the Security Council of the United Nations with the imposition of the Yugo-embargo—to stop the war—this objective remains just as unattainable now as it was the day when it was imposed on the New Yugoslavia of Serbia and Montenegro. Furthermore, far from the supposed economic embargo provoking anger and mass disturbances in Yugoslavia, leading to the downfall of Slobodan Milosevic, as the sanctions' backers may have wished, pressure from outside has unified the Serbs behind their leader under the slogan 'The Whole World is against Us.'

So, if 'Slobo'believes in God, he should spend the rest of his life lighting candles and praying for the health of those who imposed the sanctions.

BALKAN REVIEW 2/94, THESSALONIKA

Appendix 5: Emergent guidelines and conduct codes

Dr. Mary B. Anderson in the 'Local Capacities for Peace' project at the Collaborative for Development Action, Cambridge USA. Cited in *Life & Peace Review* 2/95 p. 13.

Summary of her assessment of how aid sometimes worsens conflicts based on the collective experiences of aid agencies in conflict zones:

1. Introducing resources into a resource-scarce environment where there is conflict usually increases competition and suspicion among warring parties.

2. External resources brought into war situations by humanitarian and development agencies add to overall resources in the area and , thus, free internal resources to be used in pursuit of war.

3. International assistance can result in severe distortions in local economic activities, thus reducing income and employment opportunities for some groups and, correspondingly, increasing inter-group tensions.

4. When international assistance agencies hire armed guards to protect their delivery of goods to needy recipients, they 'buy into' the terms of existing conflicts.

5. When humanitarian agencies circulate pictures or stories of war-based atrocities in their own publicity as a means of enlisting support for their work, they provide additional grist for the mill of accusation and counter-accusation which permeates conflicts among groups.

6. By working through existing regimes in order to gain access to people in need, international agencies can buttress such regimes. In some cases, such apparent support for the legitimacy of a regime can prolong oppression and resultant warfare.

7. Adopting policies of solidarity with groups fighting for their legitimate rights under oppressive regimes, international donor agencies can contribute to the will of people to engage in violent conflict over prolonged period of time.

8. By targeting their aid to specific groups in societies, international donors may exacerbate and excite tensions within that society that eventually lead to warfare.

9. Through the processes that they initiate for selecting programmatic activities within recipient countries, international aid agencies set up systems which pit groups against one another. When more than one agency works in an area, they may even become participants in the competition and furthering of inter-group suspicions.

10. Military aid, which has often accompanied humanitarian or development assistance, has left a legacy of armaments that in and of itself supports the outbreak of new violent conflicts and the perpetuation of old ones.

From Larry Minnear and Thomas Weiss 1995 *Mercy under Fire*, Westview Press:

The Providence Principles of humanitarian action in armed conflicts are:

1. *Relieving Life-Threatening Suffering*:
   Humanitarian action should be directed toward the relief of immediate, life-threatening suffering.

2. *Proportionality to Need:*
   Humanitarian action should correspond to the degree of suffering, wherever it occurs. It should affirm the view that life is as precious in one part of the globe as another.

3. *Non-partisanship:*
   Humanitarian action responds to human suffering because people are in need, not to advance political, sectarian, or other extraneous agendas. It should not take sides in conflicts.

4. *Independence*:
   In order to fulfil their mission, humanitarian organizations should be free of interference from home or host political authorities. Humanitarian space is essential for effective action.

5. *Accountability:*
   Humanitarian organizations should report fully on their activities to sponsors and beneficiaries. Humanitarianism should be transparent.

6. *Appropriateness:*
   Humanitarian action should be tailored to

local circumstances and aim to enhance, not supplant, locally available resources.

7. *Contextualization:*
Effective humanitarian action should encompass a comprehensive view of overall needs and of the impact of interventions. Encouraging respect for human rights and addressing the underlying causes of conflicts are essential elements.

8. *Subsidiarity of Sovereignty:*
Where humanitarianism and sovereignty clash, sovereignty should defer to the relief of life-threatening suffering.

From Nick Lewer and Oliver Ramsbotham 1993 *Something Must be Done : Towards an Ethical Framework for Humanitarian Intervention in International-Social Conflict* Dept. of Peace Studies, University of Bradford:

Ten framework principles for Humanitarian Intervention in International-Social Conflict:

1. *The Principle of Minimum Humanitarian Standards (Just Cause)*
'Where there is unacceptable denial or violation of human rights, actual or threatened, the international community has a duty to attempt redress and a prima facie right to intervene, subject to the condition laid down in principle nine.'

2. *The Principle of Human Flourishing (Just Ends)*
'The aim of such intervention should be the impartial promotion of sustained human flourishing throughout the affected region.'

3. *The Principle of Appropriate Means (Just Means)*
'The means employed should be appropriate—that is, they should be (a) necessary, (b) sufficient, (c) proportional, and (d) legitimate.'

4. *The Principle of Local Enablement*
'The intervention should be conducted in terms understood and accepted within the region and in such a way as to strengthen and support those working locally to resolve conflict and build peace.'

5. *The Principle of Consistency*
'Intervention should be consistent across different conflict situations and relevant experience should be cumulatively transferred.'

6. *The Principle of Reflexivity*
'Intervenors' motives and previous behaviour should be compatible with the professed purpose of their intervention.'

7. *The Principle of Complementarity*
'Intervenors' actions should be mutually complementary.'

8. *The Principle of Accountability*
'Intervenors should hold themselves accountable to the international community for their intervention, since it is from the international community that they derive the authority to intervene.'

9. *The Principle of Contingency and Graduated Response*
'Where possible, intervention should be preventative, non-violent and with the consent of all parties. Where this is not possible, additional criteria should be met as appropriate at the relevant decision-points, without prejudice as to the outcome.'

10. *The Principle of Universality*
'The principles which govern just humanitarian intervention should be endorsed by the international community.

Appendix 6

Probably, central to all the reasons for evaluating is the following kind of loop, information gathering, analysis and decision-making.

The emphasis and focus given to evaluation ought to be as natural as the process of planning training. Few would run a programme of training without adequate planning and preparation. Yet many programmes, at best, have evaluation tacked on to the programme almost as an afterthought or in some cases a token gesture. Clearly, for evaluation to be effective it should be designed as an integrated part of the training design and in accordance with an evaluation strategy with a purpose, i.e. a rational decision.

***Towards a Structure for Evaluations:* The basic framework**

The following framework gives an outline of possible training evaluation process:

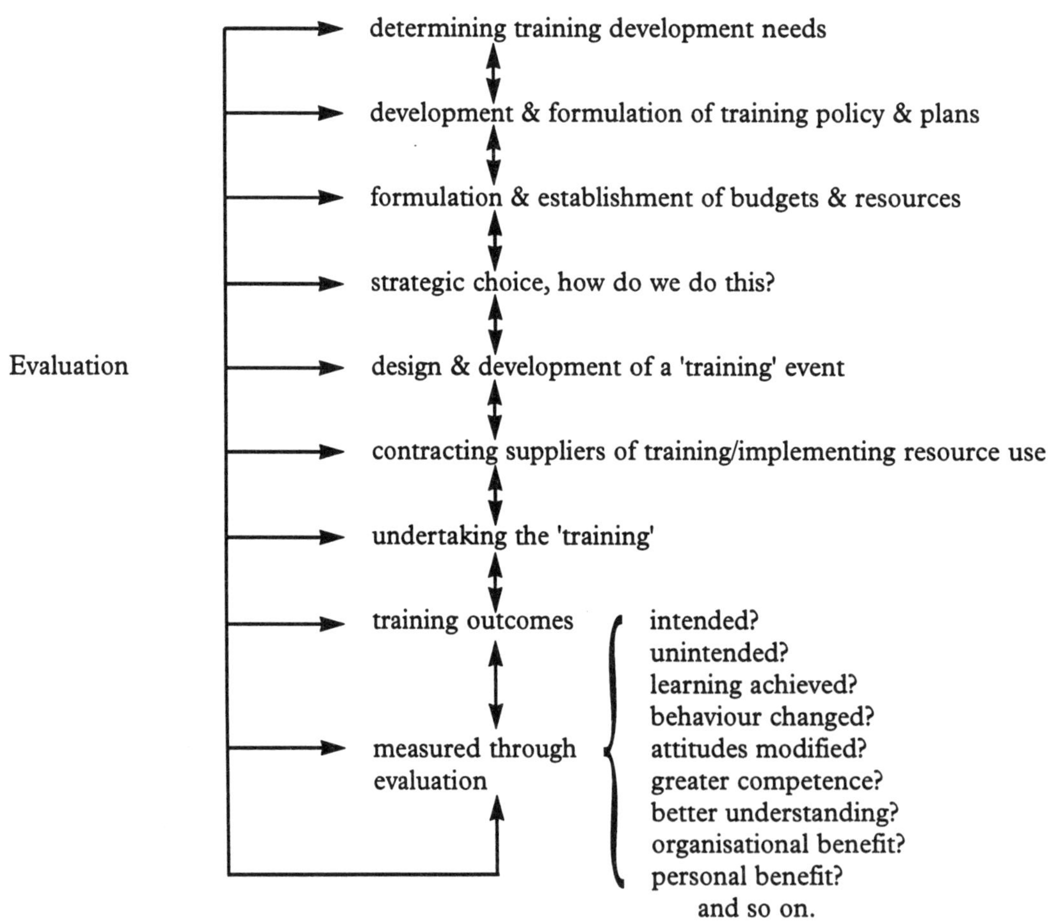

Double headed arrows simply indicate that it is a reciprocal process of mutual development and interaction. It is possible to conceptualise other arrangements but note here the great emphasis on evaluating outcomes; fine it is necessary.

Consider too that all stages of this process could be reviewed. Should there be no positive or desirable outcomes - why? Is it simply that the course or training programme was at fault? Why can't it be that the needs were incorrectly specified?

Hamblin's approach

C Context evaluation
- What changes are necessary?
- What needs are being expressed?
- To what extent can training help?
- What kind of objectives & approach would help?
- Are local contacts supportive?

I Input evaluation
- What resources do I have at my disposal?
- What opportunity costs in using them (resources)?
- How best do I use resources?

R Reaction evaluation
- Have we met expectations?
- How do participants feel?
- Do they have favourable opinions?

O Outcome evaluation at three levels
- Immediate outcomes, met objectives of my programme?
- Intermediate outcomes, training influenced "next steps"?
- Ultimate outcomes, training influenced social change?

Bibliography

Abdennur, Alexander. 1987. *The Conflict Resolution Syndrome.* Ottawa, Canada: University of Ottawa Press.

Acland, Andrew F. 1990. *A Sudden Outbreak of Common Sense.* London: Hutchinson Business Books.

Agger, Inger. 1993. 'Theory and Practice of Psycho-Social Projects for victims of war in Croatia and Bosnia-Herzegovina.' Zagreb: EC Task Force.

Ages, Ted. 1993. 'Report on Second Training in Belgrade.'

Alger, C. 1991. 'Creating global visions for peace movements.' In *Peace Culture and Society,* edited by E. Boulding, C. Brigagao and K. Clements. Boulder: Westview.

Amnesty Reports. 1981. 'Imprisoned writers, journalists and academics.' In *Yugoslavia Special Action Report.* London: Amnesty International, November 20.

Anderson, M. and Woodrow, P. 1989. *Raising from the Ashes: Development Strategies in times of disaster.* Boulder: Westview Press.

Andrejevich, Milan. 1990. 'Croatia Between Stability and Civil War, Part II.' In *Report on Eastern Europe,* pp. 42-43. September 28.

Andrejevich, Milan. 1990. 'Milosevic and the Serbian Opposition.' In *Report on Eastern Europe,* pp. 41-42, October 19.

Aron, Raymond. 1967. *Peace and War.* London: Weidenfeld & Nicholson.

Atwood, David. 1994. 'Nongovernmental Conflict Intervention: Some Observations on Two Current Experiments.' Paper prepared for the Conference 'Peaceful Settlement of Conflict—A Task for Civil Society II.' Evangelische Akademie Loccum, March 16-18.

Avruch, K. and Black, P. 1991 'The Culture Question and Conflict Resolution' in Peace and Change Vol. 16, No. 1. Jan. pp. 22—45.

Azar, E. and Burton, J. 1986. *International Conflict Resolution.* Brighton: Wheatsheaf.

Azar, E. E. 1990. *The Management of Protracted Social Conflict.* Dartmouth: Aldershot.

Baev, Pavel. 1993. 'Peace-keeping as a Challenge to European Borders.' *Security Dialogue* Vol. 24 (2). Sage Publications.

Bandura, Albert. 'On Social Learning and Aggression' in Hollander, E. and Hunt, R., eds. 1976. *Current Perspectives in Social Psychology.* Oxford University Press.

Banks, Michael (ed.). 1988 (1984). *Conflict in World Society. A new perspective on international relations.* Brighton, Sussex: Wheatsheaf Books Ltd.

Basom, Kenneth. 1996. 'Prospects for Democracy in Serbia and Croatia.' In *East European Quarterly* XXIX ,No. 4, January.

Bell, Martin. 1996. 'Conflict of Interest.' In *The Guardian,* July 11.

Bennett, Christopher. 1995. *Yugoslavia's Bloody Collapse.* London: Hurst & Co.

Berman, Maureen R. and Johnson, Joseph E. 1977. *Unofficial Diplomats.* New York: Columbia University Press.

Biserko, Sonja. 1994. 'Belgrade Peace Movement—A Society of Friends.' In *War Report* June—July, p.18.

Bloom, William. 1990. *Personal identity, national identity and international relations.* Cambridge: Cambridge University Press.

Bobbio, Norberto. 1989. *Democracy and Dictatorship: the Nature and Limits of State Power.* Cambridge: Polity Press.

Boulding, E. 1990. *Building a Global Civic Culture.* Syracuse: Syracuse University Press.

Box, S. 1971. *Deviance, Reality and Society.* New York: Holt, Rinehart and Winston.

Boydell, T. and Leary, M. 1993. *Developing the Developers* No. 4. Henley-on-Thames: Henley Distance Learning Ltd.

BPT International (Balkan Peace Team). 1995. Report: 'Balkan Peace Team International Exploratory Visit to Former Sector East.' November 13-19, Minden, Germany.

Bradbury, Mark. 'Building Partnerships for Peace and Development: A Report of a Workshop held in Borama Somaliland, 9-12 Dec. 1996.' International Cooperation for Development Publication.

Bradbury, Mark. 1993. 'Peace-enforcement, Peace-making and Peace-building. Options for Resolving the Somali Conflict.' An Exploratory Report for Oxfam.

Bradbury, Mark. 1996. 'Conflict and Humanitarian Aid. Civil Society and Our Part in its Downfall.' Paper presented to The British Agencies Afghanistan Group at the seminar: 'Good Practice in the Afghan Context: NGOs Planning and Collaborating to Strengthen Civil Society.' *Christian Aid,* January 10.

Bramson, Leon, and Goethals, George W (eds.). 1968. *War Studies from Psychology, Sociology and Anthropology.* New York and London: Basic Books Inc.

Breakwell, Glynis with Millward, Lynne. 1995. *Basic Evaluation Methods. Analysing performance, practice and procedure.* Leicester: BPS Books.

Brockner, J. and Rubin, J. 1985. *Entrapment in Escalating Conflicts: a social psychological analysis.* Springer-Verlag.

Brown, Michael E. (ed.). 1993. *Ethnic Conflict and International Security.* Princeton: Princeton University Press.

Brown, Roger. 1965. *Social Psychology.* New York: The Free Press.

Burg, Steven, L. 'International Community and the Yugoslav Crisis.' Chapter 9. In Esman, Milton J. and Telhami, Shibley (eds.) 1995. *International Organisations and Ethnic Conflict.* Ithaca and London: Cornell University Press.

Burton, J. 1990. *Conflict: Resolution and Prevention.* London: The Macmillan Press.

Buzan, Barry. 1991. *People, States and Fear. An agenda for International security studies in the post-cold war era.* Second Edition. London: Harvester Wheatsheaf, a division of Simon & Schuster International Group.

Carment, D. and James, P. 1997. 'The International Politics of Ethnic Conflicts' in *Global Society* Vol. 11 No. 2. May.

Chopra, Jarat. 1997. 'Peace Maintenance: the Last Stage of Development' in *Global Society* Vol. 11, No. 2, May 1997.

Claude, I. L. *Swords into Ploughshares: The Problems and Prospects of International Organisation.* New York: Random House.

Comatroff, J. and Roberts, S. 1981. *Rules and Processes: the Cultural Logic of Dispute in an African Context.* University of Chicago Press.

Condor, Susan, and Brown, Rupert. 1988. 'Psychological Processes in Intergroup Conflict.' in *The Social Psychology of Intergroup Conflict* edited by W. Stroebe, A. Kruglanski, D. Bar-Tal, M. Hewstone. Berlin: Springer Verlag.

Cormick, G. and J. H. 1978. 'The Ethics of Intervention in Community Disputes.' In *The Ethics of Social Intervention* edited by G. Barmant, H. Kelman and D. Warwick. New York: Halsted Press.

Cottey, Andrew. 1994. *The Pursuit of Peace.* Safer World.

Cox, Robert W. 'Social Forces, States and World Orders: beyond International Relations Theory.' In *Millennium: Journal of International Studies,* Vol. 10, No 2.

Cox, Robert. 1989. 'Production, the State and Change in World Order'. In *Global Changes and Theoretical*

Challenges: Approaches to World Politics for the 1990s edited by Ernst-Otto Czempiel and James N. Rosenau. Lexington, Massachusetts and Toronto: Lexington Books, D. C. Heath & Company.

Crawley, John. 1992. *Constructive Conflict Management.* London: Nicholas Brealey Publishing

Curle, Adam. 1971. *Making Peace.* London: Tavistock Publications.

Curle, Adam. 1990. *Tools for Transformation.* Stroud: Hawthorn Press.

Curle, Adam. 1995. *Another Way: Positive Response to Contemporary Violence.* Oxford: John Carpenter.

Czempiel, Ernst-Otto, with Rosenau, James N. (eds.) 1989. *Global Changes and Theoretical Challenges Approaches to World Politics for the 1990s.* Lexington, Massachusetts and Toronto: Lexington Books, D. C. Heath & Company.

Deacon, Bob. 1993. 'Social Change, Social Problems and Social Policy.' In *Developments in East European Politics,* edited by White, Batt and Lewis. London: Macmillan Press Ltd. and The Open University.

Demertzis, Nicolas. 1985. *Cultural Theory and Political Culture: New Directions and Proposals.* Sweden: Student litteratur, Lund.

Denitch, Bogdan. 'Tragedy in Former Yugoslavia: Nationalism Beserk' *Dissent,*. Winter 1993.

Deutsch, M. 1973. *The Resolution of Conflict: Constructive and Destructive Processes.* Yale University Press.

Druckman, Daniel. 1987. 'New Directions for a Social Psychology of Conflict.' In *Conflict Management and Problem Solving,* edited by Sandole and Sandole-Staroste. New York: New York University Press.

Duffield, Mark. 1994. 'Complex Emergencies and the Crisis of Developmentalism.' In *Linking Relief and Development—IDS Bulletin.* Vol. 25 No. 4, October.

Duffield, Mark. 1994. 'Complex Political Emergencies: An Exploratory Report for UNICEF.' University of Birmingham: School of Public Policy.

Duffield, Mark. 1996. 'The Symphony of the Damned.' School of Public Policy Occasional Paper No. 2, University of Birmingham.

Eisenstadt, S. N. 1973. *Tradition, Change and Modernity.* New York: J. Wiley & Sons.

Ellis, S. and Barakat, S. 'From Relief to Development: The Long-Term Effects of Temporary Accommodation on Refugees and Displaced Persons in the Republic of Croatia.' in *Disasters,* Vol. 20 No. 2.

Evans, G. and Newnham, J. 1990. *The Dictionary of World Politics.* Hemel Hempstead: Harvester Wheatsheaf.

Ferguson, Adam. 1966. *Essay on the History of Civil Society.* Edinburgh: Edinburgh University Press.

Fisher, Ronald, J. and Keashly, Loraleigh. 1991. 'The Potential Complementarity of Mediation and Consultation within a Contingency Model of Third Party Intervention. In *Journal of Peace Research,* Vol. 28, No 1 February.

Fitzduff, Mari. 1993. 'Approaches to Community Relations Work.' CRC Belfast. Community Relations Council.

Galtung, Johan. 1971. 'A Structural Theory of Imperialism.' In *Journal Of Peace Studies* 1 (8).

Galtung, Johan. 1994. 'Civic Approaches to Conflict.' Evangelische Akademie, Loccum Workshop Papers, March.

Gamson, W., Fireman, B., and Rytina, S. 1982. *Encounters with unjust authority.* Homewood, Illinois: The Dorsey Press.

Gamson. W. 1975. *The Strategy of Social Protest.* London: Dorsey Press.

Giddens, A. 1990. *The Consequences of Modernity.* Cambridge: Cambridge Polity in association with Blackwell.

Goodhand, Jonathan and Chamberlain, Peter. 1996. 'Dancing with the Prince: NGOs' survival strategies in the Afghan Conflict.' In *Development in Practice,* Vol. 6 No 3. August.

Goodwin, Brian. 1995. *How The Leopard Changed Its Spots.* London: Phoenix .

Goverde, H. J. M. 1990. 'The Management of Urban Conflict in Poland and the Netherlands.' Paper for European Consortium for Political Research, Bochum 2—7 April 1990.

Gow, James. 'The Use of Coercion in the Yugoslav Crisis.' *The World Today* Vol 48 no.11.

Gramsci, Antonio. 1971 (1930). *Selections from the Prison Notebooks of Antonio Gramsci.* London: Lawrence and Wishart.

Griffiths, Martin. 1992. 'Order and international society: the real realism?' In *Review of International Studies* Vol. 18 No 3 July.

Groom, A. J. R. 1988. 'Paradigms in conflict: the strategist, the conflict researcher and the peace researcher.' In *Review of International Studies.* April 1988.

Groom. A.J.R. and Webb, K. 1987. 'Injustice, empowerment, and facilitation in conflict' in *International Interactions,* Vol. 13, No. 3, pp. 263—280.

Gurr, Ted, 1970. 'Explanations of Political Violence' in *Why Men Rebel.* Princeton U.P.

Gutlove, Paula with Babbitt, E., Jones L. and Montville, J. 1992. 'Towards Sustainable Peace in the Balkans; A report on a pilot effort to introduce conflict resolution theories and techniques.' Balkans Peace Project. Cambridge, Massachusetts.

Hancock, Graham. 1989. *Lords of Poverty.* London: Macmillan.

Harriss, John. (ed.) 1995. *The Politics of Humanitarian Intervention.* London and New York: Pinter Publishers. A Cassell Imprint.

Hegel, Georg W. F. 1981 (1821). *Grundlinien der philosophie des Rechts.* Berlin: Akademie Verlag.

Hendriks, Rik and van den Berg, Dion. 1995. 'The situation of refugees in Subotica, Vojvodina, Yugoslavia.' A 'COS' report, Centrum voor Internationale Samenwerking, Tilburg.

Hewstone, M. and Brown, R. (Eds). 1986. *Context and Conflict in Intergroup Encounters.* Oxford: Blackwell.

Himes, J. 1980. *Conflict and Conflict Management.* Georgia: University of Georgia, p. 81.

Hinde, Robert. 'Human Aggression: Biological Propensities and Social Forces' in Smoker, P. et al. 1990.

Hodgkinson, Peter and Stewart, Michael. 1991. *Coping with Catastrophe: Handbook of Disaster Management.* London: Routledge.

Holmes, Jackie. 1991. 'Marching to save a nation's sons.' In *The Guardian.* September 11.

Horowitz, D. L. 1985. *Ethnic Groups in Conflict.* Berkeley: University of California Press.

Index on Censorship. London: Writers & Scholars International Ltd. 22, 2.

Jackson, Robert. 1990. *Quasi-States: Sovereignty, international relations and the Third World.* Cambridge: Cambridge University Press.

Janis, I. L. and Mann, L. 1977 *Decision Making.* New York: Free Press.

Jean, Francois, (ed.) 1993. *Life, Death and Aid. The Médecins Sans Frontières Report on World Crisis Intervention.* London: Routledge.

Jones, Sian. 1993. 'No Way Out?' In *Peace News* educational offprints 1.

Katzenstein, Peter. 1989. 'International Relations Theory and the Analysis of Change.' In Czempiel et al (1989).

Keane, John. 1988. *Civil Society and State* London and New York: Verso.

Keane, John. 1996. *Reflections on Violence.* London and New York: Verso.

Kellas, James G. 1991. *The Politics of Nationalism and Ethnicity.* London: Macmillan.

Kelman H. and Warwick, D. 1978. 'The ethics of social intervention: goals, means and consequences.' In *The Ethics of Social Intervention,* edited by G. Bermant, H. Kelman and D. Warwick. New York: John Wiley. Quoted in Lewer & Ramsbotham, p. 25.

Kirkbridge, P. and Tang, F. 1990. 'Negotiation: Lessons from behind the Bamboo Curtain.' *Journal of General Management.* Vol. 16, No. 1.

Korten, D. C. 1990. *Getting to the 21st Century: Voluntary Action and the Global Agenda.* London: Routledge.

Kostic, Branislava. 1994. 'Non-Governmental Organisations in Vojvodina.' A Report for the Agency of Local Democracy and the European Civic Centre for Conflict Resolution, Subotica.

Kosuta, M. 1993. 'Media and The War in Croatia.' In *Medicine and War,* 9: pp. 136-137.

Kriesberg, L. 1973. *Social Conflicts.* New Jersey: Prentice Hall, p.91.

Kuhn, T. S. 1970. *The Structure of Scientific Revolutions* (second edition). Chicago: University of Chicago Press.

Kumar, K. ed. 1997. *Rebuilding Societies After Civil War: Critical Roles for International Assistance.* Lynne Reinner.

Kuper, L. 1989 'The prevention of genocide: cultural and structural indicators of genocidal threat', *Ethnic and Racial Studies,* Vol. 12 No. 2, pp. 157-73.

Kuzmanic, Tonci and Truger, Arno. 1992. *Yugo War.* Austrian Study Centre Schlaining and Peace Institute , Ljubljana.

Lederach, John Paul. 1993. 'Mennonite Central Committee Efforts in Somalia/Somaliland: A Brief Overview.' Paper prepared for delivery at MCC consultation on conflict intervention. Akron, Ohio, November 1993, p. 7-8.

Levitt, E. E. 1968. *The Psychology of Anxiety.* London: Staples Press Ltd.

Lewer, Nick and Ramsbotham Oliver. 1993. 'Something Must Be Done: Toward An Ethical Framework for Humanitarian Intervention' in *International Social Conflict. Peace Research Report* No. 33, University of Bradford, Department of Peace Studies, August 1993.

Lewis, Samuel W. 1993. *Negotiating Across Cultures.* United States Institute of Peace.

Light, M. and Groom, A. J. R. 1985. *International Relations: A Handbook of Current Theory* London: Frances Pinter.

Little, R. and Smith, S. 1988. *Belief Systems and International Relations.* Oxford: Basil Blackwell.

Little, Richard. 1987. 'Revisiting Intervention: A Survey of Recent Developments.' In *Review of International Studies,* 13: pp. 49-60.

Mack, John E. 'The Enemy System' in Vokan et al. 1990.

Markotich, Stan. 1995. 'A Potent Weapon in Milosevic's Arsenal.' In *Transition,* April 28.

Marsden, David with Oakley, Peter and Pratt, Brian. 1994. *Measuring the Process: Guidelines for Evaluating Social Development.* Oxford: Intrac.

Mastnak, Tomaz. 1990. 'Civil Society in Slovenia: from opposition to Power.' In *Studies in Comparative Communism,* Vol. XXIII, no 3/4: pp. 305-317.

Matic, P. and Zivkovic, P. 1995. *History of Serbs in Baranja.* Beli Manastir.

Max-Neef, Manfred. 1982. *From the outside looking in:Experiences in 'Barefoot Economics.'* Uppsala: Dag Hammarskjold Foundation.

Mabey, Christopher, and Mayon-White, Bill. 1993. *Managing Change.* London: Paul Chapman Publishers.

McAllister, I. and Rose, R. 1982. *Can Violent Political Conflict be Resolved by Social Change?* Centre for the Study of Public Policy. University of Strathclyde.

McDonald, J. W. and Bendamane, D. B. (eds.) 1987. *Conflict Resolution: Track Two Diplomacy.* US State Department: Foreign Service Institute.

McDonald, John, W. 1991. 'Further Exploration of Track Two Diplomacy' in Kriesberg and Thorsen, *Timing the De-escalation of International Conflicts.* Syracuse University Press.

McKay, John. 1995. 'Working for a Beta Day.' In *War Report,* May.

Mead, Margaret. 'Warfare is only an Invention—Not a Biological Necessity' in Bramson and Goethals. 1968.

Minear, Larry with Weiss, Thomas G. 1995. *Mercy under Fire War and the Global Humanitarian Community.* Boulder, San Francisco, Oxford: Westview Press.

Mitchell, C. R. 1981. *The Structure of International Conflict.* Basingstoke and London: The Macmillan Press Ltd.

Mitchell, C. R. 1991. 'Ending conflict and wars: judgement, rationality and entrapment.' *International Social Science Journal.* No. 127, pp. 35-55.

Mitchell, C. R. and Webb, K. 1988. *New Approaches to International Mediation.* Westport, Connecticut: Greenwood Press, Inc.

Montville, Joseph. 1991. 'The Arrow and the Olive Branch: A Case for Track Two Diplomacy.' In V. Volkan, Montville and Julius. *The Psychodynamics of International Relationships* Vol. II Lexington: Lexington Books.

Morgenthau, Hans J. 1985. *Politics among Nations.* New York: Knopf.

Muzafer, Sherif. 1966. *Group Conflict and Co-operation: their social psychology.* London: Routledge and Kegen Paul.

Nader, Laura. 1988. 'Post-interpretive Anthropology.' *Anthropological Quarterly.* 61:156.

Pecnik, N. and Stubbs, P. 1995. 'Croatia: from dependency to development.' In *The Rural Extension Bulletin,* No. 8., Dec. 1995. University of Reading.

Poulton, Hugh. 1993. 'The Hungarians, Croats, Slovaks, Romanians and Rusyn/Ukrainians of the Vojvodina.' In *Minorities in Central and Eastern Europe.* London: Minority Rights Group.

Prebisch, R. 1964. 'Towards a New Trade Policy for Development.' Report by the Secretary-General of UNCTAD. New York: UN.

Pruitt, D. G. and Rubin, J. Z. 1986. *Social Conflict: Escalation, Stalemate and Settlement.* New York: Random House.

Pupovac, Milorad. 1995. 'A Minority Dispersed and Unprotected. The War after the war in Krajina aims to destroy any possibility for Serbs to return.' In *War Report,* October, No. 37.

Qleibo, Ali H. 1993. 'Tribal Methods of Conflict Resolution—The Palestinian Model: *Atwah* or *Sulh Asha'iry*' in *Practicing Conflict Resolution in Divided Societies,* Policy Studies Paper No. 46. Jerusalem: Leonard Davis Institute.

Ramsbotham, O. and Woodhouse, Tom. 1996. *Humanitarian Intervention in Contemporary Conflict.* Cambridge: Polity Press.

Reid, A. R. , Barrington, H. and Kenney, J. 1992. *Training Interventions.* London: Institute of Personnel Management.

Reynolds. Philip A. 1979. 'Non-state actors and international outcomes.' In *British Journal of International Studies,* Vol. 5. No 2. British International Studies Association/Longman, pp. 99-110.

Roberts, Adam and Kingsbury, Benedict, (eds.) 1993. *United Nations, Divided World: The UN's Roles in International Relations.* Second Edition. Oxford: Carlendon Press. Charter of the United Nations, Appendix B.

Rogers, Paul. 1992. 'Giant-Killer dogs of war.' In *The Guardian.* August 17 1992.

Ropers, Norbert. 1996. 'Peaceful Intervention. Structures, Processes and Strategies for the Constructive Regulation of Ethnopolitical Conflicts' Berghof Research Center for Constructive Conflict Management, *Report* No. 1, Berlin.

Rosenau, James. 1968. 'The Concept of Intervention.' In *Journal of International Affairs,* 22 : pp. 165-76.

Rosenau, James. 1969. 'Intervention as a Scientific Concept.' In *Journal of Conflict Resolution,* 13.

Rottfield, Adam. 1995. 'Europe: the Multilateral Security Process.' In *SIPRI Yearbook 1995.* Oxford: University Press.

Rousseau, Jean-Jacques. 1782. *Considerations sur le gouvernement de Pologne et sur sa reformation projetee.* London.

Ryan, Stephen. 1990. *Ethnic Conflict and International Relations.* Aldenshot: Dartmouth Pub.

Ryan, Stephen. 1993. *Grassroots Peacebuilding in Violent Ethnic Conflict.* Paper presented to Conference 'Peaceful Settlement of Conflict', Loccum, March 1993.

Ryan, Stephen. *Grassroots Peacebuilding in Violent Ethnic Conflict.* University of Ulster, Magee College.

Sandole, David and van der Merwe, Hugo. (eds.) 1993. *Conflict Resolution, Theory and Practise* Manchester: Manchester University Press.

Schapera, I. 1938. *A Handbook of Tswana Law and Custom.* London: International African Institute.

Schapiro, Leonard. 1972. *Political Opposition in One Party States*. London: Macmillan.

Schirch, Lisa. 1995. *Keeping the Peace: Exploring civilian alternatives in conflict prevention.* Life and Peace Institute: Uppsala.

Schweitzer, Christine. 1992. 'Training in Yugoslavia.' In *Nonviolence Today* No. 24 January—February 1992. Australia.

Scott, James. 1985. *Weapons of the Weak; Everyday Forms of Peasant Resistance.* New Haven: Yale University Press.

Sharp, Gene. 1985. *The Politics of Nonviolent Action.* Boston: Porter Sargent

Shaw, Martin. 1993. 'There is no such thing as society: beyond individualism and statism in international security studies.' In *Review of International Studies* vol. 19 no 2 April 1993.

Shenk, Gerald. 1993. 'God With Us? The Roles of Religion in Conflicts in the Former Yugoslavia.' *Research Report 15*, Life and Peace Institute, Uppsala. December 1993.

Silber, L. and Little, A. 1995. *The Death of Yugoslavia.* London: Penguin and BBC .

Simnel, Georg. 1955. *Conflict & the Web of Group Affiliations.* New York: The Free Press.

Sites, P. 1971. *Control, The Basis of Social Order.* New York: Dunellan Publishers.

Small, Cleo. 1996. 'NGO Management in situations of Conflict' *INTRAC Occasional Paper* No. 12. Oxford: International Training and Research Centre.

Smelser, Neil. 1967. *Theory of Collective Behaviour.* London: Routledge and Kegen Paul.

Smillie, I. 1996. 'Service Delivery or Civil Society? Non-governmental organizations in Bosnia and Hercegovina.' Zagreb: Care Canada.

Smoker, P., Davies, R. and Munske, B. eds. 1990. *A Reader in Peace Studies.* Oxford and New York: Pergamon Press.

Sorensen, Jens, S. 1997. 'Pluralism or Fragmentation?' in *War Report* May. p. 34.

Spillman, K. R. and Spillman, K. 1991 'On enemy images and conflict escalation.' *International Social Science Journal.* No. 127, pp. 57-76.

Splichal, Slavko. 1994. *Media Beyond Socialism: Theory and Practice in East-Central Europe.* Boulder: Westview Press.

Steele, Jonathan. 1996. 'Silent Sentinels for Peace.' In *The Guardian.* August 16.

Stoltzfus, Nathan. 1996. *Resistance of the Heart: Intermarriage and the Rosenstrasse Protests in Nazi Germany.* Norton Press.

Stubbs, P. 1995. 'Civil Society in Slovenia and Croatia.' In *Newsletter* No. 2 September 1995a. Leeds Metropolitan University publication.

Stubbs, Paul. 1995. 'Social Reconstruction' article in *Leeds Metropolitan and University of Zagreb Newsletter*, No. 2.

Stubbs, Paul. 'Nationalisms, Globalisation and Civil Society in Croatia and Slovenia.' Paper for Second European Conference of Sociology: Budapest August 30—September 2. 1995b Leeds Metropolitan University, UK and University of Zagreb, Croatia.

Stubbs, Paul. 1996. 'Perspectives on NGO Development in Croatia, Slovenia and Bosnia- Herzegovina: Notes from the Research.' May 1996. Background Paper for the International Conference 'Social Reconstruction and Social Development: An Agenda for Change.'

Tagirou, Tatjana. 1995. 'The Short Arm of the Law.' In *War Report* March 1995.

Thakur, Ramesh. 1995. *A Crisis of Expectations: UN Peacekeeping in the 1990s.* Boulder: Westview.

Thompson, Mark. 1994. 'Forging the War. The Media in Serbia, Croatia and Bosnia-Herzegovina.' An Article 19 Publication adapted by I.W.P.R. Inset in *Balkan War Report*, June-July 1994, No 27.

Tindemans, Leo, (Chair). 1996. *Unfinished Peace: Report of the International Commission on the Balkans.* Washington DC.: Aspen Institute Berlin and Carnegie Endowment for International Peace.

Tismaneau, Vladimir. (ed.) 1990. *In Search of Civil Society.* New York: Routledge.

Traynor, Ian. 1992. 'Ethnic terror stalks the night.' In *The Guardian.* May 18. 1992.

Vasi, Milos. 1995. 'Letter from Belgrade: Chronic War, Chronic Milosevic.' in *Balkan Quandary*, March 15, p. 29.

Vayrynen, Raimo. (ed.) 1991. *New Directions in Conflict Theory. Conflict Resolution and Conflict Transformation.* London and New Delhi: International Social Science Council. SAGE Publications.

Vico, Giambattista. 1970 (1744). *The New Science of Giambattista Vico.* Translated by Bergin and Fisch. Ithaca: Cornell University Press.

Volkan, Vamik. 1988. *The Need to have Enemies and Allies; from Clinical practice to International Relationships.* New York: Random House.

Voutira E. and Brown, S. W. 1995. 'Conflict Resolution: A Review of some Non- Governmental Practices.' Oxford: Refugee Studies Programme.

Walker, R. B. J. 1998. *One World, Many Worlds: Struggles for a Just World Order.* Boulder: Rienner.

Walsh, Martha. 1996. *Beyond Feminist and Feminine: Unpacking Women's Initiatives in Ex-Yugoslavia.* Unpublished dissertation. University of Sussex and IDS.

Walz, K. N. 1959. *Man, the State and War: A Theoretical Analysis.* New York and London: Columbia University Press.

Webb, Keith. 'Structural Violence and the Definition of Conflict.' *Encyclopaedia of Social Sciences.*

Webb, Keith with Vassiliki Koutrakou and Mike Walters.*The Contingency Model of Mediation in the Yugoslavian Conflict.* University of Kent.

Weber, Cynthia. 1992. 'Reconsidering statehood: examining the sovereignty/intervention boundary.' In *Review of International Studies.* Vol. 18 No. 3 July.

White, Stephan, Judy Batt and Paul G. Lewis. 1993. *Developments in East European Politics.* London: Macmillan Press Ltd. and The Open University.

Williams, Andrew. 1995. 'From Theory to Practice: A Personal View.' *IR Alumni Associatian Newsletter*, Vol. 1, Issue 2. December 1995. p. 3. University of Kent.

Woodward, Susan L. 1995. *Balkan Tragedy: Chaos and Dissolution after the Cold War.* Washington DC. The Brookings Institution.

Zartman, W. and Berman, M. 1982. *The Practical Negotiator.* Yale University Press.